THE DEFICIT

Other Books by Helen P. Rogers

Everyone's Guide to Financial Planning
Social Security: An Idea Whose Time Has Passed
The Election Process: A Grassroots Call for Reform
The American Deficit: Fulfillment of a Prophecy?

THE DEFICIT

TWELVE STEPS TO EASE THE CRISIS

Helen P. Rogers

WELLINGTON PUBLICATIONS

CARMEL, CALIFORNIA

Laws, regulations, economic, and social conditions constantly change; therefore, the reader is urged to use this writing as only a beginning to his own investigation.

The information presented is believed to be correct at the time of this writing. The ideas presented do not pretend to be original with the author but are gratefully acknowledged as stemming from many publications, audio and visual news sources as well as discussions with colleagues. Although I may be unaware of the origination of many ideas still I would follow the admonitions of the Talmud which says when a scholar acknowledges all his sources he brings the day of redemption a little closer.

First Edition

Copyright © 1988 by Wellington Publications

Library of Congress Catalog Card No.:87-051350

ISBN: 0-915915-06-5

Printed in the USA

This book is dedicated to J. Peter Grace because of his efforts, on behalf of all Americans, to bring some sanity to government spending.

ACKNOWLEDGEMENTS

I am especially grateful for the guidance and criticism of Craig Kaplan who corresponded with me from Carnegie Mellon University and for the good humor, intelligence and patience of Michelle Rush of Salinas, California who struggled with me over this manuscript.

CONTENTS

PREFACE

"This book was written by a *citizen*!", declared a professor recently in defense of his decision not to adopt one of my earlier books for classroom use.

It is true that I am associated with no institution of higher learning, no think tanks, and have served in no sacrosanct echelons of government, but in this nation being a *citizen* qualifies me to speak my mind. And there are others like myself, who have worked hard, raised a family and after twenty or thirty years of keeping our noses to the grindstone have finally gotten a chance to catch our breath and look around.

I have found the sight appalling! The intelligentsia have been supported by the productive public and in return have permitted an epidemic of illiteracy and allowed the ideals on which this nation was founded to metamorphize. Elected and appointed officials have encouraged government's expansion and then tried to convince us with their convoluted statutes and laws that they are in control, all the while the monster they have nurtured knows no accountability.

In the appendices you will find evidence, in the words of various members of the latest elitist establishment, the National Economic Commission, to support my accusations.

Unfortunately, awareness of a problem is far from the solution. The 1988 presidential election will determine the course of the solution. It will answer the often debated question "Did Ronald Reagan gain the White House *because* he ran on the theme that government is the problem not the solution, or in spite of that idea?".

On page 383 I claim:

> that the solution in every instance is to take the circle smaller and smaller; from federal, to state, to local governments, to neighborhoods, relatives, immediate family until it centers finally on the individual and his own conscience. The best of all possible worlds is when actions are neither controlled by mandates from government nor censorship from one's neighbors. The best of all possible worlds is achieved when a person is allowed to act freely according to his personal convictions.

I was elated that the same thought was expressed more succinctly by former attorney general William French Smith in a C-SPAN interview prior to the 1988 California presidential primary. Mr. Smith capsulized his ideology: "Final decisions should be made by the smallest unit capable of making them."

Like any ordinary citizen I want to live among others capable and desirous of making their own decisions. I want my children and grandchildren to be part of a strong and vibrant nation of individualists. As Milton and Rose Friedman pointed out in the introduction to *Free To Choose,* "...an ever bigger government would destroy both the prosperity we owe to the free market and the human freedom proclaimed so eloquently in the Declaration of Independence." Sadly, this is the legacy of future generations unless we, who are committed to less government, are successful in changing people's minds.

In the preface to William E. Simon's 1978 *A Time For Truth*, Professor Friedman warned of the problems faced by advocates of limited government

> ...the view that government is the problem, not the cure, and that the invisible hand of private cooperation through the market is far more effective than the visible hand of the bureaucrat is a sophisticated,

subtle view that is...(hard) to get across. It requires thought, not emotion, to comprehend. It does not lend itself to ringing phrases, to high-flowered sentiment, to promises to particular people or particular groups. Moreover, the market has no press agents who will trumpet its successes and gloss over its failure; the bureaucracy does.

Advocates of individual freedom often give up the fight and resign themselves to what they believe is inevitable. George C. Lodge of Harvard in his 1984 book, *The American Disease,* envisioned a "communitarian" ideology in which society's needs take precedence over individual freedom. Some of his ideas were put into practice in Massachusetts under Michael Dukakis. In the Commonwealth during the 1980s government exercised an expanded role in planning, and decisions were made through consensus among bureaucrats and business and labor leaders. Professor Lodge went even further when he suggested in his book that private corporations should be forced to choose half their directors from a government-produced list of candidates. Employees with ten or more years of service with the corporation would vote on the list of candidates to determine the company's directors.

It takes stamina to hold fast in the face of those who idolize government solutions. Grover Cleveland was once asked for what deeds in his presidency he wished to be remembered. He reportedly replied, "Not for anything I have ever done, but for the foolishness I have put a stop to." Representative Charles Schumer of New York recently declared that "The idea that government is bad is being replaced by the idea that government is needed." I resisted his words until several recent polls showed that the public's faith in government is actually higher in 1988 than it was before Ronald Reagan took office.

The next administration will face rising calls for federal assistance. Many citizens have come to take federal help for granted and politicians are betting that we are so addicted that we not only will not, but cannot give it up. David Stockman referred to the six sobbing sisters of subsidy: (1) agriculture (2) big business (3) local government (4) small businesses (5) transportation and (6) users of federal credit. That just about covers all of us. Fortunately the so-called Reagan deficits have made the unbridled spending of earlier years impossible in the 1990s. The tax reforms of the Reagan era have put the traditional means to obtain more money, that is tax hikes or inflation, off-limits. (Remember taxes have been indexed to inflation.) Unfortunately the cries for more spending on education, health care, child care etc. are being directed towards the business community.

Despite the persistent instability in the world economy, the lack of a world central bank, fixed exchange rates or synchronized international policies, trade and GNP continues to grow world-wide. Although exchange rates bear the brunt of the adjustment process as nations are forced to hedge against one another's inflation and currency rates, nevertheless U.S. economic growth, though unspectacular, has been consistent during the eighties. Still there is talk of America's decline and the need for govern-ment action. There is no doubt it would take a mammoth effort for the United States to remain number one in global competition, but not the kind of effort envisioned in the 1988 omnibus trade bill. For America to remain the world's economic leader (1) corporate taxes and capital gains rates would need to be eliminated or cut to furnish financing and incentives for new business, (2) regulations that slow productivity would have to be eliminated, (3) labor and capital would move from ailing industries into new technology with the cost of training and retraining undertaken voluntarily by both labor and management, (3) anti-trust laws would have to be modified where they inhibit competition (4) a free-trade policy without subsidies would separate the strong from the weak indus-tries and allow the former to flourish and (5) flexibility would have to be encouraged. President Reagan had the will to do these things but a U.S. president is powerless unless he has the support of Congress, the citizens and the media. All three came together in World War I and II and we proved that we were unbeatable, but such a merging of wills may be impossible during peacetime. Indeed there is ample evidence that there is a willingness on the part of the American people to trade their freedom for security— to let government control more and more of their lives.

Former President Nixon, in an address to the American

Society of Newspaper Editors in the spring of 1988, summed up my purpose in writing this book:

> Only when you're engaged in a cause bigger than yourself can you be true to yourself. This is true of individuals, it is true of nations, it is particularly true of America. To turn away from challenge, to settle for second best, to quit trying to be as great as we can be, is contrary to the American character....If the primary aim of a captain were to preserve his ship he would keep it in port forever. The seas out there may be stormy but conflict is the mother of creativity. If you take no risks you will suffer no defeats, but if you take no risks you will win no victories. We must never be satisfied with success and we must never be discouraged with failure. That is the philosophy that made America the great nation that it is today.

This is the legacy I want to leave my children and grandchildren.

Helen P. Rogers
Carmel, California

"Radicals who would take us back to the roots of things often fail because they disregard the fruit time has produced and preserved. Conservatives fail because they would preserve even what time has decomposed."

Justice Louis Brandeis

THE FIRST STEP

(RE: WASTE)

CUT WASTE
AT ALL LEVELS

THE 1st STEP

(RE: WASTE)

THE POPULAR POINT OF VIEW

We have cut federal programs to the bone and there is no fat left anywhere. We have to start means testing all programs, including Social Security.

ANOTHER POINT OF VIEW

The Grace Commission findings, with their promise of billions of dollars of savings, have not been fully implemented, nor has the potential for savings in energy been fully explored. It is not ethical to means test Social Security benefits "after the fact". It will undermine the credibility of the U.S. government and be worse for the country in the long run.

3

THE GRACE COMMISSION

My interest in cutting waste from government can be traced to 1982 and the formation of the Grace Commission. There is no doubt cutting is the approach to the federal deficit that is most easily understood by the majority of people — after all, that's how we tackle our own deficits. Like many of my fellow citizens I was anticipating a relatively quick and easy way out of our budget deficit problems, and in fact if Congress had chosen to rally around the Grace Commission's recommendations back in 1983 we would have saved over $424.2 billion every three years after full implementation.

Over its existence the Grace Commission has spent approximately $76 million dollars tracking down fraud and waste in the government; every single dollar donated by a concerned citizen in the private sector. Not bad! $76 million to save $424.4 *billion* is a pretty good investment. Remember that's $76 million *private* dollars to save $424.4 billion *public* dollars.

The Grace Commission, originally known as the President's Private Sector Survey on Cost Control (PPSSCC) was established in February 1982 when President Reagan asked prominent businessman J. Peter Grace to head a commission for the purpose of conducting a comprehensive study of government spending. The Commission was made up of 161 high-level private business executives familiar with cost control and efficiency.

The Commission was faced with a difficult task when one considers that two million federal civil servants enjoy permanent status, which means they remain in Washington protecting their programs and their jobs regardless of the administrations which come and go. On top of that, our system of government is set up to encourage our elected representatives to be concerned with the local impact of spending decisions, even at the expense of the national interest. Only one person is elected by the entire nation, the rest have to answer to and depend on the votes of their isolated localities. Pork barrel legislation is the natural result, most readily achieved by Congressional back-scratching. One Congress person or Senator will often support another's move to acquire bounty for his own narrow constituency, knowing the favor will be returned.

In the preface to *Pork Barrel,* published by the Cato Institute as an expansion of the original Grace Report, the authors, Randall Fitzgerald and Gerald Lipson, tell how Congressman James Howard of New Jersey circulated a blacklist of those Congresspeople whose own projects would be defeated if they refused to support a specific piece of legislation. Congressional blackmail![1] It seems Congress operates much like prisons, with its own set of rules that newcomers quickly adapt to or suffer the consequences.

Congress is still spending and unwilling to eliminate waste, claiming that all the fat has already been trimmed from the federal budget. Instead of tackling the tough issues, officials are still playing around with the tax code and considering sales and fees to raise additional revenue.

Certain foreign airline passengers will be assessed $5 a head to help finance the Immigration and Naturalization Services; additional court fees will help finance the Justice Department; sales of Export-Import bank loans, the Naval Petroleum Reserve, are all possibilities that, if implemented, could help bring the deficit down temporarily. But still there is little thought in Congress of permanently reducing *spending*. Slowing the increase seems to be their less than lofty goal.

"BURNING MONEY"

You may have noticed this book is dedicated to J. Peter Grace because of his efforts on behalf of all Americans to bring some sanity to our government spending. The limitless examples of waste being supported by your tax dollars makes sensational, fascinating and often humorous reading. The story has already been uncovered thanks to the diligence of members of the Grace Commission and an army of dedicated journalists. Rather than paraphrase their revelations, let me instead urge you to read what

5

has already been written on this important subject.

If you have not read *Burning Money* by J. Peter Grace you should do so immediately. It is light, humorous and above all informative. If you feel ready for something with more statistics and a little on the heavy side I recommend *War On Waste*, a condensed version of the Grace Commission's report. Whatever you do, if you haven't done so already, join Citizens Against Government Waste (CAGW).

CAGW is a bipartisan non-profit educational foundation established in 1984 by Peter Grace and Jack Anderson. CAGW has two objectives: to educate the American public on the issue of waste, inefficiency and mismanagement in the federal government and to generate grass-roots support for implementation of Grace Commission recommendations. To learn more about CAGW and how you can join the fight to end government waste, simply call CAGW's toll-free hotline 1-800-USA-DEBT or write to CAGW, 1511 K Street, N.W., Suite 643, Washington, D.C. 20005.

The Grace Commission found that the federal government has 332 separate and incompatible accounting systems and 17,000 computers so obsolete that they are (were in some cases) almost impossible to service. Jack Brooks of Texas, who was chairman of the House Government Operations Committee in 1985, was quoted as saying: "Despite tremendous advances, many government agencies are still in the dark ages in the uses of this technology." [2]

Almost all the figures uncovered in the Grace report are mind-boggling and that is why you must read it for yourself. (No, not 21,000 pages with one and a half million pages of supporting documentation, but *Burning Money* and *War on Waste*.)

THE GRACE CAUCUS

The Congressional Grace Caucus deserves mention. It consists of Congressmen who mean business in the "war against waste" and are attempting to expedite many of the Grace recommendations through Congress. (No mean feat!) Members believe that

6

Congress should eliminate government waste before it even *thinks* about increasing taxes.

George Goldberger, President of CAGW, has reported a projected savings of $110 billion in reforms already adopted. Of the 2,478 proposals presented to President Reagan 1,788 were accepted and 1,426 had been implemented by the end of fiscal year 1987. According to Jack Anderson, co-chairman of CAGW, 129 recommendations were included in the Administration's FY1988 budget and 68 more are being proposed in the FY1989 budget. It's up to the Congress. If your representatives are not part of the Congressional Grace Caucus (list in appendix) how about contacting them and finding out the reason.

PAYING TOO MUCH

The Federal Deposit Insurance Corporation (FDIC) was involved with 27,000 lawsuits in 1986, up from 4,000 just six years earlier. Ten years ago the agency had seven attorneys; in 1986 it had 245. Government attorneys ($45 an hour average) are one thing, but the FDIC has been known to pay as much as $285 an hour for outside counsel. It paid approximately $50 million to outside firms in 1986. This is more spent on legal counsel than any other agency spends (thank goodness!). The second runner up was the Federal Home Loan Bank Board which paid approximately $15.5 million on its "outside" legal tab for 1986.

The FDIC takes on a failed bank's existing lawsuits and the bad loans the bank made to borrowers who often end up in bankruptcy court. Then too it defends and initiates litigation on its own behalf. The $50 million isn't taxpayer's money (whew) at least not directly. It comes from asset liquidation and insurance funds raised via bank assessments.

We can all wonder — why hire outside lawyers? They say it's not practical to send a government lawyer to every town where a bank goes belly up, but the true test is the number of outside law firms panting at the FDIC's door to get a piece of the action. The marketplace is clearly showing signs of over-paying!

OFF BUDGET SPENDING

J. P. Boldac, Senior Vice President of W. R. Grace & Co. and former President of Citizens Against Government Waste, had this to say in 1985:

> For instance $1 million of off-budget spending authority can be spent over and over again through 'off-budget transactions' until it ends up being $1 billion, instead of $1 million.[3]

Underground Government,, published by the Cato Institute in 1983 and authored by James Bennett and Thomas DiLorenzo, reveals more about off-budget spending than you probably want to know. But you *should know* and so should your colleagues, your friends and your relatives. This is the area of government spending, more than any other, that benefits the few at the expense of the many. As Gordon Tullock of the Center For The Study Of Public Choice said in the Cato book's forward:

> Although a referendum might beat some particular expenditure, it is likely that the beneficiaries from it will remember what happened by the time of the next election, and the widely dispersed victims will not. Politically it pays.[4]

Off-budget items seldom see the light of day, which means politicians are seldom held accountable for them. The facts about off-budget spending are little known and so outrageous that a condensed version of this information will not do the job. I am again going to ask you to do some more fascinating reading. (To obtain a copy of *Underground Government* contact the Cato Institute, 224 Second St., S.E., Washington, DC 20003)

As I said, many organizations have grown up trying to "help" our politicians do what has to be done and gathering support for cuts (and in some corners, tax hikes). But cutting isn't easy — where do you begin? Ronald Reagan had 80 pages of suggestions totaling $4.3 billion which he told the nation about during his final State of the Union speech in January, 1988. If the federal deficit is ever to be taken seriously, government can not go on providing funds for items such as the following: $100,000 for "taste-aversion research", $240,000 to control the damage rats do to sugar cane and macademia nuts, $540,000 to bring legislators from developing countries to study Congress's role in budgeting and finance, $260,000 for blueberry and cranberry research, $100,000 for a guard-dog program, $40,000 to specifically control rodent damage in Vermont, $500,000 to fight potato ring rot, $350,000 for marketing research by the National Potato Council, $9.5 million for four highway safety projects in Mississippi, $225,000 for a study of cormorants, $100,000 to study how to raise red fish in ponds and on and on for eighty pages! I'm not suggesting these projects are useless but only that they should be paid for by the narrow groups directly benefited, not all taxpayers.

LET'S GET SERIOUS

Peter Grace took an army of people to show us where and how to go about cutting the federal budget with the least injurious effects, but for the most part Congress is still asking basic questions and pretending Grace's work didn't even exist. The new National Economic Commission (NEC) was recently given $1 million of taxpayers' money to find ways to reduce the deficit while stimulating economic growth. Many observers believe the NEC could turn into an advocacy forum for tax increases and industrial policy positions, as well as a platform for big-names with little knowledge of the problems and less time to find out. More hype! Aren't you tired of this nonsense? Let's get serious. Here's what we're facing:

The four largest items in the federal budget are defense, Social Security, interest and Medicare, in that order.

It goes without saying that we cannot repudiate the interest owed by the federal government although it is increasing at an alarming rate.

Congressman Larry Craig of Idaho reported that according to the National Taxpayer's Union every person entering the workforce in FY1988 would pay an additional $10,000 over their

9

entire working lives thanks to interest expense on the national debt.

On March 23, 1988 Congressman William Dannemeyer of California offered a substitute to House Concurrent Resolution 268 (H. Con. Res. 268), dealing with the FY1989 federal budget. Representative Bill Young of Florida addressed the House in support of Mr. Dannemeyer's amendment. He told House members that over an eight year period the national debt has increased $1.8 trillion. $1.4 trillion, 75 percent of the entire increase, was interest cost!

The Florida Congressman presented the following outrageous figures:

Table 1
Relation of Interest Costs to Deficit

(listed in billions of dollars)

Fiscal Year	Deficit	Interest*
1982	$127.9	$117.0
1983	207.8	128.6
1984	185.3	153.8
1985	212.0	178.8
1986	221.2	190.2
1987	150.4	195.2
1988	146.7	210.1

*(interest is on entire federal debt not the annual deficit)

We would have a surplus in FY1989 of $90.8 billion except for the $220.3 billion in interest costs.

Congressman Dannemeyer pointed out that the actual general fund deficit for FY1988 is $244.4 billion. Income from trust funds reduces it by $97.5 billion leaving the illusory figure of $146.7 billion as the ostensible FY1988 deficit. According to Mr. Dannemeyer, in 1982 it took 28 percent of all general revenue to pay our interest expense; in 1988 it takes 38 percent. The Dannemeyer substitute calls for a $25.8 trillion revenue increase in FY1989 due to a tax amnesty plan, higher GNP growth and interest cost savings of $20.6 billion. The Congressman projects that the government, by refinancing debt, could save $777.5 trillion over a ten year period. Right now the government is paying an average interest rate of 8.7 percent on a $2.5 trillion debt. Refinancing at a lower interest rate is prudent. Mr. Dannemeyer suggests that the Treasury offer gold bonds which might carry a one percent interest cost.

Representative Phil Crane of Illinois agreed that what we need is a gold backed system which would ensure consistency and low interest rates, possibly in the 2.5 percent range. We need honest money!

It may argue well for the cause to mention that Alan Greenspan, currently the powerful chairman of the Federal Reserve, wrote an article in 1981 which was published in the *Wall Street Journal* suggesting we issue bonds backed by gold. Who knows? A little name dropping can't hurt!

I don't go along with Mr. Dannemeyer's entire bill, but refinancing at a lower interest rate certainly makes sense. Also tying the dollar to a solid backing to eliminate the three or four percent premium all Americans are paying for uncertainty is worthwhile and merits a serious response. As Mr. Dannemeyer put it, "Who can be against cutting interest?" It gores nobody's ox. However, the Dannemeyer substitution to H. Con. Res. 268 was not taken seriously, as evidenced by the 347 to 75 defeat it suffered. That's too bad since the Congressman's bill was supposed to get us to a balanced budget by FY 1993. (Promises, Promises!)

One thing is certain — the federal government must maintain its creditworthiness. A government that can't borrow would have to resort to printing and I needn't tell you what a nightmare that would be!

Let's discuss Social Security and Medicare under the broader heading of social programs in general. These programs are considered by many to be untouchable. They are viewed as a right. That the poor, sick, elderly and very young are entitled to whatever resources are necessary to fund these programs is not, according to these advocates, open to debate. This is the idea behind what Jesse Jackson has referred to as "Demand-side Economics". Needs must be met. The only problem is one of semantics. One person's need is what another might refer to as a wish, desire or simply a want. To those like the Reverend Jackson, it is beyond comprehension that anything else could have a higher claim on our national resources. They figure that deficits and higher taxes are a small price to pay in order to satisfy the *demands* of those who cannot adequately care for themselves. They honestly and sincerely feel this commitment should take priority even over national defense, which of course they consider to be already more than adequate.

On the other hand, to those whose main concern is national security, the solution is equally simple. If the United States cannot defend and protect her people then there will be no social programs and no need for debate about deficits and taxes. Those whose main concern is national security are only too happy to assent to increased taxes, cuts in social programs and don't mind the increased cost of borrowing if all this will result in enough military strength to deter any and all would be aggressors.

Professor Martin Anderson of Stanford gives a couple graphic examples in a 1984 pamphlet.[5] He talks of a fluid filled ball with four sticks protruding. The ideal is to have all four sticks pushed in even with the surface of the ball. The problem is that whenever the taxes and deficit sticks are pushed in, meaning lower taxes and a reduced deficit, then the social program and defense sticks are pushed further out, signifying a cut in spending in these areas. On the other hand if we push *them* in, thus increasing our defense build up and social programs, taxes and deficits are automatically increased. There is no way to have all the sticks pushed in flush with the ball at the same time.

Cooperation among the various advocates is just as difficult to achieve. It's rather like taking the local Scout Troop to Burger King. If the dinner comes out of the general fund they order two or three of the most expensive items but if it's dutch treat they immediately curb their appetites *and the bill.* (That was a very poor example now that I think of it — as a mother of five boys, I if anyone, should realize there is no way on earth they're going to curb their appetites!!)

THE ECONOMIC BILL OF RIGHTS

In the Bill Of Rights, the people speak as a whole, rising above any combination of interest groups. They firmly, flatly, in black and white, prohibit any tampering with personal basic freedoms. The framers of the Constitution wisely did not trust elected officials. They didn't question their integrity on entering office but they were smart enough to realize forces could and probably would be generated that would make these otherwise honorable men act against the national interest when it was in their own self-interest to do so.

There are also certain elements of economic policy that are so crucial and fundamental to the proper functioning of a free economy that they should not be left to the mercies of any elected officials.

Economics may be only a part of life, but it is the part which sustains and makes possible all the rest — the intellectual, the spiritual, the cultural. If we want to be free in these areas, we must maintain economic freedom. Personal freedom can't exist without economic freedom. The more the marketplace is left alone the more prosperous the Nation will be and the more free the individual. The only alternative to the free market is force — some people telling other people what to do. That's just what we have presently. Government officials are staggering around tinkering with the system and telling everyone else what to do. The result is a mess!

The finance minister of France, Edouard Balladur recently said

> Order and freedom go together. Economic freedom will have little hope for the future unless it is based on a world order accepted by all and binding on all.[6]

13

Order need not entail meddling and force, although unfortunatedly it usually does.

SOCIAL SECURITY — A WARNING

Social Security has been pushed, pulled and twisted in as many ways as there are points to prove. Future liabilities of the system are seldom if ever mentioned as the number would terrify even the most knowledgable. But as a surplus begins to build up in the trust fund (in response to the 1983 Commission's recommendations to raise the payroll tax still higher) there are plans to take Social Security off-budget. Since it is supposedly financed by its own revenue source (the payroll tax and invested trust fund) why should this cause concern?

For years there has been little or no surplus in the Social Security Trust Funds, but by the end of this century and through the first decade of the next, a gigantic surplus will build up. It won't last long once the baby boomers begin to retire, and in fact a gigantic deficit will begin in earnest by 2018 or thereabouts.[7] In the meantime the problem is how to protect the surplus which presents a temptation, hard for politicians to resist no matter the ostensible safeguards. It's like putting a dieter in a pastry shop. These surpluses will make the overall deficit look smaller and tempt officials to finance social programs without actually depleting the Social Security Trust Fund. According to Representative Rodney Chandler of Washington, by investing government trust funds (read "Social Security") in government Treasuries (all that the trust funds are allowed to be invested in by law) we're already making the budget look far less than it is. FY1989 is really a $249 billion projected deficit if we forget about the $113 billion invested by government trust funds which amounts to a mere paper reduction. Remember Congressman Dannemyer's similar observations regarding FY1988. (See p. 10)

WHAT YOU CAN DO

Elected officials are dependent on constituents for their jobs and therefore can do little without jeopardizing their own careers unless the voters are behind them. Representatives generally hear from people who want the other guy's ox gored and won't consider sacrificing their own.   Several organizations have recently been formed in recognition of this fact and with the hope of helping politicians do what has to be done about getting the American deficit under control.

Citizens for a Debt Free America is one such organization. (See Appendix A) It encourages citizens to contribute towards paying off the deficit for the sake of future generations. It reports from 1961 to 1980 $4,842,077 was donated to the Treasury in an effort to reduce the public debt; $5,880,261 in the four years 1981 to 1985 and $2,113,709 in the single year, 1985. The dollars go to pay off the debt principal.

Somehow it makes you wonder about representative government when citizens have to take the bull by the horns and do everything themselves. But the fact that such a thing is possible — that *anything* is possible — is what makes America so special.

ELIMINATE THE INTEREST

A few years ago I tried to get people to focus on the nation's interest expense as the one item in the budget which produces no tangible benefits. I sent a chart around to the Mayors of all our largest cities with instructions on how to determine their particular community's share of the national debt and suggested they erect plywood thermometers showing the community's share of the national debt and another depicting the community's share of the *annual* national interest expense. (See Appendix B) My pitch was that these thermometers would bring reality home to citizens and serve as tangible reminders of our past fiscal irresponsibility and shock citizens into awareness that our present policy cannot

THE SECOND STEP

(RE: CAPITAL)

TEACH YOUNG AMERICANS HOW TO ACQUIRE AND MANAGE CAPITAL

THE 2nd STEP

(RE: CAPITAL)

THE POPULAR POINT OF VIEW

America's decline is inevitable as one more cycle in history. Workers, who after all determine a company's success, are exploited by those who hold capital. Workers will become more and more valuable as there will be fewer of them in the future. Foreigners are taking our jobs and "buying up" America. Full employment, better management and bringing jobs home from abroad, is the answer to our problem. There is a dangerous gap between rich and poor in this country and the middle class is shrinking.

ANOTHER POINT OF VIEW

America is on the way up and has a destiny to fulfill. Today capital is more important than labor. Wages are no longer enough — all people must learn how to obtain capital and put *it* to work. Fewer laborers will be needed in the future as robots become commonplace. A nation's prosperity will depend on its ability to attract capital. If a government oppresses entrepreneurs and capital holders they will set up shop in a more hospitable environment. The danger posed by the "disappearing middle class" has been exaggerated by a biased interpretation of raw statistics.

THE PROS AND CONS OF CONSUMPTION

In this Information Age, truth is not easy to identify. We are presented with so many statistics with such diverse interpretations that it comes down to a judgment call as to whose information we choose to believe. Some sages fear that the future is passing out of our hands — that America's day in the sun has passed. Others argue that a new day is dawning and that we must enlarge America's golden circle of opportunity and reach out to include other nations.

Peter Peterson, in an article titled "The Morning After" which appeared in the October 1987 issue of *The Atlantic,* claims that instead of the promises made by Ronald Reagan in his "It's Morning In America" campaign, we got

> a torrid consumption boom financed by foreign borrowing, an overvalued currency, and cuts in private investment, with debt-financed hikes in public spending and huge balance-of-payments deficits. It's the same script, proceeding toward the same woeful finale, that we have seen played out over the years by many a Latin American debtor. [1]

Peterson fantasizes a speech by Ronald Reagan in which the President promises to make citizens feel better by raising the real personal consumption per worker during each year of his term by diverting savings. The fantasy speech has Ronald Reagan promising to run deficits in order to attract the savings of not only American citizens, but foreigners who naturally flock to buy Treasury bonds. Peterson claims that

> behind the pleasurable observation that real U.S. consumption per worker has risen by $3,100 over the current decade lies the unpleasant reality that only $950 of this extra annual consumption has been paid for by growth in what each of us produces; the other $2,150 has been funded by cuts in domestic investment and by a widening river of foreign debt.[2]

In order to reduce our foreign borrowing by $200 billion over the next decade, ($200/year for each of 100 million workers, a figure Peter Peterson suggests as prudent) some miracle would have to take place. According to Peterson, currently our real net product per worker is $135 per year, leaving us $65 short to begin with. Add to that shortfall the $40 per year per worker that is required to service the national debt and the $60 per year per worker needed for investment to increase our productivity and we come up with a total shortfall of $165 per year per worker. Peterson concludes that every worker in America will be required to cut back on his consumption by $165 per year until our debt is squared away.

Sounds easy? Think again. During the seventies when things were "tough", the average worker's consumption *increased* by $200 per year — we're talking about a *difference* of $365 per worker per year and it will hurt the proverbial "little guy" the most. We have become addicted to consumption during the Reagan years. Peterson points out that whereas we historically consume under 90 percent of our production, under Ronald Reagan we have been consuming *325 percent of it.*

On the other hand, George Gilder, writing for the January 15, 1988 edition of the *Wall Street Journal,* says

> we have been increasing investment, employment, and yes, consumption, far faster than our European or Asian rivals. But both investment and GNP have been increasing faster than consumption for the last six years....Two-thirds of the U.S. trade deficit with Asia consists of critical components and subassemblies for U.S. manufacturers; devices designed in the U.S. and assembled or packaged abroad; unique capital equipment vital to U.S. productivity...[3]

Mr. Gilder does not even attempt to label such activity as "trade" but says it is simply the

> integration of industry across national borders...Yet a new school of accountant-catastrophists has managed to spread the erroneous idea that these fully profitable and desirable arrangements put the U.S. deeply and dangerously in debt to other nations. We must soon 'pay it back', they say, or unspeakable disasters will ensue. [4]

America's situation today is frequently compared to the decline of Spain in the late sixteenth century, France in the late seventeenth century and England in the 1920s. They too ignored the law that limits consumption to production. However, the United States of America is not a rigid monarchy and the less structure the better chance any nation has to adjust to changing circumstances.

We frequently forget that consumption, not income, is the ultimate goal of economic activity. Production, growing or otherwise, is but the means to that end. Sure, the decline in future income implied by a slowdown in growth means a reduction in potential future consumption. But even a decline in consumption over time would not necessarily mean a decline in social well-being. More growth per se, cannot be equated with improved well-being. Peterson points out the obvious, that when the same level of consumption continues with a decrease in revenue there must inevitably be an increase in borrowing which puts a real drain on investment savings. The best way to determine whether more or less growth is desirable is to let the marketplace decide. This means making public policy completely neutral with respect to saving choices.

During his annual Economic Report to Congress on February 6, 1986 President Reagan said,

> the best way for government to promote economic growth is to provide a foundation of stable, predictable economic policies, and then to stand back and let the creative potential of the American people flourish. [5]

DECLINE OR NORMALIZATION?

Isn't it normal that the share of total manufacturing output and GNP of other nations which was depressed to an all-time low in the decade after the Second World War should increase? Isn't this what Americans have been working towards for over forty years? Isn't it normal that growth rates in both the U.S. and the U.S.S.R. should slow and that their proportional shares of global production and wealth should shrink over a time period when other nations, no longer at war, catch up? Although Japan is not a Third World country it is significant that by some measurements it has overtaken in GNP the much larger, and after the Second World War, victorious U.S.S.R.

But still the laments go on around us that "America is no longer #1" — a juvenile concept at best, and in most instances not even true. At any rate no thoughtful person could believe America's #1 status could be maintained indefinitely in all areas in a less than stagnant world. We are indeed hypocrites in this country if we desire to dominate the rest of the world in all things rather than, as we have always claimed, see every nation achieve its highest potential. Foreign aid, from the Marshall Plan on down, has been a charade if we fail to rejoice when another nation whittles away a larger slice of the pie.

The problem arises from the "pie" or "zero-sum" concept which emphasizes a limited world where one nation (or person's) success is at the expense of another. Americans have attempted to show the world the fallacy of that idea, to prove that there are no limits to what can be achieved by free men. We can all have larger cuts of a world pie that is constantly growing. It always bothers me when a buyer who is overjoyed by the "good deal" he is getting turns sullen when he discovers the seller earlier received an even better deal. All of life is a trade and a successful trade benefis all parties. Today the poorest American lives better than the richest King of ancient times yet America is constantly being compared to declining empires in other ages and most recently to England. Instead of "decline" perhaps we should be referring to "normalization". What are the facts?

Let's compare the present American deficit which accounts for 2 percent of GNP to Britain's pre-Thatcher deficit. England had run its deficit which amounted to 7 percent of GNP from 1973 to 1981 when it was attacked by Prime Minister Margaret Thatcher. She cut the budget deficit by 3 percent of GNP, when the economy was already in recession, causing 365 economists to write to the *Times Of London* saying Mrs. Thatcher was commiting economic suicide. The trough of the recession came in the 2nd quarter of that same year.

Military historian Paul Kennedy, author of the provocative book *The Rise And Fall Of The Great Powers*, argues on pages

533-534 that the geographic size, population and natural resources of Great Britain suggest that it ought to possess roughly three or four percent of the world's wealth and power, all other things being equal, yet in its prime Great Britain possessed closer to 25 percent of the world's wealth and power. By the same reasoning, the geographic extent, population and natural resources of the U.S. suggest that it ought to possess 16 to 18 percent of the world's wealth and power. However, Professor Kennedy points out, the U.S. actually possessed 40 percent or more by 1945 and today we are simply witnessing a decline from that unsustainable high figure to a more natural share. To compare this kind of decline to what happened to the Roman Empire or Spain or Holland (their fall into obscurity) is to ignore certain facts. For one thing, according to the professor, the shere size of the U.S. ensures it a place as an extremely significant power in a multipolar world.

Professor Kennedy raises the possibility that

> alarmist voices are exaggerating the gravity of what is happening to the U.S. economy and failing to note the 'naturalness' of most of these developments. ...Since the American economy is so large and variegated, some sectors and regions are likely to be growing at the same time as others are in decline — and to characterize the whole with sweeping generalizations about "crisis" or "boom" is therefore inappropriate. [6]

No one would argue against the fact that the world has changed irrevocably since 1945 and the economic and productive power balances are no longer tilted as favorably in America's direction. However Paul Kennedy seems to echo George Gilder's suggestion that America's decline is perfectly natural and at any rate it is relative, not absolute.

THE LARGEST DEBTOR NATION
IN THE WORLD

(If I hear that phrase just one more time I'm going to scream. How about you?) George Gilder claims other nations raised tax rates and increased entitlements and subsidies which caused their most productive citizens to ship their capital overseas to the United States in an attempt to preserve its value. The stability and safety of our government and the initiative and industry of our people still makes America the safest place in the world to invest, at least in the minds of many foreigners.

An investment, he points out, is not something that is "paid back" in the sense that a loan is paid back. An investment pays the investor back in profits and capital gains or losses. Rhetoric to the contrary is pure nonsense. He states simply that

> If the U.S. follows bad policy, foreigners will not reinvest their earnings. But because the U.S. has sharply improved its competitiveness, foreigners are likely to continue to send us money. Fueled in part by this flow of capital, in part by still lower tax rates, in part by a dramatic acceleration of technological progress, our rising investment and industrial production will enrich both foreign investors and U.S. citizens. [7]

He goes on to vividly reiterate the nonsense being spouted by 1988's crop of dooms-day-seers as they compare the U.S. as "the largest debtor nation in the world" (Agggh!!!) to Third World countries, suffering from poverty, illiteracy, starvation and of course, a mountain of debt. These prophets-of-woe warn us of the dangers of letting foreign money into this country and agree that a ruinous binge of consumption, mostly financed by foreigners, is the cause of America's alleged decline and poses a threat to future generations of Americans.

Mr. Gilder maintains that the only way the United States might conceivably be compared to a developing nation is in its openenss and frontier spirit which continues to attract ambitious and visionary foreigners both in person and through their investments. Economist Alan Reynolds would probably agree. He has said that heavy lending by foreigners is actually a sign of strength. But even he would agree there can be too much of a good thing. It is very costly for us to borrow capital.

Peter Peterson figured at the end of 1987 there was approximately a $400 billion difference between what we were owed by other countries and what we owed them. It makes sense to conclude that the greater our debt the less credit worthy we become and that to compensate for the greater credit risk lenders will ask for more interest and at some point may refuse to lend at all. We are currently borrowing at a rate of 3.4 percent of GNP per year. Professor Peterson believes our indebtedness could reach 35 percent of our GNP which, he says, will be a burden on our nation "... on a par with Germany's reparations burden following the First World War."

Most leaders agree that such borrowing is not cost efficient and morally it should not continue. "Mortgaging the future of our children" is the phrase most often used; a bit dramatic, but unfortunately true. But borrowing is not something we can stop overnight.

We can't look to our raw materials and agricultural exports to narrow the gap between consumption and production because of world saturation in these areas; there is too much competition from other countries for us to hope to do better than maintain our 22 percent export market in these products.

The service industries are no panacea either. Since they are, for the most part, connected with manufacturing, to do any good there would have to be a real annual growth rate of 10 percent per year for manufacturing exports all during the 1990s. This is not a realistic scenario as the rest of the world wouldn't absorb such an increase even if it were otherwise achievable.

It is folly to look to an expansion of the economies of West Germany and Japan to help us out of our predicament because, as Peter Peterson is quick to point out, for a sustained one-percent real increase in economic growth in the rest of the world we could only get a two or even four-percent real increase in exports, whereas what we need is a 10 percent real increase.

Other experts look to an adjustment of the exchange rates for help, but that help, as we will see in Chapter Eight, has been slow in coming. Besides, although a devalued dollar may increase our exports to some extent, to that same extent it will *decrease* the exports of our trading partners.

Peterson gets specific and suggests a reduction in government salaries, pensions and in defense spending, as well as a reduction of wages in the private sector in order to reduce the deficit. He believes the nation should seriously consider "a diet COLA" (cost of living adjustments) of indexing to 60 percent of CPI (consumer price index) instead of the current 100 percent indexing which would save $150 billion in federal outlays annually by the year 2000 if it were instituted now. He believes pensions should start later and the retirement age should be raised. For the well-off, all benefits in excess of contributions should be taxed, which he claims would save another $50 billion annually by the year 2000. We should bring civil-service and military retirement programs in line with those in the private sector by designing a total compensation package. Government retirement plans should be made self-supporting as he points out, private plans must be. We should end "cost-plus" health care and explore cost-sharing and medical vouchers. (Such suggestions have been part of the Grace Commission recommendations for years. Why don't we demand action?)

More than one expert has suggested that cutting taxes rather than cutting government spending is the way to increase production . (On the other hand, an untold number of "experts" have suggested *raising* taxes as a way to cut the deficit). Cutting taxes would increase consumer and business demand rather than government demand. It's a version of Reaganomics that critics claim has failed, but I believe never had a fair chance.

PRODUCTIVITY
AND THE COST OF CAPITAL

The cost of capital in the United States early in 1987 was eight to ten percent compared with a rate of three to four percent in Japan. The cost of capital in this country has come down with lower interest rates but still has a ways to go to allow us to become competitive. An American firm may be forced to pay $50,000,000 more than a foreign firm to borrow the same billion dollars. This means it must become five percent more productive than its competitors.

Peterson claims that during Ronald Reagan's term of office

(until 1986) the production of the average American worker increased by about $100 billion whereas the increase in consumption by both government and the private sector amounted to close to $300 billion. This accounts for the deficits in the neighborhood of $200 billion that we have experienced annually during the same time period.

In 1984 America saved 4.8 percent of its net disposable personal income, put 18 percent of its gross domestic product into capital formation and investment and found its productivity growth between 1973-85 had grown at an average 2.2 percent a year. (To be fair, one must point out that productivity in the service industry is almost impossible to measure and more Americans began providing services in that time period.) Keeping that in mind, lets look at some comparisons: West Germany saved 10.8 percent, invested 20.2 percent and productivity grew at the rate of 3.7 percent; Japan saved 20 percent, invested 27.8 percent and grew at an annual rate of 5.6 percent.

Productivity is now, especially with the recent drop in the value of the dollar, a more important consideration with the global competition game. Data Resources offered a study in 1987 which showed Japan's unit labor cost was four percent less than the cost in the U.S. and West Germany's was fifty-seven percent more. (I read it twice too!)

According to Peter Peterson 70 percent of our GNP growth was due to increases in the size of the work force; not the kind of growth that raises a nation's standard of living. (One must proceed cautiously with statistics, aware that they're always qualified.) Such growth has been based on demographics, the fact that more workers than ever before in history were entering the workforce (divorced and single women and baby boomers). Unfortunately in the future it will be impossible to sustain growth by adding more bodies to the work force because the baby boom will be followed by the baby bust, which means there could be a shortage of workers. It looks like the only viable way to maintain growth is by raising the productivity capabilities of each and every worker. How do we increase our productivity without an increase in domestic investment? The answer brings us back to the cost of capital.

TAXES AND THE COST OF CAPITAL

Many economists expected the 1986 tax reform to raise the cost of capital by approximately nine percent. But if there is a fixed amount of savings available for borrowing, interest rates should fall by the amount necessary to offset any increased tax on capital, meaning the actual cost of capital would not change. However, as a side effect, the higher tax rate on returns from capital will encourage investors to hold on to their assets rather than sell them and realize taxable gains. Fewer sales mean less revenue. Our policymakers should remember that it is not the tax rate imposed on returns to capital that affects savings, but the tax on those returns relative to the returns from other endeavors. It is uneven, not high taxation, that distorts incentives and causes economic inefficiency.

In 1969 when the maximum rate on long-term gains was doubled, revenue also fell. But still a group of so-called experts always gets it backwards. They continually predict that a drop in the rate will mean a *drop* in revenue although invariably the opposite is true. In 1978 it was predicted that the drop in the capital-gains tax from 49 percent to 28 percent would "cost" the government over $2 billion a year. The fact is, revenues climbed from $8.1 billion in 1977 to $11.7 billion in 1979. Additionally the higher tax on capital may reduce the current capital inflow by making ownership of U.S. assets less attractive. Since the financial inflow must equal the trade inflow the effect of the tax bill on the international sector, if any occurs, would be to reduce imports and increase exports.

One might think our proclivity to spend and consume is genetic, but actually it is a condition encouraged by a tax code which rewarded consumption and punished savings. The 1986 tax reform attempted to curtail the rewards for consumption by ending the sales tax deduction. But by the same stroke of the pen, it cut back on the savings incentive by changing the 401K plans (Keogh) and IRA rules. The 1986 Tax Reform could cost business $120 billion over five years. That $120 billion could have gone into research and development, or the modernization of plant and equipment, all which would have boosted American productivity.

David Boren, Oklahoma's Senator, introduced the Equity Investment Tax Reform Act in 1986 in order to stimulate new investment. Only net new equity shares were to be eligible for dividend deductibility, meaning that stocks issued for the purpose of buying other companies or to redeem existing shares would not be eligible for the preferential treatment. The senator reasoned that America's high cost of capital was in large part the result of a preference for expensive equity financing, whereas in countries like Japan, debt financing is used. Debt is taxed once but equity earnings are taxed twice; once at the corporate level and again at the personal level when the dividends are received. Senator Boren hoped to eliminate the double taxation of dividend income, at least from the new equity stock. He figured his legislation would reduce capital costs in this country by about 25 percent, up to 45 percent for investment in long-term research and development. He figured the economy would be rejuvenated with little cost, as the revenue loss would be more than made up by the growth that would ensue. (Now where have we heard that before?)

In my first book I praised President Reagan for his short-lived desire to abolish the corporate tax. Unfortunately every reporter in the country ridiculed him and he made a hasty retreat from what would have been a sound policy.

The U.S. should eliminate or at least reduce the corporate income tax. As Ronald Reagan said, it cannot be justified.[8] The result would be a shortfall which would be compensated by more investment, more capital per employee, even higher productivity and a bigger take for the IRS. What do you mean it sounds familiar? Just imagine, if the corporate income tax were eliminated, investments with lower returns and longer pay-outs would become attractive. O.K. — you're right if you sense a little "trickle down", but the alternate is a reduced standard of living — your choice!

In a *Wall Street Journal* article on February 6, 1986 Senator Boren said,

In 1983, capital for a 10-year R&D project carried an interest charge of 10.1% in the U.S. but only 2.4% in Japan! Given the current differential in our capital costs, the Japanese can afford to invest nearly five times as much as we can in the same 10-year project.[9]

Interest rates have changed since 1983 and the dollar has fallen but nevertheless Senator Boren's words show what has led up to the situation America finds itself in today — and sheds some light on the *why* of it all.

Compare laid off steel workers of the 1980s to immigrants of a hundred years earlier. The big difference is opportunity and motivation, things better achieved by government eliminating excessive taxation and regulation as opposed to providing food stamps and subsidies. When the government taxes in order to provide safety nets, it leaves too few dollars for the individual to provide those nets for himself. Even worse, it removes any motivation for doing so. It was not without good reason that we were warned of control by those who hold the purse strings. Nevertheless, to have the government stimulate investment through tax policy is better than protectionism and direct government subsidies. Those who consider tax policy a subsidy (and there are many) and moan about how much this credit or that deduction will "cost" the government, appear to believe all income belongs to the government and that only out of great generosity are earners allowed to keep anything. In contrast, some of us believe all income belongs to the party who earned it and that if any "cost" occurs due to government's tax policy it is "cost" to the income earner, not the government. Determining who has primary call on the worker's production — the government (collective citizens) or the individual worker, is a philosophical judgment. There is no disagreement however, over the fact that profits can be increased by removing taxes on capital. Unfortunately the 1986 reform reduced tax rates for consumers and raised the overall tax on business.

AT THE MERCY OF FOREIGNERS

Many people believe our greatest problem is that so much of our debt is in the hands of foreigners. When U.S. government debt is held by American citizens it is in the family, so to speak. After all, the government has taxing power over its own citizens. There is a certain safety valve when our debt is owed to ourselves rather than to those we cannot tax. But as more of our national debt falls into foreign hands the money we disburse in interest on that debt is going beyond the reach of our taxing power. The real danger is the fear that once we allow ourselves to become dependent on outsiders to finance our debt something like the fall in our dollar (which Mr. Baker worked so hard originally to achieve) may make them flee U.S. Treasuries. That would no doubt leave us in somewhat of a pickle, but hardly *danger*. Contrary to the impression conveyed by the media, U.S. debt held by foreigners declined from 14 percent to 11 percent of all debt between 1980-1987. So although actual U.S. debt held by foreigners has rapidly increased, their percentage of total debt has in fact decreased. (The bad news is that our *total* debt continues to increase!) According to the *FRBSF (Federal Reserve Bank San Francisco Weekly Letter* 10/30/87) the United States in 1981 was a net creditor of $141 billion and in 1986 was a net debtor of $264 billion. In 1981 the gross U.S. liabilities to foreigners was $689 billion and in 1986 the gross U.S. liabilities to foreigners had grown to 1 trillion, 331 billion dollars. In 1987 foreign private investment in the U.S. slowed whereas foreign official investment in the U.S., primarily in the form of U. S. Treasuries, rose considerably. This was due to the attempts by central banks around the world to support the dollar.

Financial institutions in Japan increased their portfolio of foreign investments from six percent in 1983 to approximately fifteen percent in 1986, according to Reuven Glick, writing for the *FRBSF*. Between 1982 and 1986 U.S. short-term rates were about two percent above comparable yields in Japan — an incentive to invest, especially if stability and liquidity are thrown in. The recent deregulation of world financial markets and the ease with which capital flows across borders in the eighties, has accelerated this situation. Even so, the U.S. has absorbed only about nine percent of gross savings abroad. Foreign investors hold 44 percent of their U.S. assets in U.S. federal, state & local government securities. Domestic investors hold 29 percent of their assets in those same Treasuries. Foreign investors hold 40 percent of assets in short-term debt whereas domestic investors hold only 30 percent in short-term debt.

America became a net capital importer when it stopped making foreign loans because the collapse of inflation diminished the credit worthiness of foreign borrowers. At the same time America continued to look like a great place to invest, so capital continued to flow-in to purchase our U.S. Treasury bonds, notes and bills. The price was low, the return was high and the quality was AAA. It has been suggested that if you add the exporting of securities or IOUs associated with capital inflows to our export of goods and services, you would see that our total exports aren't really so bad.

But everybody knows we cannot depend on the inflow of foreign capital indefinitely. In early 1987 the bonds issued by West Germany and Japan offered higher real interest rates than U.S. bonds. With the added attraction of the probable future appreciation in the yen and the mark, the overall return of those investments makes U.S. Treasuries look less attractive, to say the least. It's probable that the world's private sector will not keep financing our deficit. The U.S. has attracted $500 billion in foreign investment over the past four or five years but there is nothing to prevent that wealth from leaving as opportunities open up in other countries.

TWO VIEWS ON SAVING

Unfortunately the savings that fuel investment have been decreasing from a net private savings rate of 8.1 percent of GNP in the seventies to 6.1 percent in the eighties. In 1986 the Japanese managed to rack up a net savings of $380 billion whereas Americans only socked away $125 billion. Unfortunately our 1981 tax-cut did little to relieve the tax burden on savings and to discourage consumption. A financial newsletter in Arizona predicted that the personal savings rates in 1987 would drop to 3.6 percent of disposable income, the lowest level since the 3.1 percent rate registered in 1947 when the nation's pent-up war time sacrifices ended in a full-blown buying spree. During the Second World War, aside from the patriotic appeal of savings, consumers had little to purchase so the savings rate reached an all time American high of 20 percent. On April 24, 1987 Horace Brock told the Commonwealth Club: "We are going to have to raise the savings rate to 10 percent over a period of several years. We have got to make net investment attractive."

So how does Japan do it? Japan invests about 16 percent of its GNP in domestic production whereas the USA invests a little over 5 percent of its GNP. As the dollar falls the comparable percentages begin to look even worse. Remember, the cost of capital in Japan has been less than half ours, but that doesn't begin to account for the fact that even after investing more in absolute terms than America ($300 billion in 1986 compared to $270 billion in the U.S. that year) the Japanese still had $80 billion in savings left to lend to the rest of the world with more than half going to the good ol' USA. Japan is a nation of savers, but more because of government *disincentives* to spend, rather than *incentives* to save. It is a nation, as are all nations in the world except America, dedicated to ensuring that the good of the country takes precedence over the good of the individuals who collectively make up that country.

We have consumed our domestic savings and turned also to the savings of foreigners. High interest rates, whereas they serve to attract lenders, may push one group of borrowers, the so-called lesser developed countries, over the edge as they attempt to service their already unmanageable debt. That could spell trouble and we get into a discussion in this area in Chapter Six. For the time being, it is well to remember that anything that leads to a recession, depression, crisis or whatever you want to call it, will also most regrettably lead to stricter control by government. Is that what we want?

Herbert Stein, a Fellow at the American Enterprise Institute says,

> Suppose that the U.S. is a country in which private citizens have a low propensity to save, because they are already relatively rich or for cultural reasons. And suppose also that the U.S. is an attractive place to invest, because we have lots of land, a skilled labor force, a favorable political environment or for other reasons. And suppose further that in the rest of the world private citizens have high propensities to save and the opportunities for investment are less attractive. In these conditions there will be a flow of capital from the rest of the world, and a corresponding net inflow of goods, to the U.S. The U.S. would have a trade deficit. [10]

He, like George Gilder, is not alarmed by this scenario but finds it to be both an efficient and a natural adaptation to the different savings propensies and investment opportunities found in this and other countries. Our trade deficit would disappear naturally if the return on investment capital dropped due to oversupply or the rest of the world simply decided it was time to consume instead of save and invest. What most people fear — the pull out of foreign capital — Mr. Stein welcomes. He says when the trade deficit becomes a surplus it simply means

> the rest of the world would be receiving investment income from the U.S. The U.S. will not be made poorer by paying this investment income because the income will be earned by capital that would not have been here without the prior inflow of funds from abroad...[11]

A LITTTLE HISTORY

In the eighteenth century capital was owned by roughly five percent of the population. Today approximately five percent of the population still owns most of the capital but there is a difference. Two hundred years ago capital, consisting mostly of cheap and plentiful land, was easily accessible to the other ninety-five percent of the population. To be sure it was not very valuable in relation to labor because technology was in its infancy and land was only worth what labor could produce. Early America, and in fact the entire world before the Industrial Revolution, was labor intensive. It took the emergence of machines which could do the work of many men to raise the value of the land (capital). At the end of the nineteenth century that process was well underway with the appearance of the gasoline engine in 1872, the telephone in 1876 and the incandescent light in 1879.

British historian, Arnold Toynbee claimed that the most significant aspect of the Industrial Revolution was the substitution of capital for labor as a means of getting things done. The challenge now is to make capital owners out of workers. Capitalism is well suited to the task. The great documents of this nation were written with the goal of empowering people, by men steeped in the lessons of Hume, Locke and Adam Smith.

Technology diminishes man's power to produce via his physical and mental labor. Since the purpose of technology is to reduce the need for labor, full employment is a goal that no longer makes sense. As technology multiplies it becomes worth less in relation to capital. The economy becomes capital intensive.

Karl Marx thought technology would alienate man from the fruits of his labor; instead it alienated man from the *worth* of his labor — robbed him of his chance to experience self respect and fulfillment. We have heard often enough that people don't want charity or make-work jobs; they want to be honest producers. Unfortunately, no matter how hard they work, in this age of technology their labor can never regain its productive power as against machines.

Yet the national conscience still subscribes to the old protestant work ethic which came over with the Puritans on the Mayflower. Roughly it says, "If you want something, you must earn it by the sweat of your brow". Even today our political leaders continue to preach that full employment is the answer to our income distribution problems. They fail to realize that there are two ways to produce income; by labor and by putting capital to work .

According to Louis Kelso, economist, author, lawyer and investment banker, the Employment Act of 1946 says earned

36

income or gift income are the only legitimate ways to acquire income in our free market capitalist society. This is news to many of us. Passive income has long been recognized in this country as income from real estate and stock dividends etc. and taxed as such.

We have counseled our own children that the profession they choose to follow in life should be one they are suited for temperamentally and one which they will enjoy without considering its potential for making money. Having been taught to economize, they understand they can acquire capital early through manual or mental labor, which when invested, will eventually become their *main* financial support.

Financial planners are skilled in showing people how to shave ten or twenty percent off even the leanest budget. Invested, tended and occasionally fed, that ten or twenty percent will increase through the magic of compound interest and leverage — subjects which should be taught in every high school in the country.

Nothing would benefit individuals and society as a whole more than learning how to acquire capital and put it to work. I can think of no more worthwhile goal than making it possible for the vast majority of capital-less citizens to acquire capital.

THE KELSOS

Louis Kelso has devoted over thirty years to an attempt to democratize the American capitalist system. He believes the USA is a political democracy but no longer the economic democracy it once was. Economic democracy refers to the power of production being equally accessible to all. America today is a plutocracy, where, according to Kelso, economic power is highly concentrated and capital is no longer easily accessible.

In *Democracy and Economic Power—Extending the ESOP Revolution* , written by Louis Kelso and his wife, Patricia Hetter Kelso, the authors speak about the government's "surogate responsibility" to provide its citizens with access to capital credit. There is no doubt access to capital was diminished with the coming of the Industrial Revolution, as we discussed above, but is it *government's* role to intervene and provide that access?

The Kelsos would like to see government intervention to make capital more easily accessible to everyone. They believe the federal government should establish an agency and in other ways make it possible for citizens to receive capital via a loan without going the long traditional lending route which requires collateral, credit ratings and so forth. They call this "democratic financing" as opposed to 'plutocratic financing' (also their term). They claim the "right to life" clause in our Declaration of Independence refers, economically speaking, to the right to earn income to support life. No doubt that interpretation is preferable to the interpretation which claims that some are entitled to biological life supported by the earnings of others.

It is not uncommon upon first being introduced to the ideas of Louis and Patricia Kelso, to sense a smathering of socialism or even communism. However they like to point out that the current U.S. economy, with its dependency on redistribution, is far closer to the socialist ideal than the democratic capitalist economy they are advocating.

No one makes an investment unless he thinks it will not only pay for itself, but will start working for the owner, generally within a time limit of three to five years. "If the asset is destined to be self-liquidating, as all good investments are, then why", asks the Kelsos, "do you have to already have capital to purchase it?" It should not only pay for itself but it should be throwing off a surplus within the the three to five year rule-of-thumb period, and in that sense be "working for you"—providing you with an income separate and distinct from the income from your job or other labor. The Kelsos choose to ignore the risk factor.

But life is a risk! You may not even be around tomorrow. Nothing is certain. There is then, the risk, no matter how slight, that the investment may not pay off. Sure, you can get a loan if you are willing to pay for it and the lender sees merit in you proposal, but rarely will you be given 100 percent financing. I must admit, however, that it can be done and that we have done so many times, especially as poor college students and even over a period when we were encumbered (as the bankers like to put it) with the financial liabilities of five young children and a mountain of debt from one of those investments that didn't work out as planned. But generally you will have to come up with ten, twenty or even thirty percent and/or other concessions in order to obtain financing. The Kelsos refer to this as being asked to self-insure. In other words, they say you have to be rich to get a commercial loan the way things work in the *real* USA.

However, the Kelsos overlook the fact that capital can be acquired by hard work, budgeting and investing, but most of all by disciplining oneself to postpone the pleasures of today for rewards tomorrow.

This is the fact that John La Costa exemplifies so well. Mr. La Costa arrived in this country with no money, little knowledge of the language and through careful administration and a lot of belt tightening managed to set aside some capital. It didn't matter that the original amount was small, what mattered was that this capital was put to work as soon as possible. He now heads his own organization in Brooklyn called The Better World Builders whose purpose is to help other Americans succeed.

There are countless true stories more surprising and more inspirational than fiction; stories which are being repeated by new immigrants every day. Immigrants, most recently from Asian countries, very often manage to attain independence after they are settled in this country. They don't seem to understand that they have been cut off from capital and so they obliviously pursue, and furthermore attain, economic security.

People want to earn more money. If the only way more money can be earned by an employee is by extracting higher wages for his labor, then in a world where labor is cheaper outside the USA the American employer will become less competitive. Owning capital is a way to participate in production and earn income without lessening the competitiveness of American business.

ESOPS

Louis Kelso come up with the ESOP (Employee Stock Ownership Plan) concept many years ago. Under Kelso plans, as they are sometimes called, loans are made to employees to enable them to purchase shares in their employer's business.

> Loans made to corporations to finance corporate capital transactions that raise the income-earning power of employees as consumers are safer, more secure, and promote the economy's prosperity better than loans made to finance corporate growth which raise the earning power of already overcapitalized stockholders who will not use increased earnings in the consumer markets at all. [12]

Louis Kelso has calculated that the typical equity capital owner today gets about one-twelfth of the income which flows from his capital. He takes stock of a corporation for example and shows how taxes, state, federal and payroll, take about half the corporation's net income. Seventy-five percent of the remaining half he figures is used to enhance the company's growth, leaving one-eighth which shrinks to a twelfth after management and labor get through picking it over.

Senator Russell Long of Louisiana, with considerable urging from the Kelsos, lent his powerful support to the passage of legislation designed to encourage the use of ESOPs. The 1984 law made dividends paid to employees via ESOPs tax deductible as well as permitting shareholders to defer tax when selling to an ESOP and lenders to defer fifty percent of the interest earned from ESOP transactions from their taxes. An ESOP itself is a tax exempt entity.

The 1986 tax reform also had a lot of ESOP incentives, encouraging ESOPs, some claim, at the expense of other corporate tax advantages. The 1986 reform eliminated the exclusions for capital gains, while lowering the corporate tax rates which means that all deductions are worth less. Mutual funds were permitted to join with other commercial lenders and exclude half of the interest earned on ESOP loans from taxes. Companies that leverage are now also allowed to repay loan principal and interest with pretax dollars by declaring dividends to ESOP stock and distributing them among employees These provisions were in large part due to the diligence of Jeffrey Gates, tax counsel to the Senate Finance Committee in 1986.

The hope is that expanding the ownership of capital to workers will help cut back on plant closings, raise morale and employee production, ease labor-management difficulties, provide a ready market for the company's stock, encourage local ownership and of course provide a superior form of estate planning for the participating workers. The trouble is that the risk transfers to the worker for his retirement security whereas management picks up a new powerful financing tool. ESOPs should not be substituted for pension plans, they are *additions*. It is true that even after an employee retires from the labor force, income from capital would continue. But that doesn't mean there would no longer be a need for private pension plans or Social Security benefits. It all depends on how much and how wisely an individual invests during his working years. There is a very good chance that ESOPs would provide higher benefits than a traditional pension plan because an employer could afford to put more money into an ESOP. Nevertheless, the benefits are tied to the unforseeable performance of each individual company.

According to the National Center for Employee Ownership (NCEO), in 1987 over seven million workers were covered by ESOPs. About 80 percent of all ESOPs are private and 20 percent are traded in the open market. Employees hold a majority share of the companies in only about 15 percent of the cases with a 20 percent to 40 percent share being typical. Generally employees participate in the equity (ownership) of the firm but not the management. The thought that employees might gain too much control of a company is the nightmare of both employers and their bankers, but something that seems to be of very little consequence to the employees themselves — at least so far.

Mr. Kelso refers to ESOPs as the capitalism of Marx's dreams — capitalism for the many. Few appreciated the merits of capitalism as did Karl Marx but he could not endorse it because he believed that under its dictum capital itself was held too tightly by too few people.

Today large companies are less likely to allow their employees to participate in self-directed accounts simply because the record-keeping would be unmanageable. But small businesses are increasingly permitting workers to manage their own profit-sharing money in special accounts at brokerage houses. The idea is especially attractive to individualists, but they should have some investment background or be willing to invest some time to acquire investment savy. The more people that are willing to take responsibility for their futures without waiting for Big Brother or Uncle Sam to take them by the hand, the stronger our nation will become.

The idea behind ESOPs is not new. Cooper Proctor said:

> The chief problem of big business today is to shape its policy so that each worker will feel he is a vital part of his company, with a personal responsibility for its success and a chance to share in those successes.

That was said over a hundred years ago when Proctor and Gamble introduced profit sharing.

AMERICA'S LARGE
AND UNIQUE MIDDLE CLASS

The middle class is practically synonymous with American capitalism. In most countries the wealthy minority lives in fear of revolt by the poor majority, which means the capital of those countries flows to places of stability like the United States. The rich minorities are understandably apprehensive about the safety of keeping their wealth at home.

America, through its Declaration of Independence and Constitution, offered hope to mankind. Instead of giving the people an aristocracy, the people were given opportunity. Individuals provided their own unique incentives and in time, hardwork and ingenuity gave birth to America's large and distinctive middle class. The middle class concept is an ideal; unnatural and

42

fragile and not without its shortcomings. It barely withstood the Great Depression and is suffering today from the quackery (the New Deal) which was unfortunately applied at that time.

The Great Depression in the twenties and thirties was caused by capital production in the hands of too few. (I'd also go along with journalist Alfred Malabre, Jr. who claimed "A lack of economic information is widely seen as a major reason for the depth and persistence of the Great Depression".)[13] This caused a distortion of free market principles. There was simply too much "morbid wealth"; a term used by the Kelsos to denote such an excessive amount of money that it cannot be recycled in the market place where it can do its job of pumping up the economy. Some people had more capital than they knew what to do with whereas others had needs they could not fill. (You're right — there's too much of that today.)

The New Deal was a deviation from the private property, free market capitalism which had been the hallmark of America up to that time. The solution proposed by the New Deal was redistribution — take from those who earn more than they need (according to whose judgement?) and give to those who need more than they earn (again, who is to judge?). Not really an American sounding concept but smacking a bit of fictitious old England (remember Robin Hood?) and Karl Marx ("From each according to his ability, to each according to his need.")

New Dealers failed to realize capital had replaced labor as the main means of production after the Industrial Revolution. It is too bad that those who at that time expressed alarm about government's expanded role were never vindicated. First the Second World War, then Keynesian economics (with its emphasis on increased spending by government, more programs and more taxes to keep the economy perking) and finally the rigged price of labor, all worked together to disguise the inevitable consequences of the New Deal policies.

Then and now, creating new jobs is a phony answer. Today more than half of all American families have two income earners and are no more prosperous, in the majority of cases, than their parents were with only one family member working.

The New Deal, according to the Kelsos

has resulted in higher taxes, higher interest rates, a towering debt structure, deficit spending, inflated prices, eroded purchasing power, and a massive loss of American markets to foreign producers. [14]

Since the government insists on interfering it is far better that it follow the Kelsos' perscription towards a long-term permanent solution rather than mindlessly continuing to pursue destructive dead ends. Redistributing the income others have earned and pushing for jobs which are obsolete in what should be a capital workforce, is not the answer. At least *Democratic Capitalism* is a share-the-wealth scheme where the wealth is earned, not redistributed.

AMERICA'S DESTINY

Although there is little doubt that both Conservatives and Liberals are concerned about the general welfare, Conservatives are also concerned about individual responsibility, free markets and private enterprise. The concern of most Liberals leans towards government programs and collective responsibility. The free market is tied up with human freedom, from a spiritual as well as a material point of view. There can be no freedom of spirit without first freedom in the marketplace.

Louis Kelso says,

but nature had an economic plan for world society. Nature thought that economic autonomy—i.e., making every human capable of participating in production and earning the income he needs for himself and his dependents—was a good idea. It is an idea that agrees with the inner man. But the arangement of "one person, one labor power" is about as far as nature can go. After that, it is up to government, labor and management to devise the institutions that enable us, in the advanced industrial age that we live in , to earn our income by engaging in production in ways that are consistent with economic reality. [15]

I agree with Louis Kelso that capital assets are more than

44

catalytic agents that simply raise the productivity of the workers who use them. That does not mean however, that there is a "constitutional duty" or that "due process" demands government action, as Mr. Kelso claims. He declares that,

> each household has a natural human right to participate in the production of wealth through the ownership and application of productive property, to a degree sufficient to earn for that household a decent standard of living.[16]

"Decent standard of living" requires a subjective judgment. Mr. Kelso sees a duty to act for the common good. He says society is obligated to see that every family gets its due in accordance with natural economic rights — whatever legislative regulation of economic activity it may take. "Economic right" is generally interpreted to mean man's right to property under his own labor power. But Mr. Kelso suggests the right to life is meaningless unless it involves a right to acquire subsistence by *rightful* (?) means. He claims a man who cannot find employment is unable to earn a living and therefore his right to subsistence is denied as well as his right to life.

I agree that a man's right to an earned income is a conditional right. The right imposes upon man a duty to contribute to the production of wealth and imposes upon government the duty to prevent interference. However, taking further license with the language, Louis Kelso claims the right to earn a living is a right to property in the means of production. The ownership of productive property by an individual or household *must not* be allowed to increase beyond the point where it injures others by excluding them from the opportunity to earn a viable living.

Laws to limit the concentration of capital by some, under the pretense of preserving the liberty of others, leaves us with several troubling questions. Who is to decide when *injury* occurs? Whose definition of the *common good* should be adopted? How and who is to tell when the *proper* amount of capital has beeen accumulated? Who will determine when *others* attain effective participation?

45

I disagree with the Kelsos in their conclusion that government must stop other men from obtaining more than "their fair share", and must pave the way for "favored" citizens to obtain capital. I believe if man has a duty it must be the duty to work hard, save and invest his earnings while acquiring new knowledge which will be the capital of tomorrow.

When I ask that age old question; "What do people want from life?", I come up with "self-respect, fulfillment and security". The Kelsos claim it is humiliating to possess nothing, but I disagree. Native American Indians did not require ownership to feel worthwhile nor do members of religious orders who voluntarily take the vow of poverty. Many people can be quite content with the three things I mentioned and little or no possessions. It is not "ownership" which makes a person count for something.

Although I do not agree with the Kelsos' interpretation of the U.S. Constitution or the role they outline for our government to play, I greatly admire their dedication to an ideal which has been the cornerstone of American life from this country's earliest beginnings and may well be its salvation in the competitive world of tomorrow. Capitalism has always been a beacon of opportunity to those who would discipline themselves and determine to take advantage of it. Capitalism has been summed up by such colloquialisms as "Giving your dream a shot!", "Go for it" and "The sky's the limit!". It has meant people struggling, failing and getting up and trying again and again. We should not stifle one of man's better instincts.

Unfortunately the Kelsos are correct in stating that without owning capital and letting it work for them, Americans will have little chance of getting ahead economically in the world we live in today. A world where capital, not labor, is king.

THE THIRD STEP

(RE: PRIVATIZATION)

LET THE PRIVATE SECTOR DO WHAT IT DOES BEST AND CONFINE GOVERNMENT TO ITS LEGITIMATE FUNCTIONS

THE 3rd STEP

(RE: PRIVATIZATION)

THE POPULAR POINT OF VIEW

Privatization results in higher costs, poorer quality of service, corruption, and loss of government accountability. The private sector provides lower wages, fewer benefits and less opportunity for advancement which translates to a lower living standard for workers. Government furthers many social objectives through its civil service programs.

ANOTHER POINT OF VIEW

Privatization is cost efficient and will help reduce the federal budget deficit. Without competition from government more citizens will become entrepreneurs and will better understand and participate in the free market policies of a government they formerly criticized or ignored. It is wrong for government to compete against entrepreneurial citizens or by subsidies to favor one citizen above another.

HISTORY

Privatization, selling national assets or relegating to the private sector duties formerly performed by government, is by no means a new idea; in fact it was the norm in the 18th and 19th centuries. In 1794 a group of private businessmen invested in the nation's first planned and engineered road, intending to recoup their investment from road tolls. Although it's commonly known that entrepreneurs built the railroads, it is less widely known that at one time private firms owned and operated much of New York City's subway system. In the 1890s Robert LaFollette and his Progessives gathered support for the regulation of railroads and the taxation of corporations with a call for more publicly held assets. His supporters believed that no private group should profit from supplying essential services to the public.

Misunderstanding the nature of profit, people came to hope that the public sector (government) could do things less expensively than the private sector because the government could operate without making a profit. They forgot that profitability ensures accountability. At any rate, it was unsurpressed dissatisfaction with old policies which finally culminated in the election of Ronald Reagan on a platform which promised to reverse the expansion of government and relegate it once again to the limited role which this nation's founders envisioned.

But there are modern day "Progressives". Many, like their historical counterparts, are fearful that entrepreneurs may make money from society's needs. Somehow they must be convinced that it is not a betrayal of democracy to turn tasks, now performed by government, over to the private sector. In fact, if this nation is to continue to prosper, it will have to encourage individual drive and initiative. Attacking the successful (and therefore usually the rich) may win votes, but it will not make the nation more prosperous.

GET GOVERNMENT OFF THE BACKS
OF THE PEOPLE

In an effort to ridicule conservative thinking, certain left-wing writers penned the following lines:

> If the government would just get off people's backs and free enterprise were once more allowed to spread its wings through less government interference, America would regain the growth track. Private enterprise and the market system create — through the workings of Adam Smith's mysterious 'invisible hand' — the best sort of society, one in which individuals have the liberty to do what they want, and acting as individuals, somehow produce the greatest social good. Government interferes with this process.[1]

It was written tongue in cheek but I offer it for your serious consideration.

PRIVATIZATION —
OTHER COUNTRIES DO IT!

The privatization craze that is sweeping Europe began in 1979, shortly after Margaret Thatcher came to power. Under her leadership, Britain has sold all, or part of more than 13 companies and raised the equivalent of approximately $25 billion. American politicians might take a lesson from their British counterparts who have shown that privatization is a way to keep some of their pet projects alive that would otherwise be facing the ax.

Mrs. Thatcher has had remarkable success by making certain the employees of any companies that are candidates for privatization are in favor of the plan. Without employee cooperation, as we have found in the United States, most privatization schemes are doomed. Employees bought out England's largest trucking company, the National Freight Corporation (NFC) which subsequently witnessed a 30% increased in productivity and a jump in its stock. Both the general public and the employee-owners benefited.

In 1982 twenty thousand employees bought 83 percent of National Freight for $80 million. Five years later these same employees faced the happy task of deciding whether to offer the company, which then had an estimated market value in the $400 million range, to the public. That worked out to an average equity ownership of $17,000 for each employee. Not bad, considering many of these workers had never before dreamed of owning capital assets beyond a house or automobile.

The British automaker, Jaguar, was sold by the government in 1983 and in just two years its profits climbed 142 percent. Another company to benefit from its severence from government was Cable & Wireless which more than quadrupled its old state-owned earnings.

In early 1987 British Gas was put up for sale for $7.9 billion; the largest stock offering in England's history. The offering, aided by a 57 million dollar television campaign featuring Larry Hagman, star of the American television series *Dallas,* long a hit in England, attracted 4.5 million buyers. A $237 million offering was oversubscribed in the United States. Three months after the offering, British Gas shares were up 28 percent.

Germany has followed the lead of Britain and France in denationalizing many industries. Privatizing (selling national assets to the public) is an essential part of the West German government's plan to reduce its budget deficit while at the same time carrying through its tax reform proposals. However the October stock market crash slowed the process somewhat as the government waited for the stock of some of the companies it planned to sell to stabilize.

In January 1987, the French government offered Saint-Gobain, one of the nation's most esteemed companies, for sale to the public. "One and a half million Frenchmen bought in, a number equal to the total of all French shareholders before the sale."[2] Because of the long and expensive process involved with registering stock for sale with the U.S. Securities and Exchange Commission, Americans were not offered a chance to buy Saint-

Gobain, at least on the American market. According to Shawn Tully, in an article for *Fortune,* "Even conservatives once supported France's centuries-old tradition of government intervention in business and the economy. Chirac (the former French Prime Minister) renounced that approach, dismantling the web of regulations that hampered state-owned and private companies alike. New laws make it easier for companies to fire employees and arrange workers' schedules to keep factories humming around the clock with a minimum of overtime." The French government plans to sell more than 60 companies with an estimated worth of almost $50 billion by 1991.

Spain, Sweden and Italy are the latest to begin selling off government controlled industries, following the lead of Britain, France and West Germany. In just the last four years Italy's huge holding company, IRI (Instituto per la Ricostruzione Industriale) sold 20 companies and raised more than $3.5 billion to expand and modernize others.

All over Europe a transfer of ownership from bureaucracies, with their social goals, to individuals with their eye on profits, has created a people's capitalism that even Marx and Engel's would find hard to fault. No doubt these thousands of brand new shareholders will be more likely to support free market policies now that they have a stake in the capital of the country.

THE REAGAN ADMINISTRATION
TRIES TO PRIVATIZE

But attempts at privatization in America, once the foremost bastion of an economic system based on free enterprise, have not fared well. In the fall of 1987 former Chamber of Commerce economist, Ronald Utt became the first Director for Privatization at the Office of Management and Budget (OMB). Shortly after that appointment Professor David Linowes of the University of Illinois was named as head of a 13-member commission to suggest new ways to privatize. Over the years the Reagan Administration has proposed privatizing the Coast Guard, National Institute of Health, Amtrack, the Bonneville Power Administration, Naval Petroleum Reserves, government owned housing, waste-water treatment plants, the air-traffic control system, the Tennessee Valley Authority, the post office and uranium enrichment operations. It has been studying the feasibility of privatizing veterans health-care services, the Custom Service, tax court and federal prisons as well.

Let's take the post office as a prime example of resistance to the whole concept of privatization.

Preston Tisch resigned as postmaster general after little more than a year in that position. The post office has come under increasing criticism since Daniel Oliver took over as head of the Federal Trade Commission (FTC). "The Postal Service is a glaring example of the deficiencies of government monopolies" he said in a speech on May 15, 1987 before the direct mail marketers. Mr. Oliver wants to repeal the 1872 Private Express Statutes which have been used for over 115 years to protect the Post Office Department from first-class letter delivery competition. Mr. Tisch insisted that the postal service has competition when it comes to packages and overnight and other special deliveries, although he admitted that "some specific limited restrictions" were put on the choices of the public and the business community.[3] He went on to say that tax laws and antitrust regulation already placed those restrictions on commercial intercourse, as if to say if something is harmful already what's wrong with adding a little more harm.

The postal service has once again asked for a raise in rates in order to fund its pension obligations. In 1987 it assumed between $600,000 and $800,000 in new pension costs. This need accounts for about one-third of the proposed postal rate increase with overhead costs and the anticipation of wage increases making up the other two-thirds of the increase. Unfortunately the hikes will be in the areas in which the postal service has its monopoly and cuts will occur in the rates for overnight mail so the government agency will be able to offer keener subsidized competition to private firms.

Congressman Phil Crane of Illinois has offered legislation

seventeen times which would bring an end to the postal monopoly. Postal employees, fearful for their jobs, have united to block the proposals just as the organizations who supposedly speak for the elderly have been able to successfully block any meaningful Social Security reforms. In 1987 the congressman suggested the assets of the Postal Service be turned over to a corporation owned by the otherwise threatened employees, under an Employee Stock Ownership Plan (ESOP). The Crane bill provides for a five year phase-in period with competition kept at bay, after which the postal monopoly would effectively be abolished.

The Reason Foundation recently published a paper called "Deregulating, Divesting and Privatizing the United States Postal System". It proposes that the postal system be divided into five regional operating companies, a support service and a parcel post company, all to be sold in stock offerings with postal employees being given a 15 percent to 20 percent discount on the stock.

Of course there are those who maintain that the only reason the postal system continues to work as well as it does is its monopoly status. Privatizing the postal service is not something that is likely to be decided any time soon, at least not in favor of privatization if Representative William D. Ford, chairman of the House Post Office and Civil Service Committee has his way.

SORRY — THE PRIVATE SECTOR DOES IT BETTER!

The Local Government Center in Santa Monica, California has a data base with 28,000 examples of privatization throughout the United States by cities, counties and states. Virtually every quantitative study comparing service delivery by government departments with service delivery by private firms finds significant cost savings when private contractors are used. For example, in Boston a private collection agency was used to collect parking fines and revenues went up 600 percent as the private firms collected on 70 percent of the tickets whereas the city had only been successful with 17 percent.

55

An amendment proposed by Congressman John Kasich of Ohio passed the 100th Congress and now the federal government is allowed to enter into contracts with collection agencies in order to collect some of the debt it is owed — more than $35 billion in non-tax debts alone!

Incentives inherent in public-service monopolies just can't match what competition in a free market can accomplish.

But sometimes the efforts to encourage private enterprise have been misguided. For instance the Reagan Administration has suggested limiting NASA to three space-shuttles although, according to David Gump, an expert in this area, "the shift to private launch operations ought to be based on cost, not a politically enforced scarcity of shuttle flights." [4] Mr. Gump argues that instead of undercutting would-be private competitors via gigantic government subsidies, that a private space industry could be legitimately encouraged by guaranteeing private companies a certain number of government pay loads over an agreed upon period of time.

Of course the fact that an activity is encouraged by government does not guarantee that things will go smoothly, or that the private sector will always be interested.

Information companies are balking at computerizing the government's record systems without assurances that they'll recover their expenses. Government data can't be copyrighted which means competitors can buy from the new provider and resell the information at a lower price. The investment is too risky for the potential rewards. On the other hand, where the government has induced a company to step in by awarding it a monopoly, prices have soared making it more expensive to deal with the private sector than the public. As a recent example Martin Marietta Corporation received exclusive rights to the massive amounts of farm data the Agriculture Department gathers and now customers are paying through the nose.

When Danford Sawyer took over the Government Printing Office (GPO), its document-sales operation had compiled a $20 million deficit over a three year period. It only took hints that the agency might be replaced by private printers and GPO productivity soared. But why shouldn't it be replaced by private sector competitors? Is printing and providing information government's business?

The late Malcolm Baldridge asked these same questions in March 1987, when he was Secretary of Commerce. He appeared before the Senate Government Affairs Committe and was questioned by Senator John Glenn of Ohio regarding his efforts to privatize the National Information Service. The Senator claimed since it was well run and a money maker it should be left alone. No matter that it provided unfair competition to those engaged in providing similar services in the private sector.

A couple years ago Jack Anderson used his column to explain how the Center for Disease Control in Atlanta benefits a few at the expense of all taxpayers. According to Mr. Anderson, manufacturers of medical items can have their products tested for free at the Atlanta facility and private agencies, along with an occasional private physcian, can have laboratory analysis done without charge (except to the taxpayers). In 1981 a thousand commercial products were tested in Atlanta at a reported cost of $438,000. How about charging a fee for services?

Currently government agencies are required to compare the cost of products and service in-house with those offered by the private sector and to contract-out only if the savings would be ten percent or more. Office of Management and Budget (OMB) reports that if its directive were followed, taxpayers could expect to save $1 billion a year. It's strange that no candidate for the 1988 presidential election ever mentions this billion dollar a year potential savings when asked how he intends to cut the deficit. Especially strange since they all agree that bringing the deficit under control is their number one objective "when elected"!

THE FEDERAL GOVERNMENT
IN THE LOAN BUSINESS?

Collecting and managing loans is one of those things the private sector does better than a government bureaucracy can ever hope to do. The federal government's $257 billion loan portfolio suffers from a delinquency rate five times that of the private sector. Delinquent debt owed the federal government in 1986 approximated $69 billion; more than double the amount owed just five years earlier (1981 to 1986). That should be reason enough for the federal government to get out of the loan business.

The Reagan administration has been attempting to control the explosion of federal loan programs since 1980; direct loans as well as guarantees. As direct loans are cutback guarantees increase. However many people believe guarantees may be the greater evil. A government guarantee transforms even the highest risk into a top notch security.

Take the Veterans Administration (VA) home loan programs as an example. The VA has made it possible for veterans to get a home loan with no money down and at an interest rate below conventional loans. The borrower pays a fee on one percent of the loan amount which the Reagan administration, in 1985, proposed raising to five percent. Congress howled!

The Administration was painted once again as "cruel and heartless". Somehow you never heard from your Congressmen or the media that in 1985 the VA was owed $700 million by defaulting veterans, and that foreclosures were running at a rate of 2,500 a month, and costing the agency an average of $14,496 on each foreclosed home. But that didn't stop the VA in 1986 from guaranteeing a record $21.8 billion in home loans for veterans.

Federally backed mortgages are especially vulnerable to fraud because they can easily be assumed by a buyer, often with no credit check. Yet where fraud was involved the VA didn't even attempt to collect foreclosure losses from the guilty party but instead went after the sellers.

The Federal Housing Administration (FHA) loan program has its problems also. Fraud losses at the VA and the FHA combined have reached gigantic proportions in the past few years. Since veterans pay no insurance premium the VA loan program is unattractive to the private sector. However, the FHA, which in 1985 made a profit of $162 million and had a $4 billion surplus, is a possible candidate for privatization. Privatizing the FHA, an idea endorsed by the Reagan administration, has been labeled "appalling"[5], "nuts"[6] and "outrageous"[7] by elected officials and others. Yet what is so outrageous about getting rid of a program that has only about 3 percent of the residential housing loan market, down from a 20 percent market share in the 1950s? It serves so few people because private insurers have been able to do the job faster and less expensively.

Our elected officials have freely admitted embarrassment over the number of accounting gimmicks which are constantly being considered in an effort to meet Gramm-Rudman's goals. Critics say selling loans and other government assets is just one such gimmick in a long line. They argue that although it may appear to be a painless way to raise revenue, it is in reality, short sighted. They claim that selling loans in one year may help meet specific deficit reduction targets on a one time basis but widen the deficit later on when interest and principle payments no longer bring funds into the federal coffers. But the government, in selling loans, foregos interest, as critics claim, only if the loans would have been repaid.

Those who try to blame the rush to sell government loans and other assets on Gramm-Rudman are missing the main tenent of conservative thought. Ronald Reagan was elected in large part because he promised to ask the following question over and over: "Is this legitimate government business?"

TO TURN OR NOT TO TURN
TO THE PRIVATE SECTOR?

Early in 1987 OMB attempted to implement a plan to sell direct federal debt to the private sector. Private-sector lending that is now guaranteed by the federal government, such as housing and student loans, would have been reinsured with private carriers.[8] Why not? The discounts that would be demanded by the private sector for the purchase would reveal the portfolio's true worth. Now every loan on government books is treated as if it were as good as gold whereas the fact is, some loans will never be repaid, and others will only be paid in part. Critics say that by selling loans at deep discounts the federal government is essentially giving away the nation's assets. They forget that discounts represent the value to the government of having the use of its money right away. They also reflect the market's opinion of what the loans are really worth and an assessment of their chances for payment. The difference between a discount and a nominal price reveals a subsidy. Selling government loans on the open market will permit the taxpayers to evaluate the true cost of the federal loan programs. Remember, the federal government operates over 350 such programs and has hundreds of billions of dollars outstanding and in loan guarantees.

Some headway has been made in packaging and selling government loans, and no, I'm sorry, but I'm still not satisfied. Let's start, not from what *should be* (government out of the loan business) but from what *actually is* (government already in the loan business). One would think with all our high paid civil servants the taxpayers could expect enough competence from government employees to enable them to package and market these entities without soliciting help from Wall Street. Sure, I know "Wall Street" is the private sector in whose favor I have, up to now, been arguing. But to pass the reins to private financiers who stand to make millions of dollars in commissions and have therefore been fawning over heads of government agencies with loans to sell, is ludicrous. These bureaucratic heads are supposed to appoint financial advisers to help package the loans and naturally these would-be-advisers have a strong interest in seeing that the loans are as easy to sell as possible. To that end they have suggested there be government repayment guarantees, special tax exemptions on interest payments and other benefits for the prospective purchasers of these loans. Some of our elected officials were all for the guarantee idea because it would raise the potential price of the loans and at the same time make them look as if they were working hard at getting the deficit under control. Thank goodness there were some sane heads in the administration who stood fast against such nonsense. The government, by offering guarantees and credits, would only be fattening the purse of the investment bankers while leaving the government with potential liability for defaults, less revenue from tax credits and the loss of the income from the sold assets. How could anyone conceive of persons with vested interests as advisers to government agencies anyway?

WHAT'S THE MATTER WITH VOLUNTEERS?

In September 1986, the Farmers Home Administration's (FmHA) Rural Development Insurance Fund selected Manufacturers Hanover to advise it on the packaging and sale of $1 billion in loans. The fee to Manufacturers Hanover? In the neighborhood of a million dollars! This will be repeated many times, needlessly. What did government pay the members of the Packard Commission or the Grace Commission for their advice? NOTHING AT ALL!

There are many competent individuals who can afford to and would love to help for no reason other than love of country and that they have a skill which can be put to use for the benefit of their fellow citizens. I can give you ten qualified persons to advise on packaging those loans right now.

In contrast to the current proposal to use Wall Street advisers for the sale of government loans, the Grace Commission adhered to strict internal rules shunning even the slightest hint that a conflict of interest might arise. The Commission went as far as to use Frank Cary of IBM on the HUD task force instead of taking advantage of the unique qualifications which would have made him invaluable as head of the task force on data processing. At one time Peter Grace asked, "Must it be a criminal offense to know something about the subject you're dealing with in government?"

Peter Grace was able to assemble over 2,000 corporate volunteers, including 160 of the best and brightest CEOs in the nation. After two years and $76 million worth of donated manpower, equipment and materials, these men had produced 21,000 pages of hard hitting recommendations with another 1.5 million pages of supporting documentation. No more empty platitudes about what needs to be done but 2,478 specific ways to cut $424.4 billion from our deficit over a three year period.

Unfortunately the cooperation of Congress is required to implement these recommendations and the subject successful Congressmen know most about is getting reelected. That meant, among other things, that any cut back in personnel for reasons of efficiency became "policy issues". Shortsighted Congressmen demanded the reinstatement of clearly unnecessary employees on purely political grounds.

On Nov. 12, 1985 the National Research Council released a study which cost the Department of Labor $684,000. The Council is a non-partisan, but apparently not a non-profit, private group established by Congress to advise the government. I personally would feel better about a group's non partisanship if it were also non-profit — absolutely devoid of any vested interest as was the Grace Commission. Why in the world doesn't the Congress wise up and use a group of patriotic high quality volunteers similar to the group Peter Grace was able to gather for his advisory report concerning waste in government?

Congress persons fight over $100,000 for the Phillipines, or the Contras when they could instead save that much and more if they would only give serious consideration to the consequences of their actions.

What can be done outside government? Jack and Jo Ann Hinckley (the parents of President Reagan's would-be assasin) sold their oil business and now devote their time to educating the public about schizophrenia through their American Mental Health Fund. They feel that if they had been better educated about the disease they would have recognized it in their son and been able to prevent the attack on President Reagan.[9]

The Commission for the Status of Women, formed in 1965 to follow women-oriented bills in the Legislature and to collect information on women's issues, had a $721,000 budget in 1985. Why were *federal* dollars needed if the issues were of such concern to individuals?

Why do we need government funds and organizations for displaced workers? In 1983 the National Center on Occupational Readjustment, a *business-backed* clearing house, was established in order to provide support and guidance so that the unhappy effects of plant closings could be minimized. Nancy Olsen, a counselor at a non-profit organization in Palo Alto, California, has written a book called *Starting a Mini-Business: A Guidebook for Seniors and Others Who Dream of Having Their Own Part-Time, Home-Based Business*. There is plenty of help, concern and creativity out there if government would just back away.

David Broder, in his July 9, 1986 column gave an interesting example of volunteerism and the public schools.

The Senate has approved an amendment by Sen. Daniel Evans (R-WA) requiring the Secretary of Education and the National Academy of Sciences to report next year on the feasibility of using subsidized college students, retirees, business and professional people as classroom volunteers.

But if people don't volunteer there are those that apparently feel not the slightest qualm in "volunteering them". Small-scale models of a possible "national service" program are under way in almost half the states and in many local communities. In their 1986 book *"National Service: What Would It Mean?"* Richard Danzig and Peter Szanton estimated that almost 3.5 million persons could fill useful roles, one-third of them in education, the rest in health or child-care, the environment, law enforcement, libraries and museums. The program would be neither cheap nor easy. They suggest that if it is tried at all it should be experimented with at the most local levels.

It had better be strictly voluntary, and not in the sense that *taxes* are voluntary, or forget it!

YOU BETCHA FEDERAL EMPLOYEES OPPOSE PRIVATIZATION!

Much of the cost reduction gained by privatization is due to more efficient use of personnel and the payment of market wages rather than inflated civil-service pay scales. The AFSCME (American

Federation of State County & Municipal Employees) refers to it as firing workers and lowering wages. The fact is most public services are shielded from competition by legislative fiat so that the competitive pressures for cost reduction just aren't there. Public agencies do not have to satisfy consumers in the same manner that private firms must.

The AFSCME is naturally opposed to contracting out, claiming the private sector provides fewer benefits, lower entry-level wages and offers less opportunity (not automatic) for advancement than does the public sector. Unfortunately many people believe the livelihoods of public-employee- union officials depend on continuing the delivery of public services via bureaucratic monopolies. On top of it all, in order to make contracting-out less objectionable to federal employees, the bureaucrats turned their attention to the private sector and set about reducing efficiency there by requiring private contractors to give first chance at their jobs to any federal worker laid off because of the change.

No doubt privatization will reduce the number of government jobs, but if we are to seriously attack our budget deficits we will have to stop living in a dream world and weigh cost as one item in a trade situation. Of course one person's "dream world" is anothers "nightmare". Even if it would *save* instead of *cost* money to have government employees provide all the products and services they now provide, many of us would oppose these government monopolies on ideological grounds. Always it comes down to a honest difference of opinion concerning the role of government in a capitalist society.

EMPLOYEE OWNERSHIP

But forgetting ideology for a moment, on purely pragmatic grounds if government agencies like the Tennessee Valley Authority, sections of the Coast Guard, Amtrack, the Postal Service, the air traffic controllers and military commissaries are sold to their non-military employees the taxpayer would be relieved of providing subsidies for less cost effective operations and pensions for their employees. The employees would be better off as owners of capital and the general public would be better served by a more productive operation. A 1977 University of Michigan study found that on average employee-owned companies are 150 percent more profitable than conventional companies. A similar study by the *Journal of Corporation Law* found that employee-owned firms enjoy almost double the increase in productivity as comparable traditionally owned firms. Is there something wrong with providing the Treasury with greater tax revenue if it were used to reduce the deficit? Ah, — there's the rub!

UNFAIR GOVERNMENT SUBSIDIES

There are powerful forces, other than government employees, who have grown accustomed to government subsidies in one form or another and are opposed to privatization.

In January, 1987, the Reagan administration proposed to raise the fee charged by Ginnie Mae, the Government National Mortgage Association, for guaranteeing mortgage-backed securities, from six to ten basis points. (A basis point is 1/100th of a percentage point.) The reasons for the proposal were sound. The increase was needed to reduce the federal budget deficit, to replenish reserves at Ginnie Mae and to make its fees more comparable to those in the private sector. But that was not good enough for Congressman Henry Gonzalez of Texas who offered a bill to freeeze the fee at six basis points. He called the Administration's proposal preposterous, especially when so many citizens were already finding it difficult to finance the purchase of a home. But the preposterous thing is that the federal government is competing once again with the private sector and using taxpayers' subsidies to do so.

Just as bad, the government uses taxpayer dollars to subsidize one private sector competitor against another. Two examples follow:

First, the Export-Import Bank (Eximbank) provides subsidized credit which helps foreign customers purchase aircraft, locomotives and other big-ticket items from a handful of large American corporations. Smaller companies who see their larger competitors prosper as a result of this activity are helpless. They cannot withhold a portion of *their* tax dollars, so like it or not, they end up subsidizing their competition. Although the Reagan administration suggested that the bank only subsidize interest rates from commercial lenders rather than make loans directly, Congress refused to listen.

Secondly, the residents in a small town outside Boston were certain they could do a better job of managing their water supply than the local private company. The private company, after years of cajoling by customers fed up with murky, bad tasting and foul smelling water, had agreed to build a new water treatment plant. Construction costs were estimated at $7 million. Citizens did not want to pay the increased rates a $7 million construction bill would ensure. They decided that if they banded together they would qualify for state and federal grants; the same plant that would cost a private owner $7 million would cost them only $3.5 million [10] (thanks to taxpayers everywhere).

Ain't it wonderful — better water for the same rates! And the private company? Well, what would you do? It's hard to compete when government gets into the water business, but maybe the would-be entrepreneur can find a nice comfy government job.

Subsidies put government in the___(fill in the blank)___ business in an attempt to even things out. Just because you and I happen to live in an area with a sparkling clear inexpensive water supply doesn't mean we should turn our backs on those in the Boston suburbs. And don't worry, they'll subsidize our highways even though they don't drive to work, but then we'll help out with their mass transit and they'll give a little to help Uncle Jake on the farm and we'll subsidize their student loans and DON'T WORRY — it will all even out. (Then how come our deficit is so large?!)

LINKAGE — PROS AND CONS

"Linkage" is the concept of tying a cutback in a social program with an alternate solution to the problem that needs to be tackled. Support will be greater if Great Society programs are not simply undone, but replaced by programs of the Opportunity Society. But there are both good and bad aspects to these solutions. It may be fairly easy to argue that the benefits outweigh the harm to the private sector by, for instance, passing a proposed "homestead act" to sell public housing to tenants to help soften the blow of cutbacks in urban grants.

A little trickier is the coupling of a cut in training programs with the establishment of vouchers or enterprise zones. Enterprise zones are credited with the creation of 130,000 jobs. Entrepreneurs are enticed to start new companies with offers by government of exemptions from property, sales and other taxes and credits for hiring new workers. Some communities promise loan guarantees for business starts and even child-care for employees. There is no doubt these programs are beneficial to some segments of society but how can older, often struggling, businesses compete without the subsidies being offered these newcomers?

A well meaning government finds itself favoring some at the expense of others. Is this fair? Is this government's role? It is a role that if not filled by government would, and some might argue *should,* be filled by private organizations. Men reaching out to one another is, after all, what life is ultimately about. Above all government must remain neutral — never favoring one group above another and existing only to redress grievances which arise from the private sector.

THE COST OF ENERGY
IS EVERBODY'S BUSINESS

Do you realize the federal government has made power more expensive for many citizens already?

Richard Clarke, chairman of Pacific Gas & Electric (PG&E)

claimed PURPA, the Public Utility Regulatory Policies Act, (part of the larger National Energy Act of 1978), is responsible for California consumers paying an extra $850 million a year. PG&E is forced by PURPA to purchase power from independent cogenerators. Another portion of the 1978 National Energy Act (Fuel Use Act) prevented electric utilities from installing new gas-buning generators, in effect giving a favored position to cogenerators.[11] Although cogeneration can be highly efficient, Mr. Clarke objects to government's mandate forcing him to buy power he neither needs or wants at exorbitant prices when a free market in power is not only feasible but has been practiced successfully by PG&E in San Francisco. There in its headquarters company technicians purchase power as prices are transmitted electronically from other producers in the region. Terms and conditions for purchases of power are set by state PUCs (Public Utility Commissions) and they vary around the country.

Do you realize the federal government has the power to increase the cost of your utility bill?

Privately-owned utilities serve 88 percent of electricity consumers in the United States while government owned utilities serve the other 12 percent. Private utilities operate 366 licensed hydroelectric plants serving millions of customers in 41 states. Hydroelectric plants provide a relatively inexpensive source of power which helps keep the nation's electricity bills down. However, government-owned utilities have a "preference" in the relicensing of hydroelectric projects originally licensed by the government long ago. According to a strict interpretation of an old law, government utilities could conceivably take over hydroelectric projects in their areas and monopolize the cheap power for their own customers. Such a preference could mean that cities and towns with municipal utilities would only be required to make ridiculously low payments based on the original cost of the projects — an unconscionable competitive advantage. Contrary to the public power rhetoric of the early 1900s, private investors weren't "power grabbers", but rather power suppliers. (I can't resist a pun and so will remind you that the real power grabber is government at all levels.)

STATE AND LOCAL GOVERNMENTS

State and local governments spent $100 billion in 1985 to purchase services from the private sector. Kansas City International Airport saved 55 percent by contracting with the private sector for fire protection and rescue service. Los Angeles county saved 21 percent by hiring a private firm to supply food services at its University of Southern California Medical Center. Chicago saved 50 percent on transportation for the handicapped and so on and so forth. In St. Paul, Minnesota the police and fire departments are "contracted in", meaning they serve as backups for surrounding communities and charge for their services as required.

Vehicle towing heads the list of services now provided by the private sector.

> The second largest contract nationwide is legal services, with 48%, followed by streetlight operation, 38% solid waste disposal, 26%, street repair, 26%, hospital operation, 25%, traffic signal maintenance, 25%, labor relations, 23%, ambulance service 23%, building maintenance, 19%, snow plowing, 14%, exterminating services, 13% and payroll, 10%.[12]

As was mentioned earlier, building and operating prisons and detention centers is another area ripe for privatization but thanks to strict bidding processes and government regulation, it has a very low profit margin. There is also the question of liability; what happens if someone escapes and causes harm? New Mexico and Texas have authorized the use of private prisons in their states. Tennessee and Florida both have high security detention facilities that are run by private firms.

YOU'VE GOT TO BE KIDDING

Representative Silvio Conte proposed a bill to allow the government to charge recreational boat owners a mere $20 per year fee to offset some of the costs of non-emergency services provided to them by the Coast Guard. It was a ridiculously low figure to request. Might as well have gone down for $200 as for $20 since the bill was defeated 119 to 287 anyway. The Grace Commission estimated that it costs about 12 times the cost of a private tow to have the Coast Guard engage in non-emergency towing services. Instead of a Coast Guard, the British have a volunteer search and rescue service called the Royal National Lifeboat Institution. This Institution provides services similar to those provided by our Coast Guard but uses no government funds to do so.

It would appear to the casual observer that Congress is mismanaging the Coast Guard. Cutting back their funds is one thing, but according to columnist Jack Anderson, there may have been a conflict of interest regarding boats.[13] Apparently the Coast Guard could have designed a patrol boat for a million dollars which would not have allowed drug smugglers the advantage they presently enjoy, while at the same time avoiding a $5.5 million design cost paid by Congress for an allegedly inferior design. The boat the Coast Guard was *ordered* to buy cannot be operated successfully at high speeds in high seas, develops hull problems potentially dangerous to its crews, idles high enough to sway small boats being towed, has a service life of only 15 years and if that were not enough, it is expensive to repair. How many 1988 presidential candidates brought this to your attention?

There are reasons why Congress didn't jump at the offer made by a private company to build and operate a much needed icebreaker at a fraction of the Coast Guard's cost to do the same thing, but the question is would we accept those reasons? Would it be too much to ask to save taxpayers the estimated $300 million cost of the icebreaker and at the same time shorten the delivery time? Congress seems to be a natural at getting things hind-to. Opting for an expensive private design when the Coast Guard could do better for less is mistake number one. Rejecting a private bid where the Coast Guard will take longer and cost more is mistake number two. Are there more? Do cows eat grass?

Take the air-traffic-control system as another example. It is no secret that private air-traffic control companies, commonly used at smaller airports, often provide better service at half the price.

But instead of leaning towards privatizing air controllers, the Department of Transportation (DOT) is considering a plan to make the FAA a government owned corporation.

More?

The Department of Transportation has regulations preventing communication companies from laying fiber optic cable along federal highways, although there is no safety reason and the companies would be willing to *pay* for the privilige. But who needs the money, right?!

ARE WE EXPECTING TOO MUCH FROM OUR PUBLIC OFFICIALS?

Is it possible we're being too hard on our public officials? What would you say to a business executive whose company had invested $7.7 billion in a venture and was looking to sell the same for $1.2 billion? Why should we be more lenient with public officials? Is it so easy to pretend everybody's money is nobody's money?

Since 1976 the government has poured $7.7 billion into Conrail, the government freight railroad which was formed by combining six bankrupt carriers. Conrail operates a 13,000 mile route in 15 states and employs approximately 35,500 workers. The railraod became profitable in 1981 following government spending to modernize it, cost cutting measures and concessions by labor. At one time the Congressional Budget Office (CBO) thought the government's proposed sale of Conrail could bring as much as $3 billion into the federal coffers.

Then Secretary of Transportation, Elizabeth Dole, had originally pushed for a sale to Norfolk Southern Railroad for $1.2 billion, reasoning that Conrail might not survive alone and that Norfolk could afford to keep it alive. But that $7.7 billion of taxpayer money had brought Conrail's profits up from $39 million in 1981 to $442 million in 1985. Not bad, even though profits dropped to slightly more than $431 million on revenue of $3.14 billion in 1986. True, the favorable accounting treatment that

71

helped make those profits will disappear when the railroad is no longer owned by the government and must succumb to conventional corporate accounting. Nevertheless at the end of 1986 Wall Street sages were predicting a more realistic sale price in the $2 billion range; $8 million more for the taxpayers than what our officials had been willing to settle for. Even though the Senate earlier approved the $1.2 billion sale to Norfolk, that company later raised its bid to $1.9 billion when Morgan Stanley Group, Inc. offered to underwrite a public offering geared to yield $2 billion. In the summer of 1986 Norfolk dropped out of the picture entirely.

On March 26, 1987 Conrail offered 58.8 million common shares representing the government's 85 percent stake in the company; the other 15 percent is owned by Conrail's employees. This was the largest initial stock offering by a U.S. company to date. The offering sold out in one day raising $1.65 billion for the government. When a stock is selling at a price that is so favorable that buyers cannot get all they want, any business person will tell you the price should be raised until supply and demand is evened out. Conrail was priced at $28 a share, a price/earnings ratio of less than 10, whereas non-government railroads were being offered at up to 17 times per share earnings. Other railroads trade at premiums of at least 10 percent above their book value. Conrail's book value was roughly $50 per share; considerably higher than its stock offering would indicate. Does this look like the taxpayers are getting a good deal here? Does it look like maybe *somebody else* is getting an unnecessarily large bargain? Its underwriters would argue that Conrail's markets may be contracting, its revenue falling and anticipated dividends may not be as great as other railroads. What are you, Joe and Mary taxpayer, suppose to answer? Power leaves those without it with a desperate feeling of helplessness which no American citizen should have to endure.

But we are told, "In the end, though, the $1.9 billion public stock sale left nearly everyone happy"[14] It kept service and rate structures intact which might not have been the case if the sale had been made to a private firm. By the terms of the sale changes in operations are not permitted for three years. Favorable reception of the stock offering on Wall Street helped strengthen management's hand.

No matter how you look at it, the sale was not profitable unless you simply forget the $7.7 billion taxpayers poured into it. Is that poor management or what? How much incompetence are you willing to forgive?

I think you will share my amazement that as the offering was being prepared, other officials were sabotaging the sale by suggesting renewed railroad regulation and more stringent tax treatment. Certainly the worst feature of Conrail was the subsidized competition it provided rival private sector railroads. As we discussed earlier, privatization prevents the government, which is supported by *all* the people, from favoring some over others.

A recent article in the *Wall Street Journal* [15] told of Walter Rich who owns and operates a small independent railway which he claims has 50 percent lower labor costs than Conrail because it operates with smaller crews and without Conrail's costly work rules. He convinced Conrail, in 1982, to grant him rights to haul freight trains on a Conrail track between Binghamton, New York and northern New Jersey. In 1986 Conrail raised its fees substantially in an attempt to stifle the competition Mr. Rich and his little railway were presenting. In response Mr. Rich began to renovate 70 miles of decrepit and hilly track while still using Conrail's lines (for a fee) for most of his trips. Although Conrail has a considerable advantage with a shorter direct route to offer customers, still the government controlled line throws roadblocks at the struggling entrepreneur, much in the manner of an Ayn Rand novel.[16] At Binghamton, Conrail forces Sea-Land trains to switch onto a siding to make the connection between Delaware Otsego and Guilford. This wastes countless hours and has led to at least one derailment. In still another example of one hand undoing the work of the other, Mr. Rich has been able to attract grants and low-interest loans from state and federal agencies interested in preserving rail service. "What government builds up, government tears down." How long are we going to put up with this nonsense?

73

PRIVATIZING WORKS

What if I could prove to you that privatizing works? What if I could show you that what people need and want to get done, *can* get done even without the profit motive? Hypocrisy!

The Nature Conservatory (TNC), headquartered in Arlington, Virginia, is the largest private owner of land sanctuaries in the world. It had its beginnings in 1917 as an offshoot of the Ecological Society of America. Since 1953 it has been purchasing private land to set aside to preserve endangered plants and animals. It has approximately 900 sanctuaries, more than two and a half million acres of land providing shelter for more than a thousand species of threatened flora and fauna. It was even asked by the U.S. Fish and Wildlife Service to raise $25 million to purchase land threatened by development which was home to a particular endangered reptile. Some people believe TNC's computerized list of endangered plants and wildlife species is better than that at the Department of Interior.

TNC is funded, not by the government, but by private benefactors — just people who care. In 1985 TNC had assets estimated at $457 million. A past president of the organization told a *Time* magazine reporter that the group, in 1987, had $50 million in liquid cash which enables it to jump into the real estate market competitively and quickly. "We intend to raise a billion dollars by 1995 to save what is worth saving" said Frank Boren, a former real estate executive and TNC's president.[17]

TNC is proof that the government pie is not the only pie in town. TNC shows that if government fails to do something that a large number of people feel should be done, then the people themselves will gather voluntarily and tackle the problem. There are only two alternatives. The first is to keep Uncle Sam's pie growing (Reagonomics) and although no one questions the desirability of such a plan, we have seen how hard it is to accomplish. The second alternative is to referee the various interest groups already receiving subsidies and incentives who nevertheless continually clamor for an ever bigger slice of Sam's pie. The nation continues to work toward accomplishing alternative one but in the meantime it has had to adopt alternative two. I have in this chapter attempted to acquaint you with some of the drawbacks inherent in alternative two and can only recommend it to those able to embrace the concept of centralized planning and "fair share".

A further word of advice to this group: your best course of action is to simply not let yourself even think about the federal deficit!

THE FOURTH STEP

(RE: DEREGULATION)

FREE CITIZENS FROM EXCESSIVE REGULATION AND ENCOURAGE CREATIVITY

THE 4th STEP

(RE: DEREGULATION)

THE POPULAR POINT OF VIEW

Deregulation has gone too far. Now that the Reagan era is over it is time for a reversal. Deregulation will jeopardize public safety and the environment.

ANOTHER POINT OF VIEW

Deregulation has just begun. It still has a long way to go but as unneeded detrimental restrictions are removed, industry and creativity will flourish. Deregulation will play a large part in getting this nation out of debt. An informed populace can best protect itself and the environment.

REGULATION IS COSTLY

Regulation costs in two ways; the first is money. There is no doubt about it, some regulation is well worth the dollars spent. When we get real value for the cost of regulation we make a good trade. However there are many instances when regulation does more harm than good. You will find in this chapter examples of regulations that are "not worth it".

Secondly, regulation costs those that are regulated a portion of their independence. They are asked to exchange a bit of their potential for growth and ingenuity in return for an often false sense of security. Regulated citizens are too often lulled into believing that they no longer have to check things out and make decisions on their own. They come to depend on Big Brother to do their thinking and choosing for them and if things do not turn out as expected they turn to the courts. This is the often forgotten and most dangerous cost of regulation.

A NATION OF WIMPS?

Too many of our citizens in recent years have been taught to look to government for nurturing and sustenance. Just this morning the news reported that many home blood pressure machines have been found to be inaccurate. The proposed solution? Federal regulation! The stamp of approval from Uncle Sam is supposed to reassure us.

We are changing from a self-reliant, independent populace to a conglomeration of whimpering dependents, unable and unwilling to take responsibililty for our actions and our decisions.

A lady in Pennsylvannia fell asleep with a cigarette and immediately sued the tobacco and couch manufacturers for the resultant fire. A child choked on a peanut butter sandwich and the parents sued, claiming the peanut butter manufacturer should have warned that eating peanut butter could be dangerous.

John Marshall, Supreme Court Justice 1801 to 1835, gave classic expression to the theory that the Constitution should be broadly interpreted in order that the federal government could achieve its purpose for the general welfare. From that small beginning others have chipped away over the years until the Constitution that was supposed to protect the sovereignty of the individual against the state and the state's sovereignty against the federal government has lost its potency.

Elected officials see the average American as a person with needs. Fill his needs, collect his vote and pat him on the head and before long America will be permanently and irrevocably a stratified nation; a few at the top stroking and feeding the many needful at the bottom.

We are familiar with the young men who inhabit pool halls and park benches all around the country, and in their "spare time" father five or six illegitimate babies. What do you think they would do if no agency reached out to care for their "families"? Do you think they would let them starve?

Do you believe young men today are less capable than our pioneer ancestors who had no education and nothing but their bare hands, ingenuity and love? No—they had one more thing — *freedom*. The difference today is not with people but with government's role. Government policy makes young men feel ashamed and removes their motivation to try because the government can provide more than they can. Take away government and some might cry "how cruel" — take away government and I would point out that the shiftless young men suddenly become persons of substance who are very much needed. Dignity and incentive filter through, and all those who truly believe in the *equality of men* will not be surprised that new potential is unleashed without special educational programs, without job-training, without subsidized housing or food. *Leave them alone.* I realize this is too simple for those who are addicted to controlling others and looking down on them under the cover of compassion, but believe me, it is the solution.

As you read these words there are a dozen people on talk shows across the nation teaching people how to slip into self-esteem in the eighties. How to feel good about what they may have no right to feel good about.

Drug addicts, alcoholics, the lazy, the undereducated, the timid, all repeating "I am beautiful", "I deserve", "I am worthy", "I am great" just doesn't make it so.

REGULATION MAKES
LEGISLATORS LOOK GOOD

Democrats have controlled the House of Representatives for a good many years and frequently control the Senate also. They are the majority party in both Houses of the 100th Congress, which means they have greater control than the Republicans over regulation. The Democratic Party views regulation as a way to be considered activists on popular issues without spending a lot of money. They cannot afford to be labeled as "big spenders" during this time of austerity brought on by the government's huge federal budget deficits. The Democrats want to be identified as the party that is concerned with the public interest, but in doing so they must be careful not to appear too much like the party of big government. But "big government" may no longer be the unpopular villian it was during the years of Ronald Reagan's ascendency. The change reflects reviving sentiment for a strong government role in certain areas of public concern. Many experts are declaring that the anti-government revolt that catapulted Ronald Reagan to power is now over.

Perhaps they are right. In a 1987 NBC-WSJ poll 61 percent of those surveyed said there should be more government regulation of the environment, while only 6 percent said there should be less. But then that's the environment and its regulation is considered, even by Libertarians, to be a legitimate concern of government. However the same poll showed that 38 percent of the people still believe there is too much government regulation of the economy, while 32 percent think there is about the right amount and 23 percent say there is too little. This is a more significant finding when one considers that in 1980 more than two-thirds of those polled thought there was too much regulation!

AIRLINES AS A CASE IN POINT

In July, 1987 a Roper opinion poll was released that would seem to support the contention of those who claim the trend towards deregulation has been reversed. The poll asked 1,997 adults the following questions:

Q 1—Is there too much government regulation of airlines, not enough, or about right?
In 1984 16% said not enough, 52% said about right, 15% said too much and 17% were undecided.
In 1987 35% answered not enough, 35% about right, 17% too much and 13% were undecided.

Q 2— Should airlines be free to raise or lower their fares on their own or should they be required to get permission from the government?
In 1984 53% said be free; 35% said get permission and 12% were undecided.
In 1987 43% said be free; 49% wanted airlines to obtain permission and only 8% had no opinion.

The people seem to be saying "enough already!", even though there is no doubt that deregulation has resulted in cheaper fares and more people flying. In fact a Brookings Institution study estimated air travelers save approximately $6 billion a year thanks to deregulation. Unfortunately the popular media focuses almost exclusively on the delays and crowds. The public, who might feel differently if they evaluated the entire picture, may never get that opportunity.

ARE THESE REGULATIONS "WORTH IT"?

James Bovard wrote a piece for the *Wall Street Journal* sometime ago, in which he discussed Federal Marketing Order 910, proposed for reasons technology has since made obsolete. When enacted in 1941, the regulation was intended to stabilize prices and preserve small lemon growers. It has not been successful in either endeavor; the number of growers has been drastically reduced and lemon prices fluctuate more than most fruit prices. Indeed, Mr. Bovard claims the regulation is responsible for the shameful fact that 500 million fresh lemons rot in the fields each year. Under its directive California and Arizona growers must grow three or four lemons in order to earn the right to sell one! Technology has made possible a new shrink-wrapping process for lemons which could put an end to this nonsense. However, a large company, in an effort to keep the lion's share of the lemon market, has managed to block shrink-wrapping with the help of Federal Market Order 910.

Lemons are one example of the many products that are subject to, not the producers' good sense and judgment, but to the half-wit policies of often totally unknowledgable bureaucrats. A perfect example of the misuse of power and the danger of regulation. There are many such examples.

The U.S. Dept of Agriculture defines pizza as a dough-bread product containing cheese and tomato sauce. When an innovative chef in Los Angeles recently tried to market a frozen version of a pizza using fresh ingredients instead of tomato sauce, he was told it didn't meet the Department's definition of pizza!

Here is one of my favorite examples as reported by the *Wall Street Journal:*

> let us tell you about part 1680-00-103-4974 and part 1680-00-103-4973. These are nylon-webbing leg restraints used with fighter-plane ejector seats. They are identical, and worth about $12. Part 1680-00-103-4974 is for the left leg…it's price is $102.95. Part 1680-00-103-4973 is for the right leg;…it comes out $244.[1]

The *Wall Street Journal* ridiculed the bureaucracy found in Pentagon procurement procedures in 1985, showing how similar its practices were to Soviet bureaucracy. They presented a true case history relating how two diodes that should cost mere pennies ended up costing the navy $110 each. Navy personnel consulted manuals to price every step in the procedure. They were able to determine how many hours it takes a contractor to make a purchase; this came out to be 4.5 hours; someone looked up the hourly rate for material handling which came to $18 hour; another person was paid to multiply the 4.5 by 18 to get a labor cost of $81; then the contractor's allowable overhead was added making the total $157.22 which, when added to pre-negotiated allowances for general and administrative expenses = $190.24 which, with the contractor's profit of 16 percent, made the grand total $220.68 for two diodes which, according to the article, would have cost under a dollar at any Radio Shack store in the country.

On June 22, 1987 the Federal Drug Administration (FDA) relaxed rules for the distribution of certain drugs. The new regulations allowed pharmaceutical companies to distribute experimental drugs and charge enough to recapture their costs, though not enough to make a profit. The idea is that when a person is dying and where a patient and his doctor are informed, society can afford to take a risk. That accounts for the "fast track" approval in 1986 afforded AZT, the drug to control AIDS. Many people were happy with the FDA's decision although critics are afraid that as a result the sick and dying will not be adequately protected. It's a trade off. Only an AIDS patient can tell you if it's "worth it".

ENTREPRENEURIAL INCENTIVES:
THE KEY TO AMERICA'S SUCCESS

Pharmaceutical firms were expected to invest about $6 billion in research and development in 1987.

Development of a new drug from initial discovery through testing to approval can take seven to ten years, with the approval process alone adding roughly $300 million to the cost of development. Needless to say, when talking about cures for rare diseases profits rarely enter the conversation.

In the case of AIDS, Burroughs-Wellcomes' introduction of AZT, not so much a cure as a life-extender, was met by jeers and slanderous epitaphs. Because a years supply of AZT will cost a typical AIDS patient anywhere from $7,000 to $10,000 the company was accused of greed.

The United States government has in the past appreciated the risk inherent in break-through research and has been willing to encourage entrepreneuers by gladly offering a patent. Currently such a patent is good for a 17 year monopoly which permits a firm, in most cases, to recoup at least some of its investment and doesn't completely discourage it from undertaking similar risks in the future. Because not all research leads to a marketable product, when it does it is sometimes compensated in a manner to make up for past and future losses. Nothing new here — it has worked for generations.

The Federal Drug Administration is often between a rock and a hard place; damned if it approves what turns out to be a dangerous drug (which is always sensationalized by the press) and damned if it doesn't approve a potentially life-saving drug. Part of the problem stems from Congressional hearings focusing on the problems rather than the benefits of drugs. What about the lives saved as opposed to the deaths?

It had been estimated that advances in drug therapy save 40,000 to 100,000 lives per decade, while "a very high estimate of lives lost to drug-related accidents would be 10,000 lives per decade".[2] This is another example where regulation harms more than it helps. There is no such thing as a riskless society. The FDA is a creation of Congress. You know — the people who control the purse strings.

THINK IT OVER! WHAT IF
THE GOVERNMENT STARTS
PAYING FOR PERSCRIPTION DRUGS?

Kidney dialysis costs more than AZT and so do transplants. So why have pharmaceutical firms come under attack?

You don't suppose the fact that hospital stays are paid by Medicare and drugs are paid directly by the patient has any bearing on the situation do you? No — the government would have realized the signals it would be sending out — they are "experts" at social engineering after all.

Genotech spent over $200 million developing the drug referred to as TPA which costs heart-attack victims $2,300 for a single dose. Although doctors do not uniformly agree that TPA is superior to an alternate drug which is ten times cheaper, activists are charging hospitals with discrimination if they choose not to treat poorer patients with TPA.

Should Medicare cover the cost? Think what would happen if Medicare were expanded to cover all drugs regardless of cost. This is an idea being actively pursued by those too short-sighted to see the inevitable consequences. The result would be a government subsidy of the pharmaceutical industry and bankruptcy for the nation. Nevertheless advocates of Medicare expansion have the chutzpah to argue "cost-efficiency" by claiming a $280 million savings from taxpayers picking up the tab for TPA because the drug may allow patients to return to work earlier. (Oy veh! Remember — even the doctors don't agree!)

WHERE REGULATION
HAS DONE MORE HARM THAN GOOD

Much of government's interference in the private business sector over the past fifty years has done more harm than good. Unfortunately it has been fashionable lately to let management take the blame for a lot of government's mistakes. For instance the Corporate Average Fuel Economy (CAFE) standards, enacted by Congress in 1975, which mandated that automobile manufacturers meet specified fuel-economy standards, is a case in point. After 1981 the real cost of gasoline fell by more than thirty percent which increased the demand for larger, less fuel-efficient cars. CAFE standards affected consumer choices by reducing the availability of automobiles that were less fuel-efficient and therefore more damaging to the environment.

If citizens want clean air *and* large cars they must pay the price or be forced to choose between the two. Free-loaders; those who want to drive large cars and let others pay for the pollution clean-up, can be a problem. However the government might have better luck, not by restricting their choice of automobiles, but by making them pay for the pollution consequences via the gasoline tax. The larger the car the more gasoline consumption and therefore larger share of the clean-up costs is ensured.

Contrary to popular belief, Detroit tried three times to come out with small cars, but each time the United States government signaled that energy prices were going to be kept down, that gasoline would not be allowed to rise to its true market level. Consequently, the industry was stuck twice with large unsold inventories of small cars. Our government dealt an unintended, but nevertheless devastating blow via policies aimed at other objectives.

SPECIAL INTERESTS' ROLE
IN A PLANNED ECONOMY

The steel industry is an unfortunate example of special interests at work. Special interests are not bad in themselves. They have no hold over a multitude of creative flexible individuals, but only become dangerous when they come up against a centralized entity willing and able to exchange power for power. The steel industry created a smoke screen with their lobbying efforts for quotas and tariffs on imported steel and subsidized loans to domestic steel companies. This smoke screen disguised the true state of affairs, made the situation at least temporarily palatable and enabled the industry to resist adjusting to reality. Production and employment were not cut gradually, as clear vision would have dictated, and domestic prices rose as a consequence when they should have prudently dropped.

It is common knowledge that industries that rely heavily on government — any government or centralized power — do just fine when the overall economy is good but adjust slowly to adverse conditions. Russia provides a good example. Her economy expanded at a fast clip during the fifties and sixties but faltered during the seventies and eighties. Our own deepening dependence on the federal government since the New Deal has inevitably reduced the flexibility of the American economy. Too often we find ourselves following our leaders down the path to disaster — leaders who frequently receive inadequate information and poor advice.

Why else would President Nixon panic the Japanese by proposing standby export restrictions on soybeans? In an understandable effort to avoid possible shortages from the United States, Japanese importers and trading companies responded by helping step up soybean cultivation in Brazil, and now Brazil is our biggest competitor in world soybean markets.[3]

Why else would the Reagan administration put quotas on imports of Chinese textiles? Should we be surprised that Beijing retaliated against the United States by cutting purchases of our grain and turned to other suppliers, such as Canada, instead?

Why else would the Equal Opportunity Commission (EOC) spend millions of dollars trying to make a case against Sears Roebuck, one of the nation's largest and most socially minded employers?[4] Do we really have too many good guys and too much money in this country?

THE FEDERAL TRADE COMMISSION

Speaking of good guys, Daniel Oliver, who took over as head of the Federal Trade Commission (FTC) when James C. Miller III became OMB Director (Office of Managment and Budget), is definitely in that catagory. He sees his job as one of promoting competition as the consumer's best and finest protection in the marketplace. He believes in passing judgment, not on whether a merger of businesses is good or bad, but on whether it will be anticompetitive. Mr. Oliver tends to view proposed mergers on an international scale rather than simply a domestic level, and will only bring the FTC into the picture when it looks like a monopoly might result or there is a possibility of price fixing. Whereas the Justice Department seeks criminal sanctions, Mr. Oliver sees the FTC role as a mandate to police unfair and deceptive practices using the courts only to stop mergers. He acknowledges that terms such as "unfair" and "deceptive practices" are vague, overly broad, arbitrary and probably cannot stand up to scrutiny if challenged on constitutional grounds.

Mr. Oliver is aware that anxiety and uncertainty are harmful to business and in the long-run to the consumer, his ultimate interest. A man willing to take the heat and sacrifice himself for long-range views and principles is rare. At the start of the Reagan administration many federal regulators assumed that while Congress set limits on the power to regulate, those same regulations gave them more freedom to deregulate. Unfortunately the District of Columbia courts have chosen to see it differently and have overturned deregulation actions more consistently than they did regulatory actions. The District of Columbia may be small geographically but nearly 40 percent of all challenges to regulatory agency decisions are filed there.

THE FEDERAL
COMMUNICATIONS COMMISSION

An article in *Business Week* criticized deregulation by the Federal Communications Commission (FCC) under Reagan appointed Chairman Mark Fowler, claiming the FCC may be "abandoning its duty to promote quality programming and responsible ownership of media." The same article also spoke of "public policy goals of increased diversity, competition and innovation." [5]

"Quality" and "responsible" call for a subjective judgment — made by whom? There is no omniscient, benevolent "Big Brother" or "Uncle" to turn to. Society is really using an appointed somebody to make these judgments on its behalf. This appointed somebody is supposed to do a "better", presumably "fairer" (in whose judgment?) job of ensuring "increased diversity, competition and innovation" than can be accomplished by a free marketplace. Nonsense!

The FCC originated in 1934 (hardly a surprise) and managed to effectively control competition for the benefit of those already in the broadcasting and telephone industries. In the 1960s and 70s it went to work restricting the fledgling cable-TV industry.

Luckily the "somebody" President Reagan appointed in 1981 to head the FCC, according to the same *Business Week* article, sees "...his mission as 'prunning, chopping, slashing, eliminating, burning and deep-sixing' a half-century of regulation." [6]

Under Mr. Fowler's leadership the FCC has managed to end the limits on the number of TV commercials per hour and is instead depending on the fear of losing viewers to competitors to regulate station operators. (A rather old fashioned free market tenent, too basic for some.) The FCC also tried to eliminate the restrictions on the number of radio and TV stations that any single entity can own. However on that issue the FCC was forced to compromise with Congress, agreeing that a broadcasting company could own up to twelve TV stations as long as the combined potential audience of the twelve stations didn't exceed twenty-five percent of all television households in the country. (Micro-managing by Tweedle Dum and Tweedle Dee.)

By relaxing the rules requiring TV stations to air "informative" children's programming, the FCC opened itself to a great deal of criticism. Again, on whose judgment do we rely? I guess it doesn't matter as long as the average citizen prefers to abdicate control over his own children in this, as in so many areas. Some people just can't understand Mr. Fowler's belief that the first amendment's free-speech guarantee extends to station owners as well as print publishers. Regulation of broadcast content has been based on the premise that broadcasting frequencies belong to the public and are entrusted to the station. More public trust, meaning "someone else please make decisions for us again". Something tells me my pioneer ancestors would not stand for it! This idea gained acceptance at a time when broadcasting frequencies were scarce. With satellites and other new technology, this argument, according to Mr. Fowler and others, is no longer relevant. Using this line of reasoning has allowed the FCC to attack the Fairness Doctrine which requires broadcasters to air both sides of controversial public issues. Mr. Fowler argues that this is like telling a newspaper what it can or can't print.

Promoting competition in the telecommunication industry may not have been as ideologically satisfying to Mr. Fowler. Here the FCC was forced to regulate deregulation. Most AT&T customers ignored their long distance choices in the beginning and it looked like after all the chaos of breaking-up AT&T, it would keep its monopoly by default.

Observing procedure at the FCC can be revealing. The ideas espoused by the Reagan administration may be clear-cut (critics prefer the word simplistic) and basically sound, but the implementation is often complicated and results messy. What seems to alarm many, gives me cheer; that is the "...shift in the FCC's view of its own role from a guardian of the public interest to an indifferent bystander in private business disputes." [7]

ACCRUAL ACCOUNTING
FOR "SAM'S SAKE"

From time to time legislators propose regulations to benefit themselves at the expense of citizens. The proposal to force all businesses with over $5 million annual revenue to adopt the accrual method of accounting was such a situation. Under the principles of accrual accounting, income is taxed when it is billed rather than when the cash is received, if ever. How nice for government's coffers. Naturally such a change from cash accounting to accrual could cause severe cash flow problems for numerous service businesses, but who cares? Surely not Uncle Sam, just as long as he gets his revenue a little earlier! This is an example of oppression by an unfeeling and uncaring government. The same mentality proposed taxing the "inside buildup" on whole life insurance policies. Even the previously deductible interest was sniffed out by revenue hounds as a tax bonanza!

"SET ASIDES" —
REGULATION THAT IS EASY TO
"GET AROUND"

I am continually surprised to find that so often the policies which have caused this country the most grief originated in the Nixon administration. For instance "set asides" can be traced to 1968 and the 8(a) program (referring to the federal procurement process) under the Small Business Administration. Set asides allow a minority business enterprise (MBE) or a disadvantaged business enterprise (DBE) first crack at government contracts. In many instances when government enters into a contract it is engaging in activities which should better be left to private enterprise, and when the government *does* have legitimate business to contract out, it is wrong for it to discriminate *against* white-male-run enterprises in an effort to make up for past discrimination against minorities. It can't be justified by pretending two wrongs make a right. (Ok — so you've heard that one before.)

Ironically the most damage is done by the individuals we claim to honor most; the epitome of those who in the past were responsible for America's greatness — the creative, wily, innovative entrepreneur, adept at keeping one step ahead of the policymakers and able to turn any regulation to advantage. As an example, under the 1977 Public Works Employment Act a study found thirty-two percent of the minority beneficiaries were actually sham companies owned and managed covertly by whites. A low bid white-operated company is sometimes hired by the higher bid minority company who was awarded the government contract but does not have either the skill or equipment to accomplish the task. The Government Accounting Office estimated that "...minority contracts on public works projects were 9 percent higher than low bids from non-minority companies" and 10.7 percent to 15 percent higher when it comes to highway jobs.[7] The non-minority firm gets the job that without the law they probably would have gotten in the first place and the minority firm keeps the premium the government paid. Both parties are happy; only the taxpayers lose.

Canton, Illinois townspeople lost $250,000 and more importantly perhaps, a little bit of their willingness to go out on a limb to help next time the occasion arises. The town offered a low interest loan to attract investors in order to keep a dying business (Canton Industrial Corp.) running what may prove to be "beyond its time". As reported in *Forbes* magazine⁸ the business in question had been a subsidiary of International Harvester and had at one time employed 2,300 people in the production of farm machinery.

The town was successful in its attempt to attract new plant owners who soon ran up losses of $1.25 million on sales of $373,000. Like the townsfolk before them, the new owners' thoughts turned to government as a way out of their predicament. They decided to sell the business to a woman (minority) believing "…Canton, as a woman-owned enterprise, would be eligible for priority treatment in federal government contract awards." In this case, the favorable treatment was only a suggestion that government extend favorable treatment to female-owned enterprises, a suggestion that did not carry the force of law. Unfortunately the only qualification of this second "new" owner was her sex. Not surprisingly, according to the *Forbes* account, in early 1988 the company was in "…Chapter 11, owing creditors around $1.4 million and leaving investors with stock worth about 7 cents on the dollar."

But did anyone learn a lesson from all this illusory seeking of favors? Apparently not, for as of April 1988 someone else was on the side-lines gearing up to call on Uncle Sam one more time in order to keep the charade going. The next potential saviour, "…a Puerto Rican, expects to win government business because of the law setting aside 5% of defense spending for minority-owned businesses."

We're not talking small potatoes here. Set asides totaled more than $14 billion in 1986. If, as politicians are so fond of claiming, Americans ("the American people" is the term they most often use) really want to see minority firms get a helping hand and stand on their own, they will extend that hand. If they don't, and I'm aware that many of them don't (only the politicians seem to know what *all* of the American people want) they will insist that minorities compete in the marketplace with no special favors. I personally believe a majority (maybe a small majority) *do* want to help, but *pretending* by politicians will not make it so.

A LOOK AT THE
"HARD-LOOK DOCTRINE"

In 1970 the appeals court first said that a court's responsibility isn't simply to defer to the expertise of an agency, but must take a "hard look" at regulatory decisions. The "hard look" doctrine, as it is called, is now applied to all regulatory decisions under appeal.

In a 1983 decision the Supreme Court agreed with the appeals court that judges should take the same hard look, whether at regulation or deregulation. But even under the hard-look doctrine courts aren't supposed to substitute their judgments as to the merits of the policies for the judgments of the agency officials.

To what are we, a once free people, so sheepishly subjecting ourselves and our industries? Texas Senator Phil Gramm declared at the American Gas Association on the 24th of April 1986, that "Unlimited opportunity and unlimited government are sworn enemies."

When we allow government to become entrenched in our lives, after awhile we begin to think of it the same way one thinks of a big brother, a god-father, or uncle (Sam). "See if you can get me a better deal, Sam." "They're not treating me right, Sam." "See what you can do, Sam."

DEREGULATION'S SHOWCASE:
THE STAGGERS ACT

Despite the massive deregulation by the Staggers Act in 1980, the railroads are still saddled with powerful unions and archaic work rules. The 100-mile rule, for example, holds that a workday consists of eight hours or 100 miles traveled, whichever comes first. That may have made some sense at the turn of the century but today a crew will go for 2.5 to 3 hours and hit the 100 mile limit and anything after that becomes time and a half. Workers make the equivalent of almost 2.5 days pay for a one-day run in the West. Trains can sometimes cover 300 miles in an eight-hour shift. The rule is irrational, as are the obsolete regulations regarding the necessity for having a caboose to provide a lookout at the rear of the train and mandating the size of crews.

Is it any wonder that labor expenses make up 40 percent to 50 percent of the industry's total cost; far above that of other industries? But have no fear. A recent collective-bargaining session upped the limit to 108 miles. (Full-crew laws were repealed at the federal level in 1972.) There has even been a reduction in the once bloated workforce of 10,000 employees. On the other hand, that may be a negative if you favor government work programs!

Conrail serves about 38 percent of the U.S. population. Trucks haul about 80 percent of the freight in Conrail's market area. Thanks to the Staggers Act, Conrail has been able to make its own deals with shippers, get rid of money-losing routes and experiment with better ways to distribute goods. However increased profits, the sign of its success, are being threatened by a group called CURE (Consumers United for Rail Equity). "Consumers" is a word guaranteed to elicit support from the average citizen in the 1980s but should not be taken at face value in this instance because the consumers in CURE are bulk shippers of grain, coal and electric utilities, hardly consumers as we think of them. They want to see Conrail re-regulated; shackled to their benefit rather than to the goal of maximizing profits.

Shippers saw their own profits deteriorating for a variety of reasons and figured maybe Sam could put the squeeze on the railroads. But really their cry of monopoly was misguided, because when the Staggers Act deregulated it maintained Interstate Commerce Commission (ICC) jurisdiction over captive commodities, setting limits on how much freedom the railroads had in raising rates and providing a mechanism for appeal if the shipper felt he had been wronged.

Coal shippers are the railroads' biggest customers, accounting for 40 percent of the tonnage, a quarter of the gross revenues and for even more of the profits. Because trucks are not suitable transports for coal, many shippers have few options and so the railroads, because of this dependency, are tempted to jack up the prices on their most profitable customers. Estimates of the captive population range from 5 percent to 15 percent and only those that pay rates in excess of 180 percent of the immediate operating costs are included in this catagory. Those with reasonable alternatives, i.e. other rail service, barge or truck access and those who are able to switch to a substitute product or supplier, are not considered "captive shippers".

Before long CARS (Committee Against Revising Staggers) appeared to counter CURE and try to influence Sam. It is made up of those who have benefited from competitive rail service and are naturally opposed to any plan to re-regulate the railroads. According to Holman Jenkins, Jr, in his January, 1988 article for *Insight,* the railroads have come around to negotiate fairly on their own, not because of government interference, but because of the "publicity stirred up by newspapers and legislators in the coal states." [9]

Still one must wonder whether we have given Sam too much power and influence so that everyone in the nation turns to him whenever they want something.

DEREGULATION
OF THE TRUCKING INDUSTRY:
PROS & CONS

Trucking regulation began in 1935 and was modeled on railroad regulation. At one time ICC certificate owners were allowed to fix prices and divide routes among themselves. Truckers were granted operating authority between different geographical points and had to operate a return route empty if they didn't have two-way operating rights. Rights between cities were valuable and were sold between already existing companies. After deregulation in 1980, nine major rate bureaus were started by the trucking companies themselves. These bureaus allowed for discounts up to 40 percent to attract the largest shipping contracts. Truckers were allowed to compete for return loads and not having to return to points of origin empty meant greater efficiency and cheaper prices for consumers. Of course there are problems with deregulation. There are different state regulations, lighter freight (autos dropped over 1,000 lbs each in an attempt to increase fuel efficiency) and most of all, overcapacity. The number of trucking businesses has doubled from 17,000 to 34,000 since deregulation. No wonder then, that the most forceful voice against deregulation comes from within the trucking industry, where many claim it is too easy to gain entrance. But easy entry means opportunity. Freedom to risk is freedom to fail as well as succeed. That used to be known as "the American way".

Robert Delany of the Cato Institute has estimated that federal deregulation saves American producers and distributors about $90 billion a year which translates into $80 billion a year in savings for consumers. Nevertheless 43 states regulate intrastate (within a single state) trucking despite federal deregulation. If they were to follow the federal government's example, Mr. Delany estimates $28 billion more could be saved a year.

The public's general perception is that deregulation of the trucking industry has led to more accidents. Although raw data showed a 25 percent increase in the accident rate between 1985-88 and an 11 percent increase in deaths over the same period, in reality the accidents relative to the number of miles traveled, declined. After all, deregulation did not do away with safety inspections and licensing requirements for drivers. If anything, drivers who own their own rigs have a greater financial stake in safety.[10] ASCT (Americans for Safe & Competitive Trucking), a coalition of shippers, carriers, consumer advocates and manufacturers, gathered data that showed a decline in injury and fatality rates per vehicle mile. According to ASCT, injuries dropped from 101 in 1981 to 79 in 1985 whereas deaths went from 111 to 82, against a 1974 base of 100.

These statistics are ignored by those with a vested interest in seeing that deregulation is blamed for an increase in accidents and deaths. There is reason to believe that economic deregulation and truck safety are unrelated.

CAN REGULATED ENERGY
BE ECONOMICAL?

Energy is another area where hasty regulation has produced chaos. Utility companies are naturally concerned with burning the most economical fuel available to produce power, but legislation has too often made this impossible.

The Powerplant and Industrial Fuel Use Act of 1978 was conceived during a period when experts believed the nation was running out of natural gas. It prohibited utilities from building new oil and natural gas-fired power plants and required them to have coal burning capabilities, even though coal is particularly inefficient. It has been estimated that this requirement costs the average consumer between one and two hundred dollars extra a year on his residential electric bills. Says Ruth Gonze, spokesperson for the American Public Power Association, "A coal capability amendment means that you are free to build a coal plant and free to buy more expensive fuel and burn it wastefully..." [11] Thanks to the Fuel Use Act, the natural gas industy's share of the electric generation market dropped from 24.3 percent in 1970 to 11.8 percent in1985, whereas coal's share jumped from 44.2 percent in 1978 when the Act was initiated to 56.8 percent in 1985. Unfortunately the Act *forbids* utilities the use of natural gas combined-cycle generators, thought by many in the industry to be the most efficient fuel generators in the world.

Combined-cycle plants are relatively small and quickly and inexpensively built and on top of that they have coal capabilities and the gas that fuels them is domestically produced and practically pollution free. Somehow the powers-that-be decided non-

99

utilities should be allowed to build these generators and sell their excess electricity to the utilities. Now with the recognized abundance of natural gas in this country many people would like to see the Act repealed. They argue persuasively that it unjustifiably benefits the coal industry at the expense of gas producers.

When policymakers meddle in areas where they lack expertise wrong decisions are made and many people are forced to suffer the consequences of their actions. Uneconomic energy investments make everyone pay bloated energy bills for decades to come, and make American industry less competitive abroad. Many people with expertise in energy matters deplored the loss of solar tax credits and other subsidies which expired at the end of 1985. These subsidies were meant to encourage efficiency and renewable energy sources.

Utilities continue to build power plants they don't need because of huge government subsidies. Such a bias, besides being unfair to the taxpayer, destroys competition. The stupidity of it all becomes even more apparent when you understand that each dollar of subsidy for nuclear electricity yielded only one *eightieth* as much energy as a dollar of subsidy to renewable sources would yield. Electricity is the most capital-intensive form of energy.

> counted at its heat value, (electricity) got more than 11 times as much subsidy per unit of energy as directly used oil, gas and coal, and was at least 48 times as heavily subsidized as energy-saving technologies.[12]

Every dollar spent inefficiently takes that dollar away from the task of finding cheap, efficient ways to provide the same energy. Worst of all is the knowledge that Congress is making major subsidy decisions based on information that is at least ten years out of date.

Richard Heede and Amory Lovins of the Rocky Mountain Institute in Colorado suggest that

> if the USA were as energy-efficient as Western Europe, our annual bill would fall by an additional $200 billion — enough to balance the federal budget. By the year 2000, the cumulative net savings would be several trillion 1985 dollars — enough to pay off the entire national debt.[13]

How can any legislator that is *serious* about balancing the budget and ending our deficits afford to ignore a potential savings of $200 billion dollars a year? Someone or something is terribly wrong here. Why isn't the Reagan administration, or some of the 1988 presidential candidates who hand us so much rhetoric about their desire to do something about the deficit taking Mr. Heede and Mr. Lovins advice? The promise of several trillion dollars worth of savings should not be ignored!

HELIUM AS AN EXAMPLE
OF CENTRALIZED PLANNING

The Interior Department has enough helium stored to supply the government's needs, at current rates of use, for the next 140 years.

The Helium Act of 1960, which was created to extract and store the gas, was dependent on debatable forecasts of the nation's supply and demand. A 1959 Bureau of Mines study found that U.S. demand for helium would exceed 1 billion cubic feet a year by 1967 and reach nearly 2 billion by the year 2000. In 1978, eleven years later than predicted, demand finally hit one billion cubic feet.

Throughout history sages have predicted that the world was about to run out of non-renewable resources. Such fears have, for the most part, been unfounded and greatly exaggerated. When a valued material becomes scarce, its price rises, curtailing demand and encouraging entrepreneurs to search for new supplies and alternatives. For example, in the nineteenth century whale oil became scarce and it didn't take long to replace it with petroleum. As Julian Simon reminds us in *The Ultimate Resource*, the noted economist W. Stanley Jevons, predicted in 1865 that England could not continue its "present rate of progress" because the nation would run out of coal. Yet today coal is more plentiful than ever.

In 1960 the U.S. government was the world's sole supplier of helium, having bought and dismatled in the 1930s what appears to have been its only competitor. In 1960, mining experts told

Congress that nearly four billion cubic feet of helium was being lost each year into the atmosphere; about ten times what was being consumed. Just as Social Security was billed as a self-financing program, so was the government's helium program. Self-financing is an effective sales-pitch, even though nine times out of ten hindsight proves it to be false advertising. Nevertheless the 1960 act authorized the Bureau of Mines to borrow up to $47.5 million a year to finance helium purchases under long-term contracts with suppliers and to pay for the gas itself ($11 per 1,000 cubic feet), storage facilities, and interest on the Treasury loans. The Bureau set a resale price of $35 per 1,000 cubic feet which was more than double the $15.50 the federal agencies had previously been paying and 80 percent more than the $19.50 that commercial users were accustomed to paying. By 1969 several new suppliers, knowing they could beat the $35 competition, had sprung up to serve private users. These new suppliers were able to make a profit by charging $20-23 per 1,000 cubic feet and soon captured almost half the helium market. The government, not choosing to adjust to the discipline imposed by a free-market system, soon lost all its customers except those captive federal agencies which were required by law to buy from it. Richard Stroup and Jane Shaw, in their article for the American Enterprise Institute's magazine *Regulation*, tell us the Secretary of the Interior went to court (unsuccessfully) to force federal agencies to require their contractors to buy government helium.[14]

To their credit, some of the captive federal users found $35 helium not quite as vital to their programs as $20 helium had been and turned to alternatives such as hydrogen and argon. To add to the fiasco, in 1961 Riley Ridge, a new helium-rich natural gas field was discovered in southwestern Wyoming which at present rates of federal use, could supply the government's needs for between 400 and 800 years. At the same time, technology made it economically feasible to extract leaner streams of helium from natural gas. Unfortunately, as Stroup and Shaw point out, well-meaning bureaucrats have bungled the job again:

> One of the greatest pressures for venting helium at Riley Ridge is that the gas wells there are located on federal land, and companies that hold federal

102

gas leases are not allowed to lease the rights to the associated helium. The 1960 Helium Act kept those rights in federal hands. Thus, if the Bureau of Mines does not take the helium or sell the rights to it, the producers are obliged to vent it as a waste gas, since they cannot sell it. The leasing regulations, in other words, ensure there will be a 'problem' for the government to step in and solve.[15]

The obvious visible cost of the 1960 Helium Act is the $790 million that the Department cannot repay to Treasury. The other cost is in pure waste and the spread of incompetence.

How many times must we be told that bureaucratic forecast is far more likely to be wrong than right and that once error is recognized it is far more difficult to correct than a private plan would be. This is the danger inherent in all centralized planning. Versatility is what free-markets and capitalism are all about.

I know I am on the right track when one of the most creative minds of this centruy agrees that government attempts to engineer markets are doomed to failure and that our salvation will be found in the creativity of individual citizens. Carver Mead, renowned physicist and professor of Computer Science at California's Institute of Technology, told a recent Manhattan Institute audience that

> We depend on the innovations of the citizens of a free economy to keep ahead of the bureaucrats and the people who make a living on control and planning. In the long term, it's the element of surprise that gives us the edge over more controlled economies. [16]

THEY WANT TO REGULATE
PRIVATE PENSIONS!

As we have seen, when there is a widely perceived problem, the federal legislators feel compelled to offer solutions, whether these solutions make sense or not. Sometimes they are merely cosmetic, sometimes they cost private industry dearly, and sometimes they cost the taxpayers a bundle. That's why seeing that there is less regulation is an important step which must be taken if we intend to get a handle on the deficit problem in this country.

The laws regulating private pensions have already caused a "widely perceived problem" — an unfair pension system — and now policymakers may be getting ready to add to it.

A study by the National Bureau of Economic Research found that workers who change jobs just once after age 31, reduce the value of their pensions by over 25 percent. Fair or unfair? As a society we want the best of two worlds — pensions and unrestricted mobility. To achieve this it has been suggested that a fund be set up under the auspices of the PBGC (Pension Benefit Guaranty Corporation) or the Treasury or even the Social Security administration, where matching funds are paid by employer and employee and where the employee becomes immediately vested. ("Vested" means the funds legally belong to the employee.) Some people refer to this as "fundamental fairness". Ridiculous! In the first place this is having the government interfer in the private sector to reproduce what it has already botched with Social Security — this would be almost a duplicate program. In the second place, private firms that voluntarily offered pensions, did so originally in an attempt to compensate employees for years of service and loyalty. Private pensions should be contracts between a private employer and employee, not government mandated programs to help take some of the load off a welfare state.

Mandating private contracts is just one more example of expediency taking precedence over ideology.

THE PENSION
BENEFIT GUARANTY CORPORATION (PBGC)

We have just mentioned the PBGC which has problems of its own which are not helping the nation's deficit situation.

The PBGC protects 38 million workers enrolled in private pension plans against loss of retirement benefits if their pension plans fold. The agency is required by law to regularly check underfunded plans and can terminate plans where an employer is undergoing bankruptcy proceedings in order to prevent further deterioration of the plan's financial condition and avoid unreasonable long-run losses itself.

As of June 30, 1986, the PBGC had a $1.7 billion deficit with another $2.3 billion of unfunded liabilities. Three companies caused two-thirds of that deficit; Allis Chalmers, Wheeling-Pittsburgh ($500 million in unfunded pensions) and LTV ($2.4 billion in unfunded pensions). In 1986 Congress raised the annual premium from $2.60 per employee to $8.50 which meant in 1986 the agency took in about $270 million in premiums and paid out about $200 million. The problem lies with future long-term liabilities. The annual premiums charged to the 110,000 plans the PBGC insures, has risen from $1 per participant in 1974, to $2.60 in 1977 to $8.50 in 1986. Unfortunately future liabilities are unpredictable and naturally increase as more companies go out of business. Even as I write, the premium has been raised once again to $16 per participant (1988)!

Many companies have taken advantage of legal loopholes and have used the PBGC as a dumping ground for the pension liabilities they could not or would not meet. Why should companies that fund their pensions properly be expected to pay increased premiums because of the impropriety of those who don't? (Similar to another question, "Why should savers pay for non-savers?) Executive Director of the PBGC, Kathleen Utgoff, has asked that the agency be allowed to charge risk weighted premiums so that companies failing to fund their plans properly would eventually pay appreciably more than those that do. Companies should be encouraged to look first to their banks to borrow and not to their pension plans. Currently premiums are liabilities of the plan so increased premiums serve to increase the plans underfunding — under the proposed changes the sponsor and its controlled group would be liable for premiums. Miss Utgoff also would like to see the bankruptcy law amended to give the PBGC a claim on the assets of bankrupt companies, equal to the claims of secured creditors. It's unbelievable that the law does not allow the PBGC that recourse already.

ARMS CONTROL — NOT A GOOD WAY
TO REDUCE THE DEFICIT

Try as they will, policymakers cannot, by means of regulation, deter individual citizens from doing what they want to do. It is impossible! It is no easier to deter governments, which are, after all, multiples of individual citizens. David Berkowitz, in an article for the *Wall Street Journal,* stated that if by the terms of arms control agreements countries are parted from specific weapon systems, they will simply turn to new technologies in order to obtain the capabilities they imagine they need. This means arms control can end up increasing the cost of weapons.

Mr. Berkowitz cited an example from England where, before the Washington Treaty, the price per ton of British battleships remained steady for almost 25 years. In 1921 a new 42,000-ton battleship should have had the same unit price as its immediate predecessor, but the Washington Treaty limited battleships to only 35,000 tons. The ship was redesigned using high-grade lightweight steel to meet the treaty requirements and ended up costing two-thirds more than its predecessor.

Mr. Berkowitz suggests that the limits on ICBM launchers probably accelerated the development of MIRVs. Limits on ABMs accelerated the development of particle-beam laser weapons. Limits on traditional strategic weapons such as ballistic missiles and bombers accelerated the development of cruise missiles. The lesson: limit the weapons currently being deployed, and nations will ingeniously find some other weapon on which to spend money. Mr. Berkowitz says that few economists today believe that price controls control prices and wonders why politicians believe that arms control controls arms?"[17]

The principle is the same; price controls never work. Buyers will buy what they want and sellers will find ingenious ways of charging prices higher than the government mandates. Similarly, investors will invest where the best profits can be made, despite the dictates of governments everywhere.

Those who would play 'king' are only fooling themselves.

DEREGULATION IS NOT EASY

During the French Revolution King Louis XIV tried his hand at micromanaging the country with disastrous results.

> The French weavers went through a whole season without moving a shuttle. While the people were waiting for clothes, the weavers were waiting for the government to tell them what kind of cloth they would be allowed to weave, what color it should be,..(etc.). The regulations on the textile industry alone covered over 3,000 pages, and they were different for each district. The manufacturers of Saint-Maixent, for example, had to negotiate for four years before the government allowed them to use black warp, and they never did get permission to use black woof.[18]

Congress in the eighties is going in the same direction. The Grace Commission found the Veterans' Administration, with over 200,000 employees, could not, in most instances, dismiss even one or two without first obtaining Congressional approval. Congress micromanages the employment practices of many executive agencies. Randall Fitzgerald and Gerald Lipson, report that Congress demanded that the Department of Education maintain more employees than it wanted or needed.[19] Its own Congressional staff grew in ten years by almost 6,000 employees and its budget increased 102 percent (1973-1983).[20] Civil Service regulations make it all but impossible to reduce the government's payroll after the completion of a project.

Professor Gary Becker of the University of Chicago expressed what we unfortunately know to be true even in the United States of America,

> that it is far easier to regulate and extend the state's reach than to deregulate and retrench. When the state becomes heavily involved in the economy, many special interests from the bureaucracy, business, labor, and consumer groups come to rely on state benefits. Of course, they actively oppose reforms that curtail their subsidiies.[21]

It looks like it's up to you and me to let the "powers-that-be" know we're not going to take it anymore!

THE FIFTH STEP

(RE: TAXES)

INSTITUTE
A TRUE FLAT
TAX

THE 5th STEP

(RE: TAXES)

THE POPULAR POINT OF VIEW

To the extent that our federal deficits cannot be eliminated in the near term by simply deciding to put a lid on spending we must increase federal revenue. Taxes have been cut too much in recent years anyway. Ronald Reagan's reforms have favored the rich and made our tax system less progressive. A value added tax is a good choice because it would be easiest to implement. At any rate we must all make sacrifices and cut back on consumption.

ANOTHER POINT OF VIEW

Contrary to popular belief, it may be easier in the future to cut spending than to raise taxes. People with ability will gravitate to the most opportunity and the lowest tax rates; not surprisingly the two go hand in hand. Historically lowering tax rates increases revenue. A true flat tax will reduce the need to cut consumption and is fairer than a value added tax.

ARE HIGHER TAXES
THE WAVE OF THE FUTURE?

A conference on tax policy was held in Washington D.C. in October 1987 which concluded that the entire world had better be prepared for "...more expenditures than we would like, financed by higher taxes than we would like." [1] Demographics was given as the main reason. The average age of the populations in the industrialized world is rising and that means fewer workers paying for the Social Security and health care benefits for more and more retirees. But governments will not have an easy time collecting the needed revenue.

As labor decreases in proportion to capital income, which, as we discussed in Chapter Two, it has been doing over the past couple hundred years, revenue will come increasingly from investment income. In the future, because of the ease with which business, capital and labor will move across borders, governments will be forced to try to find less mobile tax bases. They may start taxing consumption rather than income. This would generate a demand for international agreements on tax policy to keep national revenues from being eroded by competition. Unless international agreements and coordination of tax codes can be achieved, technology will make it easy to shelter investments in nations with the lowest tax rates.

The so-called brain drain is a phenomenon of the 20th century and new technology will only quicken the pace.

SIDE-STEPPING THE ISSUE

That stack of dollar bills sixty-seven miles high lamented by Ronald Reagan as an intolerable deficit in 1981 was joined, under his stewardship, by a second stack higher than the first. Raising taxes, never politically popular, is even less so in an election year. To detract from the possibility of a tax hike, one 1988 presidential candidate has been promising to collect the debt owed the federal government *before,* (not instead of) raising taxes.

112

As 1988 began, the United States government had approximately $83 billion worth of delinquent debt with the $51 billion due in IRS penalties representing the largest portion of that debt.

The following is a breakdown of the other $32 billion worth of delinquent debt.

TABLE 2
DELINQUENT DEBT
(in billions of dollars)

Farm Loans	$11.8
Student loans	5.7
VA mortgages	2.9
SBA loans	2.4
Pentagon overpayments & education loans	2.0
HUD housing loans	1.5
Export-Import Bank loans	1.3
miscellaneous	4.4

Source: OMB 1988

ARE TAXES TOO LOW?

Taxes in this country are not too low; spending is too high. Despite a massive rollback in personal tax rates and major tax reform during his tenure, federal revenue amounts to nearly as large a share of the economy as it did when Ronald Reagan took office. Nevertheless when the 100th Congress convened it didn't take the new Speaker of the House, Jim Wright of Texas, long to call for new taxes for FY1988.

Those earning $35,000 and under reportedly pay 90 percent of all taxes collected, so taxing high income earners to the hilt would not solve our problem. Peter Grace has criss-crossed the nation pointing out in his humorous and somewhat caustic manner, that if we took 100 percent — every last penny — from persons earning $75,000 and up, the government could run for only ten days on the proceeds. As for the poor middle income earner, he's seen his taxes increase 32 times as fast as his income with each increase resulting in more spending by government, not deficit reduction.

In April 1987 individual income tax payments were a record $120 billion compared with $91 billion in April 1986. (OK — partly because investors cashed in a large amount of capital gains at year's end before the special tax rate on them was raised.) Unfortunately outlays for FY1987 increased also. (OK — half as much as they did the previous year, but that still meant a rise of about 2.5 percent!)

TAX CHOICES

Today most Democrats claim a tax increase is needed to reduce the budget deficit, while many Republicans hold that tax increases will only lead to more spending, stunt economic growth, reduce revenues and actually *increase* the budget deficit. But it's the Democrats' ballgame. They are, after all, in control of both Houses, so you can expect to see the 100th Congress come up with many creative ways for "enhancing revenue". Senator Chiles of Florida, early in 1987, suggested a temporary tax surcharge to lower the deficit. Congressman William Gray of Pennsylvania came up with an even worse idea; to convert our trade quotas into tariffs in order to raise revenue. Some experts favor a new national sales tax in exchange for the elimination of taxes on capital gains and on interest received from investments. Other politicians believe a tax on gasoline might be the best of unpleasant choices. Considering inflation, the 1940's price of 29 cents per gallon was more than what we're paying today for gasoline. Congressman Tom Foley argued in favor of such a tax, claiming every penny increase in a gallon of gasoline in this country would raise $1 billion in revenue. He suggested if the tax were referred to as a user fee Ronald Reagan might come around in his thinking. Of course the obvious danger is that a penny increase could easily rise to a dime, a quarter and higher. Peter Peterson is already talking in terms of 25 cent levies.[2] It might be well to recall that when President Johnson signed the Medicare Act he quipped that an

114

extra $500 million in federal spending would be absolutely "no problem"; today Medicare costs 150 times more than estimated!

Many legislators see excise taxes as a plausible choice for revenue raising. In response to the perceived threat a group of industries that would be hardest hit by excise taxes has formed the Coalition Against Regressive Taxation which argues that the burden of higher excise taxes will fall most heavily on Joe Sixpack. Federal excise taxes on beer and wine haven't been increased since 1951 and with society taking an increasingly dim view of smoking and drunk driving, sin taxes don't look half bad to most lawmakers. However, on June 16, 1987 President Reagan specifically ruled out excise taxes as a way to cut the deficit. (Didn't he once say something about corporation taxes being unconscionable too?) Already on the state level, according to Jeff Spinner, a policy analyst for an organization called Citizens for Tax Justice, there's a lot of gasoline, alcohol and cigarette tax increases and some sales tax increases also. [3]

Taxing Social Security benefits is gaining support as a possible revenue raiser. On the David Brinkley Show on January 17, 1988, Washington correspondent Sam Donaldson said that if we have paid into the system and don't "need" the benefits when we retire we should consider that we have simply performed a social duty. He and others feel it is wrong for the wealthy to receive benefits. So what if they paid into the system? The government doesn't really mean what it says anyway! Means testing Social Security benefits undermines the integrity of the government. *This* is the real danger!

In his FY1988 budget, President Reagan held firm to his pledge to oppose any tax increase. He even opposed a major spending-reduction bill purported to save $72 billion over three years because it contained the Superfund excise tax, a one percent across-the-board tax on manufacturers to pay for toxic waste disposal.

The Reagan administration has proposed user fees for national park services, ports and waterways, meat inspection services and similar government provided services. Is this really so terrible?

Why shouldn't students be asked to pay for insurance to guarantee the repayment of their loans? Why shouldn't tourists pay for the upkeep of national parks? Why can't the meat and poultry industry pay for inspection services? What's wrong with asking yacht owners to pay for towing by the Coast Guard?

Walter Wriston, former chairman of Citicorp, reminds us that tax revenue has increased every year since marginal rates were cut and that U.S. exports are rising. He feels the best government action is "no action" and let the markets adjust naturally. (Perhaps we can get him to run for public office to prove to policymakers that less meddling is the best policy!)

A VALUE ADDED TAX (VAT)

A value added tax (VAT) adds a little to the price of goods at each step of production. People would be taxed on what they purchase not what they produce; that is the good part.

Norman Ture, president of the Institute for Research on the Economics of Taxation in Washington DC, estimates after allowing for certain exemptions to protect low-income individuals, a VAT of 3 percent would raise about $45 billion. The increased private and corporate savings rate which seems to accompany VATs is another good part. Sir Alan Walters, formerly an economic adviser to the Thatcher Government, assumed he was describing virtues when he said the VAT "... is less perceptible and therefore less painful than the income tax." This is a feature, which for obvious reasons, is highly prized by politicians.

Many people, like myself, oppose the Value Added Tax (VAT) in part because of this lack of pain. A gradual unremarkable but steady rise in such a tax is almost inevitable. Subtle taxation is to be avoided like the plague by any people wishing to remain free and in control of their own destinies. Already a good many Americans are becoming so accustomed to payroll withholdings for Social Security and income tax that they hardly notice a rise in the government's "take". If they do wonder why the harder they work the "behinder" they get, the answer is less apparent than it would be if they actually wrote a check to pay those taxes every year. A passive fleecing creates a feeling of helplessness and dependency which our government should discourage. Many taxpayers have too much money withheld, which is in effect giving the government an interest free loan. Who can afford to give interest-free loans, if given the choice? With the new W-4s, over-withholding is more likely than ever to occur. In FY1986 the IRS received 102.4 million tax returns and issued 74.2 million refunds averaging $982 each. Those refunds represent loans to the federal government by citizens of close to $73 billion.

But even more relevant to the discussion at hand is the way the 1983 Commission on Social Security master-minded the tax increase on the self employed. Those that work for themselves know that for a long while contributions were three fourths the combined employee-employer rates for OASDI (Old Age Survivors Disability Insurance) and half for HI (Hospital Insurance). Starting in 1984, both were supposed to equal the combined employee-employer contributions, but with a tax credit. Actually the self-employed pay an effective rate of 86 percent of employee-employer rates. Disguising the true state of Social Security has reached an incredibly high state of the art. To soothe the self-employed, a tax credit amounting to approximately 1.5 percent of the overage was conjured up. That tax credit allows Treasury to bring in general revenue. (The cavalry!) It's really an underhanded way to beef up Social Security, but they don't want to let anyone know it needs beefing up — yes, again! The rationale for the self-employed of an earlier day to pay only three fourths of the employee-employer combined rate was that the self-employed paid income tax on 100 percent of their contributions, i.e. they couldn't deduct the tax as a cost of doing business the way a large corporation does. Since employees don't pay income tax on the employer's deductions, employers are allowed to deduct the contribution they make to their employees' accounts as a cost of doing business. The general revenue tax credit gimmick is only good through 1989. After that, half of the self employed's contributions will be considered net earnings but he will be able to take deductions on the other half up to 50 percent — if the law remains unchanged that long!

A tax reform that is revenue neutral only when taken over a five year period; a 75 year summary statistic that masks the long term deficit in the Social Security system with short term surpluses; a subtle introduction of general revenue funds into the Social Security system to beef up reserves are all examples of what a handful of men think of their constituents. They seem to believe the people who put them in office are chumps, incapable of seeing through the smoke screens that billow out of their Congressional committee rooms.

Most countries that use a VAT, tax corporate income only once, tax capital gains at the same rate as ordinary income and have no tax on interest and dividends. Many of these countries do not allow sweeping personal exemptions for home-mortgage interest, for employer-paid health care, for unearned public retirement benefits and so forth. Japan has taxed business and capital at a lower rate than we do and consumption at a higher rate. No wonder the Japanese saved! Japan's recent tax reform involved a tax on savings in an effort to discourage this seeming virtue which the Japanese carry too far. They now want to stimulate spending.

This is a Jack Sprat situation where Japan, as Jack, could eat no fat, (couldn't consume) and the USA, as his wife, could eat no lean (couldn't save). It is not clear how long the Spratt's marriage lasted under the circumstances described, nevertheless it is popular wisdom that the United States should now encourage savings and discourage consumption.

POPULAR WISDOM

Popular wisdom is seldom sustained by facts. Let's examine the idea that Americans "need to consume less." We already took a cursory look in Chapter Two and criticized the zero-sum suppositions advanced by Peter Peterson. We saw that enjoying a higher standard of living, which some people choose to equate with consumption, is the goal of all societies and savings and investments are merely means to that goal. To say America should give up the goal (consumption) in order to emulate the means (savings and investment) is pure nonsense. In a situation where men are permitted to trade freely, supply and demand is the only regulator that is needed.

In the January 1830 edition of the Edinburgh Review we find evidence that almost 160 years ago men were grappling with a government that had overstepped its legitimate boundaries:

> Our rulers will best promote the improvement of the nation by strictly confining themselves to their own legitimate duties — by leaving capital to find its most lucrative course, commodities their fair price, industry and intelligence their natural reward, idleness and folly their natural punishment — by maintaining peace, by defending property, by diminishing the price of law, and by observing strict economy in every department of the state. Let the government do this — the people will assuredly do the rest.

Karen Penner, in an article for *Business Week,* maintains that the only action that will have an *immediate* impact on America's competitiveness in world trade is "diminished consumption."[4] Increasing investment, productivity and relying more on exports would all take time to be effective. The article goes on to talk about the necessity for lowering living standards because consumption will have to drop to the level of output minus what is needed to service the national debt. This, according to the estimates Ms. Pennar uses, means the economy must grow at normal rates while we shrink our living standards by seven percent. That assumes one wishes to equate living standards with consumption which, I might point out, isn't necessarily true. You might want to look up the article and draw your own conclusions. The article concludes that our deficit could be financed without foreign money if we consumed less and saved more — ah, such wisdom!

HISTORY

In 1894 Congress passed a bill imposing the first-ever peacetime income tax. It required all citizens with incomes of more than

$4,000, only about one percent of the population, to pay a one percent tax. The *New York Times* called the income-tax law "a vicious, inequitable, unpopular, impolitic and Socialistic scheme" and on top of it all it heaped the epitaph "unAmerican"! The *Washington Post* said the graduated aspect of the tax "represents a repudiation of the spirit as well as the letter of Democracy...it punishes everyone who rises above the level of mediocrity...The fewer additional yokes put about the necks of the people, the better for the commonwealth."

In 1895 the Supreme Court ruled that the Constitution explicitly stated that a tax should be levied in proportion to population, and not differentiate by income level. (Now why do you suppose the Constitution was so specific in this area?) Therefore, the Court ruled, the income tax was unconstitutional. The *New York Times* editorialized that the nation had seen the end of attempts to tax incomes. They hadn't counted on the affinity of elected officials to public money. An amendment which would allow taxation based on incomes was sent to the states for ratification in July 1909. The *New York Times* responded with "When men get the habit of helping themselves to the property of others they are not easily cured of it." The *Washington Post,* on the other hand, had mellowed a bit since 1894 and argued that an income tax was needed to "wipe out the deficit without impairment of the public service or calling a halt upon needed public improvements." (Sound familiar?)

The *New York Times* predicted that the new income tax had established a "rock of credit from which abundant streams of revenue will flow whenever Congress chooses to smite it...We may be sure that it will be smitten hard and always harder, until the national conscience, if there is such a thing, revolts against the inequality and injustice of such a plan of taxation."[5]

To their credit both New York and Massachusetts rejected the 16th amendment which in February 1913 became the law of the land.

But one wonders if even the *New York Times* could have forseen the acquiesence of the population to the changes that would occur in just fifty years. In 1887 there was no federal income tax and over 60 percent of the federal receipts, which amounted to only about 3 percent of GNP, came from customs. Almost all of the remaing 40 percent of total revenue came from excises on alcohol and tobacco. By contrast, in 1937 the federal government took about 5.5 percent of GNP with 45 percent of the total supplied by taxes on the incomes of both individuals and corporations. The new tax on employment (Social Security) accounted for about 5 percent of all federal revenue in 1937. Going another fifty years into the future we find that in the 1980s the federal government has had no qualms about helping itself to revenue accounting for about 20 percent of the GNP with 55 percent of that revenue coming from income taxes and 35 percent from payroll taxes. But what the *New York Times* would *really* find incomprehensible is the government's practice of spending more than it has the courage to collect in taxes.

THE 1986 TAX REFORM ACT (TRA)

The 1986 tax reform was *supposed* to be tax neutral over a five year period. The catch is no tax bill in recent memory has remained in tact for a period as long as five years. There were four reforms in Ronald Reagan's first five years in office. So, once again pushing our way through the smoke and mirrors, we see that because deductions and so-called loop-holes were removed first and rates were not lowered until much later, the 1986 reform was bound to generate close to $25 billion in new revenue the first year. (Oh Golly — I guess the reformers just didn't realize that would happen!)

During the Joint Committee hearings on tax reform in August, 1986, Senator John Danforth warned that the tax reform bill was being rushed through the committee hearings without proper caution. He called the reform a bad bill for the future of the country, warned that it hit capital intensive business, was anti-growth, anti-jobs, anti-future. He said: "It hurts people. You can't take $120 billion from corporations without hurting people's jobs." (Somebody better pass that news on to the

Democrats!) He gave the picturesque analogy of the Senate's version of the tax bill as a "fair maiden" and said when you cross a "fair maiden" with a "gorilla" (House version of the tax bill) the gorilla's dominant genes are bound to win. He warned the other committee members that they were sacrificing the future for immediate consumer gratification. He pointed to the fact that the bill put a cap on the money colleges can raise without bonds being taxable. The bill discouraged the contribution of depreciated property and stock and therefore contributions, *period.* Taxing scholarships and even fellowships would be harmful for education in his opinion, and tough in the long run on the economic strength of the nation.

You figure this one out: The tax reform of 1986 only extended the tax free status of employer-paid group legal services and educational assistance for one year. At the end of 1987 these two fringe benefits expired automatically. Yet Congress continues to talk about ways government can help education! Loss of the Investment Tax Credit (ITC) would hit heavy industry hard, yet politicians rant and rave about our loss of manufacturing jobs and the need to invest in industry in this country. More gobbleydy-gook! Senator Danforth could only see Silicon Valley (high-tech less capital intensive) and high tax paying corporations benefiting from the 1986 reform.

But even worse, according to the Senator, the committee was asked to vote on a mere summary. Senator Danforth felt committee members were being railroaded and declared there was no reason to sign the report then and there because the legislation was too important and affected too many citizens to be subjected to such speedy action. He claimed the Republican members on the Ways and Means committee were not even able to participate because so much was being done behind closed doors. He requested more time and public exposure for the bill. He claimed Secretary James Baker and Senator Bob Packwood were afraid to open the bill to public scrutiny because "people will find out what we're doing and bring pressure on us during the recess... I can't understand what's wrong with a little sunshine in government" he concluded.

122

Bill Archer of Texas didn't want to sign so quickly either. "We are going to affect the lives of all Americans." He predicted an early revision if the reform was rushed through in 1986.

The verdict may still be out on the 1986 reform but it is beginning to look like some of the concerns may have been justified. At any rate Senator Danforth in particular, put up a good fight.

Senator Bill Bradley was much more optimistic about the bill and offered some convincing and some so-so reasons. He was pleased because young workers would have less reason to concentrate on avoiding taxes (young, old and in between) and could go ahead and make money because thanks to the 1986 reform they'll get to keep more of it. He was optimistic because corporations may often pay less than before the reform; from 40 percent down to a top of 34 percent, depending on the type of activity as discussed above. Additionally Senator Bradley saw the reform as a victory for general interests over special interests. ("Special interests" are almost as nasty as "the rich" and there's always open season on them both!)

Richard Gephardt of Missouri took a philosophical approach to the bill. He said "We all understood we would have disappointments in order to restore a base of $300 billion."

Senator John Chafee of Rhode Island mused, "Tax bills aren't forever. It won't last five years — we'll fix it."

As for the role of the Reagan administration, Secretary of the Treasury, James Baker sat there and recommended the bill be signed immediately.

Senator Bob Packwood and Congressman Dan Rostenkowski, the joint chairman, wanted everyone to trust and obey.

"Trust and obey" is something Americans in every walk of life are being asked to do too much lately. The more complex those in charge make a situation, the easier it is to manipulate those they have thereby made dependent.

THE FLAT TAX

A few years ago Idaho's former congressman, George Hansen, introduced a fifteen percent across-the-board tax on all income.

Ten percent proposals were made by Congressmen Philip Crane of Illinois and Ron Paul of Texas, as well as Senator Jesse Helms of North Carolina. Congressmen Panetta of California and Duncan of Tennessee proposed virtually identical nineteen percent plans. In most "flat-rate tax" proposals, allowances are made for business expenses in varying degrees and under different guises.

For some time I have supported and attempted to familiarize people with the De Concini Bill (S.B. 2147) which I will refer to for purposes of this discussion as "the flat tax". It was proposed March 1, 1982 and developed to meet four criteria: First, that all income should be taxed once and only once and as close to its source as possible. Second, that all types of income should be taxed at one low rate. Third, that the poorest members of society should be exempt from taxes and lower income families should pay a smaller fraction of their income in taxes than should higher income families. Fourth, and finally, that tax returns should be simple enough to fit on postcards.

Keeping in mind that the 1986 reform has minimized some of the distortions the earlier system exaggerated, here's how the old system measures up to each of these four requirements:

I - ALL INCOME TAXED BUT ONLY ONCE
As long as corporations are legally separate tax paying entities some income will be taxed twice; once at the corporate level and again when received by the shareholder as a dividend.

I have several newspaper headlines dated January 28, 1983 which I keep as a reminder that occasionally all politicians think they have enough power to turn the tide and the guts to try. As it happened, an extremely popular and beloved president found the undertow, backlash or whatever you want to call it, too strong. After asking in a prepared speech in Boston "...when are we all going to have the courage to point out that in our tax structure the corporation tax is very hard to justify?" Ronald Reagan was forced to run for cover. But because the concept is not politically feasible does not make it wrong.

In their 1987 book *Showdown at Gucci Gulch: Lawmakers, Lobbyists and the Unlikely Triumph of Tax Reform,* Jeffrey Birnbaum and Alan Murray claimed that despite Ronald Reagan's earlier expressed abhorrence of the corporation tax, his administration managed to transform the 1986 reform into the largest increase in corporate taxes ever enacted by Congress. They claimed that

> By raising corporate taxes, Mr. (Donald) Regan (then Secretary of the Treasury) was able to cut not only individuals' tax *rates* but also individuals' tax *bills* by an average of 8.5%. Tax revision was turned into old-fashioned tax cutting, with corporations picking up the bill.

"Running for cover" is one thing, but this is the action of a turncoat.

The deficit-reduction accord that was hastily thrown together at the so-called "summit" (November 1987) again hit corporations the hardest. One proposal alone, increasing the coverage of the corporate minimum tax, was estimated to cost corporations over $2 billion.

Is there in this nation a man or woman with the power of his or her convictions?!

II - LOW UNIFORM RATES

When different forms of income are taxed at different tax rates, clever attorneys and CPAs (and I don't fault them; that is their job) arrange for clients to receive deductions against income taxed at the highest rates and scheme to take income in ways that are taxed at low rates. This encourages the use of stock options instead of cash wages in order to get the lower capital gains rates; or deferring income from a profitable year to the next year when a client expects to be in a lower tax bracket; or the shameful liquidation of a profitable corporation for the sole purpose of escaping the corporate income tax imposed on its earnings; or passing assets to family members in lower tax brackets when judgement, unaffected by tax laws, tells a person the timing is off. The basic idea behind the flat tax is that everyone should be taxed at the same low rate and that by disallowing deductions, exemptions and credits, the revenue base would actually be increased.

I would be the first to admit many changes in the 1986 reform went a long ways towards reducing inequities, but still the law favors those who can afford to pay creative men and women to study the new road map and come up with detours and ingenious approaches. The rules may be new but the game's the same.

Our present tax system makes us dependent on the whim of policymakers. Not long ago a group of Virginia investors intended to build a $220 million rail line to Dulles International Airport. It seems that certain provisions of the 1986 tax reform may have put a damper on things. Without the investment tax credit, stretched out depreciation periods and limited tax-exempt financing, the investment changed dramatically. I am not arguing in favor of the subsidies but am pointing out how important *consistency* from Washington D.C. is for the health of the nation. Under our present system planning cannot be done rationally because too much depends on who knows who—on the dispensation of favors and unforseeable changes in the law. A favorable push given to a competitor is a risk which must always be considered and to guard against risks is costly. But the game goes on. Similarly taking away the incentives to build low income housing only transferred the burden to the Treasury. It will be less desirable to invest in rental housing and so the four or five dollars per week saved in taxes will be overshadowed by the increase in rent. These changes could make the consumer suffer in the long run.

The National Federation of Independent Businesses (NFIB) wanted to see an expansion of the provision that would allow the self-employed to deduct a portion of their health insurance premiums. NFIB wants 50 percent to be considered deductible. Why not all of it?

Not too smart to take an industry in as much trouble as oil was and give them a three billion eight hundred and fifty thousand dollar kick in the teeth. They were only functioning at ten percent of capacity so someone came up with the brilliant idea to tax them more!

There was already concern that the nation was turning away

from capital intensive industries toward the service sector when the reformers removed the investment tax credit (ITC). Many people felt the removal of the ITC would mean less investment in plants and equipment.

At the same time the Inventory Capitalization Rule proposed in the 1986 tax reform was extremely harmful to small business. No one knew how the capitalization rules for inventory were going to work; even the staff was unclear when the bill was presented to the Joint Committee on Tax Reform in August of 1986 shortly before its' passage. (Remember, Senator Danforth tried unsuccessfully to gain time for clarification.) Many critics felt that by asking businessmen to declare the percentage of their purchases left at the end of the year (inventory) as taxable income could mean a gradual liquidation of a business over a period of years. They predicted that a small businessman might see his taxes jump as much as 50 percent with the application of the rule.

Interest deductions under new regulations are not equal; it all depends on what the borrowing is for. Credit cards, trips, car purchases are all personal interest which means you can deduct 40 percent in 1988, 20 percent in 1989 and only 10 percent in 1990, if the rules are not changed before then. However if you borrow to buy stocks or bonds all interest is deductible as "investment interest" up to $4,000 in 1988, $2,000 in 1989 and only $1,000 in 1990. Interest related to passive investments, like rental real estate, is deductible only as an offset to income generated, whereas interest on loans for business or on home mortgages is 100 percent deductible.

Changes in the 1986 Tax Reform Act limit the potential savings for people with Section 403(b) plans whose annual salary exceeds $47,500. Formerly all salary could be deferred under Sec. 403(b) and it wasn't taxed until received by the employee, usually in retirement. Sec. 403(B) only affects the employees of private nonprofit institutions (symphonys, universities, museums, hospitals etc.) Under the old law, employees of nonprofit institutions were able to defer up to 20 percent of their annual salary into sheltered annuities, depending largely on how long an employee had worked at the institution. The new law limits the annual defferal to $9,500, (20 percent of $47,500 is $9,500) less any payments to other tax deferrred savings vehicles such as 401(k) trusts and 457 deferred-compensation plans. The new law adds a 10 percent penalty for early withdrawal which makes people think twice about squirreling money away for retirement in case an emergency arises and they are unable to get to it. Tax-sheltered annuities have been a recruiting tool to attract employees to tax-exempt organizations; organizations that are often unable to pay competitive salaries. Oh well, they'll just have to find other ways to be competitive until new reformers erase new incentives and so on and so forth. Most reformers are busy people who tend to streamline their actions. They have found if they have too little time to really study the ramifications of a proposal their goal cannot be hurt much if they simply go with a kind of all purpose "soak the rich" philosophy. In the above example not many employees earn enough to be hurt by the new limitations.

III - POOREST MEMBERS OF SOCIETY EXEMPT

This has been met. The 1986 reform removed more than six million low income potential taxpayers from the tax rolls.

Income tax progressivity has increased, not decreased, (excuse me, but you're thinking of payroll taxes) since 1981, and the best way to "soak the rich" is to lower their income taxes, leading them to voluntarily reenter the taxable economy. For example, taxpayers with an adjusted gross income (AGI) of more than $1 million in 1985 paid 260 percent more in taxes than in 1981, while tax payments from those middle-income Americans earning between $25,000 and $50,000 fell slightly. Tax payments from the rich rose in every year during Ronald Reagan's first term. Correcting for inflation with the consumer price index, they rose 19.2 percent over the four years. In 1981 the rich paid $2.42 in income taxes for every dollar paid by the poor; by 1985, that ratio had risen to $3.12, an increase of 29 percent.

According to IRS records, in 1981 the top *one* percent of taxpayers, measured by AGI, paid (after allowable credits) $51 billion , whereas the lowest fifty percent of taxpayers, again, measured by AGI, paid only $21 billion. That means the top one percent of income earners shouldered 18.05 percent of the nation's tax burden and the bottom fifty percent were responsible for 7.45 percent of total taxes paid in 1981. By 1985 those numbers had changed to show an increase in the first group's share of the burden from $51 billion and 18.05 percent to $72.1 billion and 23.1 percent whereas the less affluent group, although their tax payments rose from $21 billion to $23.1 billion their percentage of the entire tax bill dropped from 7.45 percent to 7.1 percent.

In contrast to the IRS data the Congressional Budget Office (CBO) produced a study during the final quarter of 1987 which showed the "poor" paid slightly higher *average* tax rates in 1987 than they did ten years earlier before all the reform. The higher average rates were the result of the continual large inceases in Social Security taxes. No one can deny that the wealthy are paying more tax dollars now, mind you, but amounts don't count in the minds of those who weigh "fairness" in terms of percentages. It is also interesting to see how carefully results from tests must be read and how futile it is to compare, or even accurately cite, findings. In the appendix of the CBO study we find that

> The richest 10% of American families (notice *families* as opposed to *taxpayers* and *ten* as opposed to *one* percent) paid 37.5% of all federal taxes in 1984, compared with 35.9% in 1977, and they'll pay 38.6% in 1988. The bottom 50% of all families, on the other hand, saw their share of all taxes fall — to 12.9% in 1984 from 13.3% in 1977.[6]

(It's interesting to note that the CBO study only documents figures for 1977 and 1984!) Here *less* percentage-wise equates with *more* actual dollars because the income of the top 10 percent has increased about 15 percent. The study claimed the income of the top one percent will have increased 40 to 50 percent before taxes and as high as 63 percent after taxes. This is supposed to show the extent that the changes in federal tax law have benefited the rich. Taking the nation as a whole, the study found that in 1977 people were paying 22.8 percent of their income to the federal government in taxes and in 1988 they were paying 22.7 percent. No mention of state, local, excise and property taxes.

The data suggest that Ronald Reagan may have been playing

the part of Robin Hood during his presidency, but you wouldn't have learned that from most media accounts during those years.

The following is a summary of the tax *increases* which took place under Ronald Reagan:

TABLE 3
TAX INCREASES UNDER RONALD REAGAN
(in billions of dollars)

TAX	YEAR	AMOUNT
TEFRA	1982	$311
Social Security amendments	1983	377
gas tax hike	1983	28
Deficit Reduction Act	1984	101
"neutral" reform	1986	30
1987 budget accord	1987	23
miscellaneous increases		9

Table 3 fails to mention the bracket-creep due to inflation which occurred between 1981-85 when indexing began which is estimated at a whooping $650 billion. (Scream bloody murder at any hint of repealing indexing!) When all is said and done eliminating bracket creep may turn out to be President Reagan's most valuable contribution to this country.

The American people are paying a whale of amount in taxes — our forefathers would never have thought it possible. The Social Security payroll tax is admittedly a regressive form of taxation. That is where the blame should be laid by those who lament the facts that seem to show a shift of about $80 billion in annual revenue collection from progressive to regressive taxes.

The 1986 tax reform called for eventually two tax rates; 15 percent and 28 percent, but it started out with five rates ranging from 11 percent to 38.5 percent. The top corporate rate was scheduled for 34 percent but in 1987 the top corporate rate was 40 percent.

Because of the base and rate change, it means the effective rates are indeed progressive — more progressive than under former law. Those making between $20-30 thousand get a 9.8

percent cut; $30-40 thousand get a 7.7 percent cut; those making over $200,000 get a 2.3 percent cut. The wealthiest get the smallest break percentage-wise and three hundred and seventy-five taxpayers will have to pay the higher alternative minimum tax. Nevertheless it infuriates some people that sixteen percent of the tax reductions go to the half of one percent who earn more than $200,000 even though six and a half million people who last year paid the lowest taxes get 100 percent relief. Thanks to the new reform they are dropped from the roles. Of course in order to obtain the $300 billion worth of rate cuts the 1986 reform had to broaden the tax base by the same amount — $300 billion was laid on the shoulders of business. When it comes right down to it, it is tantamount to fraud to call the reform a "tax cut" for anybody. After all, business will pay the increased tax levies by raising prices and/or decreasing employment.

IV - SIMPLICITY

Since I graduated from college, and that's more than 25 years and we'll leave it at that, the tax code has tripled in size, per-capita tax collections and cases pending in the Tax Court have increased seven-fold and the number of IRS employees has grown by almost 90 percent.

Rewriting the tax code via the 1986 reform entailed training 17,000 revenue agents to understand and enforce the changes. Some observers thought it would be necessary to reassign many attorneys from other branches to the Legislation and Regulations Division. The regulation pipeline was already clogged as evidenced by the fact that some corporations have been waiting for regulations to guide them in their tax planning *since the 1969 tax bill!*

The Internal Revenue Code consists of fourteen volumes — eight for income taxes alone. A high reading and comprehension score is needed to determine eligibility for deductions, exemptions and credits. It's often hard, even for professionals, to tell the difference between constructive deductions and loopholes. In addition to the old seventeen page 1040 Form and its forty-four page instruction booklet, there are pretty near three hundred tax forms and schedules covering every conceivable transaction. No wonder six million tax payers paid commercial firms to complete their Simplified Short Forms. The 1986 Reform did little to simplify the system and in fact many tax professionals have been able to expand their practices with little fear of having to constrict in the near future.

Under the flat tax that we are discussing we are talking SIMPLE! "All Income Taxed But Only Once" is ensured by using a combination of two separate postcard size forms. The Individual Compensation Tax Form is used strictly to report wages, salary and pensions. From the figure derived from wages, salary and pensions the computed personal exemption is subtracted ($6,300 — joint, $3,800 — single, $5,600 — head of household, with each additional exemption $750. Family of four = $7,700 exempted) and 19 percent of that number is the tax due. (Actual numbers are unimportant for this illustration.)

Those simple steps are all that would be involved for about 80 percent of the population who receive no business income. For the other 20 percent of Americans, the Business Tax Form must also be filed. Although under the flat tax proposal we are discussing, the 19 percent rate is lower than the old corporate income tax in this country and in most other parts of the world, it would actually raise more revenue because of its much broader base. Although it doesn't support my point, it's only fair to mention that according to the Tax Foundation, in 1980 the corporate income tax provided 2.4 percent of Sweden's revenue, 10.1 percent of the United States' and 17.3 percent of Japan's. (N.B. Only faulty conclusions can be drawn without analyzing the tax system of these countries. in entirety.)

The Business Tax Form does not constitute a tax on "business per se" but rather on individuals at the business source. Gross revenue from sales goes on the top line. From that may be deducted the cost of foods, material and services the business purchases to make the product it sells. The tax was already paid on these things by the original seller in *his* business-tax top line. The firm can also deduct the wages, salaries and pensions it pays because the recipients pay tax on that on their compensation form. Lastly, the business can deduct its outlays for equipment, plant and land. Nineteen percent of the resultant figure is the tax due. You have probably noticed there is no deduction for interest payments, state and local taxes, charitable contributions and fringe benefits, some of which were destroyed by the 1986 reform at any rate. This is not so much to increase the tax base as it is to ensure "All Income Is Taxed But Only Once". Interest is not taxed when received because it has already been taxed at its business source by not being deducted from gross revenue.

All this is explained in the book *Low Tax, Flat Tax, Simple Tax* published in 1983 by McGraw-Hill and written by Robert Hall and Alvin Rabushka, two economists at the Hoover Institution at Stanford, California. On page 41 the authors show a tax return just this simple made out for Exxon, the largest corporation in the world at that time. For reasons explained above, the corporation ended up paying $700 million more under this theoretical flat tax proposal than under the tax laws in effect in 1982. By no stretch of the imagination is the flat tax a tax on profit. Because business can deduct the cost of land, plant and equipment, in a record sales year when the company is also expanding, it may have a negative taxable income. If so it would be handled, not by government refunds, but by carry forwards which are not limited to any number of years. The balances carried forward earn the market rate of interest. A negative taxable income is no particular problem, because when expansion slows and sales increase, the total contribution to Uncle Sam will be even greater!

A startling concept of the flat tax is its treatment of the total amount of investment as an expense to be deducted in the year it is made. No more complicated depreciation calculations, no more figuring out the amount subject to recapture, or what investment credits may be available, or whether the project can be stretched out long enough to qualify for full credit and all the other contortions which are part and parcel of our present cumbersome tax law. The concept of investment as expense is included, not for the sake of simplicity, but rather from a commitment to the philosophical concept that savings should be encouraged rather than penalized.

A flat tax would prevent persons from diverting savings from their most efficient destinations, one of the main stated goals of the 1986 reform. Here, because of equal tax rates there would simply be no need to divert into unproductive and uneconomic channels in an attempt to avoid, reduce or defer taxation. The loss to the economy from all the effort to reduce or escape taxation has been estimated to be in the neighborhood of $50 billion. Add to that the $6 billion that could be saved by eliminating 600 million hours filling out returns (figured conservatively at $10/hr). Because they will get to keep more of what they earn, ambitious citizens will be encouraged to work longer and harder. Under a progressive tax system the harder they work the more they end up paying.

Exempting investment from taxation is almost the same as exempting savings — one makes the other possible. Since consumption is the difference between income and savings, then consumption is what should logically be taxed. Consumption being what people take out of the economy and income being what they put in. The flat tax is more accurately a consumption tax rather than an income tax.

By expensing investment the double taxation of saving will be eliminated. Under an income tax people pay tax once when they earn and save and again when the savings earn a return. The flat tax abolishes the first tax. Backers of this proposed reform, with its top marginal rate of nineteen percent, claim it would balance the federal budget even if spending were not decreased. (Of course the claim was made before the budget had attained its present size.) It would reduce the need for tax shelters and eliminate the numerous economic distortions left over from the 1986 reform. The 1986 reform reduced tax shelters, but it is impossible to eliminate them as long as Americans remain creative. Unfortunately the *need* for shelters was not reduced along with the shelters themselves. The flat tax would reduce the attractiveness of the underground economy even further and help make an honest nation of us again. It would end the penalties for success, improve incentives for work, entrepreneurial activity and capital formation, all of which will, in the end, raise the gross national product (GNP) and everyone's standard of living. It could amount to an economic renaissance — not all at once, but gradually over the decade after enactment.

I admit that "good" and "ridiculous" are subjective terms but having made that concession I can say that it seems to me the "good" ideas are acted on timidly and often die off without proper discussion whereas the more "ridiculous" ones keep getting pushed through without time for clear analysis.

WHY PROMISES WON'T WORK

In order to get legislation passed, or to get elected or to be able to do whatever it is someone wants to do, fine sounding promises are made. Citizens like you and I have got to discipline ourselves to discount these promises from the outset. It's not exaggeration, stupidity or incompetence (at least not always); it's just that the future is unknowable and estimates are unpredictable, especially when they deal with the many variables in today's complex economy.

The reasoning behind the 1981 Reagan tax-cut was sound and not the voodoo economics that detractors before and since have made it out to be. As GNP rises, it is only natural to expect deficits to decrease. This is not only due to the increased tax revenues from more people working, but as employment rises the need for assistance in the form of welfare, food stamps and other subsidies diminishes. But Reaganomics never got a fair chance to work. Everyone overlooks the fact that Social Security payroll taxes rose more than income taxes fell, in effect eating up the "cut". On top of that, Reaganomics collided with the slowest growth in the money supply in twenty years. The restricted money supply meant business couldn't expand as "planned". What is it they say about "The best laid plans of mice and men"? The Reagan tax cuts were not used by businesses creating more jobs and producing more revenue; instead payroll taxes increased, as did Social Security expenditures and expenditures for defense ($146 billion in 1980 and $265 billion in 1984). Sure taxes fell from over 20 percent of GNP in 1980 to 18.6 percent in 1984. But if the economy had expanded and broadened the tax-base, 18.6 percent of a larger GNP could have meant an increase in revenue. (Imagine the headlines: **Reaganomics Succeeds**). Instead there was a loss in revenue of $50 billion.

The 1981 tax bill included a generous investment tax credit and cost-recovery system which was meant to encourage manufacturing. However, most of the increase in business investment occurred in commerical real estate and expenditures for office innovations such as computer systems. This simply shows that policymakers, no matter how determined, cannot push the American people where they do not want to go.

The 1981 tax cut was supposed to raise revenue over a four year period by about $250 billion, and that's taking a $500 billion loss from the tax cut into consideration. How was this miracle to occur? The economy was supposed to grow an average of 4.5 percent a year which would bring in $7 billion more by FY1985, which would more than make up for the $190 billion rise in expenditures over the same years. Without the 1981 tax cut a *surplus* of at least $122 billion was expected by FY1985. What actually happened? FY1985 saw a *deficit* of $212 billion and a doubling of the outstanding federal debt along the way!

TAXPAYERS BILL OF RIGHTS

Senator David Pryor of Arkansas has generated a lot of support for his Taxpayers' Bill of Rights. The bill's purpose is to more clearly define the boundaries within which the Internal Revenue Service (IRS) operates, to provide greater Congressional and independent oversight of the tax collection process and to furnish additional protections to taxpayers involved in disputes with the IRS. Only in the U.S. Tax Courts are defendants presumed guilty until they can prove themselves innocent. (The Senator's bill would shift the burden of proof in tax disputes to the IRS.) So what if the U.S.

Constitution says "innocent until proven guilty" — we're talking money here!

Many provisions in the Senator's bill deserve our support. For instance the provisions that would allow taxpayers to recover the costs of defending themselves should an IRS claim be held unreasonable and to recover actual damages if it is found that the IRS acted with "careless, reckless or intentional disregard "of rules and regulations. (I know; the average citizen naturally assumes they *already* had these rights!) One would hardly think that it would have to be spelled out that the Service be required to schedule interviews at times and places convenient to both the agents and taxpayers involved. Common sense and courtesy should have taken care of that one. Another reasonable provision is for the establishment of an independent inspector general's office to police the IRS and provide taxpayers and IRS employees with a neutral place to air their greivances.

One of the most popular provisions in the Senator's bill would prohibit the practice of basing promotions or pay raises of revenue agents on the number of levies and property seizures they make. While such a practice is already against IRS policy, no one can deny that it is common practice. There are numerous other provisions such as requiring the IRS to give the taxpayer a "simple, comprehensive and non-technical statement" of his rights and obligations at the beginning of an audit, the right to make a tape recording of the interviews, requiring the IRS to make installment payment plans available to small taxpayers who are found to owe the government money, and requiring that banks hold accounts garnished by the IRS in escrow for 21 days so that taxpayers can have an opportunity to recover their money.

No one in 1887 would believe this discussion! So what? — you might counter, they wouldn't believe Americans actually walked on the moon either. OK — I accept that criticism, but differences in technology are easier to determine as *advancements* than are differences in ideas. America's ideology is determined by the United States Constitution, yet no one can deny the changes that have taken place over the years, often with little foresight. We must determine the value of those changes. We must ask whether each change has brought us closer or pushed us further from the ideals on which this nation was founded. Only when we have the answers can we say whether America has advanced in ideology as it surely has in technology.

THE SIXTH STEP

(RE: OUR GNP)

PERMIT VOLUNTARY
NOT MANDATED ADJUSTMENTS
BY BUSINESS
IN ORDER TO INCREASE
REVENUE VIA GROWTH

THE 6th STEP

(RE: OUR GNP)

THE POPULAR POINT OF VIEW

We are becoming a nation of hamburger flippers. New jobs are low paying jobs. American companies are neglecting to educate and retrain their employees so government should jump in to encourage them. Business should be *made* to provide pensions, health insurance, leaves of absence, child care and training for its employees — it's only FAIR!

ANOTHER POINT OF VIEW

Only 10 percent of all new jobs created between 1983-1987 were menial low wage. Business does not need government interference to tell it how to interact with its employees. *Voluntarily* is the key word. Overburden business and you will destroy companies or push them offshore.

GROWTH ALONE WILL NEVER
REDUCE THE DEFICIT

Frank Gregorsky pointed to an interesting phenomenon in an article he wrote for the *Wall Street Journal* February 13, 1985. A fairly popular tenet of Reaganomics was that a one percent drop in unemployment would reduce the deficit by $25 billion to $30 billion. Since unemployment dropped from 10.6 percent in December 1982 to 7.1 percent in June of 1984 the deficit should have been reduced by almost a $100 billion over that time period according to the above theory. Instead it dropped only $20 billion. More dramatically, between FY1982 and FY1983 unemployment dropped 1.5 percent and the deficit *rose* $85 billion. It is nevertheless not illogical to believe that less unemployment and faster economic growth should lower the deficit. With fewer people unemployed there should be less dollars needed for welfare programs (transfer payments). Also there should be an increase in tax revenue as the unemployed "takers" become "givers" via their new status as employed citizens.

Gregorsky offered the following facts to back up his contention that growth alone would never be sufficient to reduce the deficit:

TABLE 4
RELATION BETWEEN UNEMPLOYMENT
AND TRANSFER PAYMENTS

	Unemployment Rate	Transfer Payments (annualized) (shown in billions)
1982 4th qtr	10.5%	$399
1983 3rd qtr	9.2	403
1984 3rd qtr	7.1	416
1984 4th qtr	7.0	424

Source: Frank Gregorsky 1985

It seems that economic recovery, (higher employment) led not to fewer transfer payments but to more.

If a patient were to tell his doctor that drinking ten glasses of water a day and eating celery led to an "interesting phenomenon"

— weight gain — what conclusion could the doctor logically draw? The same conclusion we can draw from Gregorsky's "interesting phenomenon" — absolutely nothing. We need also to know that in addition to the celery and water the patient ate fried chicken, gravy, fries and pie; that in addition to a drop in the unemployment rate the government increased welfare benefits in numerous areas. Only a blatant disregard for logic could cause one to call the "interesting phenomenon" *cause* and *effect* or to conclude, as Frank Gregorsky did, that growth alone will never reduce the deficit. At any rate I am suggesting that economic growth be considered as only one of twelve steps to reduce the deficit.

To determine the probable size of that economic growth it is necessary to explore the claim bandied about by so-called experts, that Americans are ill prepared to compete in the global economy of the 1980s. With that goal in mind it is relevant to inquire about America's current policies concerning productivity and employment and to explore the incentives and burdens placed on America's locomotive — that is, business.

REAGANOMICS IS NOT DEAD

On February 19, 1987 President Reagan presented the Trade, Employment And Productivity Act of 1987 to Congress. It's stated purpose was to: "Allow American workers and business to meet world competition head-on and win." It's five titles had to do with (1) increasing investment human and intellectual capital, (2) promoting the development of science and technology, (3) better protecting intellectual property rights, (4) bringing about essential legal and regulatory reforms and (5) improving the international economic environment.

ENTERPRISE ZONES

Although enterprise-zones[1] weren't specifically mentioned on February 19th, they have been endorsed by Ronald Reagan on

143

many occasions as an ideal business-government partnership. Enterprise-zones attempt to broaden the old industrial-development approach by putting heavy stress on freeing employers from unjustified red tape as well as from a portion of the tax burden. Although the House will have no part of them, bills to promote enterprise-zones nationally have passed the Senate on two occasions. However, letting states proceed on their own may well prove to be the best answer. Almost half the states have introduced enterprise-zone legislation and in 1985 the Department of Housing and Urban Development reported those states with programs in existence for over a year had attracted more than $3 billion in new capital investment and either retained or created a total of more than 80,000 jobs. (Admittedly the cause and effect relationship is difficult to verify.) Freeing the private business sector has always been our best hope for genuine social progress.

In August 1986, Shirley Dennis from the Department of Labor told the Urban League about Pennsylvania's many successes with its enterprise-zones. She offered evidence that the entrepreneurial spirit is as strong as ever and that what was possible at the turn of the century would be possible now except for excessive regulations.

A case in point: street gang members were able to unite and act as security guards for 43 stores; everyone was happy and everyone was benefiting. Then the regulators came along with their sheaf of rules, one which could not be gotten around (a person must be 26 years old to be an unarmed security guard) and the budding self-help security company went under.

The preceeding was only one example of the inability of old fashioned entrepreneurialism to succeed on its own without the "joint-action" by government that so many intellectuals advocate today. That "joint-action" often means undoing excessive and oppressive regulation. Not *all* regulation — only regulation that is "excessive and oppresive", and this calls for a judgment. (You thought I was going to be inconsistent, didn't you?) *Whose* judgment? I just wish at election time you would take the trouble to remember *whose* judgment!

Some licensing requirements are examples of excessive regulation. Licensing, under the guise of protecting the consumer, is often merely a device to curtail competition by those already enjoying the benefits of an established practice. It causes some of society's most talented and skilled people to work at less productive jobs and thereby reduces everyone's standard of living. Tulane professor David Young has recently written a book for the Cato Institute in which he says,

> Occupational regulation has served to limit consumer choice, raise consumer costs, increase practitioner income, limit practitioner mobility, deprive the poor of adequate service, and restrict job opportunities for minorities — all without a demonstrated improvement in quality or safety.[2]

The unemployed do whatever they can, even without the proper permits, licenses, insurance and adherence to codes and regulations. By circumventing laws they often manage to keep themselves and their families off unemployment and welfare.

The underground economy has been estimated at $400-500 billion which should be rightfully counted as part of our GNP. It means $90 billion per year escapes the clutches of the IRS. (No cheers, please) But that tax loss is less than the amount those who work underground save taxpayers by turning their backs on unemployment benefits and other subsidies. Not only are the underground workers not dependent on government social programs, but they support other businesses with their purchasing power.

A popular theory suggests that an increase in net imports causes an increase in unemployment. However there is evidence to support the opposite viewpoint. We have experienced a greater number of imports since 1980 and the private sector has managed to create millions of new jobs during that period. The increase was not even by any means, with 1.6 million jobs disappearing in 23 industries, such as textiles, electrical equipment, energy, steel and of course agriculture. Experts expect to see 100,000 more jobs disappear in 1987 because of the oil-induced recession in certain areas of the country. But on the bright side, 9.4 million new jobs cropped up in 45 other industries.

I'm not claiming a *cause* and *effect* relationship for either theory. It would be foolish to conclude that an increase in imports *causes* either greater unemployment or greater employment. My point is that those that make such claims error in doing so.

Equally pervasive, and perhaps misleading, is the idea that foreign-born entrepreneurs take income and opportunity away from native born Americans. Ivan Light, author of several publications concerning Asian and other minority businesses, sees not a shred of evidence to support such a belief.

The 1965 Immigration and Naturalization Act abolished immigration quotas based on racial and national origin and consequently from 1970 to 1980 the U.S. Asian population more than doubled. Many Asian immigrants are well educated and not surprisingly prefer entrepreneurship to jobs as unskilled laborers. They generally gather capital from friends and relatives and find inexpensive facilities in depressed urban areas where it is possible to operate a corner grocery, restaurant or liquor store on a shoestring. But as all entrepreneurs will attest, it is the long hours and willingness to sacrifice that ensures eventual success.

CREATING JOBS

England tried, unsuccessfully, a few years ago to legislate profit-sharing for employees by providing tax incentives for employers. Unions didn't like the risk factor. More recently both England and France started giving government benefits to laid-off workers who wanted to buy or start from scratch, a business of their own. In this country Congressman Ron Wyden from Oregon sponsored similar legislation. Michigan, Massachusetts and New Jersey are figuring out ways to use unemployment insurance benefits for new business start ups. The proposal quite naturally angers those who struggled and saved to start their own businesses without a handout from Uncle Sam and now could end up having to finance a competitor. The labor organizations are unhappy because they claim that already the trust funds fail to provide adequate benefits to the unemployed and certainly shouldn't be used to finance new businesses. The National Foundation for Unemployment Compensation & Workers Compensation is also worried about the cost. Despite the opposition, the Labor Department gave the state of Washington a grant to see if new *lasting* businesses will come out of such a program. During 1988 four hundred laid-off workers will be given lump-sum payments as high as $6,000 to start their own businesses. (What deficit?)

A better and less expensive way to encourage new businesses is to reduce unnecessary regulations. An American Bar Association panel has come up with a simplified registration statement so that small companies can raise up to $500,000 by selling stock to the public in various states without the cost and red tape that large companies must go through when registering their stock offerings with the Securities and Exchange Commission.

Overall business starts increased by 16 percent in 1985; bankruptcies climbed 11.5 percent and business failures increased by 9.6 percent which goes to show the climate is not so bad for entrepreneurs after all and that there's an element of truth in that ol' American adage "You win some — you lose some!"

But that's little consolation to those who want to work and can't. Between 1980 and 1986 the percentage of working age people in the population rose from 64 percent to 65.3 percent and not all could find jobs; at least not good paying ones in their old environments. Clare Ansberry wrote a story for the October 1, 1986 edition of the *Wall Street Journal* about a young man in Homestead Pennsylvania who was working 80 hours a week for $3 an hour. Not many people would do something like that, and those that do generally work for themselves, starting sometimes at a minus wage until things get going. Sometimes they succeed beyond their wildest dreams. Hewlett-Packard, Nike footwear, Apple Computer are among the most famous "garage to riches" stories, but there are many others which should be more widely publicized.

Tony and Paul Gerlardi were featured on a television show on

October 7, 1986, as owners of a business which had a $200 million revenue that year. They worked 90 to 100 hour weeks for less than $3 an hour when they first started manufacturing low cost video casettes in an old car wash in southern Maine 15 years ago. By applying creative technology and high volume the two brothers were able to successfuly compete with the Japanese and are now providing employment for other Americans.

June Collier of National Industries ($115 million/year in sales and 2,500 employees) started her company in a garage with $1,503.

A lady appeared on the November 19, 1986 Phil Donahue show who had started making brownies in her kitchen and now has forty people working in a bakery.

Arthur Imperatore, a successful trucker of "near legendery proportions" was featured in *Fortune* magazine (11/11/85). His New Jersey firm succeeded because he hired only the most qualified drivers. Once he had the "best" in his employ he retained them with perks and refreshing candor regarding the business operations. As a consequence his drivers made more deliveries than other drivers and his productivity was far above average. "Underlying everything else was his "uncanny ability to control costs." (Would anyone like to talk him into running for Congress?)

But there are some who not only believe Horatio Alger's time has passed but are convinced perpetuating the legend is harmful.

ROBERT REICH AND COMPANY

Professor Robert Reich of the John F. Kennedy School of Government refers to the self-made man as an American myth out of sync with the world of the eighties. Like so many Americans who never experience the real world except in theory, Professor Reich nevertheless offers concrete business advice. According to the Professor, today's world

requires of us a different and more subtle form of entrepreneurialism,

148

which builds upon joint effort rather than individual conquest.

But should one preclude the other?

Paul Johnson told the Institute for Contemporary Studies at the end of 1986:

> Intellectuals deduce their ideas from principles and then seek to impose them on people. Beware committees, conferences, leagues of intellectuals! For intellectuals, far from being highly individualistic and nonconformist people, are in fact ultra-conformist within the circles formed by those whose approval they seek and value.

SERVICE JOBS

Those who promote the all too popular image of America becoming a nation of hamburger flippers should check their facts. The stereotype of service work as menial and low-paying is simply misleading. Of course there are fast-food and janitorial jobs which fit into that category, but so do the jobs held by physicians, government officials, professors and lawyers.

From 1983 to 1987 seventy-five percent of all new jobs were in the professions, in management, technical sales, precision repair or skilled production. Only ten percent of the new jobs were menial minimum wage.

Labor Department statistics show America is up-grading her workers at the same time Labor Unions are losing membership.

But facts are easily distorted. (No!) The ways are infinite; for instance using the Consumer Price Index instead of the more accurate Personal Expenditure Index and picking atypical years has been known to make the incredible, credible.

For example a report released in December 1986 by Congress's Joint Economic Committee found from 1979 through 1984 nearly three-fifths of all jobs created in this country were in the lowest wage category and that a startling 97 percent of new jobs recently acquired by white males paid $7,000 or less. The report was authored by Barry Bluestone and Bennett Harrison who for many years have been arguing that the middle class was on the decline in this country. (A built in bias?) Professor Frank Levy of the University of Maryland came to similar conclusions in doing research for his book *Dollars and Dreams*. (Is it fair to cry "bias" again? I'll settle for "unreliable") Any good attorney knows it is possible to take the same set of facts, and depending on which side you represent, to *make them* support your case.

Information, like a rumor, is often embellished as it makes the rounds. On March 15, 1987, a labor lawyer argued that 44 percent of the new jobs created during the Reagan administration paid $7,400 or less and Senator James Sasser of Tennessee picked that comment up, elaborated slightly and it came out before the March 23,1987 meeting of the Economic Competitiveness Senate Committee (Government Affairs) as: "Sixty-four percent of the jobs created since 1979 pay less than $7,500/year; we're witnessing the deindustrialization of America." Unfortunately the questionable information was echoed by countless journalists and other politicians wishing to advance their own political agendas.

Janet Norwood, Commissioner of Labor Statistics, issued a warning; an old fashioned caveat emptor to concerned citizens attempting to ascertain the true state of affairs amid the conflicting information being pushed on us from all sides:

> the findings (supposed proliferation of low-paying jobs at the expense of high-paying) are extremely sensitive to the particular set of data used (as well as) the years chosen for analysis.

Actually there are approximately the same mix of high and low paying jobs as we had in this country a decade ago. How do *I* know? How's "facts coupled with common sense" as a source? It's hard to mislead the public for long as citizens will figure out the truth on their own anyway — after all, excessive borrowing couldn't account for the entire rise in real (after inflation) per-capita disposable income and there's no doubt many of the new service jobs are high paying, especially in the communications field.

Brian Motley, writing for the newsletter of the Federal Reserve Bank of San Francisco in January 1987, made a good point. He said that the rising share of service jobs may be beneficial because a more service-oriented economy is bound to be less affected by the cyclical ups and downs which are the hallmark of a manufacturing oriented society.

> Because goods are durable and can be stored, producers tend to add to their inventories when business is strong and to draw them down when business is weak. Similarly households tend to accelerate or delay purchases of durable goods in response to changes in current economic conditions.

Employees are more readily expanded and contracted which means more flexibility within the economy. Where it would be unthinkable to build or dismantle plants and machinery, it is now possible to move workers to meet changing demand. Mr. Motley sees the trend to a more service oriented society as a sign of America's strength rather than a cause for concern.

UNEVEN PROGRESS — BLACKS AS AN EXAMPLE

In 1973, at the start of the largest recession since the thirties, only 5.7 percent of black males were unemployed. In January, 1983 that number had soared to 20.3 percent only to drop to 12.7 percent in 1986, still more than double the 1973 unemployment rate for black males. Social progress is uneven. There are more geographic pockets harboring the woefully depressed or the extremely prosperous than ever before.

Take Pittsburgh Pennsylvania in 1985: black unemployment was 23.5 percent; three times that of Pittsburgh's whites and fifty percent higher than the national average for blacks. The black poverty level was 28.7 percent compared to 6.7 percent for Pittsburgh whites. The infant mortality rate was 22 per 1,000 compared to 9.7 for whites and 17.9 for blacks nationally. The median family income was $11,169 for blacks compared to $19,278 for whites and $12,598 for blacks nationally and $20,835 for whites nationally.

In August 1986 the Urban League's annual report on "Black America" emphasized traditional values and self-help.

Robert Woodson, president of the National Center for Neighborhood Enterprise and Arthur Fletcher top man in a $170 billion food preparation and service industry were both incensed that Blacks are not giving other Blacks a chance when the opportunity arises. They accused Black mayors of not putting dollars into Black neighborhoods.

Floyd McKissik, an attorney from Oxford, North Carolina, in order to make his point that welfare was intended to keep Blacks dependent, used the story of the grey squirrel who became so accustomed to peanuts that he soon forgot how to feed himself.

Carl Holman, president of the National Urban Coalition, argued on behalf of grassroots Black community learning centers and urged the audience to encourage Blacks to emulate Eugene Lang, a successful New York businessman who nurtured a sixth grade class in a disadvantaged New York neighborhood and promised them college educations if they stayed in school. Nurturing one another is what other ethnic groups did to get a foot hold in this country. There is evidence that Woodson and Fletcher are on the right track with this kind of thinking, but they may have over stepped the bounds when their rhetoric went from encouraging private businessmen to encouraging public officials to "share the wealth".

Fletcher painted California Congressman Ron Dellums as a potential Daddy Warbucks for Blacks if they would only learn how to cook. It was said the Congressman controls a $13 billion food budget and 60,000 jobs. Fletcher claimed to be in the process of training Blacks "to own and control the military food service business" with its many million dollar plus food contracts.

Fletcher pointed out that Blacks own one percent of capital assets in America and his goal is to make that ten percent. According to the Census Bureau by the end of 1985 there were 340,000 Black-owned businesses with revenue of $12.4 billion, and that's a beginning.

THE MODERN WORKPLACE

Despite the call to emulate Japanese "team-work" practices and to democratize the workplace via ESOPs and so forth, today some workplace relationships are more autocratic than they have been in years. Among employee owned ESOP-type companies there might be a feeling of working together toward a common goal, i.e. regaining or capturing market share for the good of all. But too many decentralized bargaining situations have regressed to a form of blackmail — "do this or else". Companies are able to use threats because of overcapacity. There is more ability to produce in the world today than there is capacity, or should I say wherewithal, to consume. As we discussed in Chapter Two, technology has made labor more dispensible than capital and therefore those who have only labor to offer are not in the most advantageous bargaining position. The tactics unions used when confronted by a "take it or leave it" situation in the past, will no longer work because the markets simply aren't there beckoning to business to get on with it and collect the waiting rewards.

Today national contracts are giving way to local contracts. In the past the strength in numbers prevented individual localities from reducing wages and benefits. Now almost all companies are facing unprecedented global competition and simply cannot preserve the old concentration of power that union leaders loved so much. Wages and benefits are now taking a back seat to negotiations focusing more on productive capacity and working conditions. Management, not by choice, has been left with the stick rather than the carrot. But today workers take their own kind of mostly subconscious revenge.

Research by Robert Half International discovered that the average office worker "steals" more than four and a half hours from his employer each week and that workers in general are responsible for a loss of approximately $170 billion to American business through late arrivals, feigned illness and so forth every year.

Another recent study [3] reported that 77 percent of females and 73 percent of males attempt to work out their family problems on company time. AT&T figured one way to prevent this is to give employees more flexible time. That's not a bad idea, I'll admit, but I've also got to confess my first thought was to replace them with employees who solve company problems on company time.

In 1986 one and a half million workers were working under contracts featuring the two-tier pay system. Great for employers and old employees but it may end up causing more discord on the job where workers are performing the same tasks and getting widely disparate pay.

Basing seniority on cumulative service rather than consecutive employment is a praiseworthy attempt to reduce employee turnover in order to protect the company's investment.

"Pay for Knowledge" is another innovation under which employees are shifted from job to job and paid according to their repertoire of skills. The compensation they receive is keyed to the number of skills they've mastered. Starting with training they move along adding abilities and value to the company and increase their personal pride and satisfaction.

Workers like flex-time and part-time work because it is convenient and employers like it because it provides them with flexibility and lower costs.

Companies have started creating pools of "contingent" workers to replace regular employees working traditional 40-hour weeks. The ranks of contingent employees have doubled since 1980 to nearly 17 percent of all workers. If you include employees who voluntarily work part-time then that number rises to 25 million or approximately 25 percent of our workforce. Payment of health insurance, pension and fringe benefits are often avoided by employers in this manner. The U.S. Chamber of Commerce found that average fringe benefits amounted to $8,166 per employee or anywhere from $3,500 to $13,000 or 18 to 65 percent of an employer's payroll costs.

THE MINIMUM WAGE

It is almost certain that the minimum wage, which started at 25 cents in 1938, will be raised from its present $3.35 an hour. Already various states, including California, have taken the lead in this area.

Raising the minimum wage will be an incentive for people to seek employment and get off welfare rolls, according to proponents. They argue that currently only a minimum wage earner living alone makes enough to be living above the poverty level. But remember the so-called "poverty level" is man-made and arbitrary. The 1986 poverty level for a single person = $5,469, for two = $6,998, for three = $8,741, and for four = $10,989. A full time minimum wage job yields $6,968.

Who can fault a person for making a rational economic decision to turn away from a minimum wage job toward welfare where he might find he could collect almost twice the minimum wage in AFDC benefits, food stamps and housing subsidies, especially if several children are involved? But opponents of the minimum wage insist it's not head of households who are earning the minimum wage, but teenagers and second income earners who can use the employment history as a ticket to a better job in the future. A recent CBO report showed 15 percent of those making less than $4 an hour are from poor families and 85 percent are students and second and third earners. Senator William Proxmire challenged those figures but Isabel Sawhill of the Urban Institute stood firm when testifying before the Senator's Committee in early 1987, although the Senator obviously wanted her to refute the CBO report.

Senator Edward Kennedy of Massachusetts has introduced a bill which would raise the minimum wage to $4.65 gradually over a three year period. On the House side Congressman Augustus Hawkins' bill would add to the $4.65 achieved over a three year period, on additional raise of 50 cents in 1989 and a 40 cent hike in both 1990 and 1991. This would give the United States a mandatory minimum wage of $5.05 an hour by 1992.

The Petri Bill, formally known as the Job Enhancement For Families Act, is a far better alternative to the minimum wage. It was introduced by Wisconsin Congressman Thomas Petri and would strengthen and expand the Earned Income Tax Credit (EITC). The EITC, actually a negative income tax, refunds 14 percent of the first $5,714 earned by an eligible person who provides a home for one or more children. (Maximum credit = $800)

> Expanding the EITC...would raise the worker's after-tax wages without raising the employer's labor costs...It encourages job creation, it helps those workers most who need the most help, it reduces government spending, and it has a minimal effect on the budget deficit.[4]

The Congressional Budget Office (CBO) estimates the government would loose about $1.5 billion in revenue annually by expanding the EITC. Proponents claim this would be offset by increased jobs and decreased welfare expenses whereas raising the minimum wage would increase the deficit (tax revenue loss and more government spending on welfare etc) by about $7 billion a year. (Does anyone care about the effect on the deficit?)

Those who favor raising the minimum wage point out that because of inflation its value has fallen twenty percent since it was conceived ten years ago[5]. They suggest that a raise would be a poverty program which would add nothing to the deficit.

But, as opponents point out, when an employer foots the bill the cost is always passed on to the consumer (a taxpayer by any other name...). Nevertheless small businesses, who employ most minimum wage earners, may well decide what they could afford at $3.35 an hour is unaffordable at $4.65 an hour. After all, does it really matter if no one sweeps the sidewalk, picks up trash, scrubs graffitti off a small businessman's walls, washes the windshield and checks the air, or lights your way so you avoid plopping down on a stranger's lap in a dark theatre?

The bottom line is that the 4 or 5 million people earning minimum wage may not be essential to any particular business and many of the unskilled will simply swallow their pride and go on welfare. But as the marginal jobs are cut, more and more of the "niceties" disappear from American life. Of course we'll survive but the nostalgic memories will tell us something valuable is missing.

THE DISABLED WORKER'S
CONTRIBUTION TO THE GNP

A Harris Poll showed that two-thirds of all disabled Americans want to work even though it might mean forgoing a disability check. If they should get laid off work it takes about nine months to get recertified as disabled, which could mean living on the smaller unemployment check for awhile. Many are willing to take the risk. This country has always encouraged and rewarded risk takers — let's not stop now. But are we going about it in the best way?

Ted Kennedy Jr., head of the Boston based nonprofit group called Facing The Challenge, Inc., talks about physically and mentally challenged individuals who are striving to achieve the "basic rights of citizenship". According to his article in the November 23, 1986 issue of *Parade* magazine, those "basic rights" include "equal access to education, transportation, competitive employment and housing".

Mr. Kennedy claims that the disabled are a viable lobby comparable to the senior citizens' lobby in Washington DC and that their needs should be taken seriously. He tells us that 62 percent of the disabled who are willing and able to work are unemployed and he attributes this to society's prejudices. He points out that a disabled white male earns 40 percent less than an able-bodied white male.

The question is: should what Kennedy refers to as "basic rights" be prioritized along with the multitude of society's desirable goals or should they be treated as constitutional rights and be implemented by force of law?

It is certain that no one wants to depend on others. However studies have shown it might be less expensive for society to provide a lifetime of taxi service to the few disabled persons who use the buses rather than equip all buses with costly ramps. No one would argue against the merits of devices that permit a wheelchair to take curbs in its stride or an electronic device to circumvent braille and relay information directly to the blind. However, whether we like it or not, cost does matter, even when it comes to issues that are as guilt laden as providing for the elderly, ill or disabled. Government's resources are limited and individual taxpayers have their own private priorities as to how they wish to use their earnings.

Ah, but as always there is the manipulative tax code. The Targeted Jobs Credit offers tax credits to employers who hire disadvantaged and handicapped persons. If ever there was a persuasive example of the end (opportunity and jobs) justifying the means, this piece of social engineering is it.

Taxpayers supported a man with an IQ of 28 (100 is normal) for 25 years in a public institution. At age 32 and with 3 weeks training he was able to bag groceries at $3.85 an hour. A woman with a similar IQ was able to clean offices with the help of a walkman-like device that periodically interrupted the recorded music to ask if the ashtrays and waste baskets had been emptied and reminded her to move on to the next office. In the future there will be fewer workers for low skilled jobs. Non-demanding jobs are just too boring for many people. Dishwashers usually turn over two or three times a year but a retarded worker mentioned by Roger Ricklef in the *Wall Street Journal,* had been on the job six years — happily. In his article Mr. Ricklef said that if the retarded are placed in the right environment and thoroughly trained they prove to be effective and motivated workers. Employers are delighted with the decrease in absenteeism and replacement due to job turn-over. They find that although retarded workers, or workers with other handicaps, may not be as fast as so-called "normal" employees, they are generally more dependable, cheerful and willing to stick with the job. Taxpayers are happy because these people are able to contribute to society's needs rather than draining the taxpayer by living like a vegetable in a public institution, as would have been the case fifty years ago. Most importantly, and it should go without saying, the worker himself is happier and more fulfilled.

But rather than having the government appeal to their baser natures by making the situation risk free with taxpayer subsidies, employers should be encouraged to voluntarily asume a share of the risk. If you tell me they wouldn't hire the handicapped without first receiving an offer that would fatten their own purses, I tell you that is only because they have come to expect and depend on government's bribes. Government's policies are geared to encourage greed rather than altruism. (Yes, I'm the same person who consistently claims that altruism "is not the province of government", but once government is involved it is better to be on the side of altruism than on the side of greed. Best of all, but impossible to achieve, would be no social manipulation by government.)

Actually hiring the retarded is a cost saving idea for business and government. I plead guilty in this instance of using the "blackmail argument" I so despise. That is — "If society doesn't do such and such it will cost more in the long run." However, I bring up the cost savings because I am suggesting a *volunteer* hiring by private sector organizations. The private sector, not government, will provide training and equipment. (Gotcha!)

GOVERNMENT'S ROLE?

From 1981 to 1986 a little over five million persons were displaced out of a total labor force estimated to be 110 million. *Displaced* is the buzz word which appeared in 1987, sharing the lime-light with *competitiveness.* About 15 percent of the *displaced* left the workforce taking early retirement, 18 percent joined the ranks of the unemployed (unemployed and *displaced* are not synonymous) and 67 percent found other employment. More than 50 percent of those finding other employment found jobs with equal or higher pay. According to the Bureau of Labor Statistics, 26.8 percent of those new jobs paid 20 percent more than the old; 24.5 percent paid equal or up to 20 percent more; 12.9 percent paid up to 20 percent less than the old job; 27.5 percent (yes I noticed it's the largest category by .7 percent) paid less than the old job by a margin of 20 percent or above. (8.3 percent were unaccounted for). All in all those *displaced* workers who found new employment were better off by 51.3 percent to 40.4 percent—not great, but then we have not been led to believe that *displaced* was a synonym for *promotion*, rather we have heard it used synonymously for *down & out* !

In FY1981 the Labor Department dolled out an average of a little over $3,000 cash to more than half a million displaced workers. They also spent $7.3 million training 14,000 workers in 1981, less than half the $16.5 million spent 3 years later in 1984 on training and related services.

If an unemployed person could show his job was lost due to foreign competition the length of time unemployment benefits were available doubled (26 to 52 weeks) and a worker immediately became eligible for training and other benefits. One obvious result of such a policy was to delay job searches. (Can you imagine any other "obvious results" of such a policy?)

The Job Training Partnership Act (JTPA) was started with a $3.3 billion budget. Its predecesor, the Comprehensive Employment and Training Act (CETA) had a $9 billion budget. JTPA's average training period is only about four months and the average placement wage is $4.63. Hardly a long lasting or rewarding use of funds. However to keep those funds coming, those in charge had to create an aura of success. To further that end the term "placement" was construed in so loose a manner as to be utterly meaningless. The "placement" might have been the mere promise of a job or a job that lasted only a very short period of time.

Other ideas to get people working have been discussed and some actually attempted. One plan used federal vouchers which a displaced worker could redeem for job training. Another plan would give private employers tax benefits in exchange for retraining their own or training new displaced workers who are able to meet certain qualifications. "70001" (an accounting number) helps dropouts find jobs and encourages participants to pursue high school equivalency diplomas. In 1985, 84 percent of the 4,148 enrolled completed the 70001 programs and of those 92 percent got jobs. Not bad!

On the other hand the Job Corps provides remedial education

and job training for young, hard-core unemployed and costs the government $15,000 per year for each participant. On top of that it has a high dropout rate. Not good!

The President's budget for 1988 calls for a scrapping of many of the old programs and the funding of $900 million to displaced workers who will be able to qualify for the aid under more relaxed rules.

In many states, workers who receive unemployment compensation will see it end if they decide to get training in order to prepare themselves for a new line of work. In an attempt to solve this problem, former Senator of Colorado, Gary Hart, proposed an Individual Training Account (one more idea modeled after the IRA) where both employee and employer would make contributions into a fund which a displaced worker could draw upon if he ever needed it for retraining.

To ask the employer to continually make one contribution after the other for the benefit of his employees is to discourage hiring. Why in the world can't an employee be expected to set aside something for such an eventuality (job loss) on his own initiative? It used to be called "preparing for a rainy day". Are American citizens so short-sighted, undisciplined, incompetent and irresponsible? To those who would say "yes" I would say let's change that starting now!

O BOY — A TASK FORCE!

The Task Force on Economic Adjustment and Worker Dislocation was launched by the Department of Labor and reported everything was fine, just the normal ups and downs endemic to a free competitive market.

OK, I lied. What doctor can resist prescribing at least aspirin and rest for a complaining, paying patient even though he can observe nothing abnormal? When a task force is called in on a case it cannot simply say we've looked the situation over and it's fine. That might initiate the demise of all those prestige-building task forces. So this task force suggested the addition of a new agency

161

to add to Capitol Hill's already overstocked supply of "alphabet soup". The DWU (at least the letters don't spell a cutesy word) the Displaced Worker Unit, would airlift federal and state Department of Labor workers to locations anywhere in the country where a plant closing might be taking place. Mission: to hold hands and retrain where feasible. Cost = $1 billion *initially*. (Remember, feed a problem and it will grow.)

The task force called for programs for testing, counseling and teaching job-research skills and entrepreneurial skills, all of which should provide a good bit of employment in itself. The task force also recommended income support payments and funding for business start-ups via lump-sum payments of unemployment insurance. Howard D. Samuel, President of the AFL-CIO Industrial Union Department and a member of that task force, would like to see Congress restrict plant closings in order to protect manufacturing jobs.

Former Secretary of Labor William Brock was aware that advance notice of job lay-offs or plant closings could be most beneficial to employees. Nevertheless the Labor Secretary stopped short of expressing a desire to see such notice mandated by yet another new law. But as we know too well, law makers generally favor new laws. (What would we do without the — the laws *and* the makers?)

Senator Metzenbaum of Ohio expressed a desire to see a law requiring that companies with 50 or more employees give 90 days notice for any lay-offs or closings and those companies with 500 or more employees be compelled to give 180 days notice. Sounds reasonable doesn't it? After all, folks have to make plans, and how nice it would be to be retrained for a new job and send resumes around before the old job ends. Work would cease but pay would continue for three to six months. Never mind the havoc such a law might work on an employer's attempt to refinance his business. What investor or lender wouldn't be scared away by rumors, let alone *notice* of a closing?

What if an employee sought an injunction claiming proper notice was not given? Could a court then order a company to continue operating and would the court provide the necessary money to hold the plant open as ordered?

Although the plant-closing bill was defeated in the House by a narrow margin of five votes, it worked its way into H.R. 3 — the infamous Omnibus Trade Bill of 1988.

In early 1988 a study conducted by Robert R. Nathan Associates, a Washington DC research organization, found that not only would there be a rise in unemployment but the United States would be less able to compete globally if only four of the many bills on labor's agenda were to become law.[6] These are the four proposals estimated to cost about $100 billion a year if implemented by the public *and* private sectors: ("...study estimates that employers would absorb up to $47.8 billion in additional labor costs if these four bills become law.")

(1)   High-risk notification: requires employers to notify all past and present employees who under the law's terms are considered to be at risk of developing an occupation-related disease.

(2)   Mandated health benefits: requires employers to provide health insurance coverage for employees, including part-time minimum wage workers. (Kiss those jobs goodbye!) Pre-natal and post-natal care to be part of the package as well as out-patient care and physician and hospital costs.

(3)   Plant closing: we have discussed. Already there is talk of limiting the law to plants with 100 or more employees and shortening the notice required to 60 days.

(4)   Family and medical leave: (discussed on pp. 175-178) The proposal is being modified but the idea is for employers to allow so many weeks of leave so employees can care for new or sick children or ill parents without losing their jobs or health benefits.

The larger the number of regulations the more risky ventures become, the fewer ventures that are started,   the fewer the available jobs and the more sluggish the economy. (More regulation = less flexibility, more risk = less jobs, more unemployment = less economic growth!)

LINKAGE — DOUBLESPEAK FOR BLACKMAIL

So-called linkage fees are taxes levied on downtown developers in order to ameliorate social and economic dislocations that supporters of such fees claim downtown growth creates. Forget about the jobs and economic vitality that development also creates! Certain groups seem to be concerned only with punishing, not rewarding developers!

What do you call it when in order to get a building permit a developer must agree to provide child-care facilities, sell food stamps, provide parks, low-income housing, jobs or whatever else local officials desire? I call it *blackmail*!

Peter Waldman reported in the *Wall Street Journal* that a $23 million museum in Los Angeles was built with cash extorted (my word) from developers who had the audacity to request a permit to grace the City of Angels with a $1.9 billion office complex.

Apparently San Antonio officials taught a hotel developer a thing or two about waltzing into their community without "goodies" to distribute to everybody. They forced the developer to take on an equity partner of the city's choice in order to obtain his permit to build. OK, the partner put up $1 million in exchange for the equity stake, but in the America I once knew a business person could freely choose his *own* partners, thank you!

I am going to quote Mr. Waldman directly so you won't think I'm exaggerating when you read what he claims the seat of the government of "the home of the free" wants to do.

> The District of Columbia is considering requiring outside banks that want to acquire banks in the city to establish branches in poor neighborhoods, provide up to $100 million in loans to city-sponsored projects, create up to 200 jobs and sell food stamps.[7]

My anger regarding what many like to refer to as "linkage

policies" (I still believe *blackmail* is the correct term) is mixed up with guilt because I live part time in the city where this nonsense all began — San Francisco.

In 1981, partly to assuage community opposition to downtown development and also as a means of raising money for low-income housing and mass transit, San Francisco began requiring developers to either provide housing at below market costs or money to assist first-time home buyers — all in addition to a $5 per square foot "transit impact" fee. Resonable you say? Well many think so and in fact in 1985 San Francisco's supervisors got a little more greedy and decided to add new "linkage fees" (blackmail). Another $6 per square foot was added to the "take" so the "guilty city" could offer its citizens and visitors child care (ahh!), public art (ohh—) and open space (Bravo!) ala the evil developers. (That should teach THEM!)

But, you might ask, if the developers were being victimized why did they continue to build? They had to be making money. You're right — the linkage fees were passed on to their tenants and the craziest thing happened; the city's office vacancy rate went from near zero in the early eighties to over fifteen percent today (1987).

Whether linkage fees continue to "work" or not (they have generated in the neighborhood of $30 million for San Francisco)[8] the notion that developers have a unique duty to alleviate chronic urban problems is somehow repulsive. They already pay amply for what they receive from the cities with taxes, jobs, economic activity and so forth. Why add "blackmail"? At any rate (and I know you've heard this argument many times and in every conceivable form but that doesn't make it any less true) the blackmail (tax) will be absorbed as one more cost of doing business and passed on to other segments of society. The business will be less competitive and a chill will settle on future business projects in the area. After all, business will go wherever it is the most profitable, even if it means leaving the beautiful City by the Bay or the United States of America!

165

The city council of Hartford Connecticut deserves some credit for recognizing this truth and turning down the opportunity to play Robin Hood by going after their own developers and demanding their share of "linkage fees". In Mr. Waldman's account one Hartford councilman made the rather weak point that by not giving in to the demands of the city's activists for "a piece of the pie" that the politicians would be forced to extract more concessions from future developers in an effort to show they were "good guys" after all. This was supposed to be proof that acting with character now would mean having to throw even more bones to the masses in the future. This is one more example of the emerging class system in this country; not the rich and the poor — the Rulers (arrogant legislators), and the Ruled (oblivious citizens).

Chicago really has the best idea though. Can you imagine how Chicagoans will vote when a plan is presented for their approval or disapproval that will allow them to divide $10 million a year (the projected "take" from linkage levees) to use for the local projects of their choice?

Why do you suppose our economy is so sluggish when anyone can plainly see all that is being done to, whoops — I mean for, business in this country?

WHO COULD BE AGAINST CHILD-CARE?

If a corporation believes it can benefit from helping employees handle the demands of family and work then they should help, but the company's self-interest should be the motivating factor.

Contrary to popular rhetoric, the facts show many companies are already helping their employees in this area. The Conference Board estimated 2,500 companies provided some child-care help to employees during 1985 and approximately 150 companies operate on-site or near-site child-care facilities. Unfortunately tort law has had a chilling effect on these efforts. In our litigious society the deep pockets of our large corporations makes them a target for all sorts of civil suits. Because of this potential liability their child-care facilities have become more expensive than

166

otherwise. Nor is the situation likely to improve under the 100th Congress with Ernest Hollings, the South Carolina Senator who has so adamantly opposed putting a cap on business liability, as the new chairman of the Senate Commerce Committee.

Because of the legal liability, some companies try and stimulate off-site centers via donations. AT&T is considering giving employees a building to run their own center. Whatever works as long as it isn't blackmail! And that brings us back to the City by the Bay once again.

San Francisco requires new hotels over a certain size to provide child-care services at or near the hotel or to donate $1 per square foot to a child-care fund. A predictable extension of last year's requirement that new office buildings provide child-care facilities.

A small group of men and women are re-creating the Robin Hood scenario in San Francisco and no one seems to mind an iota. The Supervisors tell a group of people who are willing to put up capital to build a hotel that they must pay a little extra on the side. Nasty venture capitalists will be permitted to proceed with their already risky project only if they ante up. The Robin Hood syndrome is a perfect example of the end justifying the means — robbery for a good cause.

In order to attract competent people to care for children the pay must be higher; if working parents are to afford the care the cost must be lower. The obvious solution is to ask for government subsidies — get all taxpayers to chip in.

The Minnesota Child Care Workers Alliance had an even better idea. Give state money only to those centers who pay above-average wage scale. A game of "who can charge the most!" What a wild idea! There's no telling where it can lead if higher pay advocates are successful in luring federal money into the game. How's this for a slogan: "One income families should be taxed to pay for day-care for two income families". Kinda catchy!

In 1983, IBM contracted with a Boston child-care consulting firm. The idea was to set up 16,000 home-based centers and 3,000 group day-care centers for IBM employees. By the end of 1986 IBM had an estimated $2 million annual budget for its child-care referral service. As if that were not enough, they also contributed to a nonprofit group that has trained 5,000 new providers to care for 13,000 children. That's less than three children per provider. As a mother of five, I wonder what special training the providers were given to look after two and a fraction children — perhaps skills in avoiding lawsuits.

In 1984 Bank of America donated $100,000 (small change when you're already headed towards a $600 million deficit) and influenced others to pony up $700,000 in order to create day-care for 1,000 children with the money to be used to recruit and train providers.

In search of answers as to how Bank of America incurred a deficit of $650 million per year one might trace one measly drop-in-the-bucket to child-care and on back to 1983 when the bank began reimbursing certain adoption expenses incurred by its employees; up to $2,000 worth. Either management *didn't* think, or thought that is what it takes to keep and attract good employees.

The Bank of America Foundation acted as underwriter for several corporations and government agencies to increase the availability of improved child-care in five California counties. In San Jose, the David and Lucile Packard Foundation and Levi Strauss & Co. provided funds for a seventeen-bed children's infirmary attached to a day-care center. It is not unusual for employers to pick up all or part of the cost of caring for the sick children of employees either by sending trained nurses or medical aides to the home or footing the bill for sick-child-day-care operations like the ones mentioned. They do it, not necessarily out of altruism, but to save the extraordinary cost of absenteeism — an incredible loss to American productivity.

Aware that child-care provisions supposedly alleviate turn-over, absenteeism and stress among employees, one small (relative) company in Roanoke Virginia spends a reported $85,000 per year on its on-site-child-care facility. Wonderful for the employees but definitely not inexpensive for the employer. But what does the employer have to worry about besides global competition? Anyway he can console himself with the thought that he is eliminating "turnover, absenteeism and stress".

Ellen Glainsky, of the Work and Family Life Studies at Bank Street, reported "Our major finding is that problems with child-care are the most significant predictors of absenteeism and unproductive time at work."⁹ *Fortune* magazine reporter, Fern Chapman, then asked "Whose problem is this?" and then proceeded to answer in a familiar manner. If you have heard the Constitution's "general welfare" clause dragged out for justification, or a criminal excused because of his poor environment and lack of opportunity then you will recall the basis was either *collective need or collective guilt.* Combining the two Ms. Chapman says, "A case can be made that it (unproductive worktime) is not only the parents 'but the employers' and ultimately society's (problem)."

Elizabeth Ehrlich in an article which appeared in *Business Week* October 6, 1986, made a similar statement. "The once-private matter of child-care has become a public policy issue that demands action."¹⁰ For the benefit of those who do not consider this notion absurd lets's examine where it might logically lead.

Let's look at society's choices:

I- LET GOVERNMENT DO IT
   A 1984-type world with kibbutz-type baby hatcheries and child rearing facilities reminiscent of *Brave New World*

II- MAKE BUSINESS DO IT
   Voluntary action is fine if it is in the best interest of business, otherwise advocates are suggesting a fascist government.

III- PROGRAMS NOT RUN BY GOVERNMENT BUT USING TAXPAYER DOLLARS
   Using the dollars of those who give staying at home and caring for their children high priority and struggle on one income to be able to do so, is clearly wrong. Why should one group give money to a group with different priorities

169

in order to make it easier for this second group to work? Tax credits, vouchers, and higher prices passed on by businesses footing the bills would do exactly that.

Ms. Ehrlich says, "No one is suggesting a uniform monolithic (*Brave New World*) federal program." She admits diversity is a strength. The problem, as Ms. Ehrlich sees it, is that we "...can't assure quality care."

When a newborn leaves the hospital quality care is not assured either. Life is not riskless. George Miller, Representative from California, has a marvelous idea: "...government has to get more resources in the system."[11] (Why didn't we think of that?) This round robin starts with the need for dollars which leads one to go to work, which leads to the need for more dollars for child-care, which leads to the need for more government revenue, which leads to a tax hike to get it, which leads to the need to make even more dollars to pay more taxes ad infinitum.

The Congressman is starting small by asking for only $300 million more per year to add to the $2.7 billion we all chip in now for child-care. That should make a clean round $3 billion. According to Ehrlich's wisdom "Society should not regard (child-care) as a luxury." Haven't we all heard that argument too many times about too many things before? But nothing beats the slickness of the following phrase: "... a system lubricated with government funds."[12] That means a group of people want to do something that is not cost efficient. Incapable of prioritizing, they find it easier to take from other people. Robin Hood is at it again!

On March 19, 1987 I heard one of those early morning TV panels discussing employer-employee relations and one gentleman suggested that employers *mandate* that each employee spend at least one hour a day with his or her children. With or without pay wasn't explicitly stated, but from the tone of the discussion I assume the employer would be expected to pay for these hours because it would be, after all, for the "good of the company".

Concern for employees' morale has taken a new twist. I remember in the fifties when large corporations made it a point to hire men with wives the company felt would be supportive. The employee's wife and home life were considered then, as now, to be important to his productivity on the job. A wife who could entertain and make a good impression was an asset to the firm and no one thought it was "none of the company's business." We seem to have come full circle only with a twist. The stabililty of the employee's home life is still a legitimate concern of the employer but we think the employer should not be able to use discrimination (refuse to hire anyone) in his search for the employee with the perfect spouse and its accompanying promise of greater productivity. No indeed, the employer is expected to take full responsibility for the morale of his employees. It would be unthinkable to hire only employees without children or with a spouse at home so that the employee would feel relaxed about the well-being of his family and be better able to concentrate on his work. If any employer considered such things he would guilty of discrimination in the workplace. (What do you mean *his* business? Just because he has invested his capital and his labor doesn't give him special priviliges, Comrade.) Instead he should provide time off for the employee to visit and spend "quality" time with his children. Naturally it would be in the employer's best interest. (Naturally!) The company would save time (time is — or used to be — money) by having a child-care center on the premises. By letting mothers bring their babies to work, and of course providing the necessary facilities to make everone happy, the employer will ensure a well adjusted workforce. (Remember he isn't allowed to consider such things *before* hiring.) Is there anything wrong with making "parents" a subsidized class of citizens?

On July 30, 1986, ABC aired a television special titled *After The Sexual Revolution*. I took the following notes:

1) 62 percent of women (out of how many?) said their jobs had not been kept open when they took maternity leave. (No mention that 81 percent of the Fortune 500 companies offered job-protected maternity leaves.)

2) A lady claimed she "had to go on welfare to be with my baby."

3) Nine million children need licensed care and it is available for only one million. As a consequence, six million children are left in unlicensed unregulated care. Studies show the seven to ten million children, known as latch-key kids, are often insecure. Some unsupervised kids even become disoriented. We must "wake up as a society" or pay the price. (The "or else" theme once again! In the past relatives watched children and still do for low-income working mothers. No one mentioned that day-care centers are used mainly by middle and upper class working mothers.)[13]

4) America is "alone among the industrialized nations" in having no policy towards family. 100 countries offer job security and pay during a woman's maternity leave. 50 countries have laws mandating day-care by government or employers. (What was not said is that many of those nations are also countries with bloated social-welfare budgets, confiscatory tax rates and a contempt for entrepreneurial energy. Parental leave is fine and I'm happy more and more companies are providing it, but it must be *voluntary*.)

5) One of every four households is headed by a single mother and 80 percent of all single mothers were once married. Alimony payments are shrinking, thanks to women's lib. Less than 15 percent of women receive alimony and the average payment is $4,000 a year.

6) We are longing for a no longer existent America. (We can make America into whatever kind of nation we want it to be.) We're a nation at risk — it's time to face reality. (Does this empty phrase say *anything* to you?) Nostalgia isn't reality. (Excuse me?) Society doesn't recognize reality; if it did it would establish child-care centers. (Ah, at last some light is shed. The speaker *defines* reality.) President Reagan doesn't want to see government get into the day-care business. Women don't want to give up having children and the Reagan administration is simply telling women "You're on your own!" (I would say" bravo", but

don't you get the feeling the speaker wants us to feel this last item in the litany is simply atrocious?)

Popular talk-show host Phil Donahue aired the child-care issue in two shows, one before and one after the ABC special.

Kate Rand Lloyd from *Working Woman* magazine was a member of the March 24, 1986 panel, along with Mary Rose Oakar, Congresswoman from Cleveland, Ohio and economist Sylvia Hewitt, author of *A Lesser Life*. Ms. Rand claimed 70 percent of all women worked out of necessity. Necessity means something different depending on whether one is talking about the need to provide items necessary to sustain life, raise one's standard of living or seek fulfillment.[14]

One middle-aged male, participating from the audience, was soundly booed when he suggested the solution was to allow men the opportunity to make a decent living so women could stay at home. He claimed to be arguing for women's *choice* to stay at home which was clearly an unconscionable position as far as most of the Donahue audience was concerned.

Despite the many arguments put forth by the clearly biased panel, several members of the audience seemed to think child-care should not be the employer's responsibility. Others felt that even if large corporations were required to provide day-care centers, that would alleviate the problem for only a small percentage of the families needing help as 80 percent of working women are employed by small companies. (Unhappily expedience, not principle, was the issue.)

On December 18, 1986, Ms. Oakar and Ms. Hewitt again told Donahue audiences across the country that it's terrible that women are required to choose between having children or a career, whereas men get both. A ridiculous statement which, sad to say, has been known to influence and mold opinions.

THE WOULD-BE ELITE ARE AT IT AGAIN

What bothers me most about HR4300, the Parental Leave bill, is

173

that a small group of people apparently consider the rest of us stupid. If providing benefits such as those proposed in HR4300 did indeed make a company more productive, don't the esteemed "know-it-alls" think business people are smart enough to consider providing such perks on their own initiative? A survey by the Bureau of National Affairs, Inc. found that 90 percent of companies grant maternity leave without the coercion of HR4300 and 40 percent already extend the leave to new fathers. Freedom, not coercion, is the essence of capitalism. Freedom to compete and/ or practice altruism..

On April 1, 1986 popular radio talk-show host Owen Spann, interviewed author Sylvia Hewitt. I was fascinated by many of the claims that were made. Ms. Hewitt argued that if the government provided more help there would be less stress in American homes. She claimed that 40 percent of today's 25 year old women would become single mothers. She then said "Today's freedom is the right to become a single mother." It occurred to me that maybe that is just one more "right" that taxpayers will refuse to support. Mr. Spann suggested that perhaps more emphasis should be placed on people trying to get their marriages to work and helping one another in the home, not pulling each other apart. I know you're tired of hearing that to make something easy and attractive assures that there will be more of it. You hear but do you believe? It works the same way whether the issue is divorce, illegitimate children, lack of adequate child-care, homelessness, or unemployment.

Although I was disenchanted with Mr. Spann's guest I was delighted with a 23 year old lady who called in to tell Ms. Hewitt that the so-called crisis had already been solved and that women simply have to exercise their freedom of choice. The non-celebrity caller advised other women to do what she had successfully done; find a company that offers what you want. The caller was a "trader" — she even used the phrase "they need us and we need them". The caller and I both agree that there is no need for Ms. Hewitt's allegedly "constructive policies".

174

WOMEN'S NEW ROLE

Many times minority groups have only been able to overcome major problems through collective action. Advisory groups such as the American Women's Economic Development Corporation (AWED) have sprung up to counsel female executives on how to solve gender-based problems. It's through a joint effort — networking — that female-owned firms have grown three times as fast as male-owned firms. In 1976 there were 700,000 firms owned by females and that number had soared to over 3 million by the end of 1986.

On January 13, 1987 the United States Supreme Court ruled that states may require employers to provide up to four months disability leave for pregnant workers. Justice Thurgood Marshall demonstrated extraordinary agility in his long stretch to find that equality in the workplace could be served by allowing women, what he argued men already had, i.e. their jobs. From the wording of that decision one would hardly have guessed that among the Fortune 500 companies, 81 percent already offered job-protected pregnancy leaves. [15]

"Let freedom ring!" I know I heard that somwhere before and it makes sense. If there's a truly good idea out there it doesn't have to be stuffed down the throats of citizens as if they were idiots. Such "stuffing" is an example of arrogant leadership. Many of the country's most successful businesses consider maternity leave as an important way to retain valuable employees and build morale. It should be considered a good business practice but not an *obligation* of the employer and certainly not mandated by government.

The National Organization for Women (NOW) was quick to realize that restricting employers in their dealing with female employees could, in the long run, increase female unemployment. Did NOW temper its demands? Does rain fall *up* ? NOW's solution was to demand a guaranteed job for *all* who leave the work place no matter what the disabiltiy. (Somewhere along the line pregnancy was transformed from a "blessing" into a "dis-

175

abililty".)

Ellen Goodman, in her column written shortly after the January 1987 Supreme Court ruling, took roughly the same position as NOW. "We need to mute any disadvantage that employers find in firing women" she said, and then expressed the opinion that disability programs covering *all* workers might be the ticket to avoid discrimination. With jobs virtually secured via the Court's ruling on maternity leave, Ms. Goodman felt it was time to press on. "We have finally begun to raise the ceiling. Now its time to raise the roof." I'd just like to caution Ms. Goodman et al, that a house without a roof isn't much good in a storm — or in global competition. Even unpaid leave is costly for employers in terms of productivity losses, retraining, overtime costs, unemployment and health insurance.

HR4300, the Family and Medical Leave Act, co-sponsored by Congresswoman Pat Schroeder of Colorado is known more familiarly as the Parental Leave Act. As orginally written it required employers of 15 or more to provide new mothers and fathers with up to 18 weeks of leave with their position, salary and health benefits in tact. A person would have to be well off financially to take that much time off work. Could it be that there are plans afoot to require the leave be "paid leave" at a later date? Normal Congressional procedure is to first enact legislation and then tack on the little details which are so outrageous as to have prevented passage if mentioned earlier.

The Newspaper Guild is outrageous right up front! It wants up to four months of *paid* maternity and paternity leave, with additional unpaid time written into its contracts with 210 newspapers, wire services and magazines around the country.

Whether children are affected adversely when raised by two working parents is, as yet, unclear, but there is considerable evidence that parenting by proxy is harmful in the case of infants.[16] To alleviate any potential ill effects, Edward Zigler of the Bush Center in Child Development and Social Policy at Yale and Thomas Gamble of the Edmund L. Thomas Children's Center in Erie, Pennsylvania recommend a few months of *paid* leave for *both* parents of infants. Supposedly the *paid* part of the leave

176

would make the parents, rather than the child happy. I suppose, however, it would be simple enough to say that happy parents make a happy child.

Making it pleasant for our children to learn what they want, when they want, has put America into 48th place in education world wide. A simple extension of this pampering philosophy to the workplace; i.e. "an employee who feels good about_____(fill in the blank & leave a lot of room) makes a better worker", should do wonders for American productivity.

IT COULD BE MERE RIGHT-WING CONSERVATIVE RHETORIC

What do you mean you doubt the ability of our companies to compete in the global market if they are *forced* to allow men and women time off to care for their children? After all, not everyone has children you know. — Oh, I see what you mean; but you're forgetting about discrimination. You know how it works: We need (ought) to give to X but then Y will have a grievance (unequal teatment) so we'll solve that by giving to both X and Y. The *cost*? Never mind the cost! People are more important than money — I mean, you can't put a value on human dignity (that one is *always* good).

In arguing pro HR4300 Ms. Schroeder points to the increase in the number of working mothers of young children over the past 15 years without giving credit to the hiring practices and voluntary benefit packages that have made that increase possible. Oh well, you can't expect to pass a bill by being fair, so I guess someone else will have to point out the survey by the National Chamber Foundation which found that out of a thousand companies more than three quarters had *voluntarily* instituted parental leave policies tailored to their employees' individual situations and the other companies provided their employees with alternate benefits at their request. Pat Schroeder told you about the survey? Nooo? It's tough when you have your heart set on being the "good guy" and you're robbed of your glory.

The Bureau of Labor Statistics figures there will be about 15 million new workers in the next decade and more than half will be women. Nevertheless, as the baby boomers begin to retire in the following decade, there will be a shortage of workers and only those companies with the most attractive policies will be able to compete successfully for the best employees. That's the free market at work — not unions and feminist groups picketing and making strident demands.

THE EMPLOYERS' EXPANDED BURDEN

Employers' resources are being diverted into areas not geared to producing a salable product. Today an employer must pay others to defend him from law suits, to insure him against loss and liability, to keep the government happy by filling out myriads of forms which benefit employees and make it easier for the IRS to fleece him, and to lobby in Washington to keep a watch on the "Clowns on the Hill" and make sure they don't change the working environment and economy beyond what is survivable. And of course we expect American business to retain its #1 position as a global competitor.

In 1986 half the lawsuits brought by labor lawyers involved employees suing employers for wrongful dismissal. In 1979 California courts expanded a legal doctrine which says that employment constitutes an implied contract and that employers must actively try to help workers who are having trouble rather than just firing them.

By dismissing an employee an employer may find himself involved in costly court action. If the employee's performance was unsatisfactory any report about poor performance to others (prospective new employers for instance) could be grounds for a defamation suit. No wonder many companies are simply refusing to divulge any information regarding former employees other than the dates worked. Without each others help, employers are finding they are having to spend more time and money screening prospective employees for incompetency and dishonesty. If an employee has to tell a new employer why he left his former job this is called "compelled self-publication" and is a cause for a defamation action unless the former employer can produce fully documented and unambiguous reasons for the firing.

There is in effect no such thing as "at-will employment" anymore. A recent California case found that "the unilateral involuntary termination of an employee is inherently unfair" and that the employer has a fiduciary duty to "return the terminated employee to the market place 'whole' ... with severance which is adequate to provide him with a reasonable chance of finding comparable employment without loss of income".[17] More and more lawyers are advising firms to provide for termination pay in hiring contracts. Before the employee ever begins working an agreement should be reached by both employer and employee that, in exchange for a specified compensation, the employer will be able to terminate without cause. Attorney Charles T.C. Compton, writing for the May 1987 issue of *California Lawyer,* refers to the provision as "no-fault" employment termination — a form of self-insurance for employers. Without such an agreement judges and juries have to deliberate over the subjective issues of "good faith and fair dealing", "implied promises" and "good cause" which have been interpreted quite broadly in the past. Mr. Compton advises employers to "look upon termination pay as the deductible they pay for insurance protection against wrongful discharge litigation".[18]

The ol' "or else" philosophy in yet another guise. In this case "pay me *or else* I'll take your time and money in a wrongful discharge suit".

In 1986 seventy of California's largest employers proposed a plan which would pressure both employers and employees to accept arbitration rather than turn to the courts. If companies refused they would become liable for the employee's legal costs: if employees refused they would give up the right to win back pay beyond the date of their refusal to arbitrate. Quite naturally the plan was opposed by both organized labor and trial lawyers.

SO WHY DOES AMERICA FIND IT HARD TO COMPETE

WITH THE REST OF THE WORLD?

AIDS is deemed a handicap under federal anti-discrimination law, meaning a worker cannot be legally dismissed or not hired merely because he/she has AIDS. The employer is faced with potential law suits from all sides.

Supposing an employer doesn't tell other workers when he discovers a certain employee has contracted AIDS. Those co-workers could sue for emotional distress. In one company in Colorado all workers walked off the job to protest working with an AIDs victim. The company was set back for a good period of time. If, however, the employer chooses to inform employees of a co-workers condition, the co-worker with AIDS could sue for invasion of privacy or breach of confidentiality.[19]

SO WHY DOES AMERICA FIND IT HARD TO COMPETE WITH THE REST OF THE WORLD?

The National Council on Compensation Insurance reports that stress related claims rose from five percent of all occupational disease claims in 1978 to fourteen percent in 1986. In 1985 California alone had over 4,000 mental-stress claims. Part of the reason is that young workers are both aware and unashamed of psychological problems and blaming them on forces outside their control has become not only acceptable, but lucrative. Employees have been known to win awards due to stress caused by job expansion, to lay offs, for distress at being reprimanded and for depression caused by working with members of another race. Under subjective tests almost any act of an employer can cause trauma to the employee. The safest way to avoid being sued is abstinence — abstain from hiring employees whenever possible.

Since California has led the nation in stress claims it is only fitting it should lead the way in reform, which it did in 1986 by passing an initiative to limit lawyer contingency fees and awards for non-economic damages such as pain and suffering.

But California isn't alone. Also in 1986 Connecticut signed legislation limiting contingency fees for attorneys. Colorado, Utah and Wyoming have done away with joint and several liability completely and New Hampshire has recently limited non-economic awards. The state of Washington passed a law in April 1986, which restricted the deep-pocket doctrine which had so often resulted in a wealthy defendant (generally a corporation or local government) in a personal injury suit paying all the damages even if another party was mostly to blame. The Washington law also capped awards for non-economic damages and disallowed payments on cases in which the plaintiff's intoxication was the primary cause of the accident.

THE GREAT 'WHOSE FAULT?' DEBATE
BETWEEN INSURERS AND LAWYERS

In 1986 the United States Chamber of Commerce reported that almost half its membership saw their liability premiums climb anywhere from 100 percent to 500 percent in one year. Under these circumstances it is only natural to look to self-insurance but first Congress has to remove some barriers. For instance the tax code has permitted deductions for premiums paid to bona fide insurance companies but not to self-insurance companies. The 1981 Risk Retention Act permits firms to join together to establish what amounts to a captive insurance company that offers owner-members product liability insurance at favorable rates. In February of 1986 Senators Danforth of Missouri and Kasten of Wisconsin introduced a bill to expand the 1981 Act to include general liability.

Towns, taxis, grocers, toy manufacturers, day-care centers, taverns, architects — even the Boy Scouts of America have seen their insurance premiums rise to such heights over the past few years that many have even resorted to doing without insurance — an extremely risky situation in our litigious society.

Businesses should be able to hire the disabled and others who want to work but can't easily leave home. Only one large U.S. company, Pacific Telesis Group's Pacific Bell Unit, has a formal program which permits salaried employees to telecommute full time although all the technology is in place to allow it. Many employers are too worried about the liability issue; who is at fault if an employee trips using a room as an office at home?

Critics of the insurance industry maintain that the legal system is not the problem but that the industry's "panic pricing" is an attempt to compensate for the industry's failure to read the financial markets properly. When interest rates were high the industry lowered premiums in an effort to attract new customers and obtain money to invest at the high rates. When interest rates fell the industry panicked.

Florida is one state that followed that line of thinking, and has responded to the insurance crisis by *mandating* a forty percent rollback of premium charges to 1984 rates. (Can they do that? Yeah, *they* can do that!)

Many states, and the public in general, tend to find more credence in the insurance industry's explanation of the problem as a litigation crisis.

Between 1976 and 1985 the property and casualty insurance industry lost some $81.3 billion on underwriting losses (made lots more on investments, but that's another story). The economics of the insurance industry forced it to keep underwriting losses in line with premiums.

Since auto accidents were once responsible for half to two thirds of all tort filings, the effect of enacting no-fault insurance in twenty-one states, mandatory seat-belt laws in twenty-three states and a 55 mph speed limit nationwide, was to put some lawyers out of business and make others more creative. The creative ones quickly turned their attention to even more lucrative cases such as medical malpractice and product liability.

Medical malpractice claims rose sharply from 385 in 1978 to 1,779 in 1985; a 362 percent increase. Those attorneys were busy; suits tripled for obstetricians and gynecologists. About 75 percent of those specialists have been sued at least once during their careers. 80 percent of such cases end in dismissal or in a no liability judgement against the doctor. Nevertheless the time and effort in preparing for trial is taken from medicine which means less medical resources for society.

In the spirit of fairness let me add that if medical malpractice awards over $1 million were not included, then the increase in average awards between 1975-85 would be 26 percent not 362 percent! Also it's only fair to point out that in our current system lawyers are the main winners; insurance companies, via high premiums charged to clients, pay more to lawyers than to the injured plaintiffs.

The fact is consumers hardly ever purchase pain and suffering insurance, yet by granting huge pain and suffering awards the courts make consumers purchase what they have shown they really don't want.

In 1986 only two percent of commercial insurers still offered medical malpractice insurance. Without insurance many medical services will simply be discontinued as too risky to perform. The few insurers still in the market have upped their premiums so that across the country the average non-specialist now pays over $10,000 per year for his medical malpractice insurance. In 1985 the average obstetrician's premium was over $51,000 in New York and in Los Angeles, anywhere from $36,000 to $61,000.

> Allowing courts to find liabililty and grant awards where no real fault by the doctor exists, amounts to a court-operated welfare system, where benefits are distributed on the basis of perceived need, and the costs of such benefits are borne by patients through higher fees for medical care.[20]

So said Peter Ferrara, a Washington D.C. attorney and author who has a plan to discourage frivolous lawsuits and the tendency for plaintiffs' attorneys to try to run up the defendant's expenses in the hope of exacting a favorable settlement. His plan is neither original nor complicated; it is simple and workable. With those two strikes against it, how does Mr. Ferrara ever expect courts to adopt the idea that winning parties should recover attorney's fees and other litigation expenses from the losing party? In 1986 the Indiana State Legislature did just that by enacting a law that allows judges to force frivolous or compulsive litigators to pay opponents' legal costs.

Another idea advocated by Mr. Ferrara is to have damages paid in annual payments rather than lump sums. This would allow for the discontinuation of payments if the plaintiff either recovers or dies. Damages in tort law are, after all, compensatory and not meant to punish. Damages should only compensate loss of income and related expenses as they occur, on a yearly basis.

The products liability attorneys weren't letting any grass grow under their feet either. Product liability actions from 1974 to 1985 increased from 1,579 to 13,554; a 758 percent rise! The Insurance Information Institute points out that since 1984 the average award in product liability cases exceeded $1 million annually. (Haven't we heard that one before?) OK — that sounds a little unbelievable and you're right, the name of the Institute suggests possible bias. In fairness again, they point out that the mean average gives inordinate weight to a few huge cases and that the median award for 1984 was $271,000, not $1 million. Moreover, they would agree that many of those verdicts are never actually paid but are cut dramatically, either on appeal or through subsequent out-of-court settlements.

But let's step back from the statistics — anybody's statistics — and you analyze your own experience. Almost every business person will attest to the fact that he is spending more and more dollars on premiums and time on litigation problems. Many of our judges have been trained over the years to spread the risk to those most able to bear it. The Reagan administration is backing a tough measure which would set up a nationwide standard of liability, cap damage awards and limit lawyers' contingency fees altogether. However such reform faces obstacles with Senator Joseph Biden of Delaware as new chairman of the Senate Judiciary Committee and, as mentioned earlier, Senator Ernest Hollings of South Carolina at the helm of the Commerce Committee. Senator Hollings has expressed his preference to regulate the insurance industry rather than limit awards and he may get his druthers.

The country is ready for reform. The following are frequently heard proposals:

(1)   Get rid of joint and several liability and find parties liable only if they truly caused the harm.

184

(2)   Encourage litigants to settle out of court.

(3)   Modify contingency fees.

(4)   Penalize parties who bring frivolous suits.

(5)   Scrap the so-called American Rule which prevents the prevailing party from recovering litigation costs.

(6)   Define the limits of product liability.

(7)   Forbid punitive damages such as treble damages except in cases of gross negligence. Leave punishment to criminal law courts.

(8)   Structure settlements that disburse payments over time so that only the actual costs incurred are compensated.

When business hurts, GNP drops, tax revenue falls and our competitive edge is dulled. And the deficit? Don't ask!

For years (ante-Melvin Belli) liability in this country was tied to fault with the not unreasonable thought that individual Americans should assume some of the responsibility for the risks of simply being alive. Justice cannot be achieved by compensating all people for all injuries whether anyone is at fault or not.

It might be well to remember that Japan is a nation with few lawyers and little litigation. The countless wasted hours spent by our business executives preparing for mountains of litigation can never be regained. The drain on our productivity and ability to compete with comparatively litigation-free countries is enormous!

A member of Congress recently joked about sending 100,000 attorneys to Japan to help us compete. So much of what comes out of Congress is a joke there may be a chance they're on to something. (As an active member of two Bar Associations, I naturally jest. Besides, don't they speak Japanese over there?)

185

OLDER WORKERS

Speaking of Japan, large companies in Japan traditionally retire workers at age 55, yet the labor force participation rate of people over 55 has been higher than in the USA because many workers let go by one company are hired by others.

In America at the beginning of this century about sixty percent of elderly men were privately employed. As they were able to retire earlier, thanks to a general increase in the American standard of living, the rate at which men over age 65 participate in the labor market rapidly declined. The participation rate of men aged 55 through 64 dropped from eighty-seven percent in 1960 to less than seventy percent today, and for those over 65 the participation rate is now under twenty percent. In 1986, according to the Bureau of Labor Statistics, of the 27.6 million Americans over age 65, both men and women, 10.5 percent held jobs (about 2.9 million) as did 6.4 percent of those over age 70 (1.2 million).

Legislation adopted in the early sixties lowered the age of eligibility for Social Security benefits for males from 65 to 62 which explains the plunge in employment at these ages. To further discourage the employment of older persons, Social Security benefits are reduced when retirees earn more than minimal income. If that were not enough, employers are less likely to prefer older workers due to a recent law which requires companies to maintain health insurance coverage for former employees for up to eighteen months. This law raises the premiums of employers of older workers as insurance companies may very well become obligated for heavy medical expenses.

Legislators are sending mixed messages. With the passage of legislation outlawing mandatory retirement, the Labor Department estimates an additional 200,000 people over age 65 will be part of the workforce in the year 2000. We are familiar with the record of government's estimates. The new federal law removes the cap on retirement but it also requires the continuation of pension accruals for workers over age 65 which will be costly for business. Removing the age for mandatory retirement was an amendment to the Age Discrimination in Employment Act, but the unfortunate provision for pension accruals was part of the Omnibus Budget Reconciliation Act. Many employers wishing to hire older workers and older workers wanting to work have been known to turn to the underground economy which makes it hard to accurately determine the number of elderly persons in the present day workforce.

Do you see anything wrong when disincentives for older people to work are coupled with legislation designed to *increase* employment for the elderly?

WELL INTENTIONED PENSION PLANS
HAVE UNINTENDED CONSEQUENCES

The Department of Labor (DOL) is supposed to oversee the financial affairs of some 770,000 pension plans and two million welfare-benefit plans. No easy job when you consider nearly $170 billion in employer contributions now flow into pension, health and other benefit funds every year. Sometimes the employer contributes so much per head and service is delivered by a clinic or other designated health provider. Often the trustees hire an outside administrator who subcontracts the services leaving an enormous opportunity for kickbacks, overcharges, rigged bids and skimming off the top all the way down the line.

The abuses are unfortunately not confined to health plans. Under the Employee Retirement Income Securities Act of 1974 (ERISA) there is no doubt about the obligation of the trustees to obtain the greatest possible return for beneficiaries of the nation's pension funds. Pension funds control almost $2 trillion in assets and own a third of the equity of all publicly traded companies. Stock ownership has become more concentrated than ever before, proving the Kelso's point (see Chapter Two). Control has shifted to the pension-fund manager whose job depends on showing immediate gains, with his own performance often judged quarterly, a situation definitely not conducive to long-range planning.

Senator William Cohen of Maine, and others, have argued that a short-term orientation puts pension managers in direct conflict with the good of the plans' ultimate beneficiaries; i.e. future retirees.

This American emphasis on short-term rather than long-term is surely one reason foreign competitors are doing so well. Anything that doesn't promise immediate gain must be abandoned under a short-term system.

SOCIAL INVESTING — PROS AND CON

In 1974, with the passage of ERISA, private pension fund managers were prohibited from using those funds for nonfinancial objectives. ERISA was silent on public pension funds so the California Legislature was able to pass a Divestment Bill mandating that its approximately $67 billion worth of pension assets (combination of the Teachers, Public Employees and University of California retirement systems) be pulled out of companies doing business in South Africa. This meant about $11 billion had to be reinvested.

Some folks don't want to invest in a company that has anything whatsoever to do with weapons, or is involved in any way with abortion or nuclear power. Evidence has shown that there are so many stocks to choose from that restrictions really do not hinder a manager's choice enough to make any difference in the ultimate profitability of individual portfolios. In fact many of the private management firms offering portfolios based on social objectives can present evidence that their funds have held their own or surpassed the profitability of unrestricted investment funds.[21]

In April 1987, at the Social Investment Forum (to promote social responsibility) it was reported that groups that promote social responsibilty saw their share of investment dollars jump from $40 billion in 1984 to $300 billion in 1986.

Proponents of social investments argue that they are not likely to be hit by liability suits. Social investments do well against other mutual funds because most firms are already "good guys" so there's not much to screen out. There is even a Council On Economic Priorities which has issued a guide called "Rating America's Corporate Conscience" for investors who choose to vote with their wallets or pocketbooks. One hundred thirty American corporations are highlighted in a manner which allows a reader to see their record regarding such things as the environment, weapons, charitable contributions, hiring practices and how they treat their employees; all in an effort to determine whether the company's stock is something one would really want in one's portfolio.

I find it hard to understand Michael Kinsley's criticism that

> The proper social role of the corporation is to produce the best peanut butter at the lowest price, leaving to individuals and to the political system such matters as support for the arts and how much we spend on defense.[22]

He apparently forgets that profit is the bottom line and if customers want to choose their peanut butter according to how many days of maternity leave a company offers its employees rather than how many peanuts in a spoonful of its product then the corporation jolly well better stop counting peanuts and start counting days. Business becomes profitable by pleasing consumers and that is what flexibility, competition and voting with our pocketbooks is all about. It's precisely because I believe companies will do what's in their best interest, without government coercion, that I favor the consumer's use of social criteria in investing, or in purchasing for that matter.

If a citizen wants to encourage the hiring of minorities then he should shop at stores that hire minority workers; if he cares about the safety of an item he should purchase from a company with an established safety record. Those that think the government ("leave it to the political system") should regulate (i.e. force) such things, suspect that if left to their own devices most people simply won't care.

If people *don't* care, then should a handful of men *pretend*

189

people do care? The fact is if a select group makes the decision that the masses (don't you love being part of a "mass"?) *ought* to care, then that's it.

Despite all political rhetoric to the contrary, our policymakers don't give two hoots what you and I really want once they have made up their own minds.

STIFLING THE GOOSE
THAT LAYS THE GOLDEN EGGS

The changes in the home and the workplace which have occurred over the past fifty years have been for better and for worse — mostly for better. Those changes that have been especially detrimental to the goal of reducing the federal deficit are the ones we want to focus on for the purpose of our discussion so that we might repair their damage.

As we have seen, a large number of citizens are already involved in work which produces no tangible product. A business that used to hire only workers to manufacture a product, now hires people to provide a nice environment for the workers, health care for the workers, to help the workers with motivation, to break bad habits, to exercise and to care for their children — all things that a worker used to do for himself on his own time and with his own resources.

I cannot over-emphasize the importance of becoming aware of and weighing the consequences of relegating one's problems to others for solutions. It is my hope that once people think about it they will be unwilling to exchange freedom and the ability to compete with other nations in the future, for limited security today.

Employers have known for years that the employee's after-work life-style is relevant to his on-the-job performance. With that in mind, the following may not be as far-fetched as it may at first sound:

Since employers have to pay health costs and other expenses

for employees besides their wages, shouldn't they be allowed to control the off-work hours of their employees? After all, unhealthy life styles will make an employee less productive on the job and may make him require more health care (at the employer's expense, remember). Perhaps employers should look carefully at the type of automobile employees drive since some cars are involved in more accidents. The baseball teams an employee chooses to root for may be an important factor affecting an employee's work because supporters of some teams tend to be more depressed and less productive on the job. Whether or not an employee has children may affect his work habits. If he engages in community projects he probably should not be encouraged to serve as chairman or in other prominent positions that take time and energy and keep him up late nights because that will be drawing energy needed on the job. The debt accumulation of employees might need monitoring by employers because controlling bad spending habits may afford the employee a certain peace of mind that will make him more productive in the workplace. If he is too obese, an employer may put him on a diet for the same reason and also in order to cut future health costs to the firm.

Are today's Americans capable of providing for themselves what government and employers are now providing? Could they handle a payroll check without Big Brother's costly withholdings and be able to pay their taxes at the end of the year? More to the point, do they want to do so?

The American worker, while demanding ever more from his employer and his government, may have forgotten there is no free lunch. Many, too frightened and unprepared to fend for themselves, are unaware that security demands a price. Restrictions, regulations and higher taxes are the price of government's protection and benefits. A less vigorous and healthy economy may well be the price of protection and benefits from employers.

Wisdom that is often repeated is called trite, (like "there's no free lunch") but the phrase was repeated so often because people saw the truth in it. It may be time to put the following trite phrase on our coins, our stamps and our doorposts to help us remember: "If we overburden business, we destroy the goose that lays the golden eggs."

THE SEVENTH STEP

(RE: TRADE)

ACTUALLY PRACTICE
FREE TRADE OURSELVES
AND THEN DEMAND
RECIPROCITY

THE 7th STEP

(RE: TRADE)

THE POPULAR POINT OF VIEW

We need a strong trade policy. We are the only nation that practices free trade and we should demand reciprocity. Our goods can compete if they are allowed into other countries. We could compete even more successfully if we emulated Japanese labor practices. The Japanese are buying up America. Foreigners are taking American jobs.

ANOTHER POINT OF VIEW

Americans can trade successfully if participants are allowed flexibility. We must stay away from central planning. We are not free traders ourselves. The Japanese have had their own labor-management difficulties. Both the Dutch and the British have larger holdings in this country than do the Japanese. Foreigners provide more jobs than they take.

SO WHAT'S THE BIG DEAL?
THE TRADE DEFICIT
WILL TAKE CARE OF ITSELF!

So often government interfers where it has no need. Take the trade deficit. We owe "them" more than "they" owe us. We used to lend and invest dollars abroad because of the good returns. Now other countries, often thanks to our previous investment and loans, are able to sell goods to us which gives them money to invest here. As they purchase U.S. securities we become obligated to pay them. The truth is we would have no trade deficit except that foreigners have confidence in the U.S. and therefore freely choose to invest here. How in the world can this indication of our nation's strength be mistaken for a sign of our weakness? Haven't we had enough of misleading, manipulative rhetoric? Borrowers and lenders, thoughtful men and women with their own money at risk, are almost certainly better informed and in a better position than the government to determine when to slow down or put a halt to the lending and borrowing.

A competitive economy does not mean simply a trade surplus. That would mean Brazil is better off than the USA. By that standard Japan would be too, yet we have created 15 million new jobs in this country since 1983 and Japan's record has been sluggish. (I bet you haven't heard "sluggish" and "Japan" in the same sentence lately!)

What would you say if I told you the United States will always be the number one place to invest on the face of the earth? Chances are you'd have no trouble believing me and might even use that information to argue that we need not fear a pull out of foreign money and can simply go on living beyond our means indefinitely because the rest of the world has enough faith in our economy and "Yankee-know-how" to let us do it.

I'm sorry to have to burst your bubble.

Business Environment Risk Information Ltd. (BERI) has rated twenty nations according to investment risk. They consider political stability, business climate, rate of economic growth, inflation, crime, labor, living costs and so forth. Switzerland was rated number one — the best place to invest (O.K., not too big a blow to America's ego) with Japan second, West Germany third, Singapore fourth (now wait a #!*&!# minute!) and Holland fifth. The United States came in sixth. SIXTH!! So, you may well ask, what about all the foreign investment dollars flooding into this country? Do they realize they might do better in five other countries?

The BERI ratings are based on investment outlooks through 1991 and may be forebodings of the future when foreign investors decide to park their money in what BERI considers to be more hospitable and less risky climates. BERI claims our sixth place showing is due to protectionist sentiments among our Congress, high labor costs, low productivity and the low dollar which we have worked so hard to achieve. And then again, BERI could be dead wrong. It happens!

Listen to the following explanation of the trade deficit by Professor Ronald McKinnon of Stanford (and I'm sure you have heard what appears to be the identical explanation from countless other people):

> The fiscal deficit creates a shortage of savings in the economy, and then we try to borrow from foreigners to cover that short-fall, and that creates the trade deficit.[1]

Perhaps the good professor has the cart before the horse — which is cause and which is effect is at least debatable.

The trade deficit is the mirror image of our net capital imports or capital surplus. Capital surpluses make people smile until they realize those surpluses are part and parcel of the trade deficit and that they are borrowed. Labels create a bias. Don't you react differently when you hear "debt to foreigners" rather than "capital imports"?

The choice of words and the way they are arranged, the frequency with which they are used, all create an image often having little connection with the truth. In a recent article in a popular magazine the trade deficit was referred to variously as "horrendous", "depressing" and "dismal". The term "competitiveness" conjures up the image of a race. Politicians, always quick to take advantage of fanciful imagery, have found that the term "competitiveness" allows them to appeal to national pride, all the while depicting themselves as heros with the proposals that will put America out front once again. But *is* America noncompetitive and weak and in need of their administrations?

Total output in this country and per-capita output are both higher now than when we enjoyed a trade surplus back in 1982. The trouble is politicians can't take credit for fixing what isn't broken! It's time to call the bluff of politicians and other officials who persist in this deception. They are either ignoramuses or charlatans.

ZERO-SUM IS NONSENSE! YOU *KNOW* IT!

Americans are used to a world of plenty. The "richest country in the world" rhetoric has left its mark. We do not like to take a backseat to any nation and are reluctant to accept the idea that in order for other nations to lift their standard of living Americans must lower theirs. Perhaps this reluctance is similar to the aversion one feels when smoking that first cigarette. The body tries to warn that smoking is not healthy. In this case the brain warns that zero-sum is false. Limits are only in the minds of small men. We share a world with limitless potential. To dwell on limited space, limited resources and most particularly, limited investment capital is to short-change human creativity. The pedestrian zero-sum philosophy makes the rounds several times in every century.

In the early 1970s the Club of Rome came out with their "Limits to Growth" forecast. Their premise stated that because there was only so much of this and that, that our worldwide resources would be used up. They failed to consider the capacity to adapt that has allowed humans to progress. We developed lighter materials and smaller cars requiring less fuel in response to the "oil crisis". There is no doubt we could develop substitutes for just about anything in short supply in the future.

This does not mean that "the sky's the limit" philosophy sanctions waste. The challenge facing all of us, individuals and nations alike, is how to maximize both human and financial resources so *all* can rise to new heights. Demanding sacrifice from a minority for the good of a majority is an old pagan custom. The acknowledgement that every individual is important and inviolate is not uniquely Christian, as some would claim, but it *is* uniquely American. Many religions recognize the sanctity of the individual but no other government protects the rights of the few in the face of the needs of many. America demands no sacrifices. John F. Kennedy's stirring and often quoted "Ask not what your Country can do for you, but what you can do for your Country" is emotionally appealing but morally and intellectually bankrupt.

In *The Mainspring Of Human Progress,* Henry Grady Weaver talks about the difference between a planned economy where security is offered in exchange for regulation. Freedom is not always easy. Not always knowing where your next meal, pay-check or hospital payment is going to come from naturally breeds insecurity. Insecurity, according to Weaver, is the price of freedom and it has molded the American character in a very unique manner.

> It...has bred a degree of human sympathy that is without parallel in the history of mankind. It is only in America that rank-and-file citizens, over and over again, have made millions of small (voluntary) sacrifices in order to pour wealth over the rest of the world, to relieve suffering in ...faraway places....[2]

Those sacrifices were made, not at the bidding of government, but as a natural outpouring of sympathy by those who have lived with insecurity and can appreciate its peaks and its valleys. Despite rhetoric to the contrary we must remember that we are not in a global fight for the biggest piece of a static pie but rather our mission is to increase the pie so that everyone in the world sees his share growing at no one's expense.

THE PACIFIC RIM COUNTRIES

Can it be done? Lester Korn, Chief Executive Officer at Korn-Ferry International thinks so. He presented some interesting ideas before the Commonwealth Club of San Francisco in a speech October 31, 1987.

According to Mr. Korn, the Pacific Rim will greet the twenty-first century as the most powerful player in the world market. Los Angeles will take at least an equal place with New York as a global center, along with Tokyo and Beijing. Mega-managers will have to create products for worldwide consumption and in order to compete on a global basis, manufacturing will increasingly take place in non-industrial countries. We did such a terrific job spreading the vitality of American capitalism to Europe, the Middle East and Asia that now thirty percent of our manufactured goods are produced overseas. Mr. Korn believes the United States will continue to dominate new technology as long as businessmen continue to reinvest in and develop new areas of endeavor based on the vast store of technology already available. Mr. Korn is, to borrow a phrase, "bullish on America". He assures us the baby boom and the educational institutions of the past forty years have given corporate America the largest best-trained corps of managers in history. (Go ahead, read it again. Someone's *praising* managers!)

But will trained managers be enough? We are constantly hearing about our failure in education, research and development. A recent United Nations report showed that the USA is 48th in a field of 159 in literacy; 48th is pretty hard to take for a nation used to considering itself number one in everything. Books have been written giving the reasons, but aside from drugs and liberal teaching attitudes one possible reason may be that Japanese children spend 240 days a year in school compared to 180 days for Americans.

But not everyone is asleep in this country. The National Science Foundation (NSF) in conjunction with the private sector, is planning 50 new multidisciplinary (chemistry, biology, computers, engineering) centers. The Reagan administration's FY1988 budget doubled the funds for the NSF and already 21 engineering centers are planned. "The economic security of the American people depends on our being able to compete successfully in the global economy." Those were the words Donald Rumsfeld, former Secretary of Defense, former U.S. Ambassador and Representative to NATO, used in addressing another meeting of the Commonwealth Club in San Francisco on March 6, 1987. Mr. Rumsfeld offered the following statistics to support his contention that America must begin to focus on research and development:

> In the 1970s, research and development, as a percentage of GNP increased by 2.3 percent in West Germany, by 1.9 percent in Japan, and by just 1.6 percent in the U.S. In numbers of scientists and engineers, West Germany: plus 59 percent — Japan: plus 62 percent — even the USSR was plus 55 percent. The U.S. had a decrease of 13 percent.

Mr. Rumsfeld agreed with Mr. Korn's earlier assessment and expressed confidence in the ability of a free market to handle the situation. He warned, however, that so-called government assistance might be analogous to bedding down with a hippopotamus; at first it feels warm and cozy and then it rolls over and crushes you. (I prefer the analogy of a Giant Panda)

COMPETITIVENESS

Some people argue that the only way to make the United States competitive is to reduce the budget deficit. So what else is new?

The Congressional Competitiveness Caucus defines competitiveness:

> The ability of a nation to improve its standard of living through current earnings, not borrowing, while investing sufficiently in plant and equipment to ensure sustained growth into the future. [3]

Treasury Secretary James Baker offers the following definition:

> A competitive nation is a nation with a growing economy that is creating jobs and lifting incomes without inflation and that is getting the most from its natural and its human resources. In short, a competitive nation is one that has what economists would call a healthy and vibrant economy. [4]

The first definition is proposed by a segment of a democratically controlled Congress. The second definition is offered by a cabinet member of a Republican administration. The first definition defines competitiveness emphasizing what is lacking in our situation today. The definition implies that since we are borrowing and are not investing sufficiently in plant and equipment, we are not competitive. The second definition emphasizes job creation, controlled inflation and a healthy economy, all hallmarks of the present Republican administration and therefore implies we are competitive. (What can I say?)

In February 1987, the Reagan administration presented Congress with a 1,000 page competitiveness proposal designed to ease antitrust and product-liability laws, raise standards in education, toughen U.S. trade laws, protect patents and copyrights, improve job training and assistance, help disadvantaged youth and overhaul the unemployment-insurance and private pension systems. It proposed also to pursue international economic and monetary cooperation.

People and capital have become global rather than national assets and will be attracted to countries and localities within those countries that offer the highest returns.

A country, like any individual, will ultimately do what it believes to be in its best interest, no matter the barriers it must circumvent in order to accomplish this feat. Meetings of world leaders can only hope to educate — to encourage international cooperation through enlightened self-interest. Countries might lower trade barriers and stimulate their economies if they could see that such policies would lead to greater benefits than the short term benefits achieved by protective tariffs and large trade surpluses.

202

HEARING ON ECONOMIC COMPETITIVENESS

Senator David Pryor of Oklahoma questioned Secretary of the Treasury, James Baker who appeared before the Senate Government Affairs Committee hearing on "Economic Competitiveness" on March 25, 1987. The Senator read to Mr. Baker from the transcript of a House Government Operations Committee which had taken place on July 24, 1986, 8 months earlier. James Miller III, Director of the Office of Management and Budget had testified on that date:

Mr. Miller: "As a general principle it is the position of this administration that supply and demand should determine which products are produced by whom. If there is an opportunity for U.S. consumers to purchase from abroad products more cheaply produced than could be produced at home, they should have a right to do that. We do have compassion and the concern for the transitional effects with respect to the oil industry, with respect to farming and other industries that are adversely impacted by events."

Mr. English: "What a minute. I want to make certain I am perfectly clear, because I want to quote you correctly..."

Mr. Miller: "We do have concern over transitional effects but basically ours is not only a free society in terms of individual freedom, freedom of expression, but it is free also in terms of what actions consumers can take and what opportunities they have and if they can purchase something more cheaply abroad they have a right to do so."

Mr. Miller's response to Congressman English was a source of apparent amazement and almost disbelief, to Senator Pryor. He incredulously asked Secretary Baker:

Senator Pryor: "Is that the policy of this administration as expressed by James Miller?"

James Baker: "Senator Pryor, I would have to say I think this adminis-
                    tration is as committed to the principles of free enter-
                    prise and the free market as any administration to date in
                    the history of this country."

James Baker, to his great credit, went on to defend Mr. Miller's comments made eight months earlier.

At the same meeting Senator James Sasser requested that Secretary of Commerce Malcolm Baldridge take a message to American businessmen telling them that they are failing. Tennessee has the largest concentration of Japanese investment in this country with 36 plants employing 8,000 workers and involving $1.2 billion. Apparently Toshiba's purchase of a Tennessee factory from an American manufacturer impressed Senator Sasser to no end. He told the committee that the Japanese had maintained as good quality with Tennessee workers as they did in Japan, which seemed to constitute proof positive that the fault in American production lie with management and not workers. (A debate between Senator Sasser and Lester Korn on this subject might be interesting.)

Senator Sasser is joined in this belief by none other that Boone Pickens — the successful businessman, noted for his take-over of companies and surely in need of no political votes. There is much to be said for his assertion that if a company is undervalued and ripe for a take-over it is generally due to ineffectual management at stockholders expense. (You don't suppose there's a bias *here,* do you?)

WHO'S A PATSY?

It smacks a bit of hypocrisy for foreigners to point an accusing finger at the United States when our deficits have been keeping them afloat. We are the world's largest market. (And thank you very much now turn the other cheek—dummy.)

The idea predominates that the U.S. has somehow suffered abuse from Japan without saying "boo". The truth is our government has complained about Japanese trade practices frequently and sometimes with results. (Suprise again!) We have reached accords on beef, citrus, steel, TV sets, microwaves, autos, cigarettes and machine-tools. Admittedly some of the agreements have been broken or adhered to ineffectively. Our government has attempted to open Japanese markets to American tele-communication equipment, baseball bats, semi-conductors, leather goods, cigarettes, wood products, medical and pharmaceutical products, electronic equipment and so forth. Both countries have continued to talk in a spirit of cooperation but have the narrow vision of their own vote wielding interest groups to consider.

In 1986 the U.S. imported twice as much as it exported with imports accounting for 37 percent of all domestic purchases. That year the U.S. consumer was responsible for $52.5 billion of Japan's $82.7 billion trade surplus. Japan increased imports to the U.S. by 23.5 percent in 1986; hard to believe and harder still to swallow. Especially when two of the largest imports were our own junk cars and garbage turned into paper and products and shipped back to us.

According to a *Forbes* editorial May 4, 1987,

> The percentage of income the average Japanese spends on American products is about the same as what the average American spends on Japanese goods.

Only, *Forbes* points out, we have twice as many people as Japan! The editorial goes on to say

> Japan suffers a horrendous deficit of its own: American companies in Japan have almost four times the sales in that country as Japanese subsidiaries in the U.S. have in ours. In 1985, American affiliates in Japan racked up sales of $54 billion; Japanese affiliates in the U.S., a paltry $15 billion. ...If you add in the billions that Japan is investing in this country, then they can claim that they are on the short end of the stick.

Many of the American products the Japanese buy are manufactured in Japan so sales don't show up in the trade numbers.

> As Ken Ohmae of McKinsey & Co. has pointed out, although American-

based businesses exported only $25.6 million to Japan in 1984, companies such as IBM, Texas Instruments, Coca-Cola and Schick with production and marketing arms in Japan produced and sold $43.9 billion in goods there. The total American "product presence" in Japan—exports plus goods produced locally—was $69.5 billion. This was about equal to the total Japanese "presence" in America of $69.6 billion.[5]

Nevertheless politicians and press alike, focus on the surface numbers and the closed markets and regulations imposed by the Japanese on American goods without pointing out the subtleties and two-way street aspects to our trade problem.

It gets even more complicated! Ninety percent of an item's components may be imported from Japan but the ten percent made in the USA may help Japan get around the protectionist tariffs of other countries. The weaker dollar may make it cheaper for the Japanese to export from America, in many instances, than to export from Japan. Oh yes — I almost forgot to mention that all these Japanese-made products get counted as U.S. exports.

Not only that, U.S. imports rose 50 percent between 1980-1985 and some estimates claim that 55 percent of those imported goods are from our own companies manufacturing abroad. That means that goods manufactured in Japan by American companies and exported to this country actually contribute to the U.S. trade deficit with Japan — at least on paper.

PAST PROBLEMS

Once again, the warning to read statistics carefully, bearing in mind that they can easily be skewed by choice of years, definitions and so forth. The fact that many of the numbers presented throughout this work differ dramatically from ones commonly recited by politicians should increase your skepticism of figures. Remember Mark Twain's observaton, "Figures don't lie but liars figure." A little common sense and actual experience goes a long way.

For instance Bethlehem Steel Corporation, the nation's third largest steel manufacturer, showed in January 1988 that its earnings had increased from 55 cents a share to $1.07 a share in the space of a year. Quotas on foreign steel and the weaker U.S. dollar played a part but the largest gain could be attributed to — are you ready for this? — *tax credits* ! [6]

As 1988 began U.S. factories, on the average, were operating at 82 percent of capacity, even steel, with paper and chemicals operating at 90 percent or better capacity. Machine tools are necessary in order to increase the efficiency of plants so that American manufacturers can compete in world markets. A greater demand is also due partially to the return of some production that was shifted off-shore temporarily when the dollar was strong as well as to the increase in foreign manufacturers who are transferring production to the U.S. to take advantage of the weaker dollar and to avoid the antidumping duties which were announced on November 19,1987 by the U.S. International Trade Commission.

Manufacturing displacement is no different than agricultural displacement which has been taking place gradually over the last couple centuries. "Gradually" is the key. Sudden displacement occurs when artificial barriers are erected so the market cannot call the shots — or even see them! Protectionist tactics shield specified sectors and keeps them from responding to otherwise discernable signals. When the automobile first appeared on the scene signals were heeded by buggy whip manufacturers who gradually shifted into other businesses. If AFL-CIO president Howard Samuel[7] had been in charge of things back then it's possible we'd have a surplus of unwanted government subsidized buggy whips today. At the very least he may have attempted to restrict the opening of automobile plants as unfair competition which would cut into the horse and carriage trade and result in undesirable lay offs.

John Young, CEO at Hewlett-Packard, an electronics firm in California and President of the 1985 Commission on Industrial Competitiveness, appeared before the Senate Finance Committee's hearing on international trade on January 15, 1987. At times it looked as if he, as a business representative, was on trial. Senator Spark Matsunga of Hawaii felt it was up to private business to promote American goods abroad. Young, like the successful American businessman that he is, was quick to assure the Senator that American business did not expect the government to act as its salesman (as the governments of other countries frequently do) but only to provide statistics (which it already does, although too often ineptly). Senator Matsunga was rather critical of American businessmen and observed that there were 3,000 Japanese promoting goods in this country compared to only 200 Americans doing the same in Japan. On an anecdotal note the Senator advised businessmen to never package anything for sale to Japan in fours as four stands for death in that country. His point relates to the finding that American businessmen generally fail to research foreign markets and become knowledgable about their needs and customs.

As 1988 began seven states had opened offices in Taiwan with several more states eager to follow suit. The three years free rent offered by the Taiwan government was not the only attraction. Taiwan had built up approximately $76 billion in foreign exchange reserves and as 1987 ended, had loosened restrictions on overseas investments. Between 1959 and 1986 only $163 million was officially invested by Taiwan's citizens in the U.S. Under the new regulations the government predicted Taiwan business investments in the U.S. to approximate $2.5 billion by 1991. Their textile industry is no longer competitive due to the exchange rates and higher wages. Many Taiwanese industries, textiles among them, decided to move to the U.S. even though production costs might be a little higher. They would save on shipping costs, import duties, avoid possible trade barriers in the future and find advantages in being closer to their supplies of raw materials and their largest market.

IF YOU CAN'T CONVINCE THEM
CONFUSE THEM

U.S. multinational companies have consistently outperformed domestic companies in other parts of the world. With both generosity and modesty many of Japan's top CEOs admit to learning about productivity first from American teachers.

If you feel a certain incredulity maybe that's because you were misled by statistics which show Japan's service productivity (1970-80) grew four times as fast as America's — but don't forget it started out way below and was attempting to catch up. Service trade accounts for about 25 percent of all U.S. trade, yet it is outside the rules established by GATT (General Agreement on Tariffs and Trade). Other countries can compete in the service economy with us — they have easy access here, yet it is hard for us to gain access abroad. Actually GATT has about as much clout as the United Nations or the World Court. (Remember our hostages in Iran?)

The American Productivity Center in Houston reports American productivity is double Japan's. Surprised? But the Productivity Center would be the first to testify that service productivity is hard to measure with any degree of accuracy — much harder than measuring manufacturing productivity. There are fluid boundaries.

According to the late Secretary of Commerce, Malcolm Baldridge, the manufacturing share of GNP in this country held practically constant in the 20 percent range between 1960-85.[8] Even today fifty-five percent of all jobs are associated in some manner with the manufacturing economy. Eighteen percent are actually engaged in manufacturing.

Even with TEFRA (1982 tax reform) which repealed ERTA's (1981 tax reform) deductions for equipment and machinery, manufacturing productivity grew faster in this country under the Reagan administration than during the average postwar expansion. According to the 1987 report of the Council of Economic Advisors, output per hour rose an average of 3.8 percent per year in the manufacturing sector between the third quarter of 1981 and 1986; more than double the average 1.5 percent rate reported for the 1973 to 1981 time period. Although between 1980-85 manufacturing lost an enormous number of jobs, productivity (hourly output) continued to rise faster than in the non-manufacturing sector. On the other hand, renowned MIT economist Lester

209

Thurow likes to talk about America's decreasing productivity; from 2.4 percent 1965-1972, to 1.6 percent 1972-1977 and only 0.2 percent 1977-1982.⁹ Between 1983 and 1985 the value of the dollar skyrocketed, certainly skewing figures and apparently making them too optimistic for Dr. Thurow's use.

A comparison with other countries shows productivity in manufacturing *increased* an average of 2.7 percent a year from 1960 in this country, whereas England's productivity *increased* 3.6 percent, France's 5.5 percent and Japan's 8 percent. In fact our productivity grew less than six other additional European countries. BUT—America is still more productive than any other nation; many others were extremely inefficient and are catching up.

In the USA over the past 5 years outmoded factories have closed and others have been upgraded. According to Charles Hanley:

> As a result America's manufacturing productivity has risen faster than West Germany's and nearly matched Japan's increase during the past two years. ...(in early 1987)...Japan's per-capita economic output eclipsed America's — $18,100 to $17,700, by one estimate."[10]

Michael Balfour shows in his 1981 book, *The Adversaries: America, Russia and the Open World 1941-1962*, that the average annual rate of growth of output per capita between 1913-1950 was 1.7 in the USA, 1.3 in England and 0.7 in France. Of course in the fifties the U.S. was still the only game in town since the rest of the world was busy rebuilding after World War II.

On page 433 of *The Rise And Fall of The Great Powers*, Paul Kennedy refers to Michael Balfour:

> As Michael Balfour remarks, for decades before 1950 the United States had increased its output faster than anyone else because it had been a major innovator in methods of standardization and mass production. As a result, it had "gone further than any other country to satisfy human needs and (was) already operating at a high level of efficiency (measured in terms of output per man per hour) so that the known possibilities for increasing output by better methods or better machinery were, in comparison with the rest of the world, smaller."

Japan's productivity is not 8 percent and ours 2.7 percent — Japan's productivity *grew* at a remarkable 8 percent rate!

But despite the rise in U.S. productivity, manufactured exports have declined over the past thirty years. The U.S. share in world markets has dropped from 21-22 percent to the 13-14 percent range which in Chapter Two we agreed was a normal drop.

The big change occurred in profits. Prices of imports declined during those years, imposing a major discipline on domestic prices and ultimately profits. Whereas the financial corporations saw profits between 1981 and 1986 increase more than 75 percent, manufacturing*profits* fell 17 percent during the same time period.

Notice the variety of years for which statistics are recited here and note that sometimes manufacturing and non-manufacturing productivity are combined and other times they are counted separately.

It makes one wonder where Peter Peterson got his figures when he claims in "The Morning After" that our productivity growth has amounted to less than half of one percent a year from 1979-1986.

NO EXCUSES!

Faulty predictions of future demands are common and damaging. An executive who can foretell the future may be worth his multimillion dollar salary only there are very few who have proven to be clairvoyant. Some steel companies that expanded had managers that failed to realize that once the initial fever of building railroads and highways in the lesser developed countries (LDCs) was over, demand for steel would slow. The dream of raising the standard of living in the LDCs came true as many of these same countries became producers themselves and even competitors. Even harder to foresee was the development of alternative materials to supplant steel.

Not to excuse American shortsightedness, but the Japanese do have advantages in the following areas:

1) lower priced capital (Japan 3%-4% vs USA 8%-10%)
2) stockholders who understand or tolerate long-term strategy; therefore fewer take-over fears
3) government research assistance
4) weak unions allowing funds to cross from wages & benefits into research & development
5) a disciplined more stratified society
6) government supported trade companies

In addition the increasingly heavy debt hindering many U.S. corporations is not shared by the many Japanese firms having little or no debt. However the Japanese treat the public shareholder not as an owner, but as a claimant whose interests are subordinated to maintenance and growth of the business, which is a less preferential position than that accorded the American shareholder. Just ten years ago U.S. companies spent 20 percent of their available cash to service debt and in 1985 they spent 30 percent. That's a lot! Toyota, on the other hand, has almost no long-term debt and enormous cash resources. We're talking about a company with annual sales over $38 billion; incredible by American standards.

Mobile technology makes it possible for anyone to reach the global market. This and low cost foreign labor, foreign government subsidies and worldwide overcapacity all make it harder than ever before for Americans to compete. The technological revolution has made it possible for a service provider to perform for a client on the other side of the world. Witness the TV ads which depict a fashion designer in the U.S. able to see and choose fabric from a showroom in France; or an architect able to submit plans from his New York office to a company accepting bids in Japan — all electronically and in minutes, thanks to over-the-wire transmissions. Physicians can even diagnose patients thousands of miles away via x-ray and CAT-scan satellite transmissions.

Unfortunately most small businesses in the U.S. don't even think about the hassles they would encounter if they wanted to compete internationally. The U.S. Commerce Department, which provides counseling and has a 120-office sales network in several countries, reports some successes by small businesses in cracking world markets. There is some question as to the agency's cost effectiveness, but ideologically it is preferable to an idea that has been making the rounds suggesting that private banks be *forced* to underwrite exports. (You read it correctly — I said *forced*) Awareness of the help exporters in other nations receive from their governments provides ammunition for those who advocate public-private partnerships in this country. Those who, as Ayn Rand so aptly put it,

> dread the competition of a free market and would welcome an armed 'partner' to extort special advantages over their abler competitors; men who seek to rise, not by merit but by pull, men who are willing and eager to live not by right, but by favor. [11]

THE EMERGING ISSUES FORUM '88

The Emerging Issues Forum '88 was held at North Carolina State University in the middle of March, 1988. Former Federal Reserve Chairman Paul Volcker was a guest speaker. His topic: "Taking Control of the Future". He told the audience that leaving the deficit to market forces alone is a possible but painful solution to our deficit problems. He advocated instead a policy which would involve spending cuts and tax increases. He suggested raising taxes on gasoline and cigarettes and cutting back the rate of increase in entitlement benefits as well as taxing the benefits of high income entitlement recipients. These relatively moderate actions he believed would do the job of insuring the economy against inflation and recession.

Increased revenue may be needed if the government is to continue its role of protector *and* provider. Those of us who believe government's role must be contracted see no reason for increased revenue. Decreased spending alone will control the deficit if government attends only to its legitimate business.

Bill Clinton, Governor of Arkansas who recently headed a governors' task force on competitiveness which issued a paper called "Making America Work: Productive People — Productive Policies", gave a dynamic presentation at the North Carolina Forum. His speech was titled "Protecting American Jobs". The Governor claimed real wages peaked in 1973, the year the post World War era ended. Real wages have declined 17 percent in real terms since then, he said, and even worse, statistics (*whose* statistics?) show that between 1981 and 1985 40 percent of American workers saw their incomes increase, the incomes of 20 percent held steady, and the incomes of the other 40 percent declined. He said the implication is that unless a change occurs the American dream will not be possible for future generations. He discussed three main causes of the reported decline in wages. First he mentioned the internationalization of our economy — the fact that foreigners can do what Americans have been doing as well as Americans have been doing it but for lower wages or even for the same or higher wages. Secondly, the labor force increased, due to the unprecedented influx of baby boomers and women into the workplace, just at the time other pressures had already gathered to reduce labor's price. Finally he told the audience that Ronald Reagan's policies and the overvalued dollar aggrevated the situation, making imports cheaper and putting extreme pressure on exporters. The Governor recited four responses we could take: (1) work smarter and become more productive, (2) switch rather than fight — move into work areas not subject to competition, (3) lose the job, the farm or cap the well, or (4) hang on by lowering pay or profits (as the Japanese are doing during the dollar's fall).

According to Governor Clinton, the challenge facing America is to build a new world economic system that works. He pointed to the fact that GATT covers less than 10 percent of the dollar value of all international trade. The free trade vs protectionism issue he referred to as a bogus debate, claiming that only England and the USA have a free trade ideology, let alone *practice* it! Our

objective must be *more* trade because without more trade we cannot have economic growth in the world, without economic growth in the world Americans will tend to have downward pressures on their incomes.

The Governor said we need new trading rules that will permit free trade and open foreign markets. He did not fail to point out that during the past eight years, while spouting our free trade slogans, the United States has become more protectionist. Twenty percent of our trade used to be covered by some sort of protection but as a reaction to the overvalued dollar that protection grew to include 35 percent of our trade. He said that the depression in Third World countries harms our exports more than anything else. He mentioned a 1986 study which found that if the growth rates in Latin America had been the same in 1986 as they were in the late 1970s we would have had a 20 percent lower trade deficit in this country, whereas if Japanese trade barriers had been relaxed our trade deficit would have been only 5 percent lower. Despite rhetoric to the contrary Japanese barriers don't cause that much damage.

Governor Clinton saw several good signs on the horizon. (1) a labor shortage by 1995 which would bid up wages, (2) manufacturing productivity which increased substantially during the 1980s (increasing at over 3.5 percent a year) transferring into other sectors of the economy in the years ahead, and (3) the dollar's devaluation. The biggest problem, he continued, was our *waste* of time and money and most of all, waste of human capacity. As examples he recited our high teen pregnancy rate, high infant mortality, high number of kids dropping out of school, high drug abuse and high adult illiteracy. Even when there is a labor shortage we'll still have low incomes, he warned, if we continue this waste of human potential. We'll end up importing workers from other parts of the world to perform the high paying jobs. "We must focus on the human aspect of our economic problems", he said. The reality of our structural federal deficit means that government has few resources to invest here and that the private sector and state and local governments will have to pick up the ball in this instance.

I found myself agreeing with Governor Clinton up to this point in his speech but had to disagree, as I must always, with those who expand the legitimate role of government. It may well be that as a nation we need to address the following problems and apply some of the remedies suggested but it is NOT GOVERNMENT'S ROLE!

The Governor told the audience of the need for states to:

(1) Make an economic connection. He advocated a state-private sector partnership to deal with quality and productivity problems of already established businesses. He suggested a task force of "advisers" — successful bussinessmen. (WHY involve government? Let the business community handle it alone.)

(2) Increase research and development, and put research centers in depressed areas. (He admitted federal dollars would be needed in this area.) He advocated the establishment of technology transfer centers to take maximum advantage of the Technology Transfer Act which was recently passed by Congress. The Act was intended to enable Americans to turn their ideas into jobs. The Governor gave, as an example, the fact that although Americans invented VCRs all VCRs are made in Japan — *only* made in Japan!

(3) Bill Clinton wants to see targeted investments ("targeting" calls for discretionary professional judgment) in every state in areas of real opportunity. (Again — "areas of real opportunity" calls for the best judgment of professional venture capitalists who have the pulse of the market.) He gave Arkansas as an example: Arkansas invested taxpayers' dollars in superconductivity research. (A lot of judgment calls and risk-taking here, which is certainly not a job for policymakers or bureaucrats, elected or otherwise.)

(4) Capital: every state should invest seed capital in small high technology businesses. The Governor didn't exactly say "because", but the "because" was implied in his pointing out that " 85 percent of new jobs in the USA over the last ten years have come in units of less than 50." He recommended that every state set aside a portion of its pension fund for reinvestment in the state. (Not a new

idea. [12] But taking money from citizens and investing it for them is not a legitimate role for government in the United States of America. Citizens should be encouraged to take charge of their own affairs and make their own investments, instead of depending helplessly on a group of "men at the top".)

(5) Bill Clinton says that we need an investment strategy that deals with the economic underclass. We need to rejuvenate the truly depressed areas. Arkansas has a Southern Development Bank which loans money to very small entrepreneurial ventures in high unemployment areas. It is based on the highly successful Southshore Development Bank in Chicago which went into a depressed area and rehabilitated 6,000 housing units by setting up scores of independent business people, carpenters, electricians, mechancis, people who were formerly unemployed. The Chicago experiment was based on an experiment in Bangladesh where 400,000 loans were made to otherwise hopeless people and where the repayment rate, according to the Governor, was almost 98 percent. It worked by teaming people with one another. If one person failed to make payments then another was denied a new loan.

I had little quarrel with the activist do-gooder stance taken by the Governor, and would agree cooperation and helping one another is the solution to the immediate problems confronting America and the entire world, but I reiterate — IT IS NOT GOVERNMENT'S ROLE. The job will be done, and not by police power (what else is government?) but voluntarily and flexibly by the private sector if the government backs off.

In his January 1987 State of the Union address President Reagan proposed initiatives to promote commercial use of high technology in general. In order to ensure that American manufacturers, rather than European or Japanese, take the lead in commercial development of superconductors, the Reagan administration proposed legislation to permit more joint ventures under antitrust law, to increase patent protection for manufacturing processes, to shift more federal research funds into super-conductivity projects, to speed up research for military applications and to negotiate with the Japanese for American involvement in their research and development programs.

Programs requiring the judgment of an elite group (Boards, Commissions, Task Forces, Advisers etc.) run the risk of corrupting officials who must continually fight against the temptation to trade favors. Governor Clinton, in his North Carolina speech, is advocating a power trip for policymakers. Such programs will encourage a class system far more harmful to America's character than the distinction between rich and poor or labor and management. I earlier mentioned the danger of strengthening the roles of the *ruling* and the *ruled* and I do not apologize for the repetition here — the peril cannot be emphasized enough!

The Governor ended with a host of programs that the government must undertake because "the future has a price". This naturally led into a pitch for raising taxes (the price). I agree, most of the programs relating to early childhood and education need to be attended to, but again NOT BY GOVERNMENT! I even agree with Governor Clinton's closing statement. (For anyone looking ahead to 1992 it is worth noting that the Governor's oratorical skills rival those of Mario Cuomo and Jesse Jackson.)

He ended by telling his audience that the nation will survive and prosper only if it considers the future to be more important than the present. Americans must believe that the future can be better than the present and every person must have a personal moral responsibility to make it so. Amen. BUT NOT THROUGH GOVERNMENT!

HOW EXCHANGE RATES
AFFECT OUR COMPETITIVENESS

As we will see in the next chapter, there has to be some kind of exchange rate stability for business to prosper. Sam Kusumoto, president of Minolta Corporation agrees.

> Because productivity is measured by the dollar value of what is produced, drastic exchange-rate fluctuations render such comparisons somewhat problematical—another indication of the need for stable rates in making business decisions.[13]

Where a manufacturer puts his plant depends on his *guessing* what the exchange rates will be in the future. It is not a simple matter to pick up and move if one guesssed wrong.

Some American businesses have developed sophisticated operations to hedge against currency fluctuations and some even make a profit at the same time. The *Wall Street Journal* (George Melloan) reported certain comments from the 1986 *Annual Report on the Worldwide Economic and Business Climate* published by the accounting firm of Coopers and Lybrand.

> currency rates, even among the two largest industrial countries in the world, can swing dramtically over a very short period and have far more impact on ultimate corporate profits than any other factor.[14]

The USA accounts for one third of all economic activity in the industrialized world. It was obvious from the outset that our problems would simply be exacerbated if American business failed to take advantage of the competitiveness gained through the weaker dollar and instead of increasing market share, simply raised prices. Donald Petersen, CEO of Ford Motor Co., claims that is not being done — at least not by Ford. [15]

In an article for the *Wall Street Journal,* David Ranson and

Marc Miles proposed a "chicken-or-the-egg" question when they suggested that it may well be the trade imbalance that first drives the dollar. They hypothesized that changes in the dollar tend to follow, not lead, changes in the U.S. trade imbalance. Historically, they maintain,

> many strong-currency countries have been surplus-prone (Germany, Japan) whereas weak-currency countries have been deficit-prone (Italy, Britain). [16]

They conclude the link between the dollar and the trade imbalance is better seen as political rather than economic — a governmental knee-jerk.

> the countries with which the U.S. encountered the largest bilateral deficit increases in 1980-84 should have been those against whose currencies the dollar rose the most,...(however) the truth is almost exactly the opposite.[17]

Charles Alexander, writing for *Time's* November 16, 1987 issue claims

> countries with strong currencies have been able to boost their living standards...Germany has become the world's leading exporter...A weakened dollar is no substitute for forceful action to reduce the budget deficit.[18]

In 1986 Taiwan showed a $16 billion trade surplus with the U.S. and Hong Kong and South Korea each showed a surplus of $7 billion. Since the dollar began its fall in 1985, South Korea has managed to increase exports by 24 percent. South Korea has been experiencing economic growth in the 10 to 11 percent range whereas Taiwan's growth has exceeded 8 percent recently. To put that in perspective, the U.S. is anemic in comparison, with a meager 2 to 3 percent growth. Taiwan increased sales to France by 71 percent and West Germany by 41 percent just in the first half of 1986.

Naturally neither the United States, Japan nor West Germany, the main players in the Group of Five who masterminded the dollar's decline, are overjoyed by the windfall being enjoyed at their expense by the "4"—Hong Kong, Taiwan, South Korea and Singapore.

The United States is demanding Korea and Taiwan strengthen their currencies. It looks like they may be complying, but just enough to appease Secretary Baker and that best friend and customer of all nations, the American consumer.

Remember a trade deficit is not necessarily a sign of weakness. *Forbes* suggests that our trade imbalance is in large part due to our growth while the rest of the world stagnated. That rosy scenario is not being bought in 1988, and even *Forbes* would admit there's a lot more to it than that.

Since early 1985 the dollar has fallen from 260 yen to under 125 yen early in 1988. This depreciation in the dollar was supposed to make American goods more attractive to foreigners (less expensive) and foreign goods less attractive to Americans (more expensive). Producers benefit from a falling dollar, but they also found the rising dollar beneficial. Between 1980 and 1985 when the dollar rose, producers had to cut their costs in order to compete and that's when manufacturing productivity made some headway. It grew at an average annual rate of 1.2 percent between 1973 and 1981, but between 1981 and 1987 it averaged 4 percent. (Be aware! Notice the different years used here and that what is being measured is "the average annual rate".) The U.S. earned $8.3 billion in 1986 from its Canadian investments which amounted to 25 percent of all American foreign investments. At the end of 1987 U.S. exports were 20% higher than they were a year earlier, attributable, perhaps, to the cheaper dollar.

Of course producers in other countries didn't just sit still during that time period. The high dollar opened doors for them and they, especially the Japanese, stepped through and convinced American consumers that Japanese products were not only cheaper but of superior quality to boot.

Unfortunately the "powers-that-be" don't want to face the fact that many Americans believe foreign products are superior and will not hesitate to pay more for them. This is especially true when it comes to machine tools and automobiles. Mercedes-Benz, for instance, can't seem to import enough cars even though the sales price increased twenty-three percent in 1986. Both the Germans and the Japanese sell more on engineering and other features; quality not price. Therefore when planners look to tax cuts, cheaper oil, lower interest rates and so forth to stimulate the economy, they are often disappointed. American consumers spend all right, but they continue to purchase far more foreign products than ever before. Charles Alexander points out that as the price of foreign products increases, Americans spend even more dollars for the same volume of goods. Meanwhile they earn fewer yen, francs and marks for U.S. products that do sell well abroad, like Boeing aircraft and IBM computers. As a result the trade deficit actually increases in dollar terms.

Martin Feldstein, past chairman of the President's Council of Economic Advisers and Professor of Economics at Harvard, says that even if faster economic growth could be achieved in other countries, it would not make up for the further decline in the value of the dollar. Professor Feldstein also argues that slow growth abroad will have relatively little impact on our export sales. In fact he claims that a two percent reduction in Japan's economic growth would only reduce imports from the entire world, not just the United States, by less than $4 billion. The Japanese, remember, aren't big spenders and generally when they buy they "buy Japanese". "Even doubling the projected real growth rates in the rest of the industrial world for this year and next would cut the 1988 U.S. trade deficit by less than $20 billion."[19] Professor Feldstein believes a further reduction in the value of the dollar is necessary in order to bring our imports and exports back into balance and reduce U.S. dependence on the flow of foreign capital. He believes that even if we wanted to stop the dollar's fall we could not do so by artificial means. He would like to see it drop to around 120 yen at any rate. In January 1988 he came mighty close to getting his wish.

But even if the dollar continues to decline it will leave a substantial portion of the trade problem unresolved. Forty-seven percent of all U.S. trade is with new suppliers like Latin America. Nevertheless we musn't give in to the temptation to turn to protectionism, but should remain flexible in order to deal with countries on an individual one to one basis.

Surprisingly our imports as a proportion of GNP have remained unchanged over the past seven years. Even though the U.S. exported to Canada more than twice what it exported to Japan, in 1986 it purchased 10 percent more from Japan than from Canada. Nevertheless our most important bilateral trade relationship is not with Japan, but with Canada. Between 1982-86 sales to Canada grew by 45 percent accounting for 20 percent of all U.S. exports. That sounds terrific doesn't it until you realize that at the same time the trade deficit with Canada was $2 billion more in 1986 than in 1985. How could that be? Between 1985 and 1987 the U.S. dollar dropped about one percent against the Canadian dollar making Canadian products more attractive to Americans.

Europe is not as dependent on us for trade but we are still one of their biggest customers. In West Germany trade with the U.S. accounted for $16 billion of their $57 billion 1986 trade surplus; not too shabby.

It has been estimated that the dollar would have to fall to almost 100 yen in order to wipe out the U.S. trade deficit with Japan over the next few years. Others insist it will take both lower interest rates and a lower budget deficit in this country to wipe out the trade deficit. MIT economist Rudiger Dornbusch has shown with a computer model

> that for every 116% gain in the competitiveness of U.S. export prices and every 8% rise in net foreign spending levels, the U.S. gains net exports equivalent to 2% of gross national product. But every six years, 1% of GNP is eroded from U.S. net exports by gains in the export capacities of developing countries. [20]

The Federal Reserve Bank is walking a tight rope. A looser policy at the Fed risks inflation and/or a weaker dollar which can end up hurting Japan and West Germany. Carl Walsh, writing for the Federal Reserve San Francisco weekly "Outlook" (3/6/87) said

> A contractionary fiscal policy designed to reduce the current federal budget deficit is one example of a policy that is likely to improve the trade balance, yet lead to slower real growth. A reduction in government purchases of goods and services will directly lower the demand for domestic output and reduce the borrowing needs of the government. A decline in the government's borrowing needs will tend to put downward pressure on market interest rates. As U.S. interest rates decline relative to rates of return available in other countries, so will the value of the U.S. dollar...

Of course we could "inflate away" the budget deficit by printing more money but it will not help the trade deficit.

Not surprisingly there is disagreement over the manipulation of the dollar. Some liken devaluing your own currency to a national death wish, while others would like to see the dollar drop lower still. Senator Lloyd Bentsen (D-TX), during an interview on Cable News Network (CNN) on January 17, 1987, echoed Martin Feldstein's wish to see the dollar drop to the 120-125 yen range. Aside from that deviation[21] the Senator seemed to agree pretty much with the administration's agenda for 1987-88. He agreed the trade situation would be helped by more stable exchange rates but added that the long-term solution to our competitiveness is more research and development, education, job retraining and making pensions more portable. Who would argue?

Significant currency depreciation can be highly inflationary. Instead of encouraging a lower dollar and thereby encouraging exports, the trade deficit could be narrowed by discouraging imports. This "pain on purpose" strategy could involve tax increases or more stock market crashes which take liquidity from the system. Loss of wealth would mean less demand for both domestic and imported products. Reducing consumption could slow the economy as could taking dollars away from non-military research and development. You got it — the danger is recession! Recession depends ultimately on policy decisions.

WHO'S AFRAID OF JAPAN?

The average American might be surprised to learn Japan's budget deficit was among the highest of the industrialized nations in 1986; $855.9 billion. It's little wonder when you consider that Japan's 1985 farm support programs amounted to a whopping $56 billion — more than double ours! But according to Charles Hanley, Mitsui Bank researchers had calculated Japan's worth at $5 trillion — more than all the developed real estate in the USA.

The Japanese believe America is in an historic decline. If they read this book — or better still, Paul Kennedy's book, they will realize America's decline is both relative and natural. We would only wish it were slower and believe now it has gone far enough and that it is time to "get tough" and make a stand.

Americans imagine themselves as "most creative" — the "Yankee-know-how" image is ingrained — but it's hard to beat Japanese ingenuity in some areas. Japan buys Canadian wheat at $122.60 per ton and Japanese wheat at $1,226.00 per ton selling a combination at $574.60 per ton. How's this for inventiveness? The Japanese renamed an area in Japan "USA" so they could legitimately (?) stamp goods with "Made in USA".

In his testimony the late Secretary of Commerce Malcolm Baldridge agreed that we had relinquished our huge export lead in the sixties and seventies when exporting became necessary to the survival of other nations. He admitted the pendulum may have swung too far but asserted that facts show since 1980 American business has been reaserting its competitiveness and, without government's foot on its back, has been making headway. Not that there haven't been problems.

Rodney Chase of British Petroleum was quoted in *Fortune* magazine as saying, "The real brain-power is still with the American firms." Perhaps, but for how long? It may cost us $100 million to produce a new pharmaceutical only to have it immediately copied by other countries. For example Lotus 1-2-3 (spread sheet for computers) can be purchased in Hong Kong for a dollar. It would be self defeating to delude ourselves. According to the

U.S. Patent Office, patent requests by foreigners have more than doubled from twenty percent to forty-two percent between 1965 and 1986. In 1986 alone, of the 76,993 patents issued, 34,606 were issued to foreigners, with the largest batch (5,983) going to Japanese inventors.

Japanese manufacturers have been hurt by the dramatic rise in the yen in relation to the dollar since 1985. Because the currencies of the 4 Tigers (South Korea, Taiwan, Singapore and Hong Kong) were closely tied to the American dollar, the yen's sixty percent appreciation meant a golden opportunity for the "4" to move in on some previously Japanese dominated markets in both the United States and Europe.

South Korea has been exporting record numbers of autos (Hyundai) videocassette recorders (Goldstar) personal computers (Daewoo) and so forth. South Korea, as the fourth largest debtor in the world, sees the increase in exports as a way to pay its debts, and one which the rest of the world shouldn't begrudge it. (Isn't it interesting that Singapore is trailing the "4" and yet it is right behind Switzerland, Japan and West Germany as BERI's pick for best place to invest in the world?)

The loss of world market share forced the Japanese to face for the first time, unemployment at home. Although a 3 percent unemployment rate would bring joy to the hearts of Europeans and Americans it is cause for concern in Japan. Again according to Charles Hanley, Japanese work an average 2,152 hours per year compared to 1,898 hours per year for Americans. They put in many hours of unpaid overtime, and offered an average of 32 suggestions per employee per year at Toyota, for example. Workers in Japan *care,* is the message conveyed by Mr. Hanley. The Japanese use four times the number of robots used by U.S. manufacturers so it is little wonder they build twice the number of cars per employee. It is interesting to note that the U.S. produced more cars in 1980 (6.9 million) than in 1960 (6.65 million) but in 1960 that number accounted for 52 percent of world output whereas it was good for only a 23 percent share of the world market in 1980. The auto and related service industries which account for 10 percent of Japan's total workforce are feeling the effects of the rising yen. Many Japanese auto makers have increased prices in the U.S. up to 15 percent on top of swallowing lower profits. Incredibly, in 1986 one out of every three cars sold worldwide was made in Japan. Japan's auto exports made up 38 percent of its 1986 trade surplus with this country. However, with lower priced imports anticipated from countries such as Brazil and Mexico, that number is expected to fall in the future.

Although Japanese exports have declined somewhat because they are more expensive for foreigners, Japanese imports have been declining even more. The Japanese are less willing to purchase foreign goods and, as strange as it may seem, the Japanese trade surplus has actually been increasing as a result of exchange appreciation.

As the yen buys more abroad the danger of inflation decreases in Japan. Fiscal expansion would raise Japanese interest rates and further drive up the yen which could realistically lead to a greater demand for U.S. goods which would help the American economy. Monetary expansion in the USA would lower interest rates which would lead to a lower dollar which should in turn lead to more exports and increased domestic growth.

The other side of the coin is monetary expansion in Japan which would lower interest rates still further in that country (on February 23,1987, rates were discounted from 3 percent to 2.5 percent under urging from the USA). The resulting lower value of the yen would probably lessen demand for American goods which would certainly not help exports in this country. Even worse, the trade imbalance would deepen and there would be slower growth in the American economy.

Japanese manufacturers would rather institute austerity measures in their factories, reduce workers and endure lower profits (and wages) than lose market share in the world. The real problem is that central planners and bankers in both West Germany and Japan prefer trade surpluses and strong currencies. Tough if it means high unemployment and a weaker economy. This is one more reason to steer away from centralization; the common-man (who ever he may be) gets the shaft every time.

Why can't these power-hungry "would-be-planners" understand that human beings are marvelously adaptable? No matter how good "the plan" or tight the regulation, citizens will find ways to do what they believe is in their best interest and "thank you very much for your task forces, commisssions, reports but..." (you know the rest).

During John Young's January 1987 testimony before the Senate Finance Committee he said Japanese banking, automobile and insurance companies have taken advantage of the strong yen and invested directly in the United States:

> not unlike (the pattern) just after World War II when American companies, armed with practically the only hard currency extant, set about in the words of one banker, to 'buy up the world'.

But even though Japan's investments in America were growing at an unprecedented pace they were still far below that of either the Netherlands or Great Britain. Alan Murray reported in the February 29, 1988 edition of the *Wall Street Journal* that

> Foreigners control less than 5% of the nation's assets. And the Japanese, who seem to raise the most concern, control less than 1%.[22]

Japan's own Ministry of International Trade & Industry (MITI) expected its country's investment in American manufacturing to increase 14.2 percent each year until the year 2000.

According to a 1986 *Business Week-Harris Poll,* if asked to choose, 48 percent of Americans would have discouraged Japanese investment and only 18 percent would have encouraged it.

Peter Drucker, professor of social sciences and acclaimed author claims

> U.S. manufacturers, despite the dollar's greatly reduced purchasing power abroad, are now increasing their direct investments abroad — and contrary to what almost everybody believes, at about the same rate at which foreigners are increasing their direct investments in the U.S.[23]

Data Resources, a research firm, reports that in 1986 new investments in this country by foreigners amounted to $25 billion whereas new U.S. investments abroad amounted to $28 billion that same year.

On the other hand, Treasury and the Commerce Department estimated that by September 30, 1987 we owed foreigners $268.4 billion and interest on it of $23.5 billion. In the third quarter of 1987 for the first time in over 50 years foreigners earned more on their U.S. investments than Americans earned on their investments abroad. According to the Commerce Department, foreign-held assets in the USA outstripped American-held assets abroad by $263 billion. Overall government debt, not just the portion owed to foreigners, has grown so that foreign debt is only about 14 percent of our total debt — no big deal — right? Not necessarily. The problem is we no longer owe the dollars to ourselves.

Table 5
DEBT HELD BY & INTEREST PAID TO FOREIGNERS
(in billions of dollars)

Year	Federal Debt	Interest
1980	121.7	12.0
1984	175.5	19.0
1986	256.3	22.3
1987	268.4	23.5

Source: Treasury and Commerce Departments 1988

This information can only be reconciled if you note the subtle differences: (1) "*new* investments" on the one hand, and "debt owed" on the other, (2) earnings *on* assets, not assets, (3) foreign domination of 14% of our total *debt* or 5% of our *assets,* (4) older American assets were valued at book value, not the current market value — new purchases by foreigners in the USA were greatly inflated by comparison.

By 1986 the Japanese had become such major buyers of U.S. government debt that any lack of buying interest in Tokyo could send the U.S. bond market reeling. The lower dollar made

America a shopper's paradise for foreign buyers, but even worse, the devalued dollar became an invitation to foreign investors to desert U.S. assets thereby sending new shock waves through our stock and bond markets. To keep foreigners interested in subsidizing our budget and trade deficit, the Fed would have to keep U.S. bank interest rates attractively high which would lower the value of stocks in comparison. Recession and even depression could be a stone's throw behind.

It was a relief then when foreign investors switched to more illiquid investments as the dollar continued to drop in value.

By 1986 500 Japanese companies were manufacturing or assembling in the U.S., Japanese investors were snapping up real estate, (the Japanese bought over $4 billion worth of U.S. real estate in 1986 and even more in 1987)[24] stocks and other equities.

It's far better from the American point of view, to have foreigners invest in illiquid real estate and manufacturing plants rather than in U.S. securities which can be withdrawn suddenly with dire consequences.

But those on the Hill often see things differently when they see them at all. Congress, increasingly uncomfortable with the sale of American assets to foreigners, proposed legislation in the summer of 1987 that would require foreigners to register with the federal government if they purchased more than $5 million worth of U. S. assets. (See p. 239)

> Ultimately, the best way to reduce the flow of foreign investment is to reduce the trade deficit. And the best way to reduce the trade deficit, as the president's Council of Economic Advisers argues in its latest report, is to reduce the budget deficit. That's the real challenge for those worried about the selling of America. [25]

HIGH WAGES BREED HIGH UNEMPLOYMENT

Three of the five nations BERI predicts will overtake The United States as investment havens are located in Europe, which may be hard to believe and maybe you'll decide not to believe it after a perusal of the following facts:

230

Employment figures released by the Organization for Economic Cooperation and Development (OECD) in the summer of 1986, show nineteen members will boost employment 0.5 percent, or almost 800,000 workers, the best performance since 1979, and a huge improvement over the *loss* of 1.3 million jobs in 1981. For 1987 the OECD predicts another 1.2 million jobs will materialize.

Europe is beginning to benefit from more flexible working hours and looser regulations. Previously unions had tried to keep companies from organizing night and weekend shifts. Now companies keep the equipment humming by arranging shifts around the clock.

Many European businesses have shied away from hiring in good times for fear of being stuck with too many workers when things slow down.

West Germany had an unemployment rate above eight percent, thanks to high payroll taxes, budget-busting subsidies to favored industries, inefficient farmers and a protectionist attitude to boot. Powerful labor unions exerted tight control over hiring, firing and wages. German employers had to go through an expensive and complicated procedure in order to fire any employee who had been on the payroll for at least six months. Luckily a new law has put a stop to that nonsense and employers are allowed to hire workers on contracts of up to eighteen months and lay them off at the end of that period without a giant hassle. These recent reforms have the West German government predicting an unemployment rate of five and a half percent by 1990.

There is a conflict in employment data. According to the projections of the United Nations, average annual increases in the Western European workforce will drop from 692,000 in 1985-90 to 365,000 at the end of 1995. A slowing of the increase but an increase nevertheless.

European manufacturing wages shot up on average 13.4 percent a year from 1971 to 1980; 3.3 percentage points above inflation. Social Security, and other indirect labor costs borne by employers, soared. In England these costs jumped from 16.1

percent of the total labor bill in 1968 to more than 25 percent in 1986. After adjusting for inflation, labor costs have risen almost fifty percent since 1970 in Europe. Now why do you suppose Europe has an employment problem? Yet popular wisdom in this country is suggesting we follow suit and raise the minimum wage. "Try it — it does wonders for employment!"

It's true, as you've probably heard, that between 1980-85, U.S. labor costs rose about five percent *under* most other industrialized countries. (But again remember where they started!) From 1982 to 1985 Japanese workers were paid fifty percent less than American workers. By January 1987, the Japanese workers were paid only twenty-one percent less than Americans. In 1985 the wages and benefits of West German workers were twenty-five percent less than those of American workers but by 1987 those wages were twenty percent *above* the wages of Americans. The USA had become more competitive on labor costs than the Europeans.

The desire for and attempt to obtain cheap labor is common to all manufacturers. Auto workers make $500 a month in Taiwan so it is not surprising that both American and Japanese capital was attracted to this small island. Ford (USA) owns 25 percent of Mazda and 70 percent of Ford Lio Ho Motor Company while Nissan and Mitsubishi each own 25 percent of Taiwan's Yue Loong Motor Company (and an affiliate); Toyota owns 22 percent of Kuo Zui Motors. Auto parts from Taiwan are replacing Japanese made parts on U.S. shelves and may soon even be imported to Japan.

In 1987 Ford planned to assemble the "Tracer" (auto) in Mexico and import it to the U.S. The Mexican minimum wage translates to $22 a week — quite an enticement. In 1986 there were approximately 800 American owned factories on the south side of the border between the U.S. and Mexico employing an estimated 250,000 Mexicans. To those who would call this exploitation I would suggest that it is impossible to exploit a person capable of exercising free will — i.e. a non-slave. (Disregard the finer arguments that may suggest that everyone is a "slave" to *something*.) To the Mexicans lucky enough to be working, this opportunity means a middle class existence in their own country. To American entrepreneurs it means a competitive edge. When both parties benefit from an agreement it can only be spoiled by the entry of do-gooders in a misguided effort to protect one party from another or to claim a third party, not involved, is somehow being robbed. At the moment, with the price of oil so low, Mexico's greatest resource is her people — yes, cheap labor. Naturally U.S. labor unions are unhappy with the situation but what they fail to understand is that companies are not trading American jobs for Mexican; American labor priced itself out of the unskilled market long ago. The trade is Asian labor for Mexican. Unskilled Mexican labor cost half that of the "Four Tigers" (Taiwan, Singapore, Hong Kong and South Korea) and one-sixth that of Japan. Now how long do you think it will take even more capital to find Mexico as long as its leaders refrain from erecting artificial barriers? This is the best thing that could happen to future Mexican-American relations; to have the Mexican economy grow. In the past Mexico's political leaders have been suspicious of any sign of expansion by U.S. business interests. Suddenly they are preaching the virtues of a more open economy. The Japanese, who used Hong Kong labor awhile back, are not letting this opportunity go by them but have also switched to the cheaper Mexican labor. If no one interfers with the natural flow of the world market it will raise Mexico's standard of living. It's Mexico's turn — while it lasts! According to Peter Drucker

> Wage levels for blue-collar workers are becoming increasingly irrelevant in world competition...blue-collar labor no longer accounts for enough of total costs to give low wages much competitive advantage.[26]

Somebody better pass the word on to the candidates for the 1988 Democratic presidential nomination — especially to Richard Gephardt and Jesse Jackson.

THE WORKPLACE

Futurist John Diebold believes it will soon be normal for people to alternate a year of work with a year of study throughout their entire lives. He believes continuing education will be the future's answer to unemployment. Instruction will cost far less than it does today and computerization will ensure a high quality and consistency in education. He sees America able to compete with the rest of the world in manufacturing because factory automation will reduce our dependence on expensive human labor. He suggests we will have 50,000 industrial robots working in our factories by 2010.[27]

It's true the high-tech workplace depends more than ever on highly trained people. Fewer may be required but those that are will be critical. Mistakes can cause enormous damage. These technologies simply cannot be operated safely with people who are not committed. More companies are installing work systems that emphasize broader-based jobs, teamwork, participative managers and multiskilled workers. The concept of semi-autonomous teams originated, in the British coal mines in the late 1940s but has been revised and refined in the last few years by the Japanese.

The Japanese team approach is very appealing to the egalitarian spirit lying dormant in most Americans. The Japanese have done away with executive privilege and its exclusive wash rooms, parking spaces and special dining areas and instead managers have become "just one of the boys". Employees (associates) are trained to perform several jobs geared to increase their value to the company and enhance their own feeling of self-worth. Because everyone performs several tasks, other team members pick up the slack if anyone goofs off, which builds peer-pressure disipline into the line. It has been found that semi-autonomous teams (teams that function without first-line supervisors, set their own work pace within limits set by management, and enjoy an input into the compensation, scheduling and hiring and firing of members) are 30 percent to 50 percent more productive than their conventional counterparts.

Talk about other countries taking our high paying jobs is nonsense. Japan and Europe are experiencing the same labor problems only whereas we blame Japan the Japanese heap blame on the Koreans.

Even Japan, the shinning example to the rest of the world when it comes to labor relations, has had its problems. Nissan, that country's number two auto manufacturer, seems to be a victim of a situation which started long before the appreciation of the yen, although the exchange rate changes have exacerbated the situation recently to be sure. In 1953 Nissan's management made a deal with union leaders giving the union a large voice in decision making. In the late 1970s the union had its say about establishing plants in Europe and the United States. In-fighting broke out which stifled the creative process. Damon Darlin, writing for the *Wall Street Journal,* reported a Nissan insider as saying "People with original ideas couldn't develop them...All the efforts were channeled at guessing what the bosses wanted rather than building the best car."[28] (Listen up America and consider carefully the examples you are constantly being told to follow!) Nissan is in a downward spiral which may unfortunately prove to be irreversible.

If you have been thinking the report by BERI might be off the mark, how about the book, mentioned in Mr. Darlin's article[29] which holds Nissan up as the successful model and Ford as the disgraceful failure? Recently Ford's fortunes have been rising. It looks like Ford may have the last laugh and we may have another example of "You can't believe everything (or almost anything) you hear".

Market share is not something that anyone expected Japanese businessmen to give up readily, no matter the aims of respective governments. *Alps,* the largest independent maker of electronic components and computer floppy disk drives, with annual sales in the area of $2 billion dollars, is a case in point. *Forbes* magazine did a piece on *Alps'* founder in which it was reported that in order to obtain the advantages of cheaper labor the firm was considering importing from Korea where it had connections with Gold Star and where it is affiliated with Tatung in Taiwan.

(Mr. Kataoka, *Alp's* founder is) stepping up his manufacuring operations in the U.S. And he's doing what the Japanese always do when under siege:

235

try a little harder.[30]

FREE TRADE? FREE TRADE?
WHOSE GOT THE FREE TRADE?

So what about the workings of the market place? True, buyers have been reduced, thanks to the LDC debt burdens and generally sluggish economies in much of the industrialized world, but why haven't the markets adjusted domestically and globally? The answer, despite avowals to the contrary, is that all governments are using tariffs, restrictions and subsidies more and more frequently.

It has been said that the market place responds to market incentives and rewards winners whereas government responds to political incentives and protects losers. The agricultural policy of the Common Market is based on gigantic subsidies. The European Economic Community (EEC) came into being in 1957 with The Treaty of Rome. Unfortunately a united Europe has come to mean little more than an expensive international social-security program for farmers. The Common Market's extravagent agriculture policy, known as CAP (Common Agriculture Policy 1962) has led the ECC closer to bankruptcy. CAP guarantees prices and offers farmers protection against imports and guarantees them a steady standard of living. Inevitably, miners, auto manufacturers, shipbuilders and other laborers are beginning to question why they, like the farmers, are not allowed to produce as much as they like and sell their surplus to the Common Market. In 1957 the countries of Western Europe were welfare states "where the national governments were considered primarily responsible for the protection and promotion of the economic and social welfare of the citizen" In 1966 the Luxembourg Compromise granted member states the right to veto any Community decision whenever they felt a vital interest was threatened. The ECC started out with 6 members then expanded to 9, 10 and now consists of 12 countries who find it all but impossible to reach any decision. In 1985 the members tried to reform the Treaty of Rome with the Single European Act which has been ratified by every member except Ireland. The Act, among other things, restricted the unilateral veto.

In response to European subsidies, the U.S. spent $20 billion on farm subsidies at home, which caused the Europeans to point a finger here and — nah, nah, nah, — what does it remind *you* of? All that's missing is the sandbox! Who cares who started it? The point is we, the great advocates of free markets and free trade are *subsidizing* !

Just look for a moment at sugar production. A worldwide surplus brought sugar to a low of 2.56 in 1985. Luckily for sugar producers, the USSR went on a campaign against alcoholic beverages and the sugar drinks that were encouraged as replacements brought the world price of sugar up to 6.56 in 1986. Then Brazil began using its sugar cane to make ethanol to fuel its automobiles, Cuba's crop was poor and a variety of events occured so that by 1987 world demand exceeded production. Not that our sugar producers ever needed to worry, mind you. Our government subsidizes our sugar producers and it is a small matter that American consumers pay 3 or 4 times the world price. The Japanese do the same thing with beef and rice. Don't worry, the leaders have it all worked out — no one ever gets hurt but the consumers of the various nations.

Spain and Portugal joined the Common Market and immediately imposed exorbitant tariffs on what had been a $1 billion trade in U.S. grain. What choice did they have? The Common Market increased Spain's tariff on corn from 20 percent to 100 percent. The U.S. threatened to retaliate with tariffs on European gourmet items which would have led to an escalation in price by domestic producers of competing items. Who would have lost? The American Consumer! Anyway Brussels gave in and penalties were removed before they were scheduled to take effect.

FREE TRADE HERE? HARDLY!

GATT requires any country that imposes tariffs to the injury of another country to offer equivalent compensation. If this is not done, under GATT regulations the injured country is justified in its retaliation. The compensation Spain and Portugal offered the

237

U.S. for higher tariffs on agriculture was a lowering of tariffs on U.S. manufactured goods, from 12 percent to five percent. However since the Common Market countries already had access without any tariffs the U.S. was still at a disadvantage.

FREE TRADE HERE? I DON'T THINK SO.

The Institute for International Economics estimated the cost in 1986 for restrictions on apparel was $27 billion to the consumer. The textile industry tried to get the Global Quota Bill through Congress in 1986 and in 1987. They are seeking protection which they don't need. The textile industry rebounded without the benefit of the Textile Bill (Presidential veto was sustained in the summer of 1986). New trade agreements with foreign producers increased efficiency and better marketing techniques all helped. Even with fewer plants, or maybe because of, the industry is now producing more and job losses in 1986 were actually less than one percent. Productivity in the American textile industry is one third higher than Japan's due in no small part to the industry's having invested in new equipment; since 1977 more than a billion dollars a year! The most dramatic gains have come in inventory control. Because of computerized control, mills are able to plan production to be completed and delivered on demand — often within 24 hours. Also the computerized checkouts at retail stores provide manufacturers with immediate feedback on what is and is not selling.

When it comes to the textile industry the government and the industry cite widely differing statistics to support their different conclusions on imports. Industry statistics show apparel imports accounted for 55 percent of the American market; textiles (non-clothing) accounted for 18 percent. The Commerce Department shows apparel imports were closer to 35 percent and private analysts claim foreign market penetration is far less. Nevertheless the 1974 Multi-Fiber Arrangement placed stringent quotas on imports and is one more piece of evidence attesting to our hypocrisy in calling for free markets.[31]

No one denies the subsidies of other nations. Australian and Dutch competitors get anywhere from 30 percent to 70 percent of their marketing costs subsidized through direct government reimbursements. Many countries provide long-term financing at below market interest rates. No matter how large an advantage an American firm might have in quality and price it is not able to respond to the financial interference by foreign governments in multilateral markets. But there are free market alternatives even to the subsidies of others. If we stopped subsidizing agriculture those remaining American free market farmers could under-cut the Europeans and force them to either increase or end their own subsidies, and the latter alternative is the more likely. Hypocrisy has never influenced anyone!

Brazil has an interesting trade policy; "If we make it you can't bring it into our market". The words and the language may differ but the message is familiar. As I said before, this is where America has the mission to be an example—deeds not words. We fault Japan for government support for their auto industry while we applaud Uncle Sam's rescue of Chrysler. Who's calling the kettle black?

In 1981 a quarter of all imports to the United States were subject to some form of U. S. government restriction. Under Ronald Reagan that philosophically distasteful policy has grown to include forty percent of all imports.

The House version of the 1987 trade bill contained a provision sponsored by Congressman John Bryant of Texas which was meant to deter foreign investment in this country. No other industrialized country has anything like it and in fact its enactment would be in violation of U.S. treaty obligations. Actually the proposal is out and out hypocritical since we recently objected to a much weaker, though similar provision coming from Canada. The Bryant provision requires detailed disclosures by foreign investors to our government and would put foreign investors at a distinct disadvantage and severely hamper investment and jobs in this country and set the stage for retaliatory action abroad. (See p. 230) We can be thankful that the Provision was deleted in 1988 from H.R. 3, the Omnibus Trade Bill which contained "everything but the kitchen sink".

On April 17, 1987 the Reagan administration imposed tariffs on some $300 million worth of Japanese imports that either contain Japanese made semiconductors or are manufactured by the same Japanese firms that make the micro-chips themselves. The actual list of targeted goods represented about $900 million worth of goods but officials pared the list to the $300 million level, the amount U.S. officials estimated American firms had lost as a result of a failure by Japan to comply with the agreement made eight months earlier in the summer of 1986. Tokyo had promised to allow U.S. producers to expand their market share of computer chips in Japan, but the U.S. share had in fact declined since the agreement. The Reagan administration intended to replace the 3 percent to 7 percent tariffs with 100 percent tariffs as a retaliatory act against Japanese semi-conductor firms whom they accused of dumping their product on world markets at about 60 percent of cost.

The strategy (threats) had worked to America's advantage on other occasions bringing concessions from the Japanese. At the end of 1985, for example, the U.S. did not have to carry through with its threat to slap tariffs on $24 million worth of Japanese imports to protest Tokyo's refusal to lift restrictions on American leather exports. The hope was that restrictions would not have to actually be implemented in April 1987 either.

However, it would have been costly for the Japanese to give in because the Europeans, with grievances of their own, were watching the situation like hawks. Although Japanese exports to Europe totaled $30.67 billion last year, that was less than forty percent of Japan's exports to this country. Europe is farther away and has weaker ties with and is therefore less tolerant of Japan than we are. The ECC (European Common Market) is not at all thrilled with Japanese assembly plants on their shores, which they believe are built with the anticipation of avoiding dumping duties. Some European observers claim that research, engineering and the higher paying jobs are performed in Japan and that every job in a Japanese-owned assembly plant in Europe comes at the expense of four and a half jobs in a European country.[32]

On the other hand the Reagan administration was reluctant to announce penalties for several reasons. First, Tokyo may have actually begun taking steps to enforce the 1986 agreement;

240

secondly, the Japanese government was, at the time, already reeling from the effects of the declining dollar, and on top of that, then Prime Minister Nakasone was considered to be a good friend in trouble on his own political homefront and this might prove to be the straw...(you know the rest). At the time analysts were not agreed whether the threatened sanctions bolstered Mr. Nakasone's hand with errant micro-chip manufacturers and therefore should be seen as an aid to the Japanese government, or if it would be taken as an insult and work to pull the Nakasone government down.

The Japanese government, like all governments everywhere, has an almost impossible task trying to make citizens do what they do not wish to do. It should be noted that the "guidance" of the Ministry of International Trade and Industry (MITI) doesn't have the force of law.

The Reagan Administration, for its part, was opening a valve in order to release U. S Congressional anti-Japanese steam which had been building to a head for quite some time. Also the administration's action was intended to have "shock value"; to tell Japan that the U.S. meant business and there was going to be "no more Mr. Nice Guy".

How can we criticze the tariffs imposed on our goods by other countries when we put restrictions on imported steel? Since 1982 the Reagan administration has negotiated 18 agreements limiting exports to the U.S. from steel-producing countries.

FREE TRADE HERE?

In 1986 the Administration pressured Japan and Taiwan into limiting their exports of machine tools to the U.S. for five years and set quotas that rolled back the exports to earlier levels on products from West Germany and Switzerland.

FREE TRADE HERE?

The U.S. also limited the growth of the "Pacific Tigers" textile exports to less than one percent a year.

FREE TRADE HERE?

Where is principle? An America that stands for nothing can hardly be taken seriously by its own citizens, let alone the rest of the world!

A record that distant from the Reagan ideology invites suspicion. Maybe one who didn't know any better might conclude that a president who has made "Do as I say, not as I do" a motto has been trying to function with hands tied by an unfriendly Congress.

But holding the President's tied hands to the fire — any President's — and making him adhere to rigid trigger responses such as those mandated by the Gephardt Amendment to the 1987 House Omnibus Trade Bill is both dangerous and stupid. America should lead the way to a solution rather than making itself part of the problem. Maybe if the United States adhered to a free market policy and refused to play ball with those who didn't reciprocate, some headway could be made.

OVERCAPACITY

Global abundance lessens the neccessity, if not the ardor, for trade. It is difficult to transcend overcapacity. With demand for the world's goods already weak, belt tightening by the world's largest consumer will only make it weaker. America has been everyone's prime market.

Overcapacity can be seen clearly in auto manufacturing. Japan's nine auto makers will be adding almost two million more cars to the already glutted market when Daihatsu Motors locates in Canada. And don't forget Korea, Yugoslavia, Thailand, Taiwan, Malaysia. Everybody and his uncle is getting in on the act! U.S. competitors will end up closing plants; does that make sense?

Take a look at the iron ore industry which spent over $4 billion in updating and modernizing its plants and equipment in the seventies, even winning the cooperation of its employees. At one operation hourly output rose more than 50 percent over a five year period. But none of that was enough to stop the rising tide of change. In 1986 the production of iron ore was less than half the 1979 production peak of 85.7 million tons. Without a healthy steel industry, iron was out and the overcapacity in the steel industry is almost obscene! John Jacobson, an economist at Chase Econo-metrics, was quoted in the *Wall Street Journal:* "... only if the entire U.S. steel industry shuts down, would demand equal supply in the non-communist world."

Four of America's seven largest steelmakers sold equity stakes to Japanese companies or formed joint ventures with them. Capital was too expensive for American steel to modernize in the late seventies when the Japanese industry had the support of its government. But to paraphrase a cliche (Is this allowed?) "Into every nation a little rain must fall" and the big five Japanese steel companies found themselves in the midst of a downpour in 1986 with combined losses of $1.8 billion.

The steel industry in this country lost a total of $12 billion between 1982 and 1986. Domestic steel producers spent $8 billion modernizing, reducing raw-steel making capacity and cutting labor costs. As a result they were able to improve their quality and reduce labor costs by, in some instances, as much as 40 percent. By 1988, U.S. costs had fallen to an average $431 per ton. The cost to Japanese steelmakers was $508 a ton, partly due to the rising yen. Naturally U.S. steelmakers picked up some lost market share.

But the ludicrous aftermath of this recent success is a U.S. steel industry currently operating at 55 percent of capacity and unable to close plants as prudence might dictate because of huge pension liabilities. "Chase Econometrics estimates the total cost of closing a mill at $75,000 per employee...a typical integrated-plant closure today would cost over $300 million." [33]

In February 1987, Nippon Steel announced the elimination of 19,000 steelmaking jobs. That announcement was followedd by layoffs by other Japanese steel producers for a total of 43,000 lost jobs. As Charles Hanley reported in the *Wall Street Journal* "The steel layoffs seem to strike at the heart of Japan's "shushin koyo" — the lifetime employment system." [34]

But as you might expect, where there is room to maneuver there is potential. Although *integrated* steelmakers in America are 30 percent less productive than their Japanese counterparts, not everyone in the steel industry is ailing. Referring to Peter Drucker's expertise in this area once again:

> Integrated steel mills still have blue-collar costs of 25%. But the "minimills" operate at blue-collar costs of 10% or less—and they now produce a fifth of all steel made in the U.S. and are likely to produce well over half in another 10 years.[35]

The chairman of the ninth largest U.S. steelmaker, Nucor Corp., wrote an article for the Wall Street Journal [36] in which he stated that his company had been profitable for years. Nucor is a minimill, a smaller group of steel producers using a different technology; the continuous casting method (as opposed to the integrated method). As other steelmakers closed facilities, Nucor had built seven advanced minimills over a sixteen year period with its only competition being other American minimills. In 1986 Nucor spent over $10 million on applied research, experimenting with a semi-continuous steelmaking process that could further reduce production costs.

Nucor, as an example of the minimills, will get into the large structural steel business in 1988 and will begin producing flat-rolled steel for the first time. Already their productivity averaged 981 tons per employee whereas the Japanese average was 480 tons. Nucor is a nonunion producer operating under a group incentive system. Bonuses are paid weekly and often run more than 100 percent of base pay.

The Nucor chairman expressed a strong distaste for protectionism which he claimed delayed modernization and cost consumers billions of dollars. He found the current voluntary restraint agreements to be counter productive and was similarly critical of the trigger price mechanism employed by the Carter administration. When the American steel industry is sheltered, world prices on some steel items are $100 to $200 a ton lower than the American price. This encourages American companies to move overseas and undersell domestic manufacturers. An increase in such imports will naturally cause the domestic steel market to contract.

The irony in protectionism is that it helps to bring about the very thing it is meant to prevent.

"A RISING TIDE RAISES ALL SHIPS"

Histroy has shown that leaders, not the people, start wars. However, when I read that workers in all countries are rededicating themselves and willingly sacrificing in the hope of long-range advantage, I fear for the future. Not everyone can win in a zero-sum competition, and everyone seems to be under the illusion that zero-sum is the game we're playing. No one is prepared to lose; blame will evitably be focused on other countries. U.S. Trade Representative, Clayton Yeutter, has already warned U.S. businessmen about arousing anti-American sentiments among lesser developed and newly developed countries.

Our own "Buy American" campaign has started off innocently enough but protectionist sentiment can easily be fanned into something more. Not long ago a lady in West Virginia suggested a *Boston Tea Party* to throw all Japanese products in the ocean. Such a suggestion was more humorous than anything else at the time but it may be well to realize it was prompted by an underlying frustration that is growing throughout the nation.

The same frustration is growing in Japan. Shortly after the April 17,1987 sanctions were imposed, the editor of the *Japan Economic Journal* was quoted: "Most Japanese regard the sanctions as unreasonable and seem to be losing patience with American demands." Sony's chairman Akio Morita reported that some Japanese regard recent trade pressures from abroad as "a second coming of the black ships" which symbolize the West's attempt to impose its will on Japan.

There will be losers in the battle for world markets and losers who have sacrificed and worked hard only to be robbed of their rewards are fertile soil for the ideas of demagogues. Just fifty years ago Adolf Hitler was successful in fanning frustration and envy into hate and war. We must act before it is too late, to give GATT some teeth and to set an example.

THE EIGHTH STEP

(RE: EXCHANGE RATES)

INSTITUTE SOUND MONEY, HOLD FLEXIBILITY IN HIGH ESTEEM AND BEWARE CENTRALIZED CONTROL BOTH DOMESTIC AND GLOBAL

THE 8th STEP

THE POPULAR POINT OF VIEW

The Federal Reserve is largely responsible for the expansion our economy has enjoyed during the Reagan years. A return to a gold standard is tantamount to a return to the dark ages. In the future we must depend on the cooperation of other countries to maintain our own economic health. Although experts disagree as to the relative merits of fixed versus floating exchange rates, it is essential that some agreement be reached among the countries in the near future.

ANOTHER POINT OF VIEW

The Federal Reserve may have too much authority and too little accountability. A gold or similar standard would guarantee stability and economic growth. The differences of opinion among experts regarding what to do about exchange rates only points out the danger inherent in centralized planning and is further proof that an international agreement should be delayed, perhaps indefinitely.

HISTORY OF THE FEDERAL RESERVE

The Federal Reserve Bank came into being on December 23, 1913, and was seen by its creators as a trusteeship dedicated to helping safeguard the integrity of money. Although independent of both Congress and the executive branch of government in the conduct of its day to day business, the Federal Reserve Bank is nevertheless a creature of Congress and can be changed at its whim.

Unhappily Congress gave the Federal Reserve (Fed) power without guidance on how to use it. The Fed's creators sought safety in numbers, hoping in that way to diffuse the power. They not only provided for a seven-member board but also directed that there be 14-year staggered terms. The main power was to reside in a 12-person committee known as the Federal Open Market Committee (FOMC) to include five presidents of Federal Reserve Banks chosen from various parts of the the country. They were to meet nine or ten times a year and decide how much money the economy needed and what price people ought to pay for it.

The Federal Reserve's (Fed's) job is monetary policy. It tries to provide liquidity sufficient for private sector growth and to prevent a banking crisis, while maintaining a steady price level. It does this primarily by buying and selling government securities. The Fed gets securities and the bank gets money that didn't exist before.

According to Washington DC attorney and author, Thibaut De Saint Phalle,

> The Fed was never intended to fund the government, only the private, productive economy.... (Now) the Fed creates money out of thin air, uses it to buy government securities, then returns the interest paid to the government. This amounts to a perpetual-motion machine, taxing future Americans because the present ones refuse to live within their means. [1]

When the Fed purchases Treasury debt it increases bank reserves allowing banks to make more loans and thereby increas-

250

ing the money supply. The Fed, of course, must buy a certain amount of Treasury securities to keep money growth on a steady path. Remember only a fraction of each deposit is held in reserve. In 1981, banks held three cents in reserve for each dollar in consumer savings accounts and anywhere from seven cents to sixteen cents for each dollar in a checking account. Even borrowed money, once deposited in a checking account, allows banks to make several new loans.

"Bank reserve credit" represents the total assets of the Fed which at the end of 1987 was estimated at $240 billion. The Fed creates money while at the same time monetizing a portion of the federal debt. To put it bluntly, monetizing the debt means printing money to pay bills. Restrained monetization stimulates the economy, but unrestrained, it increases inflation. To control inflation the Fed can constrict the money supply by selling government securities. The Fed, having first created the money to buy the securities, gets income from the government securities it holds. What a racket!

THE FED AS BORROWER

In this election year the media and half the candidates can, on any given day, be heard lamenting the deficit. It may seem strange then to point out amidst all this "doom and gloom" that a large deficit reflects the relative attractiveness of U.S. assets.

The attempt to put the United States (the "largest debtor nation in the world") in the same boat with the lesser developed countries, is ridiculous. The big difference is that the LDCs have borrowed the currency of other countries — mainly dollars — and must repay the loans in currencies other than their own. They can't print the repayment; they must make money the old-fashioned way — they must earn it! We, on the other hand, have borrowed in dollars and we can, and do repay those dollars with dollars we — ah — um ahem — *create,* and that brings us back to the Fed again. Creating money nowdays means controlling a

251

ling a money supply. Borrowed money can always be repaid by a country in the currency it controls but the value of that money is another matter.

The Fed differs from other private borrowers in several important ways: (1) its debt is of the highest quality, (2) its financing needs are larger and more frequent, (3) its financing needs are independent of the interest costs paid and can't be postponed, (4) its decisions influence the entire world, (5) its strategy reflects on current and future tax revenue.

According to Lowell Bryan, director of McKinsey and Company, the U.S. Treasury has been issuing more fixed-rate debt than the market can readily absorb. In November 1986, the difference between the 3-month Treasury bill rate and the 7-year note was about 190 basis points. (1.9% — a basis point is one hundreth of one percent.) In April 1987, the difference had gone to 250 basis points, 270 by September '87 and after the October 19th stock crash it was 340 basis points.

> Clearly, the bond market is telling us something. Institutions now holding fixed-rate debt want a hefty risk premium or they won't hold it. It may seem strange to say that Treasury debt is risky. Indeed, academicians have long referred to the rate on long Treasury bonds as the risk-free rate of return.[2]

Sir Alan Walters, formerly an economist in the Thatcher government, advises the U.S. to issue indexed bonds as Britain does. If the U.S. inflates, investors would be insured — it is a useful tool to finance the debt as it decreases the risk of uncertainty.

Treasuries, whereas they may carry no credit risk, certainly carry interest-rate risk and especially for foreign investors, currency-exchange risk. By issuing indexed notes and bonds the government would save in annual interest costs, the difference between the bill and the bond rates. For instance, according to Mr. Bryan, the government would save roughly $9 billion in annual interest cost if the proceeds from $300 billion worth of floating instead of fixed-rate notes and bonds were used, ($300 billion times the 3% differential). In fact the government would be wise to repurchase all existing fixed-rate debt and replace it with indexed instruments. Mr. Bryan points out that

> the floating rate notes and bonds...would improve the soundness of our depository institutions which could safely invest in this debt and still earn reasonable returns on capital. For example, the new capital guidelines that are now being proposed by the world's central banks are likely to require banks to keep only $1.50 to $2 of equity (or less) to hold $100 or short-term Treasury debt. If, for example, banks invested their money-market deposits in these floating-rate instruments, and passed on the entire yield to depositors less 0.75 basis point, they would earn a 30% to 50% pretax return on equity (ignoring any increase in operating costs) on the margin, depending on the final form that the new capital guidelines take.[3]

Since short-term rates would rise and long-term rates would fall, there would be less incentive for depository institutions and corporations to borrow short and take interest-rate risk. Since corporate bonds and fixed residential mortgage rates are directly linked to the rates paid on Treasury notes and bonds they too should drop. Best of all, the real cost of capital would fall to the extent that our current high level of fixed rates is due to the federal government requiring investors to assume more risk than they'd like.

(As an argument against indexed bonds, New Zealand found there was open-ended liability for the government and that the indexed bonds served to fan the expectation of inflation.)

INTEREST RATES

According to John Rutledge, President of Claremont Economics Institute, "Every 100 billion dollars of increased federal debt raises interest rates by about six-tenths of one percent". Then how do you explain the fact that government debt peaked in 1967, 1971, 1975 and 1983, all years with relatively low interest rates?

Some economists think it supports the theory that deficits have no crowding-out effect. Others claim interest rates fell

253

beause few businesses or individuals borrow during a recession.

The only certainty out of all this is that we cannot assume that the size of our deficit determines interest rates. If further proof is needed, in 1981 the deficit was $58 billion, and the prime rate was twenty percent; five years later in 1986, the prime rate was down to half that figure despite the deficit's rise to $220 billion.

Henry Kaufman, in his book *Interest Rates, The Markets, And The New Financial World,* rails against the government's excessive borrowing and argues that the Treasury should have analyzed how much lower rates would have been if the deficit had been smaller. By doubling the national debt in five years the federal government has saturated the market for long-term bonds and forced corporations to borrow in the riskier and more volatile short-term market. Mr. Kaufman joins many other economists in viewing our present economy as dangerously over-leveraged.

Until October 1979, rates had been controlled by supplying banks with enough money to avoid major rate swings. Former Federal Reserve Chairman, Paul Volcker tried maintaining a specific supply of dollars circulating through the economy without regard to the actual demand for money.

In August 1986, the Fed cut the discount rate (the fee on loans to financial institutions) to five percent from six percent. The short-term market rates declined but long-term rates rose. Unfortunately it is the long-term rates that serve to stimulate the economy rather than short-term. Some people saw the cut as a sign that the central bank was heading in an inflationary direction.

The Fed has two choices; finance the federal deficit and private borrowing by holding interest rates down (expanded money supply and increased danger from inflation might be side effects) or constrict the money supply and contain inflation (high interest might be a side effect).

But interest rates are a mixed-bag; lower rates hurt some segments of society while advancing others. Many retired Americans and others who depend on interest income have a stake in rates remaining high, whereas lower rates bolster the economy by inticing consumers to purchase big ticket items like automobiles, furniture and homes. Many analysts think that four years of economic growth means a lot of pent-up demand for consumer goods, at least durable goods, has already been pretty much satisfied, so no matter how low the Fed drops the discount rate it won't stimulate additional demand. The tax reform of 1986 which ended consumer interest deductions didn't help in this area. Lower rates also encourage business expansion and are good for holders of bonds.

In his book, *Secrets of the Temple: How the Federal Reserve Runs the Country*, William Greider views the world as "us" against "them" once again, this time the later being the wealthy with money to lend and the former being the little guy needing to borrow in order to get a chance at the wheel of fortune. Mr. Greider argues that inflation is beneficial to the little guy. No doubt it eases debt for the little guy who is big enough to have borrowed in the first place, but raises costs making it hard for the even smaller guy to just get by.

Even worse, the apparent inability of Congress to come to grips with our huge deficit discourages business expansion. Uncertainty breeds contraction, not expansion. Many business-men are especially wary when they realize that historically peace-time economic expansions last about three years and the Reagan expansion has gone way beyond that mark. The influx of new dollars made imports so cheap that our old trade surplus turned into a deficit of record proportions. Others blame the tight money policies of the Fed for forcing the nation to look to foreigners to finance the budget deficit. Conversely, lower rates and less foreign money could mean financing our deficit via money creation which would result in increased inflation. This becomes a catch-22 situation as lenders will naturally demand higher long-term rates to compensate for a predictable erosion of capital due to inflation. Rising debt costs will always mean less capital formation.

Low interest rates go hand in hand with a high standard of living, as evidenced by Switzerland. Companies can borrow from the Swiss Bank Corporation at three percent whereas competitors in the USA may have to borrow at ten percent. Surely Mr. Greider would agree that low interest leads to low cost of capital which leads to the current buzz word — "competitiveness" — which, by the way, is far better than inflation, especially for "the little guy".

THE FED AS LENDER OF LAST RESORT

Under the Depository Institutions Deregulation and Monetary Control Act of 1980, (what a mouthful!) the Fed was made the lender of last resort to approximately 40,000 institutions that accept deposits. When bankers need funds quickly they have other sources besides the Fed's discount window. They can sell certificates of deposit and borrow for a day or two in the federal funds market from banks that have extra money. But the Fed controls not only the discount rate (cost of borrowing from the Fed at the discount window) but the federal funds rate as well (cost of banks borrowing from one another).

In a simple repo (repurchase agreement), one party sells or lends a security to another party and agrees to repurchase it at a higher price, usually the next day. Players are not required to register with any government agency and enjoy immense leverage possibilities as they operate without the minimum capital requirements imposed on most other securities markets. A buyer need put up less cash than the margin requirement of fifty percent in the stock market and can even participate in "when issued" trading in Treasury securities that have been announced but not yet issued, with no cash at all. This is one of those last frontiers you hear so much about, where a man's word is his bond!

Because the prime rate was raised four times in the first half of 1984 the cost of servicing the national debt was increased by $12 billion. Perhaps it's time for the indexed bonds concept discussed above?

THE FED TO THE RESCUE

The Fed first stepped in to avert a non-banking crisis in the 1970 bankruptcy of Penn Central Railroad. Shortly after that episode it rode to the resuce of the commercial paper market, the Drysdale Securities and the Hunt Brothers' silver crisis. The Fed felt good atop the white horse and soon fancied itself as monitor and solver of financial crisis, no longer an entity involved merely in the narrow area of banking.

Once easy money lowered interest rates. Now days the slightest indication that the Fed might ease up on the money supply and investors assume the Fed is purposely going to inflate in order to finance the deficit. As a consequence, the Fed has become overly shy about buying government securities.

Uncertainty pushes interest rates up even while an influx of foreign capital works to keep them low. If foreign capital shrinks faster than the deficit our interest rates will rise.

The United States, as the world's largest debtor nation, is dependent as never before on the willingness of foreigners to bankroll its huge deficit. Many think Paul Volcker is needed to maintain foreign confidence. He carries tremendous prestige in world financial markets because of his success in curbing runaway inflation and the leadership he exercised in controlling the Third World debt crisis that erupted in the summer of 1982. His successor, Alan Greenspan, is less well known in the world banking community.

IS THE FED TOO INDEPENDENT?

It has been said that the Fed is independent within the government, not independent *of* the government — at least that's the ideal.

There have been several unsuccessful proposals to impeach the Federal Reserve's Board of Governors, the Federal Open Market Committee (FOMC) which is the Fed's monetary policy setting committee, and even to repeal the entire Federal Reserve Act. Other measures have been proposed to restructure the Fed by shortening the terms of Governors, subjecting the system to the appropriations process, making the Fed raise its monetary target to specified levels or to target interest rates rather than the monetary aggregates, making the Fed part of the Treasury, and/or by placing the Treasury Secretary back on the Board of Governors (a position which he held, along with the Comptroller, until removed by the Congress in 1936).

The Balanced Monetary Policy Act of 1982 (co-sponsored by 30 Senators) forced the Fed to set yearly targets for positive real short-term interest rates consistent with non-specified "historical levels". A similar bill sponsored by 60 House Democrats would have required the President to express his position on every vote of the FOMC and required the Fed to establish targets for long-term interest rates as well as for monetary and credit aggregates. Congressman Jack Kemp sponsored the Balanced Monetary Policy and Price Stability Act, which, in a complete reversal of the Congressman's 1980 position, directed the Fed to concentrate on lowering interest rates in order to obtain price stability and to lessen its former preoccupation with the money supply. It also called for Chairman Volcker's resignation.[4]

Jack Kemp was not alone in his condemnation of the Federal Reserve. Senator John Melcher of Montana thought the Fed was too independent in its appointments and in 1984 filed a suit claiming that his rights as a U.S. Senator to "advise and consent" on the appointment of high government officials under Article III of the Constitution had been violated by the operation of the Fed. He suggested the regional directors nominate Fed presidents, with the advice and counsel of the Board of Governors, but thought that the presidents should be subjected to confirmation hearings in the Senate. Senator Melcher said: "The country's economy is too important to be decided by invisible officials who work behind closed doors without any accountability."

Neither the Congressman's nor the Senator's action influenced Mr. Volcker. In March 1986, Mr. Volcker told a Congressional sub-committee that even though he might be trimming the Fed's budget to bring it into line with Gramm-Rudman legislation, he would not accept accounting guidelines from the Congress since the Fed's independence might be threatened.

It's interesting to remember that Paul Volcker was an appointee of the Carter administration and had no loyalty to Reaganomics. It was not the policy of the Reagan administration to turn off the money supply so abruptly. The severe disinflation that followed caught everyone by surprise and was especially hurtful to farmers and oilmen. President Reagan is constantly blamed for the deficit but it was really the Fed's policies which brought on the sudden collapse in inflation that set the dollar soaring and caused our export problems. No one had budgeted for such an unforseen situation. Mr. Greider believes a freeze should have been declared for a year or so to enable the various agencies and different departments within government to catch their breaths and adjust.

Some economists claim Mr. Volcker's refusal to purchase Treasury bonds to finance the deficit pushed rates up in the first place. They reason that when bonds are purchased by the private sector fewer dollars are available for private financing and everyone knows scarcity results in higher costs. The Fed allowed the money supply to expand in 1986 then tightened the reins in early 1987. The Fed's goal was, and is, to provide enough money to keep the economy growing but not enough to sink the dollar and encourage inflation; not an easy goal to attain.

Mr. Volcker was wise not to take "Fed bashing" personally. Blame was heaped upon his successor just as zealously by those who blamed the Fed for the October 19, 1987 stock market crash. They pointed out that interest rates had risen 40 percent over the year and yet in September 1987 the Fed again raised the discount rate causing the markets to react. Consequently, we had the crash of '87. Needless to say, an oversimplified explanation.

Mr. Greider, and others, believe the Fed may have too much power. It is true that any mistakes the Fed makes will always have cataclysmic consequences. Mr. Greider is perhaps extreme however, in blaming the Fed not only for the depression of the 1930s but for every recession that has occurred since its founding in 1913.

No one can know with any degree of certainty what the Federal Reserve will do because the Federal Reserve has unlimited discretion and little accountability. It may not be too dramatic to suggest that the U.S. Federal Reserve Bank stands as a sword of Damocles over the industrialized world. The independent central bank is accountable to no one. How can this be in a country dedicated to checks and balances? The only monetary discipline

259

that remains is achieved by market forces that cause an increase in interest rates or a flight from the dollar.

Thibaut De Saint Phalle says there is a "tried and true" way to control not only the Fed but our runaway budget also. He tells us President Charles de Gaulle of France took care of a deficit problem by notifying the Banque de France that it could not increase its portfolio of government obligations. Viola — a thirty percent cut in the country's *next* budget! Closer to home, President Truman would not allow the Fed to finance the federal debt to pay for the Korean War because he feared the chain of events that would be set off; inflation, higher interest, recession. So, declares De Saint Phalle:

> The machine can be turned off. President Reagan should propose that Congress amend the Federal Reserve Act to prohibit the Fed from increasing its portfolio of U.S. government paper. This would immediately force a sharp reduction in government expenditures. [5]

De Saint Phalle is too optimistic. Although the word "immediate" could conceivably apply *after* the Act were amended, there is certainly nothing "immediate" about the amending process itself and the persuasion that would have to take place to get the Congress to assent. Of course one would have to agree the task is less formidable than the alternative more frequently heard — the call for a constitutional amendment to balance the budget.

Meanwhile Alan Greenspan has already had occasion to match Mr. Volcker's March 1986 defense of the Fed's independence. In February 1988, he showed why the Fed's independence is good by refusing to be influenced by Michael Darby, Assistant Treasury Secretary, who in a letter had urged the Fed to ease the money supply. We can only hope that Mr. Greenspan will remember that although a certain independence is essential to enable the Fed to do the job it was created to do, it is not and should not, act as if it is a fourth branch of government!

WHATEVER HAPPENED
TO THE GOLD STANDARD?

Political bantering between the Administration and the Congress is a healthy aspect of American life. The Reagan Administration claims Congress caused the deficit by spending too much money; Congress accuses the Administration of causing it by cutting taxes and increasing defense appropriations. But few would disagree that a primary cause of our high interest rates is the skepticism of dollar creditors who have no assurance, as they had with a fixed dollar-gold ratio, that the dollar will hold its value in terms of real goods.

Lord Keynes was the chief architect of the 1944 Bretton Woods agreement, which committed the U.S. to maintain the $35 dollar-gold ratio. At that time the price of gold was controlled by the London Gold Pool which was the link between international monetary policy and the price level in the world market place. With the dollar linked to the price level through the London Gold Pool, and with other currencies fixed to the dollar, stability was established. Small changes in prices would direct goods and investments to where they were most needed and contracts could be written with some confidence.

Bretton Woods worked until the Vietnam War and its inflation and consequent downward push on the dollar. In the mid-1960s President Johnson financed the rising cost of the war in Vietnam and the equally expensive domestic Great Society program with inflationary bank credit rather than with higher taxes. Consequently the balance of payments weakened and our gold reserve declined. That led President Nixon to cut the dollar's tie to gold to allay a possible run on our gold reserves by foreigners who may have lost faith in the dollar at that tumultous time in our history.

In 1971 there was a massive outflow of gold from the United States, but unfortunately it seemed less risky, in a political sense, to our elected officials, to go off the gold standard and chance economic stagnation and a rise in inflation rather than curb government spending or raise taxes.

The prices of primary products (products from mining, oil drilling and agriculture) were bid up faster and higher than other prices and the price of the assets that produce primary products such as farmland and oil reserves, skyrocketed. Other countries were buying up dollars which were accumulating in the reserves of their own central banks because the United States was reluctant to redeem them at the gold window. Many people argued that after the closing of the gold window in August 1971, foreign monetary authorities no longer had any claim on U.S. official reserves. The claims on the U. S. Treasury may be different now, but they still have an effect on American citizens; they dilute the dollar's value and that means the average Joe-Six-Pac finds he must work harder just to stay in place.

WHAT GOOD IS GOLD?

Everything hinges on people's perception. There must be a promise of reliability which people can trust or chaos will ensue. Investors must have confidence in a fixed value. Belief in a fair and enduring value for an objective standard of economic measurement and exchange is essential for commerce. Yet what we have today is an unpredictable floating value, adjustable at the whim of the Fed. There is no legal requirement that the Fed maintain the value of the monetary standard with gold or any sort of backing. We simply will not learn from history!

Confidence in the stable future purchasing power of a convertible dollar would lead lenders to offer loans for longer terms at lower rates. Historically interest has run three points above inflation. Today loans are six percent above inflation because lenders don't want to be caught off-guard.

When you consider the low two percent interest rate that we paid on our national debt in 1945, a debt which thanks to WW II amounted to 119 percent of GNP, credit has to be given to the fixed-dollar-gold exchange rates. Experts such as Professor Mundell and Lewis Lehrman of the Lehrman Institute in New York, believe that if gold were pegged to a fixed dollar amount today, the national debt could be refinanced at a much lower interest rate.

Policymakers can make rational decisions only if the costs of making an economic choice are known and specific. A monetary unit that remains essentially subject to central bank manipulation, or to political tinkering, will not give any long-term reassurance to the markets.

"The whim of the Fed" is a definite risk; it creates great uncertainty and confusion. Investors only have confidence in a fixed value, otherwise they must hedge against uncertainty. Today there is the added risk that our government might prove to be fickle. A return to a gold standard would not work unless we made it part of our Constitution, because holders of gold would otherwise doubt the government's determination and its resolve to maintain that conversion rate. The gold standard has too easily been abandoned in the past and people would naturally fear that happening again, especially against the enormous volume of credit and paper money now outstanding. Individuals and groups are not willing to leave the problem in the hands of Congress but continue to think and propose solutions of their own.

When decisions are left in the hands of elected officials, we tend to get short-term politically expedient solutions. In the case of gold, the urgent immediate political pressures are overpowering. A gold standard makes it more difficult for our elected officials to spend and tax. You can't borrow as much, as easily, under a gold standard. Now wouldn't that be something? If you can't finance federal deficits you can't create them! The only alternative would be to raise taxes or cut expenditures. (Haven't we heard that choice before?) If fixed-rates were linked to gold, countries would be able to judge more accurately when to stimulate or contract their economies. This stability would focus the entire world away from the short-term and toward the long-term, where America has perhaps the most catching up to do.

When it comes to our budget policy we must learn to think

"long-term". That's why it's so important to work towards a gradual reduction in the deficit over the years rather than looking to reduce a certain amount by a specific date. Too large a reduction in the FY1988 budget could make the slow down worse, and so could any more changes in the tax code.

THE PLAZA ACCORDS

Around 1977 the world economy began to stagnate as a result of greater monetary, fiscal, and trade uncertainty. During the early 80s the USA acted as a locomotive pulling the rest of the world out of an economic slump. After 1980 the dollar went up and both the budget and trade deficits increased.

Before 1985 the exchange rate was allowed to find its own level and the world accepted it. In 1985, unfortunately, that changed.

The original Plaza accord which took place at the Plaza Hotel in New York City in September 1985, marked an agreement by the G-5 (Group of five: United States, Japan, West Germany, France & England) to drive down the value of the dollar. (Not that there is or ever has been a real consensus on exactly what is meant by "the value of the dollar".) Seventeen months later, this time in Paris (The Louvre) the countries pledged an end to the dollar's fall.

Both meetings were practically repeats of events that took place sixteen years earlier. In 1971 the Nixon administration thought the dollar was over-valued whereas the Europeans considered it to be under-valued. Now in 1987 some Americans see the dollar as still over-valued whereas many Japanese have joined with the Europeans to attest to its under-value. In both 1971 and 1987 the nations agreed to compromise and fix the dollar in its track. The Nixon administration imposed a ten percent surcharge on foreign imports and to counter any resultant inflationary effects, unwisely imposed price controls. The Reagan administration used less stringent methods in its attempt to control the dollar in the world market.

THE DOLLAR'S *"RIGHT LEVEL"*

Harvard's Martin Feldstein and Rudiger Dornbusch and Paul Krugman of MIT are among those who applaud the dollar's fall, whereas Ronald McKinnon of Stanford and Robert Mundell of Columbia are among those who believe the fall should have been halted much earlier. This later group talks about the *Law of One Price* which maintains that goods traded internationally should cost the same in all countries when measured in a common currency. The exchange rate that achieves that equilibrium is called the purchasing power parity or PPP. The theory says that if currencies are out of whack investments are distorted.[6] This an excellent example of an honest disagreement with highly acclaimed experts on both sides. Those at MIT say "If the dollar were fixed at its purchasing power parity, the U.S. current account deficit would grow explosively." They believe the dollar must fall before we cut spending or raise taxes. They argue that the suggestion that the trade gap can be narrowed without changing the relative prices of American and foreign goods, "... only makes sense if American and foreign goods are perfect substitutes for one another and that's obviously untrue." (Paul Krugman of MIT)

The rationale for allowing the dollar to drop until it reaches the right level is that the lower the dollar goes the less risk that it should go down further. But no one knows the "right level" of the dollar. If, however, money keeps flowing into the USA the economy will overheat. The trade balance improved by $40 billion over the last year and with the economy essentially at full employment, there is a danger of inflation. Intermediate goods, like pulp, paper and chemicals are already working at full capacity and have trouble meeting their export orders. It is not unreasonable to suggest that if the dollar overshot upwards in 1985 by 40 percent, why not down?

Pierre Reinfert, former adviser to several U.S. presidents,

265

claims it was dumb to force the dollar down. According to Mr. Reinfert, James Baker is the worst Secretary of the Treasury in history. "Knocking your own currency is pure insanity!", he said. "We should keep the dollar strong. Interest rates are going up and inflation is on the way." Supply-siders and Paul Volcker fear that a collapse of the dollar might trigger the flight of foreign capital from the USA, leaving us high and dry and forced to grapple with inflation.

Driving down the dollar temporarily improved the income statements of American farmers and international corporations, though it may also have contributed to the boom-and-bust scenario on Wall Street.

There are several indexes; some average the dollar's value against the currencies of our traditional trading partners, others include the currencies of newly industralized countries. Depending on the number and mix of currencies that are included in an index, the value of the dollar changes dramatically. When the dollar is measured against the currencies of the twenty-five countries from which the U.S. imports the most merchandise, we see that the dollar had only fallen 9.1 percent between 1985 and early 1987. When averaged against the currencies of all U. S. trading partners the drop is even less — 6.4 percent.

It's interesting that those who advocate free-markets in all other areas find no conflict in advocating an indexing mechanism. They make the case that the dollar isn't a commodity but rather it is a standard.

I tend to agree with those who say if the dollar is going lower let's get it over with. A slow supposedly painless fall only delays recovery as everyone stays on the sidelines trying to catch the bottom and sensing that it is yet to come. We have another policy induced catch-22 situation. A lower dollar would help reduce our budget deficit and a lower budget deficit will lessen the painful effects of a lower dollar. Since the Treasury would be forced to borrow less the Fed could lower interest rates and thus stimulate the economy.

FIXED OR FLOATING EXCHANGE RATES?

A free-market economy works on finely calibrated prices and comparative advantages, and the whole deck is reshuffled if exchange rates swing too far too quickly. It is important to have an objective measure of the dollar's value but almost impossible to achieve. The debate between those who favor fixed-exchange rates and those who prefer floating rates is still going on.

Milton Friedman, a supporter of floating rates, believes that nations will not, at any rate, sacrifice their own domestic policies in order to support foreign currencies which they would have to do under a fixed rate system. Business, as represented by the National Association of Manufacturers and the U.S. Chamber of Commerce, tends to favor floating rates over fixed also. After all, the discipline of fixed rates can be down right dangerous when so little is known about the "right" way to control.

In the 1920s Winston Churchill undervalued gold and over-valued the pound at the pre-war parity which raised labor-intensive export prices while at the same time lowering import prices. Historians concede that these "best laid plans..." were responsible for the underemployment that followed in Great Britain.

Orderly adjustment under the floating system has worked in the past, but many question if it is still workable today. Floating rates have been blamed for the high unemployment in Europe, instability in markets, high interest, bankruptcy and inflation. A fairly strong argument for floating rates is the fact that trade seems to do better under them than under fixed rates. The "float" liberalized the flow of capital across borders, allowing nations a latitude to borrow that didn't exist prior to the float. On the other hand, reformers argue that floating rates have become too unpredictable and tend to interject a chaotic climate among trading partners. The relative interest rates of countries entice investors to leap from one currency to another, setting exchange rates fluctuating in their wake. The Arab oil dollars made it painfully clear that roaming capital is capable of producing a great deal of mischief. Moreover free-floating exhange rates distort the democratic character of government. Instead of being merely accountable to a broad range of American citizens, elected officials

> must struggle daily to win the confidence of a minute group of traders and bankers — American and foreign — who make a market in currencies. Average Americans don't participate in these markets yet currency traders have become one of Washington's most powerful, if least visible, pressure groups.[7]

However fluctuations can be dangerous. In fact it has been determined that a 35 percent fluctuation in exchange rates over an 18 month period can destroy all other economic calculations including the price mechanism. The whole idea behind free markets is that prices direct goods and investments to their highest and best use.

Under a fixed-exchange rate funds could be channeled over time from speculation and hedging into long-term investments. The currencies could be converted directly to gold, or perhaps to a World Central Bank whose credit would act as reserves for the central banks of participating countries, including our Federal Reserve.

On the one hand, under fixed-exchange rates when we hit periodic currency crisis the whole world tends to suffer. On the other hand, without fixed exchange rates long-term investments may simply give way to short-term speculation. Many argue that fixed-rates provide needed discipline and monetary restraint. (Apparently not enough for us to keep our commitment to $35 gold.)

THOSE WHO WON'T LEARN
ARE BOUND TO REPEAT

At the height of the American Revolution there was hyper-inflation, high interest and huge budget deficits. The continental dollar was shunned as worthless paper money. This was cured by Alexander Hamilton's Coinage Act of 1792 which established a convertible dollar based on a sliver and gold standard.

During this same period France experienced high inflation, high interest and other problems brought about by non-convertible paper money called "assignats". Napoleon, like Hamilton, instituted monetary reform and a return to gold convertibility.

Unfortunately, as the philosopher George Santayana reminds us, "those who cannot remember the past are condemned to repeat it". It seems we remember the curse but take our time about recalling the cure. During the Civil War (1860s) the United States government once again issued non-convertible paper money. It should not have been surprised by the resultant high inflation and high interest. Fortunately, during reconstruction, people anticipated the return of gold convertibility, so between 1879 and 1889 interest rates were mercifully low.

POLICY COORDINATION

Both Allan Metzer of Carnegie Mellon University and William Niskanen, a former member of the president's Council of Economic Advisers and now a fellow at the American Enterprise Institute (AEI), believe discarding the February 1987 Louvre agreement may be the best policy for the nation's economic health. The Louvre Accord focused on coordinating economic policies with other countries. In order to stabilize exchange rates, the U.S. dollar would have to be kept at targeted international values. This would mean interest rates in this country would have to rise to support the dollar. You can see why so many economists are against using the dollar to determine monetary policy. The dollar's problem comes partly from playing the role of international currency, a burden Japan does not want the yen to take on. Monetarists say "let the markets decide".

If we refuse to stabilize the exchange rates via a gold or similar standard we have two other choices: (1) Japan and Germany can expand their economies or (2) The USA can join Germany and Japan in deflating.

Most economists agree that since the U.S. accounts for one third of all economic activity in the industrialized world it has to absorb and consume less, whereas the rest of the industrial world has to spend more—especially on new imports.

Professor McKinnon points out that the dollar's decline over the past three years has not been accompanied by a corresponding drop in the trade deficit. Devaluation, as well as making U.S. goods cheaper and Japanese goods more expensive, also lowers economic activity in Japan and raises it in this country. The Japanese aren't big spenders and generally when they buy they "buy Japanese". That's why Professor McKinnon believes an appreciating yen will lead to fewer imports of American goods by Japan so the only way to lower our trade deficit is to bring our spending and income into line by cutting the federal deficit.

Stephen Marris, of the Institute for International Economics, warns us that a devaluation of the dollar without the other two parts of the package — budget cuts by Congress and stimulus in Germany and Japan — is a recipe for disaster.

In the fall of 1986, Japan's ruling Liberal Democratic Party promised to raise public-works spending, but their FY1987 budget actually called for a reduction in public-works outlays. (All governments seem to have difficulty in following through on promises.) The Germans also pledged to increase an already planned nine billion mark tax cut in the hopes it would stimulate the sale of American imports within West Germany. But despite good intentions, as 1987 ended neither Japan nor West Germany showed any signs of faster growth in their economies and they rejected Secretary Baker's call for another round of coordinated interest-rate cuts.

Other countries have the right to guide their own economic policies as independent nations. International economic coordination isn't necessarily needed, according to Martin Feldstein. The USA sets its own economic agenda and, contrary to today's popular opinion, that agenda is not extremely interdependent.

Secretary of the Treasury, James Baker, advocated adoption

of "target zones" in which currency values would be permitted to fluctuate only within prescribed limits. Most other nations wouldn't buy it. Those who advocate target-zones are the first to admit that U.S. policies since 1980 would have clashed with managed exchange rates. Target zones would require the authorities to surrender independent policymaking to a global cause. It's a no win situation — when the rules become too hard to keep the players simply change the rules.

OTHER COUNTRIES HAVE
THEIR OWN SET OF PROBLEMS

In 1986 the dollar fell and frightened Germany and Japan into intervening via their central banks. In the first half of FY1987 the budget deficit was being fully financed by the world's central banks who were simply printing yen and deutsch marks to buy up the excess dollars in the world's financial markets. They spent about $90 billion in 6 months — too costly to continue.

The governments of Europe and Japan subsidize their exporters by supporting the dollar, even at the expense of their taxpayers and consumers. You and I may think that is a foolish policy, but as long as it represents the preferences of those governments and their people, it can go on and capital flows, exchange rates and trade will all adjust in a balanced manner.

The governments of both Japan and Europe are facing the burden of an aging population in the next 15-20 years and are therefore not anxious to consume. (Our "boomers" retire slightly later.) Lending abroad to build up a stock of productive assets for future retirement needs is a high priority in both countries. The USA has been lapping up their savings.

West Germany has a million vacant houses or apartments while Japan's policies have limited the land available for residential construction so that there is a housing shortage. The Germans are congratulating themselves on their trade surplus while their citizens suffer an unemployment rate of ten percent. Sometimes theorists foget that consumption is the ultimate end of all economic activity. Some even suppose it is a zero-sum game; that if we consume more there is less for others to consume. That is nonsense as Adam Smith so elequently pointed out in the *Wealth of Nations.*

Germany's finance minister, Gerhard Stoltenberg, is respected for exercising the fiscal restraint which enabled him to reduce Germany's budget deficit almost one third over a five year period. In December 1987, the West German government ok'd a $13 billion government-subsidized lending program in an effort to stimulate the German economy. It also agreed to tolerate a wider budget deficit in 1988 to support economic growth. Isn't that what we asked for? Unfortunately, due to the fall of the U.S. dollar, the enormous reserves of foreign currency held by the German central bank had to be devalued at the end of the year. The dollar fell to 1.598 marks and 123.7 yen at the end of December 1987 and the German finance minister found himself facing Parliament with a deficit of approximatley 40 billion marks instead of the 29 billion marks he had predicted in November, 1987. This didn't enhance Mr. Stoltenberg's image. There was speculation that the central bank might again purchase massive quantities of U.S. dollars in order to raise the value of that currency and thereby lower the size of its write-down, but that didn't happen.

Countries such as Hong Kong, Taiwan and South Korea have picked up their exports to the United States primarily because their currencies are so closely tied to ours and their goods have not become less attractive to American consumers. Because finished products and components are so frequently imported, American manufacturers are wearing two hats and are sometimes more importers than exporters. This means that the currency devaluation has changed little for them, perhaps in some instances even making what they must export more expensive.

Then you have the unruly businessmen who critics might acuse of marching to the drummer of greed. Instead of taking advantage of the lower dollar by expanding market share, as "planners" planned, they simply raise their prices at home to match the imports. (Oh for a totalitarian state! We'd show those

272

guys!)

In 1986 Taiwan had a $16 billion trade surplus with the USA. Foreign exchange reserves were building at a rate of $2 billion a month in 1987. Taiwan, with only negligible debt, has been storing large foreign exchange reserves estimated to exceed $40 billion, only a little less than that of West Germany. This is proof to many observers that Taiwan's dollar is grossly undervalued. In Taiwan the central bank buys all dollars and other currencies earned in trade from exporters. The NT, or "New Taiwan" dollars, were issued at an increasing rate as the value of the American dollar sank and the government exchanged them with NTs. This, of course, increases the danger of inflation. But Taiwan depends on exports so it has held the appreciation of the NT artificially low since the first Plaza Accord. This encourages capital to flow into the country in anticipation of an upward adjustment of the currency at a later date. The government can't use the foreign reserves to stimulate their own economy because if they spent much of it they would ignite inflation. Their dilema is too much liquidity and no safe way to spend it.

Naturally American companies with factories or suppliers in Taiwan haven't any incentive to press for a stronger Taiwanese dollar. In fact Taiwan's weak currency is an attraction to many and even the Japanese manufacturers are streaming into Taiwan to escape the recent rising value of the yen.

Banks during the second half of 1987, in an attempt to discourage higher deposits, increased interest rates on small deposits and lowered rates on large deposits. So in 1987 the Taiwanese dumped their money into real estate and the stock market.

The older generation, who still holds the power in Taiwan, remember all too clearly that inflation and the flight of capital played a large part in the fall of Nationalist China. So Taiwan's government is doing what governments everywhere always do when their controls fail to achieved desirable results — add more controls. To discourage currency speculation, in March 1987 the government instituted controls on capital inflows. However, the tight disciplined rigidity that built Taiwan is inappropriate to solve its problems today. People must be free to adjust!

As noted economist Gottfried Haberler told his audience at the American Enterprise Institute (AEI) on December 2, 1987,

> Markets do a better job than governments. It's in the nature of the political process that if the government makes a mistake it's very hard to admit it and even harder to change it, but the markets do change.

GLOBAL SOLUTIONS

But a "hands off" policy makes political officials vulnerable to attack by their opposition. In order to avoid appearing useless they prefer action, even ill-conceived action, to inaction.

Early in 1988 France's finance minister, Edouard Balladur, Britain's chancellor, Nigel Lawson and West Germany's president of the Deutsche Bundesbank, Karl Otto Poehl all began discussing the virtues of a fixed-rate exchange system, perhaps linked to gold. This is especially meaningful if one recalls that Mr. Poehl was one of the original architects of today's floating-rate system and has credited it with a consequential increase in world trade. As for the link to gold, the Bundesbank is said to have the second largest holding of gold in the world — 93 million ounces, so it would have no objections to such a change. Mr. Poehl is not, however, as enthusiastic as some of the other European leaders about the possibility of a European central bank or international currency.

French socialist president Francois Mitterand wants to institute a new world monetary order including the yen, U.S. dollar and ECU. The Japanese have suggested, for want of a better description, an OECD central bank.

Professor Allan Metzer of Carnegie Mellon proposes that central banks of the United States, Japan, West Germany, and the United Kingdom maintain the growth rate of their monetary liabilities, (currency and bank reserves) in relation to the average rate of growth of domestic output (measured in real terms) during the preceding three years. The relation would allow for the trend rate of growth in the demand for money relative to output and would be set to maintain an average rate of zero percent inflation in each country. Other countries could make similar commitments, or fix their exchange rates in relation to one of the four currencies, or remain outside the system. Price rates would continue to fluctuate and exchange rates would vary among the four countries but all policies would be geared to maintain noninflationary money growth. The adoption of this idea would reduce uncertainty, long-term changes would be constrained through similar monetary policies, the system would adjust gradually to changes in money demand, it would be easy to monitor and central banks would be required to control the liabilities on their own balance sheets.

Traders make money from volatility but governments need stability.

The Reagan administration has reversed its earlier stand on allowing exchange rates to be guided by the free market and has in the last couple years decided to encourage international co-ordination of economic and monetary policies. The purpose is to avoid or minimize the emergence of international imbalances such as the large U.S. trade deficits and the Japanese and German surpluses. Former Under Secretary of the Treasury (1961-1964) Robert Roosa has actively been advocating a closer economic policy coordination among the Group of Five. He testified to this effect before Congress in April 1985.

In his Feb 4, 1986 State of the Union message, President Reagan told the nation:

> The constant expansion of our economy and exports requires a sound and stable dollar at home and reliable exchange rates around the world. We must never again permit wild currency swings to cripple our farmers and other exporters....We've begun coordinating economic and monetary policy among our major trading partners.

In Zurich at the end of June, 1987 Professor Robert Mundell of Columbia expressed his view "that by the end of Ronald

Reagan's second term we would have in place not only a system of fixed exchange rates but a system anchored with gold." [8] (Wishful thinking I'm afraid.)

GLOBAL CURRENCIES

In March 1979, eight participants of the European Economic Community (EEC) agreed to establish a composite currency which they call an "ECU". Nowhere is the ECU recognized as legal tender; no ECU bills or coins exist, but its growing use as a medium of exchange and a unit of account is unprecedented.

Although compared to the eurodollar market, the ECU market is small, the ECU is currently (1986-87) the fourth most widely used unit in the international bond market, behind the U.S. dollar, Swiss franc and German mark, and the fifth most widely used unit for international bank lending, after the U.S. dollar, German mark, Swiss franc and Japanese yen.

A secondary market in ECU bonds has grown up and even ECU travelers checks are available. ECU-denominated instruments exist with floating rates and with currency options entitling the holder to either buy or sell their notes at a fixed exchange rate against the dollar. ECUs are attractive because it would be harder and more expensive for banks to construct their own basket of currencies. The ECU permits them access to currencies otherwise not obtainable, lowers their transaction costs and allows the banks greater market diversification.

It is possible, although unlikely, that the ECU would become a substitute for national currencies in domestic transactions. Since it has no national origin and is treated as a foreign currency in every country where it is used, it is likely to remain and grow only as an international currency offering a stable alternative to the dollar.

Robert Roosa was asked by *Forbes* magazine whether he thought the world would be using only one currency sometime in the future. He replied that probably as close as we'd come would be something on the order of the SDR (Special Drawing Right) which is a composite of British pounds, French francs, Japanese yen, German marks and U.S. dollars. Mr. Roosa thought that as a reserve currency held by central banks, the SDR would be effective in holding the other major currencies relatively steady.[9] But others believe the IMF's (International Monetary Fund) try at a composite currency, the Special Drawing Right (SDR), was relatively unsuccessful mainly because the dollar made up a large portion of its construction and it therefore couldn't serve as a hedge against the dollar. The relatively stable ECU currency basket completely excludes the dollar and is therefore an appealing and effective hedge against it.

According to Ramon Moreno, writing for the FRBSF's (Federal Reserve Bank San Francisco) January 23, 1987 Letter, euromarket deposits held by United States residents totaled $94 billion at the end of 1985 compared to $8 billion in 1975. It is quite possible that euromarkets could weaken the ability of monetary policy to influence interest rates.

> Euromarkets may offset monetary policy in two ways: (1) euromarket deposits held by domestic residents may partly substitute for domestic money (specifically M1), and (2) euromarket lending to domestic residents may offset the effects of monetary policy on the credit market...euromarkets have served largely as an outlet for deposits for U.S. residents rather than as a source of loans to them, probably because of reserve requirements on borrowing from euromarkets. [10]

Mr. Hale, chief economist of Kemper Financial Services in Chicago, believes the United States should start issuing debt denominated in foreign currencies in order to have financing alternatives available if another run on the dollar were to occur before the G-7 nations (U.S., Japan, West Germany, England, Canada, Italy and France) can develop a credible policy package for correcting their payment imbalances. Since right now American-Japanese interest-rate differentials are already being discounted for an exchange rate in 1997 of 80 yen to the dollar, the U.S. Treasury could save money if they adjusted their policy so that the need for such a large dollar devaluation would be unnecessary. The trick is to avoid the mistakes Britain made in the fifties and sixties when business cycles were erratic and everywhere there was an expectation of a crisis. The cost of capital was high and no one was certain how long demand could be sustained and therefore they cut back on investing for the future.

COORDINATION AND CENTRALIZED
PLANNING SAYS WHO?

Certainly the trend is towards more international economic coordination. The Chinese have joined the IMF (International Monetary Fund) and the Soviets would like to do the same. Both countries are moving towards making their currencies freely convertible to Western currencies and consider monetary integration with the West to be a valuable and achievable goal. Without stable exchange rates international free trade is impossible. Although no exchange-rate system is perfect ("The best laid plans...") many analysts believe currency convertibility is the least imperfect.

Remote currencies become significant when it is understood that Fed Chairman Alan Greenspan is toying with the idea of a price standard in currency management which he sees as the first step toward restoring stable currency relationships around the world. As 1987 ended there was talk of enlarging the network of currency swaps — the lines of local currencies central banks make available to each other. This would assure the Federal Reserve ready access to marks or yen if it needs to intervene to defend the value of the dollar on short notice.

Author and noted economist George Gilder believes the Fed should not try to promote exports or manage exchange rates but should stick to the job of stabilizing currency values.

> If the value of the dollar is stabilized against gold and goods, world flows of capital and information will tend to determine relative rates of growth and terms of trade just as they do in the continental economy of the U.S.[11]

Mr. Haberler says:

> free markets do a better job than governments in setting exchange rates. In competitive markets mistakes are quickly corrected...governments are slow to admit a mistake.[12]

He feels the system of floating exchange rates should continue although it may be sensible for smaller countries to peg their

278

currencies to that of a larger trade partner.

> But a general return to fixed but adjustable rates is out of the question for the foreseeable future because it would require a very tight coordination of policies, which simply is not in the cards.[13]

So why all the talk about getting our citizens to consume less while producing more? Who will buy our excess and what will happen to the world's economy if the USA does so?

Author, Peter Peterson is wrong to claim that the world is in a zero-sum situation where gains in our exports must mean loss in the exports of less wealthy nations.[14] Without barriers to trade and restrictions on the movement of capital it would be possible for economies all over the world to increase their output and raise the standard of living of their citizens. Contrary to what Pete Peterson says, this is not a zero sum situation at all!

According to distinguished economist Martin Feldstein, we must abandon the policy of international macroeconomic coordination and remind ourselves that each government has both the ability and the responsibility to deal with its own problems. He believes it's nonsense to presume that "international economic coordination" is crucial to a healthy international economy in general and to continued U.S. growth in particular — there's no justification to sustain such a belief according to Mr. Feldstein. There is little evidence that the pace of economic activity in Japan, Germany and the other industrial countries has much effect on U.S. exports and the American economy.

> We should continue to cooperate with other countries by exchanging information about current and future policy decisions, but we should recognize explicitly that Japan and Germany have the right to pursue the monetary and fiscal policies that they believe are in their own best interests ...we are not hostages to foreign economic policies, ...the U.S. is the master of its own economic destiny, ...our government can and will do what is needed to maintain healthy economic growth."[15]

BRAVO!

THE NINTH STEP

(RE: RESPONSIBILITY)

ENTRUST LDC DEBT TO THE MARKETPLACE, NOT TO TAXPAYER SUBSIDIES AND ADJUST OUR GLOBAL COMMITMENTS

THE 9th Step

(RE: RESPONSIBILITY)

THE POPULAR POINT OF VIEW

Americans are being played for a chump. We are picking up the tab to defend other nations while they use the money they save to compete with us economically. Other countries should provide a reverse Marshall Plan to help us out of our troubles. The key to avoiding recession is to make certain Third World countries have the money to purchase American products. We must pressure American banks, to forgive Third World debt and encourage the World Bank and the IMF to make more loans to these countries.

ANOTHER POINT OF VIEW

America must learn to balance the need for security (defense spending) with the need for commercial competitiveness. If Third World countries have more money there is no guarantee they will use it to purchase American goods. Many people believe the policies of the World Bank, the IMF and other such organizations, do more harm than good.

THE RHETORIC FROM BOTH SIDES

The larger the deficit the more aware citizens and politicians become of American dollars going to foreign countries. In February 1987, Senator Ernest Hollings said,

> We're paying for Japan's defense and education. We pay seven percent of GNP on defense whereas Japan pays one percent of GNP. Forty-five percent of the students in our graduate schools are foreigners; in engineering that percent rises to eighty. Since education in this country is about forty percent government subsidized, in one way or another we are subsidizing our competition.

On January 13, 1988 former Navy Secretary James H. Webb told his audience at the National Press Club that our European allies must assume a greater share of their defense as the United States was overcommitted around the world and it was time to start pulling back troops from Europe, and start worrying about our own hemisphere.

According to Senator Les Aspin of Wisconsin, a member of the Armed Services Committee, in the seventies we made a conscious decision to no longer play the part of "policeman to the world" but the cutting back on defense spending that is going on in the latter half of the eighties is strictly due to lack of money.

By 1970, according to author Ronald Steel, the United States had

> more than 1,000,000 soldiers in 30 countries, was a member of four regional defense alliances and an active participant in a fifth, had mutual defense treaties with 42 nations, was a member of 53 international organizations, and was furnishing military or economic aid to nearly 100 nations across the face of the globe.[1]

Yale University military historian Paul Kennedy worries whether the United States in the eighties has the where-with-all to keep all these commitments. He suggests that this country may be following in the footsteps of once great powers like Imperial Spain around 1600 or the British Empire at the dawn of the twentieth century whose commitments, made decades earlier, proved too burdensome to be successfully handled. (Everyone is in the "comparisons from history" game.) In his best selling book, *The Rise And Fall Of The Great Powers* , Professor Kennedy points out that America today has roughly the same number of military obligations around the world that it had 25 years ago, but its share of world GNP, manufacturing production, military spending, and armed-forces personnnel are far less now.

> given the worldwide array of military liabilities which the United States has assumed since 1945, its capacity to carry those burdens in obviously less than it was several decades ago, when its share of global manufacutring and GNP was much larger, its agriculture was not in crisis, its balance of payments was far healthier, the government budget was also in balance, and it was not so heavily in debt to the rest of the world.[2]

Others believe the decline of the United States of America is more fiction than fact. Sure there is a decline in family stability, educational standards, morals and psychological health, but that's not the economic decline that is being forecast. According to Herb Stein of the American Enterprise Institute (AEI),

> Our economic strength has not allowed us to dominate our allies. It has permitted, and in a sense required, us to bear burdens that others did not. And if we would now like others to take on more of these burdens it is not because our weakness makes that necessary but because their strength makes that possible and fair.[3]

The dollar's decline has hurt Japanese and European investors more than anybody else. Maybe, as Herb Stein suggests, "We can chalk that up as their contriubtion to the costs of the U.S. defense program that is defending them as well as us."

THE FACTS

Politicians are especially receptive to ideas to reduce our deficit in ways that will not hurt constituents. It is only natural then that plans to "make-foreigners- pay-more" are so popular.

West Germany may well be the country that can best afford to take America's place as Military Godfather, but its history has made the very idea distasteful to its own citizens as well as to its neighbors. Japan also, while economically suited for the job, would face opposition from nations such as South Korea and China, who have memories of Japan as an aggressor. Nobody, including the Japanese, wants to see Japan become a military power. Both Germany and Japan were discouraged from rearming after the Second World War and Japan's Constitution and the will of her people has restrained military spending. Nevertheless, according to Katsuro Skoh of the Heritage Foundation, if Japan's defense spending were calculated the way NATO countries calculate, including veterans' benefits, it would be closer to 1.5 percent of its GNP or the equivalent of $32 billion making Japan the third largest spender on defense in the world, only after the USSR and the USA.

Paul Kennedy warns that,

> *if the two superpowers* continue to allocate ever-larger shares of their national wealth into the unproductive field of armaments, the critical question might soon be: *Whose economy will decline fastest, relative to such expanding states as Japan, China, etc.?"* A low investment in armaments may, for a globally overstretched Power like the United States, leave it feeling vulnerable everywhere; but a very heavy investment in armaments, while bringing greater security in the short term, may so erode the commercial competitiveness or the American economy that the nation will be less secure in the long term.[4]

A few years ago most of our major allies were spending two to five percent of their GNP on defense; we were spending about six percent and the Soviet Union was spending over fifteen percent.

According to Joel Katkin, editor of *INC* magazine, who appeared on CNN's televisions show "Firing Line" on January 12, 1988, Europe's defense is costing the USA approximately $133 billion a year whereas the Europeans themselves are paying only $83 billion. On page 518 of his most recent book, Paul Kennedy says,

According to some arcane calculations, in fact, 50 or 60 percent of American general-purpose forces are allocated to NATO, an organization in which (critics repeatedly point out) the other members contribute a significantly lower share of their GNP to defense spending even though Europe's total population and income are now larger than the USA's own.[5]

We are subsidizing Europe's defense more than Japan's but with less complaining. Even Canada might be considered a freeloader. According to commentator Pat Buchanan, Canada spends only one percent of its GNP on defense, knowing we would come to her aid if the need ever arose. (N. B. In 1985 our Defense Department said Canada spent 2.2 percent of its gross domestic product on defense.)

Some western countries are demanding larger fees for our right to maintain military bases on their soil. In 1987 Turkey, almost doubled its fee, demanding about $600 million in military and economic aid. On the other hand, Japan now contributes over a billion dollars a year to maintain the American bases in that country, and according to the January 14, 1988 edition of the *Washington Post,* recently decided to make an even larger financial contribution to the upkeep of the 55,000 U.S. troops stationed there.

Another surprise may be the fact that the Soviets have occupied four strategic islands in Japan, known to the Japanese as the "Northern Territories" since 1948. Two of the islands, Kunashiri and Etorofu, house a 16,000-man Red Army division including forty MiG-23 jet fighters. Another Japanese island, Sakhalin, is home to seven Soviet airfields and three naval installations.[6] Who's bolstering whose defense against whom?

In 1976 Japan's government decided to limit defense spending to under one percent of GNP. But what most people don't realize is that because its economy has been growing so rapidly, Japan has been increasing military spending at about six percent a year while keeping the proportion to GNP roughly the same.

The Japanese increase in military spending is in contrast to the slight decrease, (taking inflation into account), in defense spending in this country over the past two years. We have heard so much about Japan not carrying her share of the defense burden and not rearming after the Second World War that it is a surprise to some people to know that Japan is the eighth largest military power in the world today.

Left to themselves, the Japanese would prefer to be self-sufficient in defense and not dependent on other countries. The Japanese Defense Agency has proposed building a new jet fighter with Japanese technology rather than importing the fighter from the U.S. The proposal brought an agitated response from Senator John Danforth of Missouri, the state where the FSX (Fighter Support Experimental project) manufacturers are located. The Senator estimated that the planes would cost the Japanese the equivalent of $10 billion if they build them from scratch themselves or $4 billion if purchased from the U.S. Senator Danforth's figures may have been a bit distorted in the heat of the moment but everyone agrees that whatever the actual costs for the planes in each country the $1 billion that Mitsubishi claims it can develop the FSX for is far too low.

One moment we are urging Japan to be self-sufficient in her own defense and the next exhorting her to come to the USA to fill her needs. We need the trade — it's as simple as that. If the shoe were on the other foot you can bet we'd see things differently. Meanwhile our policymakers are hoping the Japanese will be able to "balance their pride with diplomacy", as they put it.

But Americans have no monopoly on self righteousness. Some legislators are getting irritated by the self righteousness expressed by many of our allies with regard to balancing our budget, and recently they have been coming up with ways out of our problem that may not please the hecklers. There may be as much as $40 billion in user fees that can be charged to our more affluent allies for their defense. Our Defense Department issued the following figures showing what was paid for defense in 1985 by our allies as a percentage of their Gross Domestic Product:

Table 6
Defense Allocations As A Percentage of GDP

Japan =1.0	Luxembourg=1.1	Denmark=2.2
Canada =2.2	Italy=2.7	Spain=2.9
Belgium =3.0	Netherlands=3.1	Portugal=3.1
Norway =3.3	WestGermany=3.2	France=4.1
Turkey =4.5	Britain=5.2	US=6.9
Greece =7.1		

Source: Defense Department

Congresswoman Patricia Schroeder has proposed the Defense Protection Act which would impose an import fee on our allies based on defense spending as a percentage of gross domestic product (GDP). The fee would be the difference between the allies' spending and our spending. For example Spain spends 2.9 percent of GDP on defense whereas we spend 6.9 percent; the fee Spain would have to pay under the Schroeder plan is 4 percent—the difference. For Japan, who pays only 1 percent for defense, the import fee would amount to 5.9 percent and so forth.

A California Congressman, Fortney Stark, would impose a user fee on allies for their share of the U.S. military protection in the Persian Gulf based on the amount of Persian Gulf oil they receive. He estimates the NATO nations would be billed $20 billion and Japan would be charged $14 billion under his plan.

It is clear that nations that are now strong enough to take on a larger share of their defense and the defense of the western world, should do so. But they are not children and should not be subjected to some neat little plan hatched by a group of autocratic American politicians. This is not an area for legislation but should be left to diplomacy.

IF ONLY...

Even if, as I hope, we decide to let other nations slowly work out their relationship to us and other countries and voluntarily accept more of, what we popularly call the "burdens of a good world citizen", there are still other quicker ways they can help reduce our help them become credit worthy so they can purchase our products. They become strong so we can regain our vitality and we all co-exist on planet Earth as one happy family forever and ever. There are numerous ways to reach this Utopian condition.

First of all the leaders in lesser developed countries (LDCs) could encourage domestic and foreign investment through legislation, including few regulations and low taxes. This would stop capital from fleeing the country and attract new capital. Foreign aid, especially loans from the World Bank and International Monetary Fund is another source of capital. Of course it is not enough to provide capital; it must be used wisely by the leaders and, as we will see in our discussion, this is not something a lender can control even though attempts along this line have been made.

Presently it is fashionable on Capitol Hill to talk about relieving LDCS from oppressive debt so they will be free to purchase — purchase what? Let's hear it again for **AMERICAN GOODS!** But we forget there are other goods in the marketplace which many consumers believe are superior in quality or may be preferred for other reasons.

Perhaps you are recalling all you've heard about "the best laid plans" and you are right to do so. Let's examine this road to Utopia step by step.

CAPITAL FLIGHT

Misguided government practices send capital fleeing to safer havens and better opportunities. But it is often foreign investment and aid to developing countries that makes capital flight possible. Without capital inflows LDC savers would find it almost impossible to get the dollars or other Western currencies to send out of the country. Instead real goods or assets would have to be exported and this would improve the LDCs balance of payments and debt position, as export earnings would rise. It's the age-old question which all "do-gooders" must continually ask — "What *kind* of difference am I making? Would adjustments take place without my interference that would result in *better* long run results?" Unfortunately most of the capital lent to or invested in many LDC nations doesn't increase production in those countries. This means the LDC gets the worst of all possible worlds: a skyrocketing level of debt and little real productive economic expansion that could service that debt.

During 1986 an estimated $650 million left Brazil, just before that country called for a moratorium on its interest payments to American banks. Brazil, the largest of the so-called Third World debtors, interrupted payment on its debt to private creditors back in February 1987. It owed about $113 billion to foreign banks, governments and international agencies. In November, 1987 Brazil's interest arrears to U.S. banks between February 20 and December 31 was estimated at $4.5 billion on $67 billion debt. In an effort to avoid downgrading its loan, something neither Brazil or American creditors wanted, a plan was suggested whereby U.S. banks would pour two thirds of the interest owed into an escrow account as new loans and Brazil would add one third to it. Nothing was ever settled, but in February 1988 Brazil was making peace with its creditors, promising to bring payments up to date while at the same time requesting additional loans of some $7 billion. During the moratorium Brazil was forced to finance its trade without outside help and found it was unable to get good returns on its international reserves. Brazil's leaders saw that playing ball with their creditors was in the country's best interests and it began actively encouraging foreign investment for the first time. No country can afford to repudiate its debt because access to private investment and the world capital markets is necessary for long term growth.

Between 1974 and 1982, Argentina borrowed $32.6 billion, although capital flight from that country over the same period was between $15 and $28 billion. Capital flight amounted to between half and four-fifths of the country's inflow.

Venezuela, during that same time period, had a capital flight estimated between $12 and $22 billion and an inflow of $27 billion. Mexico's inflow between 1976 and 1984 was $79 billion and the capital flight was estimated between $26 and $54 billion.

And, according to Steven Plaut, writing for the January 8, 1988 FRBSF Weekly Letter "…some analysts believe even these figures are too conservative."[7]

Why does the capital flee? Fear of inflation, high taxation and even expropriation—not uncommon outside the United States of America. As Mr. Plaut points out:

> In unstable political regimes and in some stable ones, (like Hong Kong) wealth is not secure from government seizure, especially when changes in regime occur. Savings may be shifted to overseas institutions to protect them.[8]

Increased activity in the underground economy usually accompanies capital flight. Even in this country the Board of Governors of the Federal Reserve System estimated the size of the underground economy at "…two-thirds of recorded GNP." Imagine what it must be in many of the developing countries where citizens have more reasons to hide assets. The IMF estimated that the private citizens of debtor nations may have had as much as $200 billion stashed in assets outside their countries at the end of 1985.

As for capital flight from the good ol' USA, according to Mr. Plaut:

> We know the total stock of U.S. dollars outstanding based on Federal Reserve bookkeeping (currently about $200 billion). But according to household surveys, Americans report holding only about one-sixth of the currency notes that they should be holding based on the quantities of minted notes out-standing. So where's all the cash?[9]

No, Americans are not shipping their dollars out of the country to hide them from Uncle Sam — at least not in such quantities and not yet. Perhaps if the *Nation's* Arthur Carter had his way the story would be different. Mr. Carter had an op-ed piece in the *New York Times* in September 1986, proposing a one percent annual tax on capital which he argued could generate revenue of $100 billion a year and thus cut the federal deficit in half. He forgot to tackle the problem of illiquidity that would confront those taxpayers whose capital was tied up in something like real estate. This is a perfect way to encourage capital flight! It seems, however that the most likely answer to the puzzle of the "missing cash" is that foreigners are just holding dollars — a flight from their own currency but not going beyond their borders. After all, dollars are used for transactions in many foreign countries — above and underground (drug trade for instance).

If capital that has fled could be repatriated, this would improve the credit rating of the developing country and reduce its "national debt" (gross debt minus gross holdings of foreign assets by citizens). Citizens will only bring their funds home when they are convinced that they will be safe and produce rewards at least equal to those available abroad. Of course one of the rewards might well be the knowledge that one is helping his country recover and grow. (Who's an idealist?)

HISTORY OF THIRD WORLD DEBT

Before beginning our discussion of the ways in which the LDCs obtain capital, let's digress a moment to retrace the steps that brought us to this point. If you will remember, the Third World debt problem was started by excess oil money. Petrodollar recycling has been compared to a shell game. OPEC money came to the banks, who loaned it to the Third World, who bought energy (oil) giving it right back to OPEC and so on round robin.

But the real trouble began in the early seventies with the misguided policies of guess who's administration? Funny how so much trouble can be traced to Richard Nixon's doorstep, but here we are again, this time bemoaning the price controls and increased money supplies that led to inflation that made borrowing so inviting to the Third World nations and everyone else at that time.

Latin American imports from the USA rose 36 percent during the sixties and 338 percent during the seventies. In the eighties a reversal occurred with the U.S. importing goods from Latin America. Latin America supplies us with over $20 billion in manufactured goods, and buys $25 billion of our manufactured

293

goods annually. Walter L. Shipley, CEO of Chemical Bank, reminded his audience at a New York Board of Trade dinner on November 10, 1987 that

> *less developed* Mexico exports to us more manufactured goods than Italy, Hong Kong or France... In six month's time, *less developed* Brazil makes over 600,000 automobiles and exports 200,000 competing directly with our own auto industry... The economies of 15 major debtor nations are now growing faster than we are... (we need) freer trade, lower government deficits, looser controls on industry, coordination of policies for growth, support for the multilateral agencies and, as appropriate, additional bank lending.

Substituting *they* for the developing world and *we* for the developed, Mr. Shipley went on to say

> They and we face the task of rebuilding crumbling schools, and of ending illiteracy and poverty. They *and* we struggle to have stable economic growth. They *and* we share the responsibility of maintaining geopolitical stability in this hemisphere.

Now let's get down to business and examine the various sources of LDC capital, which, rightly or wrongly, policymakers are suggesting is the road to Utopia.

WORLD BANK

First let's examine the World Bank and the manner in which it provides capital to the LDCs.

The World Bank, formerly called the International Bank for Reconstruction and Development, was yet another brainchild of the Bretton Woods Conference in New Hampshire which, as you will recall, was convened to develop ideas to assist reconstruction in Europe after the Second World War. Currently the purpose of the 152-nation organization is to finance loans to developing countries. How? By first borrowing itself! It obtains funds in various countries, including Western Europe, the United States and Japan, through the sale of its debt issues. In FY1986 the bank lent over $16 billion, quite an increase over the less than $1 billion which it lent in the sixties. It is a tenet of the World Bank that political distinctions should not be considered when making loans. Even though the U.S. representative votes against lending to the communist government of Ethiopia, every year money is sent to that country. (A veto is only good when it comes to major *policy* changes.)

Critics think the World Bank should cut back on its staff which was increased dramatically under Robert McNamara in 1972. The Bank now supports economic policy in borrowing countries rather than financing construction, irrigation and other specific projects which require a large number of specialists. The Bank no longer needs a lot of people and could probably get along quite well without its current sixty-one office directors and twenty-one vice presidents.

Others feel the true worth of the Bank is its 7,000 member staff which spreads its expertise throughout the world. Supporters feel that although aid to China made up only .2 percent of China's gross national product, the country was strongly influenced by the Bank in other ways. Although it is supposed to have a somewhat neutral ideology, many observers believe the free market economics which recently surfaced in China can be traced directly to the Bank's influence. Others are skeptical since the original ideology behind the Bank is hardly capitalistic. The philosophy upon which the World Bank was founded maintains that as a matter of course the richer nations have an *obligation* to transfer resources to the poorer nations.

MORE HARM THAN GOOD?

There are many that would say that overall the World Bank has done more harm that good. In that vein, many critics of the World Bank accuse it of standing by to lend new money when debtors get into trouble, which only encourages more policy failures. Short term suffering may be relieved but long term incentives to change are stifled. Why should a country change its policies if it is rewarded with bail outs despite mistakes? British economist, P. T. Bauer, voices the more capitalistic point of view when he says that "To support rulers on the basis of the poverty of their subjects, effectively rewards the policies that cause impoverishment."[10]

Foreign investment was banned in many countries on the grounds that it was neocolonialist. Of course this cut off equity financing and venture capital where an entrepreneur makes a profit only when a venture is successful. Instead the countries turned to debt financing where the risk is on the borrower because the profit (interest on the principal) must be returned to the lender whether or not the venture succeeds. Prohibiting foreign investment also kept technology and skills out of the country that would have been a beneficial by-product of equity investment. But times change, and countries, just like people, learn. Indonesia relaxed its investment laws recently, and now allows some foreign ownership within its boundaries. The U.S. seems to be a slow learner in this area and instead of reversing course after past mistakes seems determined to follow policymakers down the wrong path for all the right reasons. (Aren't Americans supposed to be the biggest-hearted people in the whole world?) But there are optimistic signs too. Take the fiasco in Brazil:

One fifth of the $500 million World Bank contribution to develop the Amazon region (Polonoroeste) was guaranteed by American taxpayers. The Polonoroeste belonged to Brazil's lower classes much as the Western frontier beckoned to many of our pioneer forefathers, only, unhappily in Brazil, the land turned out to be hopelessly infertile. A failed scheme, which could never have taken place without our commitment, was stopped thanks to Congress — at least that's how Representative James Scheuer of New York sees it.[11] (He somehow forgot to mention it couldn't have started but for Congress.)

Currently there is some doubt about the wisdom of damming the largest west-flowing river in India. It is a project costing half a billion dollars and guaranteed to displace approximately two million Indians, flood 360 square miles and destroy 81,000 acres of forest cover and possibly increase all sorts of waterborne diseases. (Aren't you glad we're thinking it over?!)

Hundreds of billions of dollars were squandered on mismanaged government projects that stifled economic progress. Countries whose citizens still traveled in ox-drawn carts were overnight owners of jet airlines. Money was set aside for defense, state pensions and subsidies for government employees and nationalized industries. The litany of destructive policies many governments followed would include tariffs, export taxes and exchange control, high marginal tax rates, minimum wage laws, regulations against lay-offs, compulsory marketing for export crops, control of interest rates and detailed centralized planning.

Much of the policy instituted by Third World countries was brought home by bright young people who studied at one time or another at the London School of Economics and were exposed to what is frequently referred to as the "British Doctrine". The doctrine maintains that wherever possible private ownership should be replaced by public and that an emphasis should be put on redistributing wealth rather than creating it. Property rights were irrelevant in the grand scheme of things. (It's not a misprint — I said "London", not "Moscow".)

Some people believe that the World Bank's original reason for being is now obsolete and that the private sector should take over in helping the developing nations as many religious and other private organizations are already doing. If this were done Americans would not have to witness the dollars they give in an attempt to relieve suffering, going instead to fund socialist enterprises and oppressive regimes. Perhaps the private sector would not have funded many of the projects which have turned out so tragically.

DOES FOREIGN AID WORK?

But this isn't to say that foreign aid, although it sometimes works against planners, doesn't also work *for* them. British scholar Robert Cassen recently published a report titled *Does Aid Work?* He found that in the majority of instances it did. Twenty-five to thirty-five percent of the projects were unsatisfactory, which seems to me to be a pretty high rate of failure and one which could probably not be tolerated by a *private* fund-raising organization. I suppose it is another case of "Is it half full or half empty?" and to be fair, sixty-five to seventy-five percent satisfactory is more than half.

The so-called "power of the purse-strings", also referred to by critics as "blackmail", has worked so well at home that U.S. leaders are hoping to import it to the World Bank and other foreign aid entities. The Bank used to lend for specific projects but now lending is geared toward a country's economic policy. Money is made available in exchange for a commitment to reduce tariffs, or adjust exchange rates or lessen the commitment to socialism. There is no doubt the World Bank is attempting to influence policy-making in the developing world. Whether this is right or wrong, good or bad, is certainly debatable, but more to the point, it has little chance of working. Malcolm Gladwell, writing for *Insight* magazine, would seem to back up my contention:

> The World Bank has always, of course, tried to bring some broader influence to bear with its money, but policy lending is a much blunter instrument, one that could conceivably upset the delicate balance that has existed between the Bank's clout as a lender and adviser and the sovereignty of the recipient country.[12]

At the end of 1986 the United States agreed to reduce its World Bank voting power, which is based on contributions, in order to allow Japan to increase its contributions from 5.9 percent to 7.4 percent. The United States has enjoyed a veto power which, by the terms of the Bank's charter, was afforded to those countries who contributed at least twenty percent to the Bank's financing. If the Japanese contribute more, U.S. contributions, as a percentage of the whole, would drop to about 18.5 percent. A proposal in the charter would change the veto threshhold to 15 percent if this were to happen. (Any comment?)

THE INTERNATIONAL MONETARY FUND

The International Monetary Fund (IMF) is another source of LDC capital. The IMF was founded at the same time as the World Bank and functions as a monetary proctor providing loans to countries with temporary cash problems. During the Venice Summit in June, 1987, Japan proposed to recycle part of its trade surplus to poor nations and the French and British proposed to increase aid flows to poor African nations through the IMF. (Do the politicians bring this up? No — they carry-on about the need for "America to make other industrialized nations shoulder more of the burden", then forget to tell you when they do.)

The IMF recently made a $442 million "policy loan" to the Phillippines in exchange for the government's promise to work on tax reform and liberalization of its trade policies. Most recently the IMF has acted as a broker, coaxing banks to renew defaulting loans in exchange for promises by the debtor nations to practice economic austerity. These austerity programs have been accused of causing social turmoil in the debtor countries and making it hard for the governments to make any headway. Others claim the governments came to the IMF when trouble was *already* brewing, and after disaster struck the IMF's austerity programs were viewed as convenient scapegoats. Nevertheless if given their druthers, most countries would prefer to borrow from the World Bank rather than the IMF because of the conditions that attach to IMF loans. But as we have discussed, the World Bank is trending towards "policy lending" also.

In a free-market environment conditions on loans are set by the market and not a group of men. If policies are correct they will attract investors—that's the only condition that matters. What seems to work the world over is private ownership. Governments in Mexico, Brazil, Chile and even in some African countries are returning state-owned industries to the private sector.

The Russians would like very much to join the IMF and World Bank. The Comecon bloc, the integrated economic system run from Moscow, is $127 billion in hard-currency debt. Providing funds for such an unproductive system would ultimately hurt the world economy. The Soviet economy is essentially unbankable, but worse it is still an aggressive regime. Borrowing, for whatever reason, (and remember 15 percent of its GNP goes into weapons) would be taking money from hard-working capitalists. (Lenin's prediction!) The most we could hope from the Russians, in exchange for financing, would be the offer here and there of small political concessions to Western governments. Nevertheless Moscow has been successful in getting loans at only an eighth of a point over LIBOR (the London Interbank Offered Rate), relying on its credit record and gold holdings. (See p. 330.)

Perhaps North Korea's default on much of its commercial debt to Morgan Grenfell & Co. in London, and Australia & New Zealand Banking Group Ltd. should be a warning to other lenders. North Korea's creditors relied on gold as collateral, but most of the gold is still in the ground. The contrast between South and North Korea holds a lesson for would-be lenders. As the *Wall Street Journal* editorialized in the summer of 1987:

> The government in Seoul was faced with a relatively difficult time following the 'oil shock' of the 1970s. But South Korea adjusted. Today it is bulging with reserves. North Korea, with its rigid command-econ-omy doctrines and state bureaucracy, is incapable of that kind of rapid adjustment. The same thing applies, to a greater or lesser degree, to other Communist systems.[13]

THE EXPORT-IMPORT BANK ETC.

We'll briefly mention a few more lending sources for LDC capital and then get on to a discussion of debt relief proposals.

Ain't it just grand? We lead the LDCs down the garden path and then spend time and concern, not to mention money, to extricate them from *their* folly.

The Ex-Im Bank was founded in 1934 to promote trade with the Soviet Union; an elusive purpose. It draws funds from the Treasury Department and provides rock bottom financing for American exports. It made a modest profit until the late seventies when the difference between the agency's borrowing costs and lending rates hit six percentage points. The Ex-Im Bank was forced to borrow from the Federal Financing Bank at high interest rates but had to lend at lower rates agreed upon by members of the Organization for Economic Cooperation and Development (OECD). Not surprisingly it managed to incur consistent losses over the past decade. Losses have amounted to more than $1.5 billion since 1982. In the beginning the bank was supposed to provide the long-term financing needed for developing nations to buy American big-ticket items, something the private sector was reluctant to provide. (Do we wonder why?) But many experts believe that capital-intensive industries cannot reach the scale needed to stay healthy and profitable by ignoring world markets. Before long another purpose became apparent; to counter subsidies provided by the governments of other countries. Critics like to point out that in recent years the Ex-Im Bank has been subsidizing large profitable companies such as Bechtel, General Electric, Westinghouse and Boeing. In fact, according to journalist Holman Jenkins, the financing of aircraft sales has earned the agency the nickname *Boeing Bank* in certain circles. But Congressman Robert Garcia of New York defends the Bank, insisting that it is attempting to help all U.S. exporters, regardless of their size.

Besides subsidizing "Big Business" in this country, the Ex-Im Bank has been accused of

> foisting costly boondoggles on poorer countries. ...You've got these tiny countries that can barely balance their books, and suddenly they wind up with a national airline financed by Ex-Im Bank.[14]

Loans and guarantees dropped from $12.8 billion in 1981 to only $6 billion in 1986. The agency never writes off bad loans to other governments, preferring to keep up the charade that they will somehow be paid by a new regime in the future. The General Accounting Office has estimated that almost a quarter of the Bank's portfolio is of questionable worth, nevertheless it refuses to put reserves aside to cover these loans. Strange then that John Bohn Jr., president of the Bank can so confidently ask Congress for $3 billion in 1988. Our huge trade deficit makes the refusal of such a request politically impossible. Right now it is almost sacrilege to deny anything that anyone might conceivably claim could enhance trade. After all, the government is supposed to see that the United States sharpens its competitiveness — at least there has been a lot of rhetoric from Washington in that vein. Many free-traders want none of this, claiming that

> subsidizing exports is a sucker's game, one that takes money out of the pockets of consumers and taxpayers, serving it up to a handful of big corporations and tin-pot dictators.[15]

The mood in Congress in the late eighties is anything but hospitable towards requests for foreign aid. Barber Conable, former Congressman from New York, was appointed president of the World Bank in July, 1986. His earlier affiliation with Congress has made it no easier for Mr. Conable to wrench money from that Body, and indeed Congress seems to be taking a coward's stand and putting on a show of budget slashing in foreign aid only. The Reagan Administration requested $183 million for the World Bank in a recent budget and was forced to accept a sixty-nine percent reduction as Congress only approved $56 million.

In1987 the United States pledged to increase its contribution to the International Development Association (IDA), a World Bank affiliate, by an additional $58.3 million. As I write, this pledge has yet to be approved by Congress, and when it comes to foreign aid, Congress has little to fear from American voters by electing to cut back on funding.

It came out during the 1987 Venice Summit that in 1970 the industrial nations agreed to target .70 percent of their GNP to foreign aid. Currently the U.S. donates only .24 percent of its GNP to foreign aid and it is unclear how many governments, if any, have managed to reach the target they set for themselves eight years earlier.

Multi-lateral development banks (MDBs) would leverage additional funding to provide stability and growth in LDCs. At the beginning of 1987 appropriations looked particularly dismal for

302

foreign aid and especially for the MDBs. Congress wasn't in the mood to increase foreign aid while decreasing domestic programs. Although most everyone would agree that foreign assistance is related to our self-interest and is not a welfare program, nevertheless Americans aren't anxious to provide public money to other nations when there are those who are "hurting at home".

The $58 million requested for the Inter-American Development Bank (IDB) was reduced seventy-two percent by Congress. The IDB was created in 1959 as an international financial institution to help accelerate the economic and social development of its members in Latin America. It generally finances only about 50 percent of the cost of a project. Its critics have charged it with lending new money to a member so the member can pay off its delinquent loans. The IDB has 44 shareholders consisting of finance ministers of the governments represented and of these, 12 are executive directors. The directors are chosen 8 from borrowing countries and 4 from nonborrowing countries. The USA has 34.5 percent of the vote as the largest nonborrower, and the other 3 representatives of the nonborrowing countries (Canada, Japan and the representative chosen by Israel and 16 European countries) have 12 votes between them. The 8 Latin American borrowers have 53.5 percent of the vote. Guess who contributes the most to the IDB? Right — the country with the largest vote, but not a vote large enough to control who gets how much to do what. (Why do we do this to ourselves?) According to the Heritage Foundation in Washington D.C., the IDB has extremely socialistic policies, but bank officials refute that. Secretary James Baker has tried to obtain more influence for the United States but without much luck. In 1987 the USA contributed $31.6 million as paid-in capital and $25.7 million for the Bank's fund for special operations. According to Derk Kinnane-Roelofsma, writing for *Insight,* [16] the United States is arrears $31.6 million in paid-in capital payments which it has already pledged and $63.7 million behind in payments to the special operations fund. (I hate to bring this up, and I'm not suggesting a repeat, but the fact is in the 19th century, when our country was younger and more immature, we did stiff the British on our railroad bonds.)

303

Under the restrictions of Gramm-Rudman legislation, foreign aid is going to get cut first. Americans are skeptical about the results of government sponsored foreign aid, a skepticism which was certainly not allayed by the Marcos affair and the whole Phillipine fiasco. Ask the man on the street and he'll tell you that foreign aid goes into the pockets of the leaders in most underdeveloped countries.

YOUR DEBT OR MY DEBT?

Where does all this foolishness inevitably lead? You're right — to more foolishness!

On December 1, 1987 a Senate subcommitte approved a provision concealed in a $13.6 billion measure to finance foreign aid operations in FY1988; part of a larger deficit-reduction package. This provision would allow countries, like Israel and Egypt, to refinance billions of dollars of debt which was issued when interest rates were far higher than they are today. The United States has approximately $19 billion in loans outstanding to foreign governments who used the loans to purchase military equipment and services. The debtor countries naturally would benefit, some estimate to the tune of $1 billion plus. And who else would benefit? The investment bankers who would make plenty underwriting the refinances, *and* the politicians brazen enough to claim the procedure reduces the budget deficit. It does if you think it's fair to use disapearing ink. The government's loans are paid off in cash up front during the current fiscal year and constituents are somehow not told that the money was loaned right out again only at a *lower* interest rate. (Gramm-Rudman, doesn't allow refinancing to be *counted* as savings, but what do constituents know?) After all, our politicians are trying to help other countries get out of debt. What about our own debt? Oh, don't you remember — this is one of those steps that will eventually get us out of debt too — a little patience please!

THE BAKER PLAN — "DEBT-ON-DEBT"

The Baker Plan, named for Secretary of the Treasury James Baker, is the first of many versions of LDC debt relief that will end in a Utopian world. (Do you believe it?)

The Baker Plan was first announced in October 1985. It has since been given many popular names; one, "debt on debt", describes the basic idea. The Baker Plan urged commercial banks to keep lending to debtor nations "for their own good" — "it's in the bank's own interest" is the pitch. (Sound familiar?) Under the Plan, U.S. commercial banks, and banks of other industrialized nations, were asked to lend money so foreign debtors could keep up their debt payments and banks wouldn't be forced into writing-off the loans. Of course that would increase the likelihood that in case of default industrialized nations would be forced to bail out private banks after encouraging them to go out on this limb. This ritual rescheduling of debt whereby we continue to lend debtor nations the money to make their interest payments has been called the "new world of international finance." Former Secretary of the Treasury William E. Simon recently referred to it as "the old world of bankruptcy". The biggest problem is the possibility that the rest of the world would view the United States as having railroaded the LDCs into taking on more debt and adopting policies that are politically unpopular with their citizens. For the United States this is a *no win situation* !

Naturally international commercial banks are not too unhappy with the thought of World Bank guarantees for the loans required of them by the Baker Plan. However if the possibility of governments bailing out private banks got poor reviews, just think how the spectacle of the World Bank doing the same thing will play in Peoria! In 1985 the World Bank guaranteed a small portion of Chile's commercial bank loans but that was billed as an "extreme circumstance". No one is doubting commercial banks could benefit from the guarantee, but the World Bank's credit rating could be hurt in the international capital markets by guaranteeing too much Third World Debt. After all, the Bank doesn't grow its money on trees but is a borrower also.

In early 1987, seventeen of the most deeply indebted LDCs owed about $450 billion to Western banks. To meet the interest payments on all that debt, most embarked on "austerity" programs, meaning they cut back on imports and started concentrating only on exports. This also means they are buying less from this country and, if one were to believe New Jersey's Senator Bill Bradley, there has been as a consequence a loss of 200,000 export related American jobs. (Who can prove cause and effect?)

THE BRADLEY PLAN — 'DEBT RELIEF'

Senator Bradley has a solution: simply forgive a portion of the debt — forget it — write it off!

On October 20, 1987 (right after the stock market debacle) Senator Bradley spoke before the International Investors Convention. His topic was "Third World Debt".

He asked the now familiar question, "Is Third World debt to the world economy of today what reparations were to the world economy of the 1920s?" He stated the not unique opinion that austerity plans were little more than recipes for recession or revolution and said that the debt presently overhanging Latin America is greater than Germany's reparations burden after World War I. The Senator claimed that a million jobs were lost over the last four years in this country because Third World countries couldn't afford to purchase our exports. (Isn't that 800,000 more than he mentioned earlier? Oh well, what's a million more or less? This is one of those statistics no one can prove anyway.) LDCs have had to concentrate solely on exporting goods in order to pay their debts. Import sensitive industries in this country have lost also. We are warned that Third World debt could be responsible for turning the people of the developing countries away from democracy and driving them into the arms of right-wing dictators who promise to improve the quality of their lives. Anyway, as Senator Bradley pointed out, there is always the possiblilty of a Marxist gaining power in one of these countries and simply repudiating the debt. The Third World debt is powerful propaganda in the hands of the Soviet Union. It can be used to drive a wedge between countries.

The Senator believes the only way to give developing countries room to grow is to offer them debt relief — both on the principal as well as forgiving interest. He mentioned the 2.25 percent above LIBOR loans to the USSR and wondered why Third World countries shouldn't get at least the same break. In fact he mentioned that a syndicate of U.S. banks was willing to lend the Soviets at one eighth of one percent above LIBOR! (See p. 330.)

Instead of waving the carrot of more commercial bank loans in front of debtor nations as an incentive to reform, the Senator wants debtors to have the money to purchase U.S. exports. ("Let them eat cake!" — or do I mean "Have their cake and eat it too"?) This, he argues, will lift the U.S. economy. An analogy might be a candy store proprietor standing at the school gate and passing out quarters to improve business at his candy store. Senator Bradley has suggested providing up to three points of interest-rate relief and a three percent loan write-down per year. Critics say this makes it too easy on the debtors who would be getting a deal while either the bank shareholders or ordinary American taxpayers, or both, would be left holding the bag. Of course if you're going to reward the slaggards you darn well better reward those who have managed to keep up with their payments or...(you get the picture!)

The funniest thing of all is that our "leaders" (and I use the term very loosely) expect banks to make new loans after they have forgiven old! The saddest thing is that these leaders of ours are setting themselves up as scout masters or grammar school teachers over sovereign nations. Offering debt relief (other people's money) for good behavior (who's to judge?) as if they were distributing so many merit badges or brownie points. I don't know how long citizens in the lands to the South of us can continue to live with American pomposity and arrogance — wrapped of course, in the traditional "do-gooder's" trappings.

Just before Thanksgiving 1987, Senator Terry Sanford, chairman of the Foreign Relations Subcommittee on International

307

Economic Policy, held a hearing on "Central American Assistance".

The Chairman must have had many previous conversations with his colleague, Senator Bradley, because Senator Sanford pointed out that the United States helped Japan and Europe recover after *the war* and they should now take a turn at helping the Third World, especially Central American countries, for altruistic reasons. We helped them so it's their turn to pass it on. Senator Sanford seemed to think Japan's actions in South America were scandalous. He told those at the hearing that Japan lost money in loans to Mexico and has an imbalance because it needs Mexico's oil. In denigrating tones he spoke of Japan telling other South American countries "help me with Mexico and I'll help you out."

Unbelievably the Committee also seemed to find this appalling. They seemed unaware that the basis for any good relationship is trade — you benefit, he benefits, I benefit. Altruism alone is a feeble reason to act and to expect other nations to act wholly out of altruism is folly. It is far better and more certain to have nations and people acting because it is in their interest to do so. With leaders who fail to understand this basic truth it is little wonder that America so often ends up playing the fool in global exchanges. If we keep it up we'll be walked on just like any doormat. It's time we wised up! Altruism is the province of churches, private organizations and the individual — it is not the province of government — not any country's government. An altruistic person should support the Red Cross and World Relief Organizations.

The following is a classic example of the "holier-than-thou" rhetoric I am talking about:

> Ultimately, (debt relief) must be about what we owe one another as human beings and, in this case, what we owe one another as neighbors.[17]

Balderdash (or worse)!

We owe one another only autonomy; an understanding that we will keep our noses out of each others business. Any other so-called obligation is nothing more than self-imposed pomposity. Mandated debt relief will ensure that the dead-beat LDCs will be cut off from all future funds and so the plan will ultimately be self defeating. Of course there's the central consideration of whether under the U.S. Constitution the government has the right to force private creditors to relinquish their claims to loan repayments in the first place. Creditors too have rights — specifically in this situation, property rights. If compensation is provided, guess who ends up holding the bag? The good ol' American taxpayer once more. (On the other hand there have been court rulings lately — the Hawaiian Land Cases, for example — that say forget the compensation. But that will keep until another day.)

THE MARKET APPROACH PLAN

Meanwhile the ideas for LDC debt relief and their promise to reduce our own budget excesses continue.

Congressman John J. LaFalce of New York would like to see what he calls a "debt adjustment facility" operated through the IMF. It would provide a secondary market for these bank loans creating a manner in which losses can be spread over a significant amount of time and among all the creditor banks. Its purpose would be to restructure the outstanding debt from banks and to purchase loans at a discount and pass the discount on to developing countries. Banks would take somewhat of a loss but would shed the burden of continually renegotiating debt and in the process gain some liquidity.

Financing for the "new facility" would come from the countries running strong current account surpluses. That would mean selling the idea to Japan, the holder of sixty-five percent of the world's current account surplus and West Germany, the country with the second largest surplus. Of course the United States would have to participate, regardless of its trade deficit, meaning taxpayer money would still be used to separate the banks from their bad loans. Is this fair? There's no guarantee simply because the debt has been reduced in size, that the debtor country will pay the taxpayers anymore than they would have paid the banks.

We get back to the underlying premise that Americans shouldn't mind putting up money because if the Third World can become consumers once more it would help our trade deficit and the global economy. Fine, except as we mentioned, there are other reasons foreigners are not buying American products. (See Chapter Seven) What's to prevent them from taking American money and buying German, Japanese or even South Korean products? When it comes right down to it, this is merely another one of of those pitches like the pleas for educational grants to prevent juvenile delinquents from growing into hardened criminals. SOCIAL BLACKMAIL! There seems to be no end to the payoffs demanded for "our own good". Aren't you getting tired of their *"or elses"*?

THE FREE ENTERPRISE PLAN

What we had in early 1987 is the Baker Plan, referred to as a "debt-on-debt" plan; Senator Bradley's "debt relief" and the relatively new "market approach" plan. A plan which I feel is superior to any of these was suggested to me recently by a successful businessman. It is a variation of the market approach but I call it the "free enterprise plan". Simply put the idea is to let commercial banks write-off and buy each others loans without referring to any governmental or centrally controlled entity — period! Yeah, I know — it's too simple to fly! But debt-equity swaps come pretty close to this ideal.

DEBT-EQUITY SWAPS

As former Federal Reserve chairman Paul Volcker pointed out in testimony before Congressional Committees in 1987, the relative exposure of American banks declined about fifty percent between 1982-1986. This made cooperation more difficult for either the

310

IMF or World Bank in putting together a "rescue package" simply because there was in the beginning of 1987 less interdependence than before. The "hottest proposals" since 1987, as far as the banks are concerned, have been the various "swaps".

Although most purchasers in debt-equity swaps are multinational corporations, banks are beginning to realize that an equity investment is a better asset than a note. In December 1986, First Interstate Bank of California exchanged Peruvian debt for minerals and asparagus. (Asparagus?) Bankers Trust Company has an equity position in a Brazilian auto parts company, and also owns 96 percent of Chilie's largest life insurance company and 40 percent of the largest pension fund in that country, all in exchange for debt. Not only does a bank rid its books of a bad loan, and a nation gain relief from burdensome debt, but the economy of the developing country is given a shot in the arm from new investment. The biggest risk is that these governments are not above slapping state controls on foreign investments at a moment's notice, or even confiscating assets. The other thing to consider in the enthusiastic embrace of debt-equity swaps, is that there is far more debt than equity. There's only so much that foreigners would want to purchase and only so much that foreign governments will permit them to acquire. Most experts figure that only about 15 percent of all outstanding debt can be handled by debt-equity exchanges and so other solutions must be pursued concurrently. Debt-nature swaps also have limited application but show the creativity that is out there if we stay away from centralized planning and give it free rein.

DEBT-NATURE SWAPS

Conservation International (CI) is a non-profit conservationist organization which recently purchased $650,000 of Bolivia 's foreign bank debt from a Swiss bank for about $100,000 and then exchanged it with the Bolivian government for approximately 4 million acres for wildlife conservation. Instead of a debt for equity trade, the CI-Bolivia agreement is one of the first debt-for-nature trades and something most LDCs are anxious to pursue as enthusiastically as the environmentalists. In an effort to service their debt, many countries are tempted to exploit their minerals, timber and other resources, which environmentalists want to see preserved. This is the type of solution to the Third World debt situation where there are no losers — no taxpayers to ultimately foot the bill — just winners on both sides. U.S. banks could take a charitable deduction equal to the fair market value of the local currency it received. They could also take a loss equal to the difference between the fair market value of the currency and the original amount of the loan.

Unfortunately, as mentioned earlier, these swaps will only handle a very limited amount of debt so we must continue to explore somewhat less ideal solutions that can be more widely applied.

THE MEXICAN-DEBT SWAP

At the end of 1986, Mexico's $100 billion in debt outstanding included about $78 billion bank debt, of which $24 billion was owed to U. S. institutions. Under the Mexican debt-swap plan arranged with Mexico by J.P. Morgan & Co., creditor banks would be able to exchange a part of their Mexican debt at a discount for Mexican bonds which will be backed by a U.S. Treasury guarantee. (Translation: You and I will see that Morgan & Co. doesn't lose anything!)

However several of the larger U.S. banks were reluctant to accept losses as high as 50 percent and worried about the marketability of the new securities. They saw the risk not only as a loss on the proposed exchange itself, but as an additional loss from the discount which would be demanded by investors who would buy the new securities from them. They pointed out that if the losses together exceeded 50 percent they would be better off selling their debt directly in the secondary market. Of course if all Mexico's debt was exchanged for bonds at a 50 percent discount, interest costs would also be cut in half, making Mexico's overall debt burden much easier to meet. Some authorities believe the banks themselves should decide the discount at which they are willing to swap their loans; others think it would be better to fix the interest rate on the bonds at below-market rates.

On December 29, 1987, Mexico offered its creditor banks the chance to tender their Mexican government loans at a discount for as much as a total $10 billion of new Mexican government bonds collateralized by U.S. Treasury zero-coupon bonds. Mexico hopes to retire as much as $20 billion of debt in this manner. Although the zero-coupons don't pay interest, at maturity they would pay off the bonds' principal.

Many experts think this idea is better than the Morgan plan because it would allow the borrower to get real debt relief, allow the banks to replace some of their bad loans with securities that other investors would likely find more attractive than the interest-bearing Mexican bonds. Instead of having to purchase a "guarantee" this approach would allow the replacement of bad loans with highly safe marketable securites.

But wait — your government is at work! At the moment U.S. banks have no incentive to be realistic regarding the actual value of their loans to the LDC countries because they would be hurt by the prevailing tax and regulatory treatment they would receive if they had to write portions of the debt off. The SEC ruled that even if banks made bids that *weren't* accepted by the Mexican government, they would have to write down the difference between the carrying value of the loan amounts tendered or increase reserves allocated to the debt to reflect the difference. If the banks did nothing they could carry the loans on their books for full face value. What would you do? So much for government regulations! Currently banks can't own more than 19.9 percent of a non-financial company and can only be 'passive investors'. On top of that the new securities were not to be issued as bearer bonds but the owners were to be registered and identifiable. Rating services such as Moody's regard the bond debt of LDCs as far more credit worthy than their bank debt, making the securities just that much harder to sell. Here is another example of the U.S. government undoing with one hand what the first hand is attempting to do — unfortunate, but not unusual![18]

THE IDEA EXTENDED
TO OTHER THIRD WORLD DEBTORS

Some people would like to see the debt of all developing countries exchanged for bonds, but critics point out that it would be difficult for some countries to buy the collateral needed. Supporters answer that The IMF or World Bank could lend the necessary sums to these countries. (Here we go again!)

Richard Flamson III, chief executive with Security Pacific Corp., a California bank with over a billion dollars in Brazilian loans, believes that private banks have had too little to say about solving LDC debt. After all they hold almost three quarters of the total amount owed, whereas governments, the World Bank, the IMF, multilateral agencies and other development banks hold only one quarter. Don't you think Mr. Flamson has a point? He thinks the goal of any policy should be to make the LDC debt marketable. Yet he has little faith in the ability of bureaucrats and economists to solve these problems, especially alone. (Wonder what happened to his faith?)

THE IDEA EXTENDED TO CREDITORS
OUTSIDE THE USA

The Japanese banks have the second largest Third World debt exposure, just below the exposure of United States banks. The Japanese have been unwilling to recognize losses on their LDC loans because they haven't been able to count the losses against profits for tax purposes. (Shades of our own SEC regulations.) That may change early in 1988, however.

Americans are not the only people ingenious enough to get around a law which prevents them from doing what they want to do. A group of Japanese banks set up a company in the Cayman Islands in March, 1987 and sold that company over $800 million worth of debt. The Cayman Islands caper was an attempt to skirt Japanese regulations that would have prohibited them from writing off any part of their debt if they sold only some of it.

SCHEMES OF DESPERATION

Another plan bandied about is to have the World Bank purchase debt at a discount and give it to the countries that are constantly rescheduling their debt. Paul Volcker, when he headed the Federal Reserve, was suspicious of the idea because countries are so different and such a plan would not be flexible enough.

Another variation is the "callable capital approach". Even proponents admit it requires mirrors to make it work. Roughly speaking, if a debtor country asked for an additional $40 billion loan and the World Bank agreed to the debt increase, it wouldn't require a "pay in". There would be no actual outlays only the credit commitments; mere shuffling of paper.[19]

Even less substantial is a proposal by the United Nations World Institute for Development Economics Research that a "Japanese Marshall Plan" be established whereby the Japanese government would grant new loans to the debtors and subsidize and guarantee the loans. (Something you don't voluteer someone else for!)

It is politically tough to talk about committing taxpayer dollars when we are supposed to be cutting back on our own debt. Americans are no more ready to subsidize the debt of other nations and make them more efficient than they are to increase foreign aid. It was interesting that the only person to understand that, at a Congressional committee meeting early in 1987, was the non-elected head of the Federal Reserve. Mr. Volcker labeled these ideas "schemes of desperation".

THANK GOODNESS
FOR AN INEFFICIENT GOVERNMENT!

The LDC debt problem is a powerful force limiting world economic expansion. If the debt issue isn't resolved we could end up with a worldwide recession, but that doesn't mean *any* action is better than no action at all — far from it!

Congressman Walter Fauntroy of Washington, D.C. is a

perfect example of why the ordinary citizen fears efficient government. Even though there is clearly strong disagreement as to the best way to handle Third World debt Mr. Fauntroy is quoted as saying,

> We may not agree on the specifics of what (the) solution should be, but we do agree that something must be done and be done before it is too late.[20]

Oy Veh!

THE TENTH STEP

(RE: BANKING)

REFORM OUTMODED LEGISLATION TO ALLOW U.S. BANKS A FIGHTING CHANCE TO COMPETE IN WORLD MARKETS

THE 10th STEP

(RE: BANKING)

THE POPULAR POINT OF VIEW

The U.S. government (taxpayers) must bail out troubled banks. American banks are the safest and highest rated in the world. The banking sector is making too much money and regulation is needed to keep them in check.

ANOTHER POINT OF VIEW

Bankers are paid for taking risks, therefore it is not right for taxpayers to subsidize banks. The Japanese banks are the most highly rated banks in the world. American banks are at a disadvantage with their competitors because they are regulated in ways their competitors are not.

THE FDIC AND FSLIC

Bank regulators from around the world met in Amsterdam at the end of 1986 and expressed their concern about the dangerous banking practices which they feared might have the potential to touch off a global banking crisis.

According to L. William Seidman, Chairman of the Federal Depository Insurance Corporation (FDIC), banks have recently been folding at an ever faster clip; from 49 in 1983 to 138 in 1986; 80 percent taken over by healthy banks and 20 percent liquidated. According to a report issued by the House Government Operations Committee in Washington DC, of all the banks that failed between January 1980 and June 1983, 61 percent were involved in actual or probable criminal conduct. But to avoid distorting the picture with one-sided statistics, it should be said that 1,700 *new* banks were founded between 1981 and 1985. Nevertheless many experts believe the nation's banking system is resting on quicksand. The collapse of one large bank could lead to the failure of many more interconnected banks; business credit would be constricted and surviving banks would be unable to purchase the bonds that major corporations depend on to finance their operations and expansions. As desperate bankers tried to stave off collapse, loans would be "called in" causing defaults and bankruptcies throughout the economy. Not a pretty scene to contemplate. Additionally, the FDIC could not afford to pay off all the insured accounts.

In the banking industry, deposit insurance, introduced in the 1933 Glass-Steagall Act, is the distorter. The Fed was established in 1913 to see that sound banks didn't fail. The number of bank closures during the Great Depression bears testimony to the fact that it didn't do its job. When one agency fails to do its job the usual government solution is to add another agency and so we got the Federal Depository Insurance Corporation (FDIC) and the Federal Savings and Loan Insurance Corporation (FSLIC). Unfortunately deposit insurance has encouraged poor management.

Equity accounts for about five percent of all funding sources for banks and savings and loans; fifteen percent for consumer finance companies and seventy percent for non-financial companies. Bankers have argued for the inclusion of subordinated debt as well as equity in the regulatory definition of "capital".

Regulators tend to look at capital as a buffer to absorb credit losses, whereas banks view capital as an expensive source of funds. Deposit insurance may act as an incentive for bank managers to resist capital regulation. There is little doubt reform guidelines, which specify different levels of capital requirements for different risk assets and off-balance sheet commitments, will introduce a new dimension to decisions about loans. Banks may continue to take excessive credit and interest-rate risk, but under a new proposal all private loans are to have the same capital requirements whether the borrower is a triple-A company or a potential bankrupt. Government borrowings will have far lower capital requirements which will encourage banks to put their money in high-yielding government instruments. Because under the new guidelines banks won't be able to securitize many types of loans, they will have to supply more capital than required by their actual exposure to loss. Already most U.S. banks are over-capitalized relative to the risks to which they are exposed. A bank has an incentive to either guarantee all of a loan or to retain the loan and the related exposure. Therefore, while there may be far too much capital in the banking system as a whole, there may be far too little to protect the FDIC from experiencing catastrophic losses in a severe nationwide recession. According to financial consultant Lowell Bryan, having everyone raise more capital is not the answer — specific institutions, not the entire industry, is where the problem lies. Congress has over and over again shown its propensity for blanket legislation rather than targeting needs.[1]

The FDIC considers a bail out only when it would be cheaper than closing the bank and that means the largest banks are almost guaranteed a rescue. But as a matter of public policy more banks will be saved in the future out of a desire to give small banks the same type of protection afforded the large ones. The overall cause for concern is that the federal government (read here taxpayers) may well end up bailing out *all* the banks.

In the summer of 1986 federal bank regulators decided to spend $130 million to salvage the failing Bank of Oklahoma; only the eighth bank to be saved since 1933. First Republic Bank of Dallas, which was formed in 1987 by a merger of Republic Bank and Interfirst, was in 1988 turning to the federal government for relief. Reportedly 16 percent of its loan portfolio was "bad", leaving bond holders and shareholders at risk. (The FDIC only protects the depositors.) But FDIC protection didn't stop depositors from withdrawing $600 million from the bank in the first quarter of 1988.

Professor George Kaufman of Loyola University in Chicago came up with a plan calling for a quick closure of a troubled bank while there are still resources to pay depositors and creditors — when the bank's net worth is zero rather than sub-zero. Timely closure would allow more equal treatment of banks regardless of their size, location or nature of their business.

No bank would be too large to fail....The challenge is not to eliminate bank runs, but to harness their power in such a way that the financial system will be both safer and more efficient. [2]

First Republic's size makes it highly unlikely that it will be purchased and absorbed by another bank, the fate of many small banks that encounter trouble. First Republic is the same size as Continental Illinois was at the time of it's rescue by the federal government in 1984. You can bet there will be more such bail outs in the future. And it's not just banks; savings and loans are involved. For example in early 1987, Vernon Savings and Loan in Texas reported $1.35 billion in assets but about $1.7 billion in liabilities. The trouble, according to a report of the Federal Home Loan Bank Board, was "Imprudent and Risky...Lending Practices". Since FSLIC's losses are usually double the amount of a failed institution's negative net worth, in Vernon's case we're talking about $700 million from the FSLIC.[3]

Orginally the Federal Depository Insurance Corporation

(FDIC) was supposed to stop runs on banks, but instead it has effectively stopped depositors from keeping an eye on their savings.

Best selling author and former banker Paul Erdman, on March 5, 1987, told his Commonwealth Club audience that

> Every money center bank in the U.S. gets over half its deposits from abroad...the consensus of the Wall Street types is that it (run on U.S. banks) has a 25 percent chance of occurring.

But no big deal, he says, even if it occurs — the world's money has no better place to go!

FDIC insurance now covers any deposit up to $100,000. If a deposit remains under that $100,000 level it is the responsibility of Uncle Sam to monitor bank judgment. It's time this boondogle for the few (after all, how many people do you know with $100,000 sitting in the bank?) were examined and something was done towards gearing bank premiums to risk and perhaps even trimming the guarantee from $100,000 to a modest sum more in keeping with the average man's savings.

The FDIC presently insures 14,822 institutions with over $2 trillion in deposits. In 1987, for the first time since its founding, FDIC reserves of slightly more than $18 billion were in danger of running out. The FSLIC (Federal Savings & Loan Insurance Corporation) which insures 3,200 savings and loans, was technically bankrupt as 1987 began. Since its beginnings in 1943 the FSLIC has supported itself with premiums from institutions it insures and with income from investments. Even though it has the authority to borrow up to $750 million (that used to be a large amount) from the Treasury, it has never before needed to do so.

The Depository Institutions Act was passed in the summer of 1982. Under its guidelines certain thrift institutions can receive federal promissory notes for amounts equal to 50 to 70 percent of their operating losses if their net worths fall below a specified level. If the losses eventually resulted in the institution's collapse the taxpayers would be left holding the bag. This open-ended liability with no limits to future costs needs to be reconsidered.

The FSLIC is controlled by the Federal Home Loan Bank Board which admits that $6 million a day was going down the drain because of the sick institutions it was keeping alive in early 1987.

The 99th Congress was unable to pass legislation which would have pumped $15 billion into the ailing FSLIC and would also have permitted regulators to sell failing institutions. Mr. Seidman wanted authority to sell failing banks to out-of-state holding companies. Opponents argued that additional legislation wasn't necessary since many state laws already allow such sales. The U.S. League of Savings Institutions incorrectly estimated the FSLIC would have $17.42 billion to cover what is now expected to amount to $16 to $25 billion in payouts over a five year period.

Legislation to raise in the neighborhood of $25 billion over a five year period was put before the 100th Congress. Under the Treasury's plan the Federal Home Loan Banks would have sold debt, backed by zero-coupon bonds, for about $15 billion over a five year period with an additional $10 billion to come from income from other investments and special assessments on federally insured thrifts. What Congress actually passed in the summer of 1987 was considerably less ambitious. The banking-reform bill provided a $10.8 billion industry-financed package for the ailing Federal Savings and Loan Insurance Corporation, banned the creation of any more limited-service banks and prohibited banks from entering any securities businesses until March, 1988.

Some people have suggested that merging the FSLIC with the FDIC would provide nearly $29 billion to handle bank and savings and loan failures over the next five years without dipping into the corpus of the FDIC fund. Former head of the FDIC, William Issac, was not one of them, nor was his successor, William Seidman. Both men were against a merger.

Commercial banks are afraid a merger might mean an increase in their deposit insurance premiums and would amount to the bankers' bailing out the thrifts. The savings and loans are not exactly overjoyed, fearing a merger may mean their ultimate extinction or at least stricter controls. That's chutzpah! It's not as if they were doing such a great job regulating themselves. All in all a merger looks like an idea to please no one.

DEREGULATION

It's an unending circle. Institutions do a lousy job regulating themselves so government steps in. Regulating is the easy part; everyone loves to tell everyone elso how to act. The hard part is deregulation. A lot of people have a stake in maintaining federal and local regulation. Deregulation on the other hand, is like moving a mountain. John F. Kennedy gave it a try when he was president but it took the OPEC created inflation of the 1970s to give deregulation any kind of momentum. First it was the airlines and trucking and then financial institutions — all discussed in Chapter Four.

Regulation Q was a prime example of unhealthy interference by government. Banks, under Regulation Q, were only permitted by law to pay 5 to 5.25 percent to depositors when the prime (most favorable interest rate) was as high as 21.5 percent! Inflation meant that savers were getting less real dollars back than they put into the banks in the first place. Usury laws kept credit cards at eleven or twelve percent in some cases when borrowing elsewhere cost eighteen to twenty percent. When deregulation overtook Regulation Q it was way overdue.

Now critics are claiming deregulation has been the cause of many of our problems and must share the blame for the recent instability in the U.S. financial system. These same critics argue that deregulation allowed banks to venture into riskier activities that they often knew little or nothing about. The present trend is away from removing regulatory oppressions and toward the imposition of new safeguards aimed at ensuring the safety and soundness of the banking system. Now who could be against "ensuring the safety and soundness of the banking system"? Deregulation has become yet a another chicken or the egg question — which is the cause and which is the effect?

Perhaps there is a clue in the fact that only one Canadian bank failed during the 1920s and 30s. Bert Ely, who has written a book for the Cato Institute which details the banking collapse in America in the early 1930s, attributes the Canadian immunity to the fact that ten banks operated 4,000 branches throughout Canada. This gave Canada's banks a broad geographical dispersion for their banking risks. The independent bank, far from being the strength of small town America was its greatest weakness according to Mr. Ely. He believes the banking collapse in America in the early 1930s was caused, at least in part, by the restrictions on branch-banking which kept U.S. banks unnaturally small. In 1930 there were 23,700 banks and only three percent of them had any branches at all. In the early thirties the typical bank failure could be traced to fraud or a local economic disaster (true also today). In 1933 the Glass-Steagall Act became law. Of the 4,800 bank failures during the Great Depression era, most banks were too small to carry on investment-banking activities and therefore there was really no justification, Mr. Ely points out, for enactment of the Glass-Steagall Act which mandated separation of commercial from investment banking.

THE GLASS-STEAGALL ACT

The Glass-Steagall Act keeps the big commercial banks from underwriting corporate securities in this country and competing with the investment bankers. If a transaction is successful the bank is often able to make money from the management fees and also from the profit on the deal itself. The difference between the additional fee income and interest income alone explains why investment banks enjoyed an average return on equity of 26 percent over the past five years while commercial banks had to settle for an average return of 14 percent. But these off-balance-sheet deals stretch the bank's capital in ways the traditional ratios fail to measure. The problem is the commercial banks would be risking depositors' money. The challenge is to restrain their enthusiasm and temper their greed with good judgement in order to avoid results similar to those which came from their earlier plunges into real estate, energy and Latin America.

David Silver, President of the Investment Company Institute, in his article for the April 1987 edition of the *Financial Planning News,* expressed a fear that Congress might be getting ready to repeat what he referred to as the disastrous 1927 McFadden Act. The McFadden Act first permitted national banks to exercise securities powers. Mr. Silver reminded us that the same sensitivities are being appealed to now. Sob stories about bank failures and the inability to compete opened the way for the McFadden Act. (So, is there such a thing as an unbiased viewpoint?) [4]

Although commerical banks currently are allowed to underwrite government guaranteed mortgage-backed securities, such as Ginnie Maes, they generally can't touch collateralized mortgage obligations (CMOs). CMOs are bond-like securities backed by a pool of mortgages whose cash flows are repackaged to obtain securities of mixed maturities. CMOs allow investors and underwriters some protection against prepayments by mortgage holders. If Congress won't let them compete more freely some banks may simply give up their banking charters so they will be free to diversify into other businesses.

It's true that the nation's largest banks have applied for an expanded role in the underwriting of securities. Underwriting involves purchasing securities in a block from the issuing corporations and selling them in smaller denominations to a variety of investors. It's also true that Congress has been urged to pass legislation that would overhaul the Glass-Steagall Act and permit banks to engage in underwriting of commercial paper, mortgage-backed securities, revenue bonds and mutual funds. In contrast to Mr. Silver, Federal Reserve Chairman Alan Greenspan believes commercial banks need more latitude in order to compete against freewheeling foreign institutions and Wall Street firms and therefore hopes Congress will overhaul Glass-Steagall. [5]

The Glass-Stegall Act prohibits banks from being "principally engaged" in underwriting "ineligible" securities. To show that they are not principally engaged banks have proposed ceilings to demonstrate that underwriting in no way makes up the principal part of their securities activities.

At the end of 1986 the New York Banking Department, ignoring the old Glass-Steagall arguments that suggested the largest banks, if not severely restricted, could end up controlling industry, decided both J.P. Morgan and Bankers Trust New York could underwrite corporate equity and debt, commercial paper, municipal bonds and other activities formerly the sole province of the investment banker.

Needless to say investment bankers were unhappy. They claimed the state's action would result in depressed underwriting profits for everyone and that new investment banking talent would be that much harder (and more expensive) to attract.

William Proxmire, chairman of the Senate Banking Committee, plans to retire at the end of 1988 and would like to leave a dismantling of all or part of the Glass-Steagall Act as his legacy. The Senator would like to see new legislation permitting banks to deal in mutual funds, mortgage-backed securities, commercial paper (short-term corporate debt) and some type of municipal bonds.[5]

SECURITIZATION

Over the past few years bank regulators have forced commercial banks to increase their ratios of equity capital to loans (debt). Naturally that gives banks a strong motive for trying to beef up earnings without expanding their loan portfolios. Only a few years ago hocking portions of a bank portfolio was unthinkable. But it makes a lot of sense now when banks want to get loans off their books.

"Securitization" (another new buzz word you are soon to grow tired of hearing) is the packaging of loans for sale to investors. First mortgages now account for $300 billion-plus with securitized auto loans making up another $10 billion annually. Other consumer loans are being considered for securitization; boat loans, mobile home loans, home-equity loans, second mortgages, credit-card loans and even non-performing loans are all examples. The trouble is the best loans are the most marketable and banks are often left with the most risky loans in their portfolios.

Securitization is an idea that has caught on because there is something in it for everybody. Bank regulators were skeptical in the beginning but in 1986 ruled that banks can eliminate the loans

328

through a securities sale as long as the buyers are not given recourse to the bank that first made the loans. Issuers get a financing source which allows them to take the assets off their balance sheet and thereby increase the return-on-asset and capital-to-asset ratios. Investors get a higher yield than they could get with comparable securities. Consumers, because securitization provides greater pools of money for lending, should reap the benefits of lower interest rates on consumer loans.

At the beginning of March 1987, Bank of America announced a $400 million public offering of securities backed by credit-card loans. In this instance investors will recieve the cash flows from repayments but must absorb any losses if the default rate on credit-card loans runs unexpectedly high. Account holders should not detect any difference because the bank will continue to service the credit-card accounts the same as always.

The sale of these loans give banks additional room under regulatory capital-to-loan guidelines to make new loans. In 1987 the capital rules meant that for every $100 in loans a bank must keep $6 in capital.

According to Randall Pozdena, in a article for the Federal Reserve Bank of San Francisco Newsletter,[7] there is a difference between the way leverage is viewed and used by private corporations and the banking industry. In a corporation increased leverage (greater debt to equity) raises the expected return (earnings per share) to shareholders which makes those shares more valuable. On the other hand, reliance on debt weakens the private firm's ability to survive fluctuations in asset value without default and subsequent bankruptcy. Of course tax policy distorts the picture somewhat since interest payments on debt are deductible against corporate income and dividend distributions whereas retained earnings are not.

SHOT IN THE FOOT AGAIN

The United States sometimes seems to be running the race in the wrong direction. First Chicago Corporation in the spring of 1987 announced a $200 million loan to the Soviet Union at 1/8th over LIBOR.(LIBOR=the London interbank offer rate) As the *Wall Street Journal* editorialized on July 20, 1987

> this is a net transfer of resources to an unfriendly adversary at terms many domestic U.S. customers can only dream about. The banks need to wonder who they're going to send as collection agent if these loans go bad.[8]

This is an example of sabotage by a private entity. Now let's examine an example of government meddling guaranteed to dull any competitive edge.

The Community Reinvestment Act (CRA) was enacted in 1977, supposedly to encourage the banking industry to actively participate in economic development activities at the community level. In effect it provided a legitimate avenue for blackmail. The CRA provides the umbrella under which groups protest the merger and expansion of financial institutions. The protests are generally designed, not so much to deny, but to delay the "revenue-generating endeavors" of institutions. According to William Harvey, professor at Indiana's University School of Law and former chairman of the Legal Service Corp's board:

> Demands usually include an assorted menu of below-market interest-rate loans, specific geographical and dollar-amount lending targets, minority business loan emphasis, and outright cash grants to the protesting coalition. Such demands benefit specific interest groups, to the detriment of the community as a whole.[9]

Unfortunately the banking community has found it cheaper to give in to the protestors' demands than to fight them. Not surprisingly, as the victim repeatedly caved in, the number of extortion attempts increased.

> According to Federal Reserve Board statistics, the number of CRA protests filed in 1987 was more than 10 times the number of all protests lodged in 1984.[10]

According to Professor Harvey, although the Legal Services Corp. is private it received more than $2.5 billion in direct

Congressional appropriations during Ronald Reagan's presidency. The Professor claims the worst part of the situation is the fact that taxpayer-funded attorneys (funded by the Legal Services Corp. so ultimately by the taxpayers) not only represent protestors in many CRA cases but often initiate the protests themselves and *get paid.*

> These protests often amount to nothing more than straight transfers of wealth from a productive sector to a non-productive set of individuals. In most cases, the end product actually inflicts economic harm on the poor, who can ill afford the higher cost of banking.[11]

FOREIGN COMPETITION

American banking regulations benefit foreign competition. Thanks to the International Banking Act of 1978, approximately fifteen large foreign banks were exempted from the provision in the 1933 Glass-Steagall Act which prevents American commercial banks from underwriting corporate debt or equity offerings in the United States. This unfair advantage has contributed to today's situation where only one U.S. bank, Citicorp, can be found in the ranks of the ten largest banks in the world (as far as assets go). Last year a subsidiary of the Union Bank of Switzerland managed debt issues for Borg-Warner Acceptance Corporation, Transamerica Financial Corporation and Allied Signall — all in New York. Those foreign banks not grandfathered[12] into the underwriting business in this country have been buying shares in American investment banking establishments. Recently Sumitomo Bank of Japan purchased a $500 million share in Goldman Sachs, one of Wall Street's more prestigious firms in order to break into investment banking in this country.

Foreign banks have had an unfair advantage over domestic banks in another way. Foreigners can own banks in more than one state with no problem whereas it has been illegal in some instances, for a domestic bank to act in the same manner. In 1987 twenty states had reciprocal privileges which permitted any state with the same policy to allow its citizens to hold banks in its state as long as the privilege was reciprocated. The federal government has been blind to this injustice, so it has been left to the individual states to correct the situation — which they did, striking one more blow for federalism in the process.

Many experts believe the banking system's troubles stem from overcapacity — too many lenders chasing too few borrowers.

> Bankers figure that in order to cover reserves, deposit insurance, and other requirements, they now have to build about 1.25 percentage points into the rates they charge customers on their loans. Foreign and nonbank competitors, however, are spared those costs....According to the New York Fed, large U.S. corporate customers now borrow $4 from foreign banks for every $10 they get from major U.S. banks.[13]

Nine California banks now are Japanese-owned.

Former Federal Reserve chairman, Paul Volcker, Douglas Barnard of the House Banking Committee and Senate Banking Committee Chairman, William Proxmire all agreed in 1987 that we needed to allow U.S. commercial banks to compete or we were going to lose our market place to the Japanese and Europeans. Ralph Ziegler, Vice President of the Union Bank of Switzerland in Tokyo was quoted as saying:

> Japanese banks have a market-share-driven strategy world-wide, and it works...I have absolutely no doubt that in the battle for global supremacy the Japanese are going to make it.[14]

The Japanese have about a third of their assets tied up in the Tokyo stock market, which means the Japanese banking system is vulnerable to a stock market crash. (In comparison the U.S. has no assets in the market and West Germany has 2.5% of its assets in the market.)

Last year Japan's banks overtook their American counterparts as the world's largest international lenders, with $650 billion in loans outstanding, compared with $600 billion for American institutions. The Japanese have established banks in Australia and London where some 35 Japanese banks account for 20 percent of all British banking assets. The United States is now host to 38 Japanese banks, including the five largest banks in California.

In February 1988, J. P. Morgan Co., the last of the American companies to enjoy a triple A rating, lost it.[15] About the same time Federal Reserve Board Governor Martha Seger appeared on C-SPAN.

Martha Seger disavowed any protectionist sentiments but expressed anger because of the "unlevel playing field" on which American banks are forced to compete. She declared that the Bank Holding Company Act which controls how foreign banks operate in the United States should be scrutinized in view of the fact that in Japan U.S. banks are not treated on a par with Japanese banks whereas Japanese banks are treated better than U.S. banks when they come to this country.[16]

WHY JAPANESE BANKS CAN LEND SO CHEAPLY

After the Second World War Japan had a very tightly regulated financial system. In an attempt to prevent the concentration of capital in the hands of a few institutions the Japanese put into their banking law a word for word translation of the American Glass-Steagall Act which prohibits banks from underwriting corporate securities. But they did not mimic all American banking regulations. For instance, the Japanese have lower capital requirements than do American banks. While the Federal Reserve Board insists U.S. banks set aside cash, bonds and other low-yielding capital, equivalent to 5.5 percent of their assets, Japanese banks often keep about half as much in capital. That means they can often lend more cheaply; clearly an advantage which is upsetting to American competitors.

Between 1933-47 debt to equity ratios soared in the U.S. but dropped under the pressure of capital regulation in the fifties. The ratios climbed again as deposit protection expanded. Central banks have been talking about making this ratio of capital to assets uniform worldwide. In December, 1987 the Cook Committee for Bank International Settlements announced standardized capital guidelines for banks operating in 11 or 12 countries.

Opponents fear that higher capital requirements may cause

banks to invest in riskier assets in an attempt to maintain a given rate of return on equity. But according to Michael Keely and Frederick Furlong

> the value of the deposit insurance guarantee to the bank rises as asset risk increases....increasing leverage by increasing deposits relative to initial assets also increases the value of the deposit insurance guarantee.[17]

That means a bank, if allowed, can increase the wealth of stockholders by either increasing leverage or asset risk. However any incentive to increase asset risk declines as leverage declines. According to Keely and Furlong, as the capital of an insured bank increases, the bank's incentive to increase asset risk falls. Therefore banks with the lowest capital ratios have the greatest incentive to assume risky asset portfolios. Keely and Furlong take that to mean that the incentive to increase asset risk falls as capital increases (leverage declines) and that more stringent capital requirements would not give banks more of a reason to invest in riskier assets. On the contrary, they claim it would give them less of an incentive to do so. Insured depositors are naturally not concerned with bank risk-taking and are willing to lend to banks at a risk-free rate since their deposits are insured. This provides banks with an incentive to increase asset risk or leverage, leaving the deposit insurance fund (taxpayers) with unconscionable liability. The liability can be lowered by reducing asset risk.

When OPEC money came pouring into this country in the late seventies it had to be recycled and the bankers decided that a lending spree to the Third World countries would do the trick. At the end of 1982 the nine largest U.S. banks had lent 146 percent of total capital, reserves, equity and subordinated debt, to Latin American borrowers. At the end of 1986 the list of problem banks totaled 1,484. Experts set to work trying to reach a consensus as to the amount of capital that might be needed according to the risks taken by each bank. The catch is not all risks are known. Increasing capital requirements at higher-risk banks might well make those banks more careful *if* they and their risks could be identified. The problem stems from off-balance-sheet items and the interdependency of foreign banks, many unregulated, with U.S. regulated ones. Unfortunately it's what you don't know that ends up causing the most trouble.

Japanese banks have picked up large market shares where low interest rates are more important than innovation. This is especially true in the state and local government market where Japanese banks sell letters of credit which enhance the credit rating of the municipality or agency wishing to float bonds or notes. The more a bank is able to increase the issuer's credit, the less the issuer has to pay to borrow money. Japanese banks can offer high credit ratings because the Japanese government can be counted on to bail them out.

The state of Michigan was saved from a budget crisis in 1982 when the Mitsubishi Bank agreed to guarantee $500 million worth of the state's bonds. In 1986 the Bank of Tokyo lent $5 million to a group of New York developers who were building an office complex in a run-down section of the Bronx. The city of Boston, also in 1986, solicited competitive bids on a $100 million note. The three lowest bids were Japanese with the best U.S. bid twice as expensive as Sanwa, the winning Japanese bidder. City officials estimate Sanwa's bid saved the Boston taxpayers somewhere between $130,000 to $400,000 in fees. And Boston's experience was not unique. In December 1986 the Arkansas Development Finance Authority found its three best bids were Japanese and that the winning bid from Sumitomo Bank saved it just under $2 million in reduced interest costs and other fees over a three year period. Sometimes the Japanese earn less than one-tenth of a percentage point for supplying credit, less than half what an American bank might consider to be profitable.

We hear so much about American loans to Latin American countries but the Japanese got burnt in the same market ($40 billion to our $100 billion) and are therefore leary of risky or relatively unknown borrowers. Lending their credit ratings to American state and local governments is a low-risk business where the default rate is far lower than for commercial loans.

Even the most westernized Japanese bankers disdain U.S. and European notions of what constitutes an acceptable profit. The

335

Japanese are willing to forebear profits for ten years in order to build up business. This used to be pretty standard operating procedure for any new business in this country also. However, most of our banks are not new to the market and are being forced to compete with these foreigners who are willing to lend on much more favorable terms. Some Japanese banks offer loans to U.S. businesses at between 1/8 percent and 1/4 percent below the savings rate at American Banks. A deal too good to turn down! Consequently, by the end of 1986 Japanese banks held 8.4 percent of all commercial loans in this country.

The Japanese economy as a whole is a low-profit operation. Sumitomo Bank returns a mere thirty cents on each hundred dollars of assets whereas Citicorp returns 75 percent. (We know where you would want to borrow but where would you want to invest?)

JAPANESE INVESTORS

You might wonder why the Japanese people save so much, especially as restrictive regulations are responsible for the rock-bottom interest rates the Japanese pay their own citizens on savings accounts. You would hardly think this would be an inducement for the Japanese to save, but for them there is little alternative. For instance, buying a hundred shares of a $50 stock can cost a Japanese investor as much as $63 in fees. Between their commercial bank's low government controlled rates of interest and the high fixed commissions charged by the securities firms, there is little choice.

On the other hand, you have probably heard more than you care to about the deplorable savings rate in this country and the disincentives to save built into our tax code and social policies. Saving is for American fools! For instance those prudent enough to have saved rather than practice the "enjoy-as-you-go" philosophy are the ones that end up paying taxes on their Social Security benefits. The savers are never rewarded in this country, but end up footing the bill for the non-savers, who may or may not have been profligate spenders in their youth. When will our policy-makers understand that we get what we encourage?

But in opposition to the message delivered in our social and tax policies, the government urges the purchase of savings bonds. Employees of many companies purchase savings bonds through automatic payroll deductions, a program which raised $5 billion in 1985, enough to cover about 2.5 percent of new government debt. Savings bonds have to be held at least five years to avoid ending up with a return as small as four percent — still twice the best return many young people are expected to get from their Social Security contributions. If held ten years to maturity the rate is higher (varies) and may be a viable vehicle for conservative investors, especially when you consider the tax on the interest is deferred until the bonds are redeemed. U.S. EE savings bonds had a minimum 7.5 percent guaranteed interest rate for quite some time but that was cut near the end of 1986 in order to save the government money and to reduce competition with private offer-ings. In the first half of 1988 a saver could receive 8 percent on a 5 year Treasury and a 30 year zero coupon Treasury (non-callable) was paying 9 percent. At an interest rate of nine percent, savings double every eight years.

In 1983 foreigners added $17 billion worth of Treasuries to their holdings. In 1985 the Japanese increased their holdings of U.S. Treasury bonds by $19 billion, triple the previous year's rise. At year-end 1985, the Japanese held $47 billion of the U.S. government's $2 trillion debt. That was up from $27 billion a year earlier. At U.S. Treasury bond auctions, the Japanese have been known to gobble sixty percent of a new offering. The Japanese and West Germans buy the Fed's newly created dollars in order to protect their export industries and to ensure the value of their own dollar holdings.

Until 1986 Japan's foreign financial investments were limited almost exclusively to the purchase of Eurobonds and U.S. Treas-ury issues which offered a secure return of eight or nine percent, which was a full four percent higher than the yield on comparable Japanese bonds.

However, in the summer of 1986, the yield on long-term

Treasuries, at about 7.1 percent, was low for the Japanese. They generally invest in U.S. securities only when the yield is at least 300 basis points (three percentage points) above Japanese government bonds, which were then yielding about 4.5 percent. Nevertheless that year Japanese banks purchased about a quarter of all U.S. Treasury bonds; in effect funding our deficit.

However as our interest rates began to fall and our dollar continued its precipitous slide, the Japanese suddenly began losing their appetites for our Treasury bills and started buying up prime U.S. real estate and other equities.

In the first quarter of 1987 the Japanese took advantage of the forty-five percent drop in the dollar relative to the yen (from its 1985 high) and began buying our blue chip stocks at a rapid clip (556 on the dollar afterall). All in all our stock market was too good to pass up with American stocks offering higher yields than the Japanese home markets (seven percent vs. little more than half of one percent) and much lower price-earnings ratios (16 vs. 49). Before the October, 1987 stock market plunge, many Japanese brokers had estimated that by 1991 Japan's total holdings of U.S. equities would reach $100 billion or about four percent of all U.S. equities.

Not long ago Japan's seven trust banks and twenty-one life insurance companies were the only entities authorized to manage tax-exempt pension funds in Japan. Japan's pool of retirement savings amounts to over $50 billion and is expected to skyrocket in the next decade as the aging workforce sets aside more and more for their retirement years. The average Japanese retires at 55, earlier than in the United States and can expect to live longer. With a greater need for retirement income and the poor returns that have thus far been produced by their own Japanese trust banks there is a blossoming interest on both sides for American access to those pension funds.

We are seldom told that the need has been on *both* sides; the need for the U.S. to borrow and Japan to lend (invest). The coffers of Japanese banks have become so overladen thanks to Japan's huge trade surplus that the Japanese have no way to invest all that money domestically. In 1987 Japanese banks, insurance companies and brokerage houses were flush with more than $500 billion for investment in foreign countries.

At the end of 1986 the Japanese Finance Ministry liberalized capital flows from Japan. The Japanese postal insurance fund, which is managed by the Post and Telecommunications Ministry, used to be allowed to invest a maximum of 10 percent in foreign bonds. The ministry doubled the amount allowable and also made it possible to invest in foreign corporate bonds. Formerly investments were allowed only in bonds issued by foreign governments and public organizations.

Of course the fact that investments are less restricted abroad has been partially responsible for Japan's recent large scale overseas investments.

Now it is up to policymakers in this country to loosen the bonds they have placed on American financial institutions and to allow them to compete on a level playing field. In an unregulated market place borrowers and lenders are free to make their own decisions and innocent taxpayers are not made to pay for the mistakes of professionals.

THE ELEVENTH STEP

(RE: THE BUDGET PROCESS)

REFORM
THE
BUDGET PROCESS

THE 11th STEP

(RE: THE BUDGET PROCESS)

THE POPULAR POINT OF VIEW

President Reagan consistently submitted higher budgets than the Congress approved. The line-item veto is an essential tool to help control the budget. Accounting practices should be determined by professionals and citizens should not be concerned.

ANOTHER POINT OF VIEW

Ronald Reagan has used his veto power far less than his predecessors. The line-item veto, while desirable, is not essential to balancing the budget. Better, would be a return to impounding. The choice of accounting methods is political. The federal government follows deceptive practices which it would not tolerate from other entities.

WHAT DEBT CEILING?

The permanent debt ceiling was set at $400 billion 1n 1971 and remains fixed at this amount. That's absolutely amazing when you consider our national debt has risen to over two trillion dollars (acknowledged) and that the annual interest ($190 billion in FY1986) is almost half the 1971 authorized limit. How can this be when the Treasury may legally issue no more debt than authorized by statute? Why doesn't Congress come clean and make the government honest by raising the permanent debt ceiling?

Elementary, my naive friend. As a tactic to assure approval of ever higher debt, two-thirds of the national debt has to be *renewed* at least annually. If the old debt is not renewed (never fear, Congress is here) the Treasury would be in deep trouble. If however, current debt were made permanent it would not have to be *reauthorized* and votes on the debt ceiling would be for or against new debt, not a rollover of past debt. Such a vote would be straightforward and easily understood by the taxpayers. You probably weren't even aware Congress raised or extended the temporary debt ceiling thirteen times during the 1960s and eighteen times in the 1970s. As things stand now, if the debt were not renewed (impossible to imagine) Congress would have to cut expenditures (tell us about it) and actual tax revenues would have to be divided among competing programs or raised and everyone remembers what happened when Fritz Mondale sang that tune. At any rate there is no way politicians would take the blame for the extensive and disruptive shutdown of services that would result from a vote *not* to reauthorize the debt. Someone else will have to destroy that protective curtain if we ever hope to get our elected officials out in the open where we can monitor their simple yes or no votes concerning new debt.

Holders of Treasury debt have a legally enforceable claim against the Treasury to compel payment of interest and principal on the maturing debt. This gives Congress another compelling reason to reauthorize. Treasury has to sell securities to get cash to repay holders of maturing debt and cannot do this without continually raising the temporary debt ceiling. If however, the debt ceiling on the permanent debt was raised from the $400 billion authorized in 1971 to an amount that would cover all existing debt, a semblance of honesty would be introduced into this deceptive budget process. True, it would really only be renaming the same set of circumstances but there is something good about calling a spade a spade.

IS THE BUDGET PROCESS RESPONSIBLE FOR THE DEFICIT?

In June 1985 David Stockman, then director of OMB, denied the Budget process was responsible in any large way for the government deficit and that in fact the deficit had its origins in major policy decisions and economic trends established and carried out in the seventies and early eighties. However Mr. Stockman's replacement at OMB, James Miller III, *does* blame the budget process for much of the country's deficit woes. Mr. Miller would like to see the line-item veto adopted as well as a capital budget which would spread outlays for a long-lived investment over a period of years. Expenditures could be labeled "long-term investments in the nation's future", rather that "current operating expenses". The former would not be counted when figuring the deficit. (Remember, accounting is essentially a labeling game.)

The Impoundment and Budget Control Act of 1974 was supposed to bring expenditures into line with revenue. It established the current budget process by creating the budget committees, the Congressional Budget Office (CBO), budget resolutions and the reconciliation process. The Act called for Congress to pass each year 13 different appropriation bills. Congress continually ignores its own law (as usual) when it ignores the 13 appropriation bills and instead passes continuing resolutions and gigantic omnibus bills. Why in the world doesn't the president simply delete items as he sees fit and let critical Congress persons take him to court. This issue needs to be reviewed by the highest court in the land — and the sooner the better. Observers other than Mr. Miller have pointed to the passage of the Congresssional Budget and Impoundment Control Act of 1974 as the number one reason and main culprit responsible for the deficit's phenomenal growth.

It is now commonly acknowledged that the passage of the Budget Control Act was an attempt by Congress to wrest power over the budgetary process from the executive branch of government. The Congress had been trying to weaken the president's authority over budgeted spending items for more than fifteen years and succeeded when President Nixon was stuck in the mire of Watergate.

According to constitutional historian Professor Forrest McDonald of the University of Alabama, in the early days of this nation it was understood that Congress was to provide lump-sum ceilings on expenditures and the executive branch was to determine how the funds would be spent.

> Most important, until 1974 presidents repeatedly 'impounded' appropriations and refused to spend them; Congress had no recourse. Thus from the inauguration of Washington until Richard Nixon's last year in office, presidents employed several means to exercise what amounted to an absolute "line-item veto.[1]

GENERALLY ACCEPTED ACCOUNTING PRACTICES

We'd like to think if the general public had all the facts it would act rationally and preserve the politicians (and the nation) from both themselves and the influence of powerful groups vying for an ever bigger piece of the economic pie. Unfortunately we can't test this premise because there are presently no accounting and reporting systems in place to accurately inform the public, or the politicians for that matter, about the financial health of the nation.

The Reagan administration has suggested moving federal credit activity onto the budget and instituting a separate capital budget. So far the suggestion has received mixed reviews. The idea is to separate the federal budget into two components; an operation budget, much like a private firm's profit and loss statement, and a capital budget, similar to private industry's balance sheets. This would give a much clearer picture of the true budget (and deficit). Borrowing to finance investments would be out in the open where it could be fairly considered.

Right now the federal government doesn't follow generally accepted accounting principles (GAAP); it uses cash-basis accounting although it prohibits publicly traded corporations from doing so. In 1975 the federal government even predicated bailout loans to New York City on that City's changing to accrual-basis accounting (GAAP). The 1988 reconciliation bill even barred large farms from using the cash method of accounting.

GAAP would show that Reagan administration deficits are lower than those of the Carter administration. According to New York Congressman Joseph DioGuardi the cash basis deficit of President Carter's last year (1980) totaled $93.5 billion, whereas the estimated GAAP deficit for that same year was a whopping $408.3 billion. Ronald Reagan "took the heat", as the Congressman put it, for the rise in the cash basis deficit from $93.5 billion to $185.3 billion whereas under GAAP the deficit actually declined by almost $75 billion, from $408.3 billion to $333.4 billion.

> Mr. Carter's total estimated GAAP deficits over the 1977-80 period were $56.5 billion higher than Mr. Reagan's total for 1981-84....A significant portion of Mr. Reagan's cash-basis deficits is actually the liquidation of liabilities incurred by the Carter administration, but whose costs were not recorded at that time because of the cash-basis system.[2]

It seems that President Reagan spent more on capital items whose cost should be amortized over a period of years than did his predecessor.

(Why isn't this common knowledge? Where is everybody?!)

Under accrual accounting (GAAP), used by all publicly-held companies, revenues and liabilities are put on the books as they are earned or incurred, rather than when the cash actually changes hands. A properly implemented capital budget would transform the budget process and officials would have a very much improved accounting, reporting, priority-setting and fiscal-policy tool providing a more accurate reflection of all government liabilities. Cash-basis accounting treats huge investment expenditures whose value is in the future as current expenses. It then disregards anticipated loan defaults, recording only net-losses on loans, ignores accounts receivable and accounts payable, provides no reserves for bad debt, treats the sale of assets as income and fails to depreciate capital assets entirely. Of course it is difficult and results are at best highly speculative when it comes to evaluating assets and calculating future liabilities. It is impossible to plan intelligently under a cash-basis system. Everything may look like it is in tip-top shape because future liabilities are ignored. One accounting firm estimated by failing to use GAAP sixty percent of the true 1984 deficit was hidden because unfunded Social Security liabilities were excluded.

Social Security is a perfect example. As young Americans pay into the system the governnment accrues stupendous liabilities against the day when they will retire and collect the promised benefits. This claim against future taxpayers, according to the Department of Treasury, passed the eleven trillion dollar mark in 1987 and is still rising. But there's more!

At the end of FY1985, almost three years ago, liabilities of the militalry, civil service and other retirement systems, stood at $1.252 trillion. Just imagine what it will be tomorrow and the day after and the day after that.

Under the present federal government accounting system the $40 billion in new loans that the federal agencies make each year are counted as outlays for that year. There are more than 350 federal loan programs of one sort or another, all laudable and sound when enacted but many long since transformed by the need and greed of competing groups. Most of them do not show up "on budget" as normal credit activity because many federal agencies can make, even direct loans, completely "off budget". The millions of loans made by private lenders and guaranteed by the federal government represent a contingent liability and one more burden for future taxpayers. The federal government insures not only bank and thrift deposits (FDIC & FSLIC) but also private pension plans (PBGC). The federal government is the country's largest insurer guaranteeing loans to home buyers, veterans, farmers, students, small business people and a multitude of other groups. At the end of FY1985 this liability was estimated by OMB to be over $3 trillion.

It has been suggested that such loan guarantees be redesigned to require current-cash outlays thereby putting the subsidy explicitly on budget. Better still the federal government should be directed to purchase private loan insurance for borrowers rather than guaranteeing loans itself (on behalf of all taxpayers). Best of all, the federal government should clear out of the loan business and leave it to the private sector. (Although it has not been very selective lately judging by default rates as we saw in Chapters Nine and Ten.) There are many organizations that would step in to take care of those who would not qualify for commercial banks loans. Even now religious, cultural or work-related organizations offer free (no interest) or low interest loans to members or act as guarantor in many instances.

Borrowing by the government, however, is another matter. If the borrowing is to finance public investments it need not be a sign of trouble. Deficit financing is common and although many government investments may prove worthless, synfuel as an example, most become assets, like highways. Deficit financing shifts the cost of paying for highways to future taxpayers who benefit from the roads when they are completed and in use.

There is no doubt we need uniformity and more openness so that better informed choices can be made. Although Special Analysis D of the federal budget separates investment and operating outlays, it is only used as information, having no policy significance of its own. We have nonsense like oil and gas leases, categorized as "offsetting reciepts" and treated as outlays instead of revenue. We can't expect miracles from accounting and procedural changes in the law, but changes may make costs more visible and thereby provide an opportunity for more effective management of federal budgeting.

Everyone agrees that cash-basis accounting encourages deficit spending by underestimating the acutal deficit. As we have seen, cash-basis reporting and budgeting largely ignore depreciation, accounts payable and other long-term costs making it easier for officials to adopt programs that provide benefits up front without providing funding until years later when the appropriating official is long since gone. You would think then, that the Reagan administration would be pushing harder for the enactment of accrual accounting (GAAP). Why not? Probably because no elected official is anxious to have American citizens, let alone the rest of the world, take a look at what would be at least a doubling of our debt in one fell swoop through a change in accounting methods.

I think we have had our fill of illusion and deception. Senator John Danforth admitted publicly that the Senate in 1986 had been looking at "phony numbers" — and *knew* it! Senator James Exon told his colleagues in March 1987 that "We knew last year's numbers were phony...Let's get honest with ourselves." If honesty is what they're after you might think that the good Senators would be in favor of a capital budget (GAAP — accrual accounting) but that is not necessarily true.

Senator Paul Simon joined with Senator Exon at the Budget Mark-Up Committee (March 1987) to vigorously denounce accrual accounting. (Not that anyone thought there would be smooth sailing with accrual accounting. There are admittedly problems that would have to be overcome.) Opponents argue that since the system is already prone to vast overspending, cash-basis budgets allow more control. If accrual accounting were adopted the determination of whether outlays are placed on the capital or operating budget would be based on political considerations. Imagine, if you will, politicians falling over one another in an attempt to have their pet projects classified as capital outlays so they will not have to be paid for by current taxes and would not ostentatiously add to the deficit. Such a classification could mean the difference between acceptance or rejection of a program. One could easily argue that more spending on education is an investment in the future; that agricultural subsidies are a long-term investment in a way of life. No one could deny that environmental issues fit the bill.

A fool-proof process has thus far eluded us. Under cash-basis accounting no financial statements are available for citizens to judge the actions of officials and under accrual accounting an official may have been replaced by the time his deeds are discovered. But as Senator Paul Simon has said so often during the 1988 presidential campaigns, I know we can do better than this!

THE FEDERAL FINANCING BANK

Remember the Nixon watch; that era when so many seeds were planted that are bearing troublesome fruit now in the eighties? In 1973 the Federal Financing Bank (FFB) was created within the Treasury Department. By law its budget authority and actual outlays are excluded when the unified budget is totaled. Richard Nixon may have talked tough on occasion but he let Congress get away with murder. Many of the loans we discussed earlier were made via the FFB. All a government agency had to do was guarantee the loan then the FFB could provide the funds by selling Treasury debt to the public. Simple and underhanded. Another way to grant favors to certain groups via subsidized loans without appearing extravagant. As easy as 1-2-3 the FFB can turn high-risk agricultural or student loans into zero-risk Treasury bonds.

SUPPLEMENTAL APPROPRIATIONS

Supplemental appropriations is the code name for a device Congress has used successfully for the past few years to appropriate money out of public view. The Congress has gotten sneakier and at the same time more defiant in its expanded use of devious tactics. It commonly underestimates the cost of a program, suckers the program's constituency in and then when the higher and true costs are revealed the program has become a fait accompli and the exorbitant costs are no longer a barrier. Congress has more than once created the illusion of a budget cut and then when the spotlight has been removed managed to fund a desired program via the back door. One example is the shennanigans that occurred

351

during the FY1983 resolutions. It appeared that Congress had agreed to a cut in the food stamp program but when funding ran short nine months down the road a supplemental appropriation kept the program going — business as usual.

THE BOMB! (BLOATED OMNIBUS MONEY BILL)

In the fall of 1986, eighteen days into FY1987, for the first time in history Congress didn't pass separate appropriation bills but instead sent a single $576 billion omnibus measure to President Reagan. This 1986 legislation was aptly nicknamed BOMB (Bloated Omnibus Money Bill). Omnibus spending practically eliminates the executive role in the budget process.

The founding fathers believed (I bet you wish you had a dollar for everyone who professes to know what the founding fathers believed!) that giving each department the means to check the others would oblige the government to discipline itself. The veto was intended to force the executive and legislative branches to set priorities and to negotiate with each other. That is not what happened on October 18, 1986. It seems the Congress has found a way to give the executive all or nothing choices with no chance to negotiate and compromise as our forefathers intended. (There I go again!) Congress is the body that initiates the law-making process by passing a bill and also has the last word with its power to override any presidential veto. However that presidential veto provides an opportunity for a second look, a pause for all concerned parties to reconsider. It was intended as an effective check to prevent hasty legislation. Today it is ill suited to the budget process. It is an ax where a scalpel is called for, and yet it is often the only tool available to the executive branch. One solution is the line-item veto; without it the power imbalance will continue. The line-item veto would allow a president to object to specifics within proposed legislation without destroying the entire bill. Without the line-item veto he is held hostage, forced to ratify that which he does not sanction, or alternatively, face the music for blocking good and usually direly needed legislation. Congress has found it useful to wait to the last minute before introducing "loaded" bills, knowing a delay will cause harm which the executive will want to avoid. The executive's party will not let him take that chance (even should some brave soul want to do so) and here you and I sit; citizens of a government run by clever, deceptive clowns! On November 17, 1986, shortly after Congress delivered its BOMB, Ronald Reagan tacked the following statement onto his signature ratifying H.R. 5363:

> Although I am signing this bill, I am very troubled by the inclusion of an unrelated, last-minute amendment to the Bankruptcy Code. The Congress' decision to link such provisions to otherwise desirable and useful legislation is but one example of the highly objectionable practice of combining unrelated legislation in a single bill. This practice, at a minimum, violates the spirit of the Constitution by restricting the President's veto power. [3]

I wonder how many people realize it is a crime, by statute, for a president to spend funds that have not first been appropriated by Congress? There is no doubt the Congress has the upper hand when it comes to the budget process. Even though the government will spend in the neighborhood of $1 trillion in FY1987, the appropriation is merely a formality. Almost half the money was committed long ago and its dispersal is pretty much automatic. The dispute centers on about $560 billion of discretionary spending. Continuing resolutions are most commonly used to authorize ongoing programs at old funding levels until new appropriations can be approved. This is where the notorious "special interest amendments" get tacked on.

(I referred to them earlier as "loaded" bills but they have been called other names!)

LAWS SEEMINGLY MADE TO BE BROKEN

The Gramm-Rudman-Hollings Balanced Budget and Emergency Deficit Control Act of 1985 (Gramm-Rudman) was an amendment to a measure raising the ceiling on the national debt. Simply

353

put, Gramm-Rudman originally called for the reduction of annual federal deficits in stages until no deficit exists in 1991.

Many look on Gramm-Rudman as an act of legislative desperation. The public wants deficit reduction but abhors cuts in its favorite programs. The Democrats are going to have a hard time convincing folks (although Speaker Jim Wright has already tried) that a tax hike is the answer, when a NBC/WSJ 1986 poll showed 62 percent of the public believes the deficit can be reduced without a rise in taxes.

Most likely Gramm-Rudman will not be taken seriously by our elected officials. Laws have been on the books since 1950 requiring all government agencies to prepare GAAP-basis financial reports and they have been intentionally circumvented. Section 7 of Public Law 95-435 (Bretton Woods Agreements Act) which was approved on October 10, 1978, states that "Beginning with fiscal year 1981, the total budget outlays of the Federal Government shall not exceed its receipts." Public Law 96-5, approved the following year in 1979, said essentially the same thing because no one seemed to pay any attention the first time.[4] "Hello, are you there?"

A paraphrase of Gramm-Rudman:

O.K. guys, the 1981 deadline for zero budget deficits kinda slipped by us awhile ago so let's see if we can get serious about this new 1991 deadline. That's giving us a ten year extension.

Please, as a former late night TV celebrity used to say, *can we talk?*

For sometime now both the White House and Capitol Hill have merely shuffled paper and called it deficit reduction. It has not gone unnoticed and a lot of us out here beyond the beltway are thoroughly disgusted. Are we supposed to tolerate confessions like this one by a former public official?

We have increasingly resorted to squaring the circle with accounting gimmicks, evasions, half-truths and downright dishonesty in our budget numbers, debate and advocacy. Indeed, if the SEC had jurisdiction over the Executive and Legislative branches, many of us would be in jail.
(David Stockman, former head of OMB)

354

LEVEL-HEADED PROPOSALS

In his January 7, 1987 column, David Broder laid out the following level-headed proposals by Alice Rivlin, former head of CBO and presently hard at work at the Brookings Institution:

(1)   Two year cycle for the budget and even less frequent revisions of the tax code. (To which I say "amen". Under one-year budgeting the relative cost-effectiveness of a program is difficult to determine and can easily lead to a reduction in the budget of certain programs while expanding others on political as opposed to economic grounds. Not surprisingly, many politicians would prefer "political grounds". The Federal Aviation Board, by the terms of the FY1988 budget, is to get $25 million for an industrial airport to be built near Ft. Worth ,Texas. This was offered as an example of pork barreling, this time on the part of Speaker Jim Wright. Eighty-six percent of all Congressmen polled recently expressed a desire for a two year budget which they believe will cut back on the pork barreling.[5]

(2)   A return to federalism (The federal government should stop micro-managing.)

(3)   Combine the Treasury Department with the Council of Economic Advisers and the Office of Management and Budget and call the consolidation the new Department of Economic Affairs. (Enough already of everyone either duplicating or undermining each other.)

(4)   More consolidation; replace the separate authorizing and appropriating committees with a single committee in both Houses to handle each major area of public spending. (The Kassebaum-Inouye bill introduced into the Senate in 1987, would establish legislative committees that have the power to authorize and appropriate so that only one bill goes to the floor. It would also put the budget process on a two-year cycle and reshape the budget committees themselves.)

(5)   The Federal Reserve Board should keep in closer touch

with the congressional budget committees (new) and the new Department of Economic Affairs.

(6)   More consolidation: one good economic forecast for the government. (The trouble is no one trusts any of the present sources. It is better to have several to choose from, no matter how divergent or confusing; besides competition keeps them *trying* for greater accuracy.)

(7)   Enforce fiscal neutrality; every proposed increase in spending must be accompanied by a revenue proposal or compensating cut in another budget item.

You have probably noticed that #7 is a feature of Gramm-Rudman which I believe will be ignored on the Hill.

I would like to add another proposal. If Congress has not been obeying its own legislation (see p. 354) then there must be a way citizens can enforce compliance. Congress has been mighty hot under the collar lately and very self-righteous smelling impropriety in the Iran-Arms-Sale scandal. It is doing a zealous job of watch-dogging the executive branch. Don't you think it's about time the judicial branch of government put the same squeeze on the legislative branch? It sure looks like some laws are being broken and those responsible had better prepare to pay the piper.

I was disappointed to see the line-item veto was left out of Ms. Rivlin's proposals. But perhaps she realized that the veto would have a negligible effect on the $1 trillion budget because truly discretionary spending amounts to under 15 percent of the entire budget at any rate. The other 85 percent of the budget is made up of military expenditures and sacrosanct domestic programs. When viewed in this light the fight for a line-item veto becomes a tempest in a teapot.

SOMETHING BETTER THAN THE LINE ITEM VETO

As mentioned earlier, the Congress has been able to get presidents since Richard Nixon to accept large appropriation packages with things they didn't favor included because that is the only way presidents could get the appropriations they did in fact want.

Forty-three out of fifty states give their chief executive the line-item veto. Numerous scholars have testified to the necessity for the item-veto and it is favored by the majority of the American people — the supposed leaders of this country.

The way it stands at present, the president submits his budget proposals to Congress and they add or delete (mostly add) whatever they want and send it back to the president. It's currently impossible for the president to veto relatively small items without vetoing the entire appropriation. The line-item veto would let him veto specific additions only. The Congress could put the vetoed items back in the appropriation bill by a 2/3 vote which is necessary to override any presidential veto.

The Congress has always had the power to counter any runaway spending tendencies of a president. The time is long over due when the president should be given back the budget power he needs to counter the runaway spending of the Congress. Better than the line-item veto would be the return of his impounding powers. Impoundments were never subjected to overrides by Congress so they provided a greater presidential power than any line-item veto.

In an editorial on March 7, 1988 the *Wall Street Journal* told us that:

> Jefferson made the first impoundment of $50,000 appropriated for gunboats on the Mississippi; FDR impounded $500 million for public works; John Kennedy cut spending by 6% through impoundments, and Richard Nixon impounded up to $18 billion a year from the budget.

Congress used the Watergate scandal as a pretext to substitute recissions and deferrals for the impoundment power. If Congress fails to do anything a president's recission vanishes after 45 days. As for the ability to defer, President Reagan was sued after requesting that $251 million for Urban Development Grants be deferred in 1986 and the House Appropriations Committee had voted to kill his deferral authority. This recital of "made-up-as-you-go-along" rules sounds like the Mickey Mouse government of a tiny Third World Country.[6]

THE FY1988 SENATE
BUDGET MARK-UP COMMITTEE

Professor Paul Craig Roberts of Georgetown University has urged Congress to couple a proposal to freeze spending authority with faster economic growth — somewhat harder to pull off than the freeze itself. Of course he's right. If we could elect someone with a magic wand, that combination would cut the deficit in-no-time-at-all and enhance our economic credibility both at home and abroad.

But maybe something less than a magic wand will do the trick. An organization called Citizens for a Sound Economy has had nothing but praise for New Mexico's Senator Pete Domenici's proposal for a freeze on spending authority.

> 'This single step would allow Congress to meet the Gramm-Rudman deficit target without threatening to throw a sluggish economy into recession by raising taxes,' says Daniel J. Mitchell at Citizens for a Sound Economy.[7]

When I read that I felt like I did when I read the Michigan University report claiming Charles Murray was all wrong and welfare was working just fine.[8] I'm afraid my hopes will be dashed this time too. Let me share parts of the FY1988 Senate Budget Mark-Up Committee meeting with you:

Senator Ruddy Boshwitz of Minnesota argued that the key is to slow spending growth. He did not favor a freeze or cut.

Senator Charles Grassley of Iowa said that in 1982 he proposed an across the board freeze when the deficit was a comparatively modest $96 billion — it would have balanced the budget in 1984. Now that the deficit is twice as large, a two year freeze would barely put a dent in the deficit. The problem is to find ways to shave $63 billion off the projected FY1988 deficit. (Projected deficit of $171 billion and Gramm-Rudman target of $108 billion).

Many Senators spoke, of course, but these were the only two who spoke directly to the freeze proposal, not counting Senate Budget Committee Staff Director, Steve Brandon. Mr. Brandon presented five ways to reach the FY1988 Gramm-Rudman target using CBO estimates as of March 1987. He started with the freeze but I will include the other proposals so you will see creative juices are flowing even though none of the alternatives appear very palatable. Remember we're looking for creative ways to trim $63 billion form the FY1988 budget in order to reach the Gramm-Rudman target.

Table 7
FIVE WAYS TO REACH FY1988 G-R TARGET
USING CBO 3/87 ESTIMATES

(1)   **FREEZE Domestic and Defense**

save $8 billion in outlays
save <u>$2 billion</u> in interest
$10 billion
means we still need to cut $53 billion

(2)   **50% from Defense and 50% from Domestic — No New Revenue**

DOMESTIC CUTS	DEFENSE CUTS
$31.5 billion in outlays	$31.5 billion in outlays
$40 billion in authority	$60 billion in authority
means a 25% overall cut	below CBO base line
(except for excluded programs)	means would have $342
	billion left in defense
	budget authority

(3)   **If 3% real growth in Defense is allowed.**

DOMESTIC CUTS	DEFENSE CUTS
$71 billion in outlays	$7.8 billion in outlays added
$99 billion in authority	

means a 58% cut (except for excluded programs)
means a 32% cut (if medicare is cut also)

(4) 1/3 REVENUE PLUS	1/3 DOMESTIC CUTS	1/3 DEFENSE CUTS
$21 billion	$21 billion in outlays	$21 billion in outlays
	$29 billion in authority	$42 billion in authority
	means a 16% cut	means a 14% cut

(5) **Half Revenue Half Cuts**

REVENUE	DOMESTIC CUTS	DEFENSE CUTS
plus $31 billion	$16 billion in outlays	$16 billiom in outlays
	$22 billion in authority	$32 billion in authority
	means 12% in cuts	means 11% in cuts

Source: Senate Budget Committee Staff Director, Steve Brandan's presentation (televised by C-SPAN)

CREATIVE — CREATIVE!
WHO WANTS CREATIVITY?

In November 1987, motivated by the stockmarket plunge a month earlier, leaders from both parties met with the President to work out a deficit reduction compromise. What emerged was referred to by Senator Bill Armstrong of Colorado as "a lead ballon...one part tax hike, one part defense cut and enough cheap cosmetics to make Mae West blush."[9]

Senator William Roth of Delaware, although not as colorful, was also derisive. On December 3, 1987 he had this to say:

According to news reports, the package will cut discretionary spending by $2.6 billion, defense by $5 billion and entitlements by $4 billion. In reality, discretionary spending is projected to grow by $7 billion, defense by $3 billion, and entitlements by $37 billion. These are increases of 1%, 4% and 8%, respectively, over last year's level....despite suggestions to the contrary, federal spending will still increase by $50 billion if this plan is enacted.[10]

While ostensibly saving $2 billion in Medicare expenditures, if one were to look closely the so-called savings were to be achieved by stretching out the time government takes to reimburse hospitals and doctors. (Yeah — more accounting gimmicks!)

Guess how the great negotiators proposed to save the Pension Benefit Guaranty Corporation $400 million? You got it! By increasing the insurance premiums paid by employers. (Clever rascals, aren't they?)

Oh yeah, and the $250 million saved under the Guaranteed Student Loan program? That's achieved by increasing the lenders' risk.

Who says politicians aren't creative?

THE FY 1988 RECONCILIATION BILL

Many people believe the Gramm-Rudman bill is misleading. Cuts are not "cuts" as you and I would refer to them but a little less increase than might otherwise occur. I'm not kidding. A decrease in the increase — that's it! Let's look at the final outcome for our FY1988 budget and see beyond all the rhetoric to what really happened. (It's possible? Um, probably not, but let's give it a try.)

Table 8
THE FY 1988 BUDGET - WHAT REALLY HAPPENED

A) Internal affairs   = a real increase of $4 billion
B) Energy   = reduction of $1 billion
C) Science, space and technology   = $1 billion increase
D) Natural resources, environment
    and agriculture   = same as FY1987
E) Commerce Housing credits   =$500 million increase
F) Transportation   =$1 billion increase
G) Community & Regional Development
    of education and training.
    Employment and social services   = $1 billion increase
H) Health   = $4 billion increase
I) Medicare   = $4.5 billion increase
J) Income Security programs   = $9 billion increase
K) Social Security   = $13 billion increase from
    FY1987 outlays

OUR ELECTED OFFICIALS CONTINUE TO SPEND MORE THAN THEY COLLECT:

	Revenue	Spending
1981	$599 billion	$678 billion
FY1987	$855 billion	$1.2 trillion

THEY MAKE PROMISES THEY CAN'T KEEP

PROMISE
$960 billion in tax cuts over 5 years via the tax reform of 1981

ACTUAL

Increases in Social Security taxes and bracket creep	=	$660 billion
1982 tax increase	=	229 billion
1983 gas tax increase	=	16 billion
Deficit reduction tax Oct 1984 resulted in an increase	=	50 billion
Continuing Omnibus budget resoluton of 1986	=	6 billion
tax reform 1986	=	29 billion
Total increase		$990 billion

The actuality resulted in 30 billion more in *increased* spending than we were promised in *cuts* !

In 1982 in order to obtain the necessary votes for a tax increase the promise was made to cut $3 in spending for every $1 increase in taxes. We acutally got $1.14 in spending *increases* for every dollar raised by taxes.

Whom do you trust?

According to a *Los Angeles Times* poll, 64 percent of Americans don't want higher taxes to correct our deficit. Do policymakers care?

JAPAN'S DEFICIT COMPARED WITH OURS

Japan's deficit in the early 1970s coincided with a sharp rise in its net-private-savings surplus. Japan's shift from budget surplus in the early seventies to a series of deficits, peaking at an equivalent of 5.5 percent of GNP in 1978, did not result in foreign capital inflows into Japan and associated trade deficits. Instead a moderate fiscal policy brought the deficit down to the equivalent of approximately 1.5 percent of GNP. Strong growth in the money supply left Japan with interest rates as low as 2.5 percent in 1987. This raised domestic demand 4 percent in 1986 although GNP grew only 2.5 percent. As a consequence there was a deline in Japan's trade surplus in 1986. Slower economic growth in Japan is the result of less foreign demand because of the appreciation of the yen — it has nothing to do with a reduction in domestic demand.

By way of illustrating the "headway" we have made in correcting our own deficit woes, the late Secretary of Commerce Malcolm Baldridge before the Senate Government Affairs Committe hearing on Econcomic Competitiveness on March 25, 1987 offered the following statistics:

FY1983 GNP = $3.3 trillion   FY1983 deficit = 6.3% of GNP
FY1987 GNP = $4.5 trillion   FY1987 deficit = 3.9% of GNP

Most everyone agrees that the most alarming feature of the U.S. deficit is not its size but its structural nature; the gap between income and outgo.

NO ONE'S RESPONSIBILITY
AND UNDER NO ONE'S CONTROL

In "The Morning After" Peter Peterson reminds us that until fifteen years ago most federal spending was discretionary and unindexed. In the early 1970s we decided to transform non-poverty benefit programs such as Social Security, into untouchable and inflation-proof entitlements. Consequently "Our deficit has thus become no one's responsibility. It is subject to 'projection' but no longer to control."[11]

THE TWELFTH STEP

(RE: LEADERS)

*CHANGE THE PLAYERS
ON CAPITOL HILL
UNTIL WE GET SOME
IN OFFICE THAT CAN DO THE JOB
THAT HAS TO BE DONE*

THE 12th STEP

(RE: LEADERS)

THE POPULAR POINT OF VIEW

The longer an official holds office the more experienced and effectual he or she becomes. It takes time to "learn the ropes" in Washington, D.C. Longer terms and public financing of campaigns means incumbents don't have to "waste time" in search of funds to wage battle for Congressional seats. PACs (Political Action Committees) should be curtailed because they corrupt the political system.

ANOTHER POINT OF VIEW

Rather than *extend* terms of office, the number of terms that can be served should be restricted. If public financing were provided for Congressional races, incumbents would be almost impossible to unseat. If officials can be corrupted by groups pleading their causes and requesting favors then those officials should be punished and replaced, *not* PACs! If elected officials cannot balance the budget they should step down and let others try.

IT'S NOT ENOUGH

So what if we privatize and reduce government's functions, review the role of the Federal Reserve and stabilize exchange rates, enact banking reform and undo excessive regulations, make capital more widely available and cut back further on waste, require that other countries do more economically and even pass a flat tax, encourage economic growth, make adjustments that will permit us to compete more effectively in the global market and reform the entire budget process — none of it matters an iota unless we also change the leadership that has led us down the garden path!

The inefficient and incessant spending of our dollars did not happen by itself. OUR ELECTED OFFICIALS ARE AC-COUNTABLE. NO TWO WAYS ABOUT IT!

A talk show host on a popular San Francisco radio station a few years ago ran a half-hearted campaign to unseat all incumbents. A bit mindless and undiscriminating perhaps, but when it comes down to it, even those who are trying to do what is right (in each voter's subjective opinion) may deserve to be ousted for lack of competence in convincing their colleagues. Starting over with fresh new leaders may be just the antidote this nation needs for its ills.

The Honorable Russell Long of Louisiana retired after 38 years in Congress to standing ovations and accolades galore. When asked about his philosophy he summed it up, "to adjust ourselves to what we think is the best for the most".[1] America was once unique in her beacon-like refusal to become a collectivist society. How then did someone occupy a Senate seat for 38 years being guided by "the best for the most"? "The best for the most" is at best majority rule which tramples the individual and at worst it is communism. Columnist James Kilpatrick told of a recent poll that showed that a large percentage of our fellow citizens thought that "from each according to his ability, to each according to his need" was part of the United States Constitution.

The president needs someone besides himself looking out for the good of the entire nation; ideally that would fall to the Senate.

368

Members of the House are expected to more narrowly represent their districts although we should be able to expect that over time even they will exchange any provincial short-range thinking for long range more encompassing viewpoints.

Upon his retirement in 1986, Senator Barry Goldwater of Arizona gave an interview to Haynes Johnson of the *Washington Post* in which he provided his own set of facts which back up my contention that many Congressmen don't work as hard as they use to and not as hard as a lot of their constituents. He mentioned three day weeks — late to meetings — staffs that have grown from approximately 2,000 twenty-five years ago to over 30,000 today.

Some officials suppose they were elected to write more regulations in the form of bills and amendments, much the way some doctors feel compelled to write a prescription to give you your money's worth.

Senator Goldwater recalled that in 1952 the Congress voted on fewer than 200 bills and in the 1980s Congress has consistently voted on closer to 800 or 900 each session. But the Senator hadn't, as you-know-who says, seen anything yet. According to James Kilpatrick, *by the end of its first day* the 100th Congress (and with Senator Goldwater no longer there to hold back the tide) saw the introduction of 500 bills in the House and 283 in the Senate.

Senator Goldwater seemed to think people's low perception of Congress, and politicians in general, was deserved. A shock to most of us who go about criticizing, considering it more sport than substance. It ties with baseball as the great American pastime. We are usually too far away to know if it is deserved and so send barbs "just in case". That's why when Senator Goldwater volunteered, "I don't think I've served in many good Congresses" it was truly sobering.

MONEY TO RUN

Senator Barry Goldwater advised a change in election practices. He believes good people are prevented from running for office because of the inordinate amount of money they are required to raise.

In the 1986 election everyone would probably agree that too few issues were discussed and too much money was spent; over a billion dollars by some accounts, with over $200 million spent on political ads on TV. Members of both parties say they don't like constantly begging for more money and the lobbyists they often hit up agree change is in order. Figures vary widely, but I've seen estimates that an average campaign for the Senate now costs over $3 million and for the House about $340,000; not to mention 75 percent of the candidate's time taken to raise the money. (California's 1986 Senate race cost *each* candidate about $11 million!)

Incumbents tend to pile up huge campaign bankrolls "just in case", raising in 1986 for example, $19 million more than they spent on campaigning. These "war chests" are one reason why relatively few strong candidates challenge incumbents. Only six incumbents in the House were defeated in the 1986 general election.

In a great effort to nullify the incumbency barrier a 63,000 member organization (AMPAC) that contributed over $4 million to various candidates during the 1986 campaign suggests that:

1-Incumbents shouldn't head their own PACs.
2-Incumbents shouldn't raise funds more than two years before a reelection bid.
3-Incumbents should specify the office being sought.

Incumbents have a good many advantages that are not available to their challengers. They have the ability to reach constituents without cost and the ability to attract press coverage, both by virtue of their elected office. Use of computers, free mail (franking privileges) and personal staff all constitute a big advantage over challengers. As computers and staff churn out solutions to constituents' problems they also churn out the loyalty that eventually translates to volunteer commitment when election time comes around. The government (taxpayers) pay, but the gratitude goes to the incumbent. Right after the Second World War Congressmen had an average of three personal staff members; in the 1980s the average was up to 17 (meaning some had a lot more!). A political scientist at the University of Maryland, Michael Malbin, found that when allowance was made for staff, office expenses, phone, travel, computers, mailings and so forth, an incumbent came out an estimated one million fifty thousand dollars ahead of any challenger. It's really not surprising then, that normally 95 percent of all House incumbents win re-election. 1986 was a record year when 98 percent of all incumbents were returned to office.

The Conservative Digest estimates that the typical Senate freshman will be committed to raise $125,000 *every month* for the next six years (length of his first term) to keep up with campaign costs and prepare for a challenge. Early and constant fund raising is not good for the country as it consumes too much of an elected officials's time and energy. Early fund raising allows incumbents to wave checks around and scare off potential challengers.

But the most money does not always win!

The National Association of Realtors spent $496,000 to run its own campaign (in order to get around contribution limits) in an unsuccessful attempt to help reelect former Senator James Jones of Oklahoma. ("Former" tells the whole story!) The American Medical Association had a similar experience in Indiana in its effort to defeat Andrew Jacobs who opposed higher Medicaid fees for doctors. They spent $315,000 without success whereas Jacobs spent only $8,000 and won. Such examples give a certain amount of credence to the statement that the amount of money spent is not the determining factor in winning elections.

No doubt TV has changed campaigning. In a state as large and populated as California it is the most efficient way to reach the greatest number of people. Unhappily we are all too often subjected to slick media presentations by public relation firms rather than issues and positions. According to a 1986 study conducted at the University of California Irvine, there is evidence that "looks and image" matter. (Of course not to you or me!) Since 1900 the taller candidate has won every presidential race except one. In 1976 Jimmy Carter defeated the taller Gerald Ford. (Did you know Gerald Ford was taller than Jimmy Carter? Would anybody care to back Paul Volcker? How about Senator Bill Bradley?) Researchers found that even when a candidate's stand on issues was the same, different photos of the same person produced striking differences in the voters' reactions. In all cases, except one, the most favorable photographs garnered the most votes.

Paul Kinney, a campaign consultant, had one candidate shave off his mustache and switch to contact lenses "to look cleaner". Moustaches supposedly convey a picture of sleaziness. Mr. Kinney noted that, "It's a very negative comment on society, but politics is just a microcosm of society at large."

In the *American Commonwealth*, written in 1896, Lord Bryce noted that when it comes to a choice between a meritorious candidate or a meritorious president, the former would always win out. Lord Bryce thought that meant Americans were doomed to suffer under second rate leaders. He observed that obscure men tend to make fewer enemies and for that reason make better candidates.

We lost a good man with business acumen and both political and international experience when Donald Rumsfeld withdrew from the 1988 presidential race long before it should ever have begun back in April, 1987. Actually the race began for Mr. Rumsfeld in the summer of 1985, more than three years before the presidential election. It took time to collect a war chest of $4 million and promises of more, but in the end the sums appeared inadequate to the job of campaigning for almost thirty months. Few knew better than Mr. Rumsfeld what he as an outsider (not current office holder) would be up against when it came to raising money. He is active in Citizens For American Values, an organization to help nonincumbent Republicans run for office and to keep the system open to newcomers.

With Iowa and New Hampshire holding caucuses and primaries in February and twenty states following suit in early March, the list of candidates is trimmed early. Something needs to be changed when our two most populous states are not even given a chance to say yeah or neah to 3/4 of the candidates. Not to belabor

the point but THE ENTIRE ELECTION SYSTEM IS
WEIGHTED HEAVILY IN FAVOR OF INCUMBENTS AND
THOSE ALREADY KNOWN TO THE ELECTORATE.

COMPENSATION FOR ELECTED OFFICIALS

It may seem simplistic, but many ordinary citizens don't get paid
unless they do a good job and some even get their pay docked if
they cause damage (breakage etc.). How should these people feel
when they are told Richard Nixon did a poor job rushing through
the contracts for our embassy in Moscow in 1972 and now we've
got to tear it down and start over?

> Mr. Nixon, Sir, deposit at least $190 million please— maybe more since
> that was the cost of the unusable embassy and starting a new embassy from
> scratch in 1988 is bound to bring the cost of your mistake even higher.
> Thank you.

The prevailing folklore in this country seems to be "You get
what you pay for". Witness the defeat of the proposition to limit
officials' pay in California in 1986. Most people seem to believe
for what our government officials do they get very little compensation. On the other hand how many people would take over their
positions gratis? Right now remember, it cost over $3 million and
years of pleading to attain a seat in the Senate. The opportunity
to do something worthwhile and with a lot of ego gratifying
glamour and glory is compensation enough for 99 out of 100
persons. Have you ever heard of a shortage of candidates and if so
would the reason really be too little compensation? I doubt it.
Many citizens believe the vast majority of officials in Washington
DC have done a terrible job and should be fired, not given a raise
in pay.

Popular columnist James Kilpatrick speaks of the economic
and moral considerations that must be understood in determining
the pay for public officials. He says,

> It is impossible to say what salaries are necessary to prompt talented men

373

and women to run for Congress, to seek places on the federal bench or to accept top positions in executive agencies. (But then he goes on to admit)...Able men and women always will aspire to the prestige of the federal bench. A vacancy has only to develop before a dozen candidates make their ambitions known.

As Mr. Kilpatrick pointed out in his column, many Congress people are clearly worth twice their present pay and many aren't worth half the original amount. What makes one worth more than the other?

Section 311 of the 1,194 page continuing resolution that was presented to the president as 1987 ended contained a 20 percent pay increase for House and Senate staff. (Now how do you suppose?) Apparently it went undetected for two months, and when discovered the "deed was already done". (Who do you imagine uncovered it?) The problem, pointed out in a *Wall Street Journal* editorial is not so much the money as

the potential effects on government morale. Paper shufflers hidden in the labyrinth of Congress now can earn more than important officials running large government agencies and departments...In Washington, the people who do important jobs are paid for too little and those who do unimportant jobs are paid for too much.

Showing up for work and doing homework is an admirable trait but how about talent, skill, and experience? How valuable are the latter and how can we tell who possesses them?

I don't know about you, but I don't take advice from anyone who has not succeeded at what he preaches. I remember a few years ago the anger of an audience, as evidenced by their questions after sitting through a "how-to" type lecture given by a young *single* man who spoke about the many ways to ensure a long happy marriage. This line of reasoning would naturally lead one to conclude that only a person who has successfully managed large amounts of money and honed his negotiating skills would be qualified to sit in positions of power in our government. Perhaps

374

it's time those attributes were sought along with the compassionate nice guy characteristics.

IF YOU CAN'T BEAT THEM JOIN THEM

At the Center for Excellence in Government in January, 1987, Harry Hughes, ex-governor of Maryland advised that no one who has ever run against government and bureaucracy has accomplished anything. You can't break the system you have to use to get things done. Who can argue?

I'm often asked why I don't run for office.

> But with the real possibility of reductions in retirement and pension programs, education and health-care funding, and national defense spending, as well as additional taxes, it is important that public officials also share in the sacrifice.
>
> Congressman Leon Panetta

What can I say? I've got a model Congressman!

During his first nine years in Congress, Leon Panetta returned to the Treasury a total of $511,151 in office and payroll savings and the return from many of those years of his own pay increases. The savings came from such economies as limiting districtwide mailings, using reduced-fare flights, low-cost rentals of office space and equipment and careful management by his Washington and district field offices. All that and my Super Congressman was present for 96.2 percent of all House votes during 1985.

Your Congressperson or Senator could "read-like-this-too" or he could fly the gang to Ireland, the Far East, South America or wherever on "fact finding trips", otherwise live as high on the hog as regulations will permit and seldom show up for his obligations on the floor.

It may not be true that an elected official must curry favor with the folks back home in order to remain in office.

The Center for Naval Analyses, a Washington DC research firm, found pork barrel spending or protecting against spending

375

cutbacks was not helpful in getting an incumbent reelected.

Professors Robert Bernstein and James Payne of Texas A & M drew the same conclusion from their separate studies. Once elected and in office representatives are able to do as they please without checking with their constituents. Even those who voted against spending back home were not punished as is generally believed. The "why not?" is revealing. It was found that most constituents could not even recall their representative's name let alone his/her voting record! The excuse that politicians must spend and spend to please their constituents or risk being replaced is nothing more than a myth — but one that the majority of politicians have swallowed hook, line and sinker and that the minority simply don't care to disturb. Rather than educate the entire American population to the necessity for budget cut-backs, it may be easier to educate, at least the more receptive members of Congress, to the fact that by doing their duty and trimming the deficit they are not commiting an act of political suicide.

CAMPAIGN REFORM PROPOSALS

The House recently passed campaign reform bills on two occasions but neither got through the Senate. Currently (1987) the Senate is making reform noises with Senators Dodd, Simon, Proxmire and others waving proposals.

The Senatorial Election Campaign Act (S.2) would establish a voluntary system of campaign spending limits. "Voluntary" is an attempt to side-step first amendment problems. By its terms, in order to qualify for public financing a candidate for the Senate would have to raise $250,000 with no more than $20,000 coming from his immediate family.

Public financing for presidential elections is a child of the Watergate reform. The funds are available thanks to the number of people who check the box on their tax returns which allow $1 to be contributed to the Federal Election Commission (which, by the way issued the lowest figures for 1986 campaign spending that I found anywhere).

One suggestion for campaign reform is to set up a national payroll withholding system for voluntary contributions. Employees would sign a card authorizing $1 a week of their pay to be directed to the party of their choice. (Quite a jump from the modest $1 a year contribution on the tax return. You don't suppose *that* hasn't been *enough* now do you?) Employers could send the money to the IRS along with periodic income-tax and Social Security withholding, to be forwarded to the parties. I can't remember who to credit with the scheme — er — idea, but I think he thought up chain letters and some games having to do with Ponzi's shells or something.

Professor Ogden O. Allsbrook, Jr. of the University of Georgia has another idea. He has suggested a constitutional amendment to limit all elected representatives to one term in order to foster a genuine concern for the health of the nation and to remove the distraction of future elections. He points out that so far incumbent politicians have found deficits a more palatable alternative than defeat at the polls. (The *myth* again) Three 3-year terms for Representatives and three 6-year terms for Senators with a limit of 18 years of service is an alternate suggestion which has been making the rounds on Capitol Hill.

There are others that believe that the framers of the Constitution, by perscribing a two year term for Representatives, intended to make certain there was a constant supply of fresh faces in Congress. (I'm still hoping for that dollar for every person who professes to know what the Founding Fathers intended!) Certainly they never intended influence to be wielded for ten or twenty years in the capital by a single individual, far less a family. Article 1 Section 4:2 of the Constitution states that Congress shall assemble at least once in every year. There seemed no need to limit terms of office. Public service in a country founded on the premise that "the best government is the least government" was never meant to be a career. (Forget "a dollar for every person professing to *know* the mind of the Founding Fathers. I'll settle for a quarter each time that knowledge is personally revealed to me!)

Yet there have been several "dynasties" over the years on Capitol Hill extending between generations. For instance former Senator Albert Gore Senior's political career in Washington spanned 32 years (1939-71) and his son, while at the beginning of his career today, has already added another ten.

Some observers think there should be stricter limits put on political contributions and expenditures and even suggest candidates be given planned access to the public in the form of free TV time.

In a *Wall Street Journal* article on November 18, 1986 Arthur Schlesinger, Jr. pointed to recent elections in Brazil as an example for America to emulate. For two months before the election "... every Brazilian television network gave the parties free time every night from 8:30 to 9:30."

I have my doubts about requiring a business to provide services without compensation. I don't wholeheartedly subscribe to the old saw that "the airwaves belong to the people". Someone's energy and capital makes it possible to harness those airwaves. I would like to see a payment from taxpayers (stop that hissing) for the time provided. My other dilemma concerns the manner in which that time should be acquired. When one is in a position of power, as our elected officials are, it is easy to forget that this is first and foremost a free country. It is inconceivable to me that every station would willingly provide, even for a fee, prime time for political debates. Especially when citizen apathy is high, as evidenced by the two thirds of those eligible to vote who chose to ignore the 1986 elections entirely. Just consider the ratings a maverick station could pile up by showing *anything* else if all other channels were covering the candidates between 8:30-9:30 every night for two months!

If one station dissents then others would quickly follow and instead of accepting a patriotically modest fee, those stations willing to cover candidates would demand exorbitant fees as compensation for their probable fall in the ratings.

Another idea is to provide in the federal budget for a special TV channel to be used only for election coverage. This might be a better use of public money than the present system of providing qualifying candidates with matching funds. The debates centering on the issues, would also be carried by private TV, radio and local papers as they saw fit. Not everyone would tune into the election channel just as not everyone tunes into beauty contests, Academy Awards, baseball or anything else. So what else is new? C-SPAN (Cable Satellite Public Affairs Network) although it is available only through a paid cable TV subscription, already provides that kind of coverage as a public service.

Where's the weakness in the proposal? Maybe a lot of political hopefuls would end up eating less chicken and peas and have more time for things that matter. The millions of freed dollars ——? Didn't someone mention something about a deficit?

Everyone agrees our present system of PACs, Parties, primaries, caucuses and electoral votes has resulted in a system where years are spent campaigning and raising money — an unfit job for any fit person! Having put two to six years of a life into successfully traveling around asking for money and making promises, the person becomes an incumbent.

A man from Mars might suggest our system of choosing *Miss America* makes more sense.

WHAT DIRECTION?

Thomas Mann, executive director of the American Politicial Science Association believes the problem in this country is not with our inefficient separation of powers but the problem stems from a disagreement about the principles the country should follow. With a consensus on principle, institutional hurdles can be easily scaled. Once we as a nation have *the will* we can do anything.

Most legislators believe the problem lies with the special interests which prevent action for the benefit of the general welfare. (Remember, "special interests" and "general welfare" are subjective terms.) Special interests work harder because they have more at stake in any given situation. Ten people, in an effort to save one thousand dollars each, will do far more than a million people will do to save a penny each. Principle, logic or any thought process is completely ignored and laziness allows greed to take over. We should learn from the comment attributed to Adolf Hitler: "What luck for the rulers that men do not think." Democracy's greatest enemy is ignorance coupled with a lack of caring and concern for principle. America's strongest trait is pragmatism and expediency — it runs even stronger than generosity, and although the latter is a virtue the former will be America's downfall. Without principle a nation is adrift without a rudder and is easily tossed about by the glibbest talker. We need substance and determination, two traits sadly lacking in American leadership in the 1980s.

On January 8, 1988 Walter Hoadley, Senior Research Fellow at the Hoover Institution, addressed the Commonwealth Club in San Francisco.

In discussing the difference in leaders a generation ago and leaders today, Dr. Hoadley referred to the former as "depression scarred" and the latter as "inflation scarred":

> The differences in leadership attitudes are profound. Inflation-scarred men and women fear rising prices, interest rates, and taxes. In contrast, depression-scarred individuals fear recession, unemployment, and falling rates and prices.

He told his audience that America's educational achievements will be pitted against the achievements of other nations , where far more discipline, family support, pride and economic desire exists.

> Historians have noted that a nation's future often can be foreseen in the fears of its young people. Traditional fears of hunger, joblessness, eternal damnation, public shame, and war have led to hard work, institutional loyalty, greater acceptance of spiritual precepts and values, stronger moral values, and a ready willingness to defend themselves and their country.

He said that polls of young people show that what they fear today is nuclear holocaust, failure to 'make it big', personal rejection, AIDS, competition, urban congestion, and loss of pleasure time.

We need to look at America's philosophical evolution over the past 200 years. Not to try and bring back the past — we're a different nation with different needs than we had 200 years ago. But just as we must examine our past so we don't repeat our mistakes, so must we examine it so we don't loose what it is that was responsible for our greatness.

Most people are too busy with their work, family and friends to stop and on their own analyze where America as a nation is headed and whether they approve or not. Yet if we don't do it who will? Politicians are notoriously short-sighted, generally seeing only from election to election. It is up to the people to take that long-range view to see that the America we envision is preserved for future generations.

We have had enough of your standard officials, dependent on every shift of popular opinion. We need a new breed of politician; representatives willing to sacrifice their popularity for a principle; willing and able to go beyond the pious slogans and empty promises.

It is not hard to enlist public support for painful, short-term specific policies and to convince constituents such programs are necessary in order to strengthen and preserve America's economic and political system. I first wrote "it is not easy..." but that is the real myth — that it is not easy to face citizens with the truth. Truth is always easy to deal with — to tell and to hear — *lies* are difficult. People respond to truth. Any disaster and they're there. A story of a robbery or fire goes on the air and people bombard the stations with offers of donations. Report the tragedy of an abandoned child and everyone in the community rushes to take the child to their hearts. If statistics show otherwise it is only because regulations won't permit people to follow their hearts. During a drought some years ago in the San Francisco Bay Area customers conserved water so far beyond the expectations of the troubled Water Company that the utility had to ask them not to be so conscientious — the utility was almost put out of business by the public's zeal.

Give people a good cause — a reason to do something that they can both understand and believe in and there's nothing they can't do!

In other countries and under other forms of government the public has little reason to act as watch dog; their input is either not allowed or disregarded. That is certainly not the case in the United States of America. Congress is inundated with cards and letters. Take California's Senator Pete Wilson as only one example. In 1985 he was receiving 4,000 letters each working day, 20,000 a week. That's not apathy! That's also not the whole picture. Many American citizens feel powerless and sense that it is futile to expend energy trying to make their voices heard. As federalism declined centralization grew; centralization robs the ordinary citizen of power. Even though there may not have been an actual erosion of power there is a creeping feeling of powerlessness.

Americans pay more than they'd like to in taxes and they'd like to be able to leave the governing to others as a fair exchange. It is both a blessing and a curse that in order for our form of government to function properly the citizens must continually act as overseers. This is time consuming, often boring and we feel we are being gyped. After all we voted "them" into office and provide "them" with good salaries and all kinds of perks and then we're expected to keep "them" in line. We want to be able to trust "them" to do a good job.

Unfortunately we are becoming a nation of cynics. In the fall of 1986 polls showed many Americans believed journalist Nicholas Daniloff, who was accused of spying by the Soviets, was indeed a spy, and this despite assurances to the contrary from the magazine he worked for, his colleagues in Moscow, the Secretary of State and the President himself. As David Broder remarked in his column in October 1, 1986,

> When the public distrusts what its elected and appointed officials say and what its journalists report, the chances of maintaining a healthy democracy are sharply diminished.

Under our form of government people do not always do as they should and the temptation is strong to *make* them do what "we" know is right. Freedom is a very precious, precarious and often cumbersome thing. Coercion, on the other hand, is efficient. "Make all stations provide free coverage between 8:30 and 9:30 every night". It may be true that many people who would otherwise switch channels if given a choice, would be exposed to the issues via mandates. An enlightened populace is likely to lead to less apathy and result in a greater voter turn out which is definitely a desirable outcome.

A good many things have been done in the last fifty years using the end to justify the means. Already elected officials have decided we are too stupid, weak and undisciplined to provide for our own retirement years (Social Security is mandatory); to budget so that we can meet our tax obligations at the end of the year (automatic withholdings allows government to use our dollars all year); to care about our own safety (seat belt laws) or the comfort of others (smoking outlawed in many public areas).

How long before government, in the name of the public good and for the sake of efficiency and greater productivity, issues clothing (no time wasted shopping — China tried it for awhile) removes from the market place alcohol (attempted briefly 1919-1933) tobacco, sugar, fats and other products consumers prefer but which tests have determined are detrimental to health?

But if we deny the use of coercion what then? It was not that long ago that public opinion was the means used to the end of keeping people in line. In its favor is the fact that the penalties for ignoring public opinion are less onerous than those encountered by ignoring government's mandates. Ostracism was what kept homosexuals in the closet, illegitimate births down, unhappy couples married and even front lawns mowed. It was not so much the concept of using ends to justify means that people turned from, but rather they found these ends no longer desirable.

The solution in every instance is to take the circle smaller and smaller; from federal to state to local governments, to neighborhoods, relatives, immediate family until it centers finally on the individual and his own conscience. The best of all possible worlds is when actions are neither controlled by mandates from government nor censorship from one's neighbors but when a person is allowed to act freely according to his personal convictions. This is not something that we are likely to achieve in this imperfect world, but as Americans we at least have the opportunity to try. America is after all, a tribute to the truly free human being and all his potential.

Unfortunately it is only too true that we get what we deserve. By refusing to exercise even a little self control in order to influence the conduct of others, we are condeming ourselves and our children to a second rate world where shoddiness prevails. If we voice our opinion by tuning out stations that refuse to cover elections, if we didn't applaud mud-slinging and purchase pornography we would change things by our actions and not have to subject ourselves to the heavy hand of the law.

Public opinion over the last twenty years has come to mean no opinion — everything goes! In a choice between tolerance and intolerance, I, along with most people, would choose tolerance every time. But the tolerance we have been practicing in this country has gone beyond the "live and let live" stage into the territory of "I don't care". If we don't take a stand we will be stood on. Some small group is attempting to run this country whether you care or not. Unfortunately the brightest and best are not attracted to such a situation. Our problem is how to reach them before it's too late.

ABBREVIATIONS

AEI	American Enterprise Institute
AFDC	Aid to Families with Dependent Children
AFSCME	American Federation of State County & Municipal Employees
AGI	Adjusted Gross Income
AIDS	Acquired Immune Deficiency Syndrome
AMA	American Medical Association
AWED	American Women's Economic Development Corp.
BERI	Business Environment Risk Information Ltd.
BOMB	Bloated Omnibus Money Bill
CAFE	Corporate Average Fuel Economy
CAP	Common Agriculture Policy (of ECC)
CARS	Committee Against Revising Staggers
CBO	Congressional Budget Office
CEO	Chief Executive Officer
CETA	Comprehensive Employment Training Act
CI	Conservation International
COLA	Cost Of Living Adjustments
CPA	Certified Public Accountant
CPI	Consumer Price Index
CRA	Community Reinvestment Act
C-SPAN	Cable Satellite Public Affairs Network
CURE	Consumers United for Rail Equity

DBE	Disadvantaged Business Enterprise
DOL	Department Of Labor
DOT	Department Of Transportation
ECU	composite currency used as a medium of exchange and a unit of account
EEC	European Economic Community
EOC	Equal Opportunity Commission
ERISA	Employee Retirement Income Securities Act (1974)
ERTA	Economic Recovery Tax Act (1981)
ESOP	Employee Stock Ownership Plan
EX-IM Bank	Export-Import Bank
FAA	Federal Aeronautics Administration
FCC	Federal Communications Commission
FDA	Federal Drug Administration
FDIC	Federal Depository Insurance Corp.
FED	Feceral Reserve
FFB	Federal Financing Bank
FHA	Federal Housing Administration
FmHA	Farmers Home Administration
FOMC	Federal Open Market Committee
FRBSF	Federal Reserve Bank San Francisco
FSLIC	Federal Savings & Loan Insurance Corp.
FSX	Fighter Support Experimental project
FTC	Federal Trade Commission
FY	Fiscal Year
GAAP	Generally Accepted Accounting Practices
GAO	Government Accounting Office
GATT	General Agreement on Tariffs & Trade
GDP	Gross Domestic Product
Ginnie Mae	Government National Mortgage Association
GNP	Gross National Product
GPO	Government Printing Office
G-R-(H)	Gramm-Rudman-(Hollings) legislation to curtail government spending
G-5	U.S., Japan, W.Germany, England, France
G-7	U.S., Japan, W.Germany, England, France, Italy and Canada
HI	Hospital Insurance
HR4300	The Parental Leave Bill
HUD	Department of Housing and Urban Development
IBM	International Business Machines
ICC	Interstate Commerce Commission
IDA	International Development Association (a World Bank affiliate)
IDB	Inter-American Development Bank

IMF	International Monetary Fund
INS	Immigration & Naturalization Service
IRA	Investment Retirement Account
IRI	Institute per la Riconstruzione Industriale (Italy)
IRS	Internal Revenue Service
ITC	Investment Tax Credit
JTPA	Job Training Partnership Act
LDC	Lesser Developed Country
LIBOR	London Interbank Offered Rate
MBE	Minority Business Enterprise
MDB	Multi-lateral Development Bank
MIT	Massachusetts Institute of Technology
MITI	Ministry of International Trade and Industry (Japanese)
NAR	National Association of Realtors
NASA	National Aeronautics & Space Administration
NCEO	National Center for Employee Ownership
NEC	National Economic Commission
NFC	National Freight Corporation (Britain)
NOW	National Organization for Women
NSF	National Science Foundation
NT	New Taiwan (dollar)
OASDI	Old Age Survivors Disability Insurance
OECD	Organization for Economic Cooperation & Dev.
OMB	Office of Management & Budget
OPEC	Organization of Petroleum Exporting Companies
PBGC	Pension Benefit Guaranty Corporation
PCE	Personal Expenditure Index
PPP	Purchasing Power Parity
PPSSCC	President's Private Sector Survey on Cost Control
PURPA	Public Utility Regulatory Policies Act
SBA	Small Business Administration
SDR	Special Drawing Right
SEC	Securities Exchange Commission
TEFRA	Tax Equity & Fiscal Responsibility Act (1982)
TNC	The Nature Conservatory
TVA	Tennessee Valley Authority
VA	Veterans Administration
VAT	Value Added Tax
VCR	videocassette recorder
"4"	South Korea, Singapore, Hong Kong, Taiwan
401K	Keogh Plans (pension)
403b plans	pension plans for employees of nonprofit organizations

GLOSSARY

Accrual accounting• A capital budget which conforms to generally accepted accounting principles as opposed to cash-basis accounting.

Adam Smith• 18th century Scottish philosopher and economist; best known as the author of *TheWealth of Nations.*

American Rule• A rule which prevents the prevailing party in a law suit from recovering litigation costs from the losing party.

At-will-employment• Employment which lasts as long as both employer and employee are mutually satisfied and can be terminated when that satisfaction ends on the part of either party.

Austerity programs• Programs which usually involve tax and trade reforms and require belt tightening (cutting imports and concentrating on exports) by the citizens of less developed countries in exchange for aid.

Baby boomers• A term which refers to persons born between 1946 and 1966.

Baker Plan• A plan of continued lending proposed by Secretary of Treasury James Baker and designed to lessen the onerous debt burden carried by the lesser developed countries.

Bank Holding Company Act• Legislation which controls how foreign banks operate in the USA.

Basis point• 1/100th of a percentage point.

Belli, Melvin• A San Francisco attorney responsible for the expansion of judgments awarded for tort damages.

Bretton Woods• An international conference held in New Hampshire in 1944. Its purpose was to develop ideas to assist reconstruction in Europe after the devastation of the Second World War.

British Doctrine• The doctrine, which originated at the London School of Economics and maintains that wherever possible private ownership should be replaced by public and that an emphasis should be put on redistributing wealth rather than creating it.

Cafeteria-style employee benefit programs• A program designed to allow employees to fashion their own benefit programs by choosing from a variety of possible benefits.

Callable capital approach• Refers to a far fetched plan to ease the LDC debt problem.

Cap damages• Means to set a limit on damages awarded in a lawsuit.

Capital budget• A budget that considers outlays for capital assets as long-term investments and labels them accordingly.

Capital flight• Refers to the practice of sending money out of the home-country to another country for investment where it is presumably safer.

Capitalism• An economic system which governs itself through unplanned personal choices and achieves for its practitioners the greatest personal freedom and material production.

Cash-basis budget• A system of accounting which is currently used by the federal government in which everything is counted as an expense. It does not conform to generally accepted accounting principles.

Central banks• Banks supported and controlled by governments.

CMOs• An abbreviation for collateralized mortgage obligations which are bond-like securities backed by a pool of mortgages whose cash flows are repackaged to obtain securities of mixed maturities in order to provide investors and underwriters some protection against prepayments by mortgage holders.

Comecon bloc• Refers to the integrated economic system run from Moscow.

Commercial paper• Short-term securities sold at a discount and issued mainly by industrial corporations, utilities and bank-holding companies.

Commonwealth Club• An educational public affairs forum which features notable speakers and is headquartered in San Francisco.

Communism• A political, economic and social system characterized by the absence of classes (in theory only) and by common ownership of the means of production and subsistence.

Community Reinvestment Act (1977)• A law ostensibly to encourage banks to participate in local communities but which is used by groups to impede the growth of financial institutions

Compulsive litigators• Those who constantly bring suit.

Conrail• A railroad which was 85% owned by the government until its recent sale.

Continental Bank• An Illinois bank that was saved from failure by the government's bail-out in 1984

Contracting out• Refers to the practice by government agencies of hiring private firms to provide goods or preform services instead of having the job done by government employees.

Sword of Damocles• Signifies the permanent threat of an impending disaster. Legend maintains that Damocles was made to sit under a sword suspended by a single hair.

Debt adjustment facility• Facility operated through the IMF to provide a secondary market for LDC debt (loans).

Debt-equity swaps• Creditor to exchange debt for equity assets in the debtor country.

Debt exposure• Amount of outstanding loans.

Debt-nature-swaps• Exchange debt for land or resources set aside in the LDC to be dedicated to wildlife conservation.

Debt-on-debt• Another name for the Baker Plan to lessen the impact of debt on LDCs (keep lending money).

Debt-relief plan• proposed by New Jersey's Senator Bill Bradley—suggests banks "forgive" an amount of LDC debt.

Deep pockets• Refers to the practice of pursuing the defendant in a civil lawsuit who has the greatest ability to pay damages.

Default• Occurs when one is unable to keep commitments. Usually involves the payment of money.

Discount rate• Cost of borrowing from the Fed at the discount window.

Disinflation• The downward movement of inflated prices to a more normal level.

Displaced• Employees who left the work force. The assumed reason is that the jobs were taken by other workers or machines as opposed to voluntary retirement or routine firing.

Double taxation of savings• Dollars are taxed when earned and those after-tax dollars are taxed again when they are included in investment income at a later date.

ECU• Composite international currency used as a medium of exchange and unit of account offering a stable alternative to the dollar.

Engels, Freidrich• A 19th century German socialist leader and thinker who collaborated with Karl Marx.

Enterprise zones• The availability of government subsidies as incentives to encourage economic development in certain depressed areas

Equity partner• An investor who receives an ownership percentage of the investment as opposed to a fee for his contributions.

ESOP• Employee Stock Ownership Plans enable employees to acquire ownership shares in their employers' business.

Eurodollar• Refers to U.S. dollars that are held by foreign banks, specifically in Europe.

Exchange rates• Rates which signify the difference between the value of various currencies at different times.

Excise tax• A tax on a specific product.

Expensing investment• Deducting the cost of an investment from one's tax bill by counting it as an expense of doing business.

Fairness Doctrine• Requirement that broadcasters air both sides of controversial public issues.

Federal Financing Bank• Its existence allows for spending by government entities which never shows up on the unified budget.

Federal fund rates• Refers to the price banks charge when borrowing from one another.

Federal Open Market Committee• A 12 person committee which sets the Fed's monetary policy.

Federal Reserve Bank• U.S. central bank established by Congress at the end of 1913 whose purpose is to safeguard the integrity of money.

First Amendment• Amendment to the U.S. Copnstitution which guarantees basic freedoms of speech, religion, press and assembly as well as the right to petition government for redress of grievances.

Fiscal neutrality• Guarantees that any spending proposal must be accompanied by a spending cut proposal or balancing revenue source.

Fiscal year• An accounting period. The accounting period used by the U.S. government is October 1 to September 30.

Fixed-rate• A rate of interest that does not fluctuate over the duration of the loan.

Flat tax• Although there are many variations the term generally refers to a single tax rate for everybody with no exemptions, deductions or credits.

Floating rates• Rates of interest which fluctuate according to some predetermined index.

Franking priviliges• The privilige granted to members of Congress and others which permits them to send certain material through the public mails without payment of postage.

Free-enterprise-plan• The idea that LDC debt should be treated as any other debt and that the market place alone should decide its value.

Free trade· Trade absolutely free of government interference. (An utopian condition which exists only in theory!)

Freeze· To keep at current or specified level.

Frivolous lawsuits· Lawsuits obviously ("on its face") without substantive merit and used to delay or embarrass an opponent.

Fuel Use Act·1978 law which prohibited utilities from building new oil and natural gas fired power plants and required them to have coal burning capabilities.

Ginnie Mae· The Government National Mortgage Association which provides a secondary market place for mortgages.

Glass-Steagall Act (1933)· A law which, among other things, prohibits commercial banks from underwriting corporate securities.

GNP· The market value of the goods and services produced by a nation over a year.

Grace Caucus· A group of congresspersons dedicated to expiditing many of the Grace recommendations through Congress

Grace Commission· A group of prominent businessmen gathered by J. Peter Grace in 1982 to study government spending and make recommendations to the president on how waste in government could be cut.

Gramm-Rudman· An amendment to a measure raising the ceiling on the national debt which called for the reduction of annual federal deficits in stages until no defict exists.

Grandfathered· An exemption. Refers to any provision in a new law or regulation which exempts those already doing the thing regulated.

Great Society programs· Social programs (most notably Medicare) initiated in the mid 1960s during Lyndon Johnson's tenure as president of the United States.

Group of Five (G-5)· England, USA, W. Germany, France & Japan

Group of Seven (G-7)· England, USA, W. Germany, France, Japan, Italy & Canada

Hard Look Doctrine• Maintains a court's responsibility isn't simply to defer to the expertise of an agency, but it must take a "hard look" at regulatory decisions.

Holding company• A company which holds the controlling shares in the stock of another company.

Impoundment• Refers here to the president's ability to withhold funds at his discretion. The Congress felt the power was abused under Richard Nixon and through legislation substituted recissions and deferrals for the impoundment power.

Indexed bonds• Bonds whose rate of interest fluctuates according to a predetermined index.

Inflation• Rising prices in an economy which decreases the purchasing power of a nation's currency.

Information Age• Refers to the late twentieth century and the expansion of technology as it relates to all fields of communication.

Infrastructure• Refers to facilities and basic structures such as roads, bridges and dams which are essential for the growth and normal functioning of a nation.

Interest-rate risk• The risk that interest rates may fluctuate and change the investment scenario.

Intermediate goods• Pulp, paper and chemicals are examples. They are intermediate products as in a chain from a tree to paper to a book.

International Monetary Fund• An multinational organization which functions as a monetary proctor providing loans to countries with temporary cash problems.

Interstate• Between states

Intrastate• Within a state

Inventory Capitalization Rule• Requires business to declare inventory at the end of the year as taxable income.

"Invisible hand"• Refers to the central theme in *The Wealth of Nations*, which asserts that if men are left to pursue their own economic interests without government direction or restraint the whole community will benefit. It is as if

395

a multitude of individual non-directed decisions were guided by a wise and benevolent "invisible hand".

Jack and Jo Ann Hinckley• The parents of John Hinckley, Jr. who was found not guilty by reason of insanity on all 13 charges of shooting President Reagan and three others on March 30,1981.

Jack Sprat• Character from the nursery rhyme: "Jack Sprat could eat no fat, his wife could eat no lean. But between them both they licked the platter clean."

Joint and several• Liability is joint and several when one or more of the parties to such liability may be sued separately, or all of them together at the option of the plaintiff.

Keynesian economics• An economic system advocating government spending in order to stimulate the economy. John Maynard Keynes endorsed both government deficits and surpluses as counter-cyclical measures.

Laissez faire• (French for "let do".) The reference is to letting people do things for themselves without interference by government.

Law of One Price• Maintains goods traded internationally should cost the same in all countries when measured in a common currency

Legal Services Corp.• A government subsidized group of attorneys who are supposed to represent the interests of low income persons.

Leverage• Refers to the ratio of debt to equity. The greater the debt the greater the leverage.

Line-item-veto• This is a tool desired by the executive branch to enable it to deny parts of legislation without throwing out the whole.

Linkage• The concept of tying a cutback in a social program with an alternate solution to the problem.

Linkage fees• Linkage fees are taxes levied on developers in order to ameliorate social and economic dislocations which development is said to create. The temptation is for officials to abuse the power and turn it into a form of social blackmail: "You can have our permission to do this only if you promise to give us that." Elitist rule as opposed to laissez faire.

Litigation crisis• Refers to the increased number of law suits filed in this country.

Litigious• Refers to a society where people are only too ready to sue one another.

Loopholes• Provisions in the tax code which can be used to avoid or defer taxes.

Macroeconomic• Refers to large economic aggregates such as total employment, production and the consumer price index for example.

Margin requirement• The amount of money which must be tendered when purchasing a stock.

Mark-up committee• An intermediate stage in the budget process where members of Congress reconcile appropriations and allocations.

Marshall Plan• Plan instituted after WWII and named for General George C. Marshall to help ravished countries recover economically

Marx, Karl• 19th century German philosopher and political economist generally assumed to be the father of communism.

McFadden Act• A 1927 law which first permitted national banks to exercise securities powers.

Means testing• Determination based on a person's wealth

Medical malpractice• Suits brought against physicans charging incompetence.

Mexican-debt-swap• Exchange of Mexican debt for discounted Mexican bonds which will be backed by the U.S. Treasury

Microeconomic• Refers to the study of particular markets and sectors of the economy as opposed to macroeconomics.

Micromanaging• Pervasive and detailed management and regulations imposed by government.

Minimills• Steel mills using the continuous casting method of producing steel.

Monetarists• Economists who stress the monetary causes of cyclical fluctuations and inflations and therefore favor monetary policy rather than fiscal policy as a stabilizer.

Moody's•An organization which rates the credit of potential borrowers.

M1• Currency in circulation plus checking accounts, ATS, travelers' checks and NOW accounts.

M2• M1 plus savings and small time deposits, Eurodollars, overnight repurchase agreements and money market mutual-fund balances.

M3• M2 plus large time deposits, term repurchase agreements and institutional negative only money market mutual-fund balances.

National debt• The term is misleading as it refers only to the amount of U.S. government securities outstanding. True debt would take into account all liabilities of the federal government.

New Deal• Refers to the government policies and social programs introduced during the administration of Herbert Hoover in 1929 but generally attributed to Franklin Delano Roosevelt's presidency.

No liability judgment• A term applied when a defendant in a tort case is found not to be liable for the alleged injury.

Non-callable• Absence of a call provision which is the right of the issuing company to pay off obligations (preferred stocks and bonds) before maturity.

Off-budget• Spending that occurs but does not show up on a conventional budget.

Omnibus bill• A bill which is a conglomeration of many items.

"On capital budget"• Counted as an investment

"On operating budget"• Counted as operating expense

Opportunity Society• Refers to social programs in the 1980s touted by government as helping people help themselves. Examples are training programs, enterprise zones and helping tenants purchase public housing.

Over capitalized• To place an unreasonably high value on the nominal capital of a business or property or to contribute an excess amount of capital to an enterprise.

PACs• Political Action Committees funnel money and energy to candidates and issues which concern PAC members. They encourage participation in the political system and are feared by corruptible incumbents.

Packard Commission• President Reagan's 1985 Blue Ribbon Commission on Defense Management, chaired by David Packard of Hewlett-Packard, an electronics firm headquartered in northern California.

Panic pricing• Refers here to excessive charges by insurance companies.

Per capita• For each person.

Permanent debt ceiling• Limitation imposed by law on the amount of government debt. In 1988 it remained at $400 billion as authorized in 1971.

Petrodollar• Dollars generated by oil transactions.

Plaza Accord• Refers to the September 1985 meeting of the G-5 countries at the Plaza Hotel in New York City. They agreed to drive down the value of the dollar.

Polonoroeste• Amazon region.

"Pork Buster"• Legislation proposed by Senator Daniel Quayle of Indiana in 1985 and 1988. (Federal Spending Control Initiative) It would guarantee Congressional action on executive proposals to reduce or eliminate line-items in specific appropriation measures. It does away with the 45 day automatic lapse used by Congress to shirk their duty to review presidential recision proposals. Hundreds of President Reagan's recision proposals were simply ignored by Congress and allowed to expire. (See recision.)

Primary goods• Products from forestry, mining, oil drilling and agriculture

Prime rate• The interest rate commercial banks offer their most credit worthy borrowers.

Private Express Statutes• 1872 legislation giving the U.S. Post Office a monolpoly over first class letter delivery.

Private prisons• Privatization of the prison system may be the wave of the future. In 1987 TX, MN, MA and TN had laws allowing privately operated state prisons. In Feb. of that year The Criminal Justice Division of the American Bar Association launched a comprehensive study of the issue.

Privatize• Let the private sector rather than the government do "it".

Product liability• Liability of a manufacturer for injury resulting from his product regardless of negligence.

Progressives• Persons advocating political reform; generally liberal. Original Progressive Party was organized under the leadership of Theodore Roosevelt in 1912. A party with similar goals was headed by Robert La Follette in 1924. In 1948 Henry Wallace led a Progressive Party.

Progressive tax• A graduated tax structured so that the wealthy pay not only more nominal taxes but a larger percentage of their income.

Protectionism• Barriers erected by governments as obstacles to free trade.

Public housing• A 1930s program designed to provide *temporary* housing for the unemployed during the Great Depression. The structures weren't built to last and the program was not supposed to be permanent. However in 1986 there were over 3,000 independent public housing authorities operating 1.3 million dwelling units in this country.

Public Law 95-435 (1978)• Section 7 says starting in FY1981 total budget outlays of the federal government should not exceed receipts.

Public Law 96-5 (1979)• Ibid

Punitive damages• Money awards meant to punish the defendant rather than compensate the plaintiff.

Purchasing Power Parity• Refers to a theory that maintains if currencies are out of whack investments are distorted.

Rand, Ayn• Contemporary Russian born American philosopher and author, best known for Objectivism and works such as *The Fountainhead* and *Atlas Shrugged* .

Reaganomics• The idea that reducing taxes will stimulate the economy enough to make up for the loss in revenue

"Real" vs "nominal"• As used in the text, "real" takes inflation into account whereas "nominal" doesn't .

Reason Foundation• A California think tank that espouses Libertarian ideals.

Recision• An annulment or cancellation. Coupled with "deferment", recision is one of the means Congress has created for the executive to make narrow changes in the budget. Unfortunately each recision vanishes after 45 days if it fails to receive the approval of Congress. (See "Pork Buster")

Reconciliation process• A process which relies heavily on continuing resolutions to authorize ongoing programs.

Regressive tax• A tax that falls most heavily on the poorest people.

Regulation Q• Refers to a regulation that limited to 5.25%, the interest banks were allowed to pay depositors.

"Repo"• A repurchase agreement where one party sells or lends a security to another party and agrees to repurchase it at a higher price.

Return• Refers to the amount of profit, in interest or equity, generated by an investment.

Revenue neutral• Refers in the text to a change in tax law which neither increases nor decreases the amount of tax collected.

S.2• Senate campaign reform bill (1988) blocked by Republicans. It allows for public financing for Senate campaigns, curtails PACs and contains campaign spending limits.

Schizophrenia• Refers to a group of psychotic reactions characterized by withdrawal from reality. Generally accompanied by highly variable affective, behavioral and intellectual disturbances.

Securities• Refers to stocks and bonds and is literally the written evidence of either ownership or creditorship.

Securitization• Refers to the packaging of loans for sale to investors.

Self-insurance• Setting aside a sum of money in order to pay possible damages which may arise in the future. An alternate to paying premiums to commercial insurance companies. Sometimes a small group of "like-minded" business-men join together to self-insure.

Service work• The term refers to employment which results in a service as opposed to a manufactured product. It includes services such as food preparation, counseling, teaching, health care etc.

Silver crisis• Refers to the danger faced by silver traders if attempts by Bunker Hunt and his family to corner the silver market in 1979-80 had been successful. However the Hunts were not able to come up with enough money to accept delivery of all the contracts they were holding and so that crisis was averted.

Sin tax• Refers to a tax on alcohol or tobacco.

Social blackmail• "If you don't do this something worse will happen and you'll have to pay (or suffer) even more." Assumes an obligation on the part of taxpayers to compensate for the alleged problem.

Social investing· Investing to promote social goals.

Socialism· A political and economic system in which the ownership and operation of the means of production and distribution is held by society or the community rather than by private individuals although private property is recognized. All members of the society or the community share in the work and the products. The socialist slogan is "From each according to his ability, to each according to his work."

Special Drawing Right· The International Monetary Fund's composite currency.

Staggers Act· 1980 legislation which deregulated the railroads to a great extent, although not completely, or enough, in some people's opinion and too much according to others.

Targeted Jobs Credit· A government program that offers tax credits to employers who hire disadvantaged and handicapped persons

Target zones· An area in which currency values would be permitted to fluctuate only within prescribed limits.

Taxpayers Bill Of Rights· Legislation designed to clearly define the boundaries within which the IRS operates and provide better protection to taxpayers.

Telecommute· Communication technology such as computers, Fax machines and conference telephone calls which allow an employee to work from his home and interact with co-workers almost as effectively as if he had commuted to the office.

Temporary debt ceiling· Amount Congress reauthorizes each year over and above the permanent debt ceiling of $400 billion set in 1971.

Termination pay· A sum of money agreed to at the beginning of the relationship to be given the employee by the employer on the former's dismissal.

Third World debt crisis· Refers to the amount of debt owed by the lesser developed countries.

Tort law· Refers to the branch of law dealing with private or civil wrongs or injuries, other than breach of contract, for which the court will provide a remedy in the form of an action for damages.

Treasuries• Used in text to refer to securities issued by the U.S. government.

Triple-A• Refers to credit rating-AAA being the highest and signifying that a company is the safest credit risk.

Underground economy• The trading of goods and services; transactions which are never reported to the Internal Revenue Service and which consequently escape taxation.

Underwriter• An entity which guarantees to furnish a certain sum of money by a definite date to a business or government in return for an issue of bonds or stock. In reference to insurance, an underwriter is the one who assumes a specified risk in return for the payment of a premium.

Unilateral involuntary termination• An exalted term for old fashioned firing of an employee by an employer.

User fee• The fee paid by individuals when and as they use a service or facility provided by government.

Value added tax• A tax which adds a little to the price of goods at each step of production.

Venice Summit• The meeting of world leaders which took place in Venice, Italy in June 1987.

Vested• Refers to the time at which rights to pension benefits legally belong to an employee.

Wealth of Nations • Acclaimed work by Scottish economist and philosopher Adam Smith, first published in 1776 and believed to have influenced the fabric of the U.S. Constitution. It provides the theoretical justification for free-market capitalism.

"When issued"• The term refers to securities that have been announced but not yet issued.

Workers compensation• Refers to benefits that are paid to workers who are injured on the job.

Zero-sum• Theory that claims there is only a limited amount of X, there-fore taking by A detracts from what is available to B and C and so forth.

4 Tigers• South Korea, Taiwan, Singapore and Hong Kong.

APPENDICES

APPENDIX A
CITIZENS FOR A DEBT-FREE AMERICA

You are invited to participate in a historic endeavor.

To honor our predeccessors, to insure hope and opportunity for ourselves and our children, to restore a legacy of liberty and initiative for future generations, citizens of the United States of America have begun to voluntarily retire the public debt of the federal government.

In proportion to the success you have achieved by the exercise of your talent, energy and freedom as a citizen of this nation, make your tax deductible gifts payable to the U.S. Treasury, Public Debt Reduction Fund.

Furthermore, it is anticipated that our leadership and purpose will inspire our public servants to meet the challenge of the future with competence, efficiency, and thrift.

Contributions may be sent to:

> Bureau of Public Debt
> Department G
> Washington, D.C. 20239-0601

Citizens For A Debt-Free America
2550 S. Sunnyslope Road
New Berlin, Wisconsin 53151
(414) 782-1305

APPENDIX B
GRACE CAUCUS

CITIZENS AGAINST
GOVERNMENT WASTE
1-800-USA-DEBT

Congressional Grace Caucuses
100th Congress
As of March 25, 1988

Caucus Co-Chairmen	NUMBER OF MEMBERS		
Sen. Dennis DeConcini (D-AZ)		SENATE	HOUSE	TOTAL
Gordon J. Humphrey (R-NH)	REPUBLICANS	21	93	114
Rep. Beau Boulter (R-TX)	DEMOCRATS	12	38	50
	TOTAL	33	131	164

	SENATE CAUCUS	HOUSE CAUCUS
Alabama	Howell Heflin (D)	H. L. "Sonny" Callahan (R)
Alaska	—	—
Arizona	Dennis DeConcini (D)	Jim Kolbe (R)
	John MCCain (R)	John Kyl (R)
		Bob Stump
Arkansas	—	Tommy F. Robinson (D)
California	Pete Wilson (R)	Robert E. Badham (R)
		Jim Bates (D)
		William E. Dannemeyer (R)
		Robert K. Dornan (R)
		David Dreier (R)
		Elton Gallegly (R)
		Duncan L. Hunter (R)
		Ernest L. Konnyu (R)
		Robert J. Lagomarsino (R)
		Bill Lowery (R)
		Dan Lungren (R)
		Carlos J. Moorhead (R)
		Ron Packard (R)
		Norman D. Shumway (R)
Colorado	William Armstrong (R)	Hank Brown (R)
		Daniel L. Schaefer (R)
		Patricia Schroeder (D)
Connecticut	—	Nancy L. Johnson (R)
		John G. Rowland (R)
Deleware	—	Thomas R. Carper (D)
Florida	—	Andy Ireland (R)
		Tom Lewis (R)
		Bill McCollum (R)
		Connie Mack (R)
		Buddy MacKay (D)
		E. Clay Shaw, Jr. (R)
Georgia	Wyche Fowler, Jr. (D)	Doug Barnard (D)
	Sam Nunn (D)	George W. Darden (D)
		Charles F. Hatcher (D)
		J. Roy Rowland (D)
		Ed Jenkins (D)
		Patrick L. Swindall (R)
		Robert Lindsay Thomas (D)
Hawaii	Spark M. Matsunaga (D)	Patricia Saiki (R)
Idaho	James A. McClure (R)	Larry E. Craig (R)
	Steven D. Symms (R)	Richard H. Stallings (D)

State	Senate Caucus	House Caucus
	Paul Simon (D)	Terry L. Bruce (D)
		Philip M. Crane (R)
		Richard J. Durbin (D)
		Harris W. Fawell (R)
Illionois		Lynn Martin (R)
		John E. Porter (R)
	—	Daniel R. Coats (R)
		John P. Hiler (R)
	Charles E. Grassley (R)	Jim Lightfoot (R)
	—	Jan Meyers (R)
Indiana		Robert Whittaker (R)
	—	Larry J. Hopkins (R)
Iowa	—	Richard Baker (R)
Kansas		Clyde Holloway (R)
	—	—
Kentucky	—	C. Thomas McMillen (D)
Louisiana	John F. Kerry (D)	Chester G. Atkins (D)
	—	William S. Broomfield (R)
Maine		Bob Carr (D)
Maryland		Paul B. Henry (R)
Massachusetts		Carl D. Pursell (R)
Michigan		Bill Schuette (R)
		Guy Vander Jagt (R)
	Rudy Boschwitz (R)	Timothy J. Penny (D)
		Arlan Stangeland (R)
		Vin Weber (R)
	—	Trent Lott (R)
Minnesota	—	Bill Emerson (R)
		Harold L. Volkmer (D)
	—	—
Mississippi	—	—
Missouri	Chic Hecht (R)	Barbara Vucanovich (R)
	Harry Reid (D)	
Montana	Gordon J. Humphrey (R)	Robert C. Smith (R)
Nebraska	Warren Rudman (R)	
Nevada	Bill Bradley (D)	James A. Courter (R)
		Dean A. Gallo (R)
New Hampshire		William J. Hughes (D)
		Matthew J. Rinaldo (R)
New Jersey	—	Joe Skeen (R)
	—	Joseph J. DioGuardi (R)
		Hamilton Fish, Jr. (R)
		Amory Houghton, Jr. (R)
New Mexico	Jesse A. Helms (R)	Cass Ballenger (R)
New York		Howard Coble (R)
		J. Alex McMillan (R)
		Stephen L. Neal (D)
North Carolina	—	—
	—	Dennis E. Eckart (D)
		Edward F. Feighan (D)
		Marcy Kaptur (D)
North Dakota		John R. Kasich (R)
Ohio		Donald E. (Buz) Lukens (R)
		Bob McEwen (R)
		Clarence E. Miller (R)
		Michael G. Oxley (R)
		Donald J. Pease (D)

	Senate Caucus	**House Caucus**
Oklahoma	Don Nickles (R)	Mickey Edwards (R)
		James M. Inhofe (R)
Oregon	—	Les AuCoin (D)
		Denny Smith (R)
		Robert F. Smith (R)
Pennsylvania	Arlen Specter (R)	William F. Clinger (R)
		Thomas Foglietta (D)
		George W. Gekas (R)
		Paul E. Kanjorski (D)
		Doug Walgren (D)
		Robert S. Walker (R)
Rhode Island	John H. Chafee (R)	Claudine Schneider (R)
South Carolina	Ernest F. Hollings (D)	Elizabeth J. Patterson (D)
	Strom Thurmond (R)	Arthur Ravenel, Jr. (R)
South Dakota	Tom Daschle (D)	—
Tennessee	—	Bart Gordon (D)
		Don Sundquist (R)
Texas	Phil Gramm(R)	Michael D. Andrews (D)
		Richard K. Armey (R)
		Steve Bartlett (R)
		Joe Barton (R)
		Beau Boulter (R)
		Johnt (D)
		Ronald Coleman (D)
		Jack Fields (R)
		Thomas D. DeLay (R)
		Ralph M. Hall (D)
		Lamar Smith (R)
		Charles W. Stenholm (D)
		Mac Sweeney (R)
Utah	E. J. (Jake) Garn (R)	Howard Neilson (R)
	Orrin G. Hatch (R)	Wayne Owens (D)
Vermont	—	James M. Jeffords (R)
Virginia	Paul Trible (R)	Thomas J. Bliley (R)
Washington	—	John R. Miller (R)
West Virginia	—	—
Wisconsin	William Proxmire (D)	Toby Roth (R)
	Robert W. Kasten (R)	Steven Gunderson (R)
		Gerald D. Kleczka (D)
		Thomas E.Petri (R)
		James Sensebrenner (R)
Wyoming	Alan K. Simpson (R)	—

APPENDIX C

National Economic Commission May 1988
Conversation of Commissioners

(Transcribed from C-SPAN taped record)

Senator Pete Domenici of New Mexico:

It's very important that we understand that the Congress of the
United States has evolved from a period in its history when it had
only one committee structure and those who authorized legislation appropriated for the legislation. That means if you were a
committee on education, you drew the laws and you paid for the
program. We arrived at a dramatic point in history when that was
perceived to be in desperate need of reform. ...The Nation
thought that the committee proposing policy had a vested interest,
and therefore they'd spend too much money and, believe it or not,
the first reform process evolved and it was called the appropriations process. And so we had authorizers, which we still have,
who draw laws and set policies and, I remind you, that to this point
I have not discussed entitlements. Let's leave them alone for a
moment. We had authorizing committees and the reform process
of one committee in each house that paid for the programs called
the appropriators. Quite by coincidence, when I arrived in the
Senate, the very year I arrived with 17 new Senators, we had those
two processes and we came on the scene and said this is really not
possible that we run our Government this way, because we had no
way, you see, in advance of the year, of finding out how much we
were going to spend, because the only document was a presidential budget which was advisory, and appropriation bills which
spent money. And, I remember vividly, all 17 of us signed a letter
to the leadership saying no one runs their business or their
government this way. We need an adding machine and as you
bring us these appropriation bills we have got to know how much
we have spent and where does it end. Well, suffice it to say that
we didn't reform anything, we left those two in place because they
are very vested processes in this institution and you all know how
much committees covet being in charge of education programs
and you know how much appropriators covet being able to say
where you are going to spend it. So we dreamt up a third process.
And the third process is called a budget process. But essentially
all three are the processes by virture of which we spend money.
Because the appropriators appropriate, authorizing committess

411

draw entitlement programs which spend automatically, And then the budget process, l2 years ago, came along and imposed itself on top of all of that. And we made some very very significant compromises to the other processes so that we had sort of all of them being in some respect equal. ... The Congress of the United States only lately (4 years) has even concerned itself about outlays. We also dealt in program authority and we guessed the outlays. But outlays by the year yield a deficit, if you are looking at one year at a time, and so we had three processes going plus the opportunity on the part of a committee to draw an entitlement program which paid out automatically.

An agricultural committee could draw an agricultural program that needed no appropriating and if the farmer met the bill, he got money. And if a citizen with the right color of eyes and hair and the right age was entitled under this statute, they got a check. So, we had all of those evolving at the same time, and they are here and now before us. And then we found, believe it or not, that with all of that, we had to put an outside force on top to keep the pressure on, and therein was the evolution of Gramm-Rudman-Hollings. For it said, we will set annually a limit, and if you exceed it, there will be an automatic cut to achieve it. It was the outside pressure to impose a mandatory type ceiling.

Now, I have only given you a very cursory history. It is filled with nuances beyond anything that I want to bore you with. But let me just give you an example. Cap Weinberger, Secretary Weinberger, will understand this one very clearly. You pass a budget resolution. And, let me just say, you establish through negotiation and fussing and fuming that you are going to spend $200 billion on defense and that's the budget resolution. I hope you all understand that until this year in the economic summit, when we agreed on numbers, that the appropriators were not bound at all by that number. In other words, they would take from Defense and spend somewhere else so long as the overall total was right. And for the first 8 years of the process, believe it or not, there was no regard for the outlay effect of transferring money from one program to another. So you could take from Defense or Housing, which spend very slowly, and spend on something that is spent very rapidly so long as you used the total program authority in a consistent manner. So I submit, that while we are not going to spend a great deal of time suggesting reforms, nobody, (I don't think we are, but some might assume) I hope no one thinks that this process works very well. Now let me also say, reconciliation is both, on the one hand, a magnificent tool; on the other hand it's an abomination because it has created some rules that protect

412

legislation beyond anything we assumed and Congress hardly gets to debate, and, you pass things you don't even know you're passing. An, secondly, there is little or no control on the second, third and fourth year effect of legislation that you pass in the first year.

You can think you're saving money 'cause you pass a measure that says "we're cutting and we're only going to spend $50 million". But that program may, by its very nature, cost $700 million three years from now. And none of these processes that we are talking about, save for one very esoteric rule, that you can't pass an entitlement without a budget resolution, that's the only one and that's very very strange and we used it effectively and conned a parliamentarian into ruling on it and so it's been effective. But other than that, there is no way, even under this process, that you ...(can) put in money this year that will (not) grow dramatically in the out years and no one has anything to say about it.

So, I hope that you understand that this has been a very evolutionary process and I am not so sure, in spite of the plaudits, we did some good, with a process called a budget process. Surely we would be in worse shape if we didn't have it, but clearly there is a very big vacuum in terms of setting real mandatory goals at one point in time, even yearly, much less every couple of years and then being bound by them and seeing that they happen. ... I think it's relevant that, when you look at the nature of the deficit and the nature of the tax cuts that have been eluded to, and I am in no way complaining about the way anyone explained them, but I think it is also imperative that we look at the ultimate. And I think you will find that after five or six years , that the taxes on the American people, in spite of having the great reductions in '81 and '82, the total tax on the American people has not gone down. Because we have dramatically increased the tax for social security and if you want some charts on that you can ask them for them, but the tax on the average working man and woman is higher than before we cut taxes because of the social security tax that has been imposed which is reather dramatic. Now there is a sliver at the top of the income bracket that may come out with some cuts when the last reform package reaches its total fruition and you'll have to wait and see. But the total tax on the average working man and woman is not down as a result of the dramatic tax cuts, but rather is higher than it was. And the GNP proportion of tax take is not down, it's higher.

Now I don't know if that means anything, but it surely does not

413

mean that the tax cuts are substantially responsible for the deficit, as I see it, in terms of the total tax on the American people and I think he can show you that in charts

Felix Rohatyn:

I'm trying to learn about this process but it seems to me there is one set of numbers that sort of lives a life of its own here which we learned about in New York which is called interest on debt. And, if I just quickly add up the interest outlays for the last 7 years or '80-87, they add up to about $700 billion out of $1.9 trillion of debt, so that about 35 percent of the existing debt has been borrowed to pay interest. And then if I just look at the projections, whether they are OMB (Office of Management & Budget) or CBO (Congressional Budget Office) deficit projections, and I just take the mid point, I mean just an easy average, there is another $800 billion of debt coming in between now and '93 on which we will probably pay another $200 billion of interest, roughly. At which point, the debt, if I'm correct, will be roughly $2.7 trillion and the accumulated interest will be about $1 trillion. And we will be paying $200 billion a year interest, annually. And I just want to leave those numbers there. They have nothing to do with politics, programs, any kind of authority, but it seems to me that these are sobering numbers.

Pete Domenici:

I think that's why there's a Commission.

Carol Cox: (Ms. Cox, Executive Director of the Committe for a Responsible Federal Budget testified before the Commission)

It's what I call the Pac Man effect in the budget. Interest keeps eating everything else because you have to cut programs or raise taxes just to pay more interest every year.

Cooper Weinberger :

Mr. Chairman, I'd like to agree with Senator Domenici that the characterization of the budget process as a splendid rosey one is, uh, I think, ah, extraordinarily, well the kindest most polite way to say it is, extraordinarily optimistic or extraordinarily kind. The budget process is one of the things that I hope the Committee and the Commission here is going to spend a great deal of time on, because I think...one of the problems that we face is caused by the budget process. We were given some charts here and these are helpful except that they are very much like a text book from someone who never had anything to do with government because they totally fail, unless I have been unable to find it, unless I have been wrong in being unable to find it, I don't see the word authorization mentioned here once. And Senator Domenici correctly identified a very long sluggish delay in the whole process that is caused by the authorization committees to get around to giving their recommendations which are then regularly disregarded and which regularly cause all kinds of contentions, disputes, and jurisdictional fights and ultimately, because everyone is not only tired because the government is grinding to a halt, something is enacted. That's what happened all last year and, to be perfectly frank about it, if we want one of the best or one of the worst examples of what the budget process produces, and I'm not passing any judgments, because we've just started, it's the way this Commission was formed. This Commission was formed by a piece of paper that was handed across the desk at somewhere along close to midnight, ... maybe it was 11 pm on December 23rd or December 16th or something. There was no debate or no committee hearings. There may have been a couple of words of explanation. It was adopted. Some people are worried a little bit about the fuzziness of the charter. I think it is a remarkably clear charter in view of the circumstances of its birth. But the fact that you can have that kind of a bill of some 2,300 pages which was not even printed when it was adopted, and that horrified me a little bit more, I supppose, than most, because I used to be a member of the California Legislature, and we had a rather conservative state rule out there, that you had to have things printed before you voted on them.

All of that is an example of what we have come to and why we don't have a good budget process and why we can have some really terrible results. And I don't think that fixing the process is necessarily going to fix all the results, but it certainly is going to remove a lot of obstacles. The process, as someone pointed out, I think Chairman Gray a moment ago, works if you have total agreement on all of the policies and all of the basic overall trends. And then the process, at that point, doesn't get in the way of it because there is no need to call on the process. But if you have any kind of disagreement, which policy processes are supposed to resolve, you can't get them by this system that we have now.

415

You have six committees and frequently at least two or three others will get into it so that there are about eight. You have to give the same testimony about eight times, or six times at least, and you don't get any kind of decisions until you have to consolidate everything into one big bill and leave the President with a lot of unpalatable choices. One of which is letting the government stop, (a choice) which he has been strongly tempted to take many times. So I think we have to, if we start out with any assumption or any testimony that this is a good process and we don't have to worry much about it, then I think we need another midnight amendment that makes a few changes in our charter because we cannot do anything, I don't think, constructive until we fix that process. That isn't going to be a guarantee that we will do anything constructive, but it is a guarantee that at least you will remove some of the formalistic procedural hurdles and obstacles that make it virtually impossible for any kind of ...(rational) approach to these problems to be taken within the year. When I was Director of OMB we were all told that the real problem was that the Congress couldn't be expected to enact a budget by June 30th and so if we'd fix the fiscal year and move it up to October everything would be all right. We fixed the fiscal year and moved it up to October and everything slid three months to the right and then we come out in December instead of October with nothing done. You have to do something more basic than that. There are a lot of things that you can do and a lot of things that we can draw very constructively on if we look at state processes. No responsible large state of the United States is allowed to run its fiscal affairs in this way. And so I think we would do well to look at things like item vetos of course, single budgets, budgets that are heard by single committees and processes that enable the legislature to know what's the total amount that they're appropriating and how much revenue they have and to get it done within a reasonable period like six to eight months.

I didn't plan to go into any major exposition of that kind, Mr. Chairman, but I couldn't, as Pete Domenici could not, I 'm sure, sit by idly and hear the budget process praised when I think it is so much responsible for so many of the problems we have now.

Don Rumsfeld:

Well, just a brief comment. It seems to me that since the beginning of this Commission I have been expressing a concern about the need to look at the process and ask the question, "Are there things that we can do that would improve it so that the outcomes might

416

be somewhat better?"

If the situation's as serious as Felix suggests, and if the process is as is imperfect as some of the experts here have suggested, one has to ask the question "Why isn't there accountability?" , "Why hasn't something happened before things became quite as serious as they seem to be?". It seems to me, that in one respect the process is very good - that is to say, by its very complexity it prevents the American people from being able to hold anyone accountable for the impossible and imperfect results. And that is about its only virtue. And I would think that what we ought to do as we ask outselves these questions about the process, is to ask ourselves how we might begin to re-establish some form of accountability in the process. And I think the very complexity of it works against that.

APPENDIX D

Testimony before the National Economic Commission in May 1988 by Stanley Collender, Director of Federal Budget Policy, Touche Ross & Co. and editor of the Federal Budget Report

Let me just go back a few years. There are 4 major acts that are currently in effect. The 1921 Budget & Accounting Act really was directed at executive branch budgeting. .... It was the first time in American history that the President was required to submit a budget. Up until that time, agencies and departments submited their requests directly to Capitol Hill. As you can imagine, as the requests started to get bigger and as the agencies realized that there was no one overseeing their requests, Congress found itself incapable, or unwilling to deal with the varying priorities, so it asked the President to put ...(something) together. To help him in that fight Congress took the Bureau of the Budget from the Treasury Department and transferred it to the executive office of the President. In 1970 that became the Office of Management and Budget. As Senator Domenici suggested, Congress really didn't have a formal process for dealing with the budget all the way until 1974 when Congress passed the Congressional Budget Impoundment Control Act. The Impoundment Act created most of what we know today as the budget process. It created the House and Senate budget committees whose job it was to look at the big picture as opposed to individual subject areas. It created the Congressional Budget Office to give Congress an independent source of information on budget matters. And it created the budget process, the timetables, the deadlines, which at the time were thought to be fixed, hard and impossible to get around. As we see, in the meantime, it's not only easy to get around them, it's too easy to get around them. The important thing I think to keep in mind about both the '21 and the '74 budget acts, and from today's prospective it's a little hard to believe, is that neither one of them was designed to deal with a deficit. They were both deficit-neutral. They were used during their entire history to increase and decrease spending; increase and decrease taxes. They were simply procedures that would enable Congress and the President to get a better hold on what they wanted to do and, if necessary, to implement that. Why then was the '74 Act blamed for the deficit problem and why was it changed? Well the problem was, I think, with the '74 Act, that the deficit increased almost continuously during the time that it was in place. It increased from about $73 billion in fiscal 1976, which is the first year it was in effect, to $212 billion in 1985. Although the process, as I said, was not created to deal with the deficit, it was blamed. As a result the thing that was changed as the deficit started to get larger, was the process itself, and that's what got us to the current budget process, Gramm-Rudman-Hollings.

419

The major difference between Gramm-Rudman-Hollings and the two previous budget processes is that GRH starts by defining the deficit as being bad. It says it's bad, should be eliminated and except in the case of a war or an economic downturn, Congress and the President have no choice as to either how large the deficit should be every year or how much it should be reduced. Both are given them. There is such a thing created as a maximum deficit amount which is what the President must live up to when he submits his budget, what Congress must live up to when it passes a budget resolution and, in theory, when it implements that through the authorization and appropriation process. The Congress and the President do not agree on a plan or fail to implement it in some way that will bring the deficit down to the maximum, then this thing called sequestration, the automatic spending cuts, will be triggered and federal spending will be cut according to a very specific formula in Gramm-Rudman itself. I like to think of Gramm-Rudman as the most cynical law that has ever been created in the history of the United States. On the one hand, it doesn't trust lawmakers to come up with the appropriate fiscal policy of the United States, so it gives it to them. Then, on the other hand, it doesn't trust them to live up to that fiscal policy so it hangs a large club over their head and says either do it or else. It is, in many respects, really an admission of failure that if left on their own, policy makers will not reduce the deficit. Therefore they are told what to do and, unlike the '21 and the '74 Acts where there was lots of discretion, there is no discretion given to them at all.

In addition to the maximum deficit amounts in sequestration, Gramm-Rudman-Hollings strengthened a lot of the other procedures created by the '74 Act. In particular, reconciliation, which we talked a great deal about this afternoon. Under the '74 Act, reconciliation was voluntary. It was only if Congress decided to use it. The only time it was used before 1981 was in 1980. A lot of that was because the budget committees were worried about whether or not it was going to be complied with. A lot of that was simply timing, it was basically created to be used late in the year so it really wasn't used until the very end of the Carter administration and was only marginally effective. They certainly cut less than they had planned.

But as far as the deficit is concerned, the most important thing that has happened is the maximum deficit amounts. These were rewritten when Gramm-Rudman I was revised in September, 1987. The original Gramm-Rudman targets, particulary the first year, was shown to be unattainable almost from the very beginning. The fiscal 1986 target was $171.9 billion and when the actual numbers came in, it was exceeded by almost $50 billion. While that itself was terrible, the real problem is that it made the 2nd, 3rd, 4th, 5th and 6th years of Gramm-Rudman I impossible to achieve. To get from $221 billion, which was the actual deficit, to the original target for 1987 of $144 billion, would have required a $77 billion reduction, by far the largest reduction in history, had it occurred. The previous record was a little over $30 billion. The

Supreme Court, in the meantime, had declared that "club" to be unconstitutional, so it wasn't really surprising that Congress decided to revise Gramm-Rudman-Hollings, and in particular, in addition to of course, meeting the Supreme Court's objections, revised the maximum deficit amounts. The maximum deficit amounts for this year was changed to $144 billion. Quite frankly, I'm not sure that's going to be reached. The $144 billion number is, in my estimation, a phony number; more of a public relations stunt than anything else. Really what Gramm-Rudman said was sequestrations for this year would be avoided if the deficit was cut by a net of $23 billion regardless of the actual deficit that left.

According to my calculations, and I suspect that everyone's got different ones, that will leave the 1988 deficit at about $160-165 billion. For next year Gramm-Rudman requires (that's fiscal 1989) the current version of Gramm-Rudman requires that we go from $160 billion to $100 billion, or a $60 billion drop in one year. Again, that will be the lagest one year drop in American history, and, I think, rather unrealistic. I think what this really shows, however, is that if you examine the entire scope of federal budget acts from 1921 to 1987 to 1988 where we currently are, that (1) the process doesn't make very much difference. If the '74 and the '21 Acts were up to the discretion of Congress, they were used to increase and decrease deficits as Congress either felt like doing or didn't feel like doing. Gramm-Rudman has made some inroads, but it is fairly clear that even ... with (the) specific deficit reduction amounts that it puts in place, (it) cannot force the kind of changes that it would like to have on an annual basis. So I think there are several lessons that I think the Commission should draw from this. Let me just read these briefly.

First, the budget process is not the problem. Whatever process you put in place, whatever process is ultimately used in any particular year, it will always be subservient to whatever the budget politics are that year. No budget process of any kind, by itself, will guarantee the results this Commission has been created to find.

Second, deficit maximums are not really bad. Although they have put a lot of pressure on Congress, I think that pressure is good because at least it gives you something to shoot at and gives you a way of judging how well you have done. Before, in the '74 process, Congress and the President could agree on a deficit target, come close to it and declare victory. Now you really can't declare victory until you get within $10 billion of the maximum deficit amount that Gramm-Rudman states, so at least you have a way of knowing whether Congress and the President are doing their job.

Third, however, deficit maximims are of no use when they require spending to be cut or revenue to be increased so much in any one year that the goal is unachievable. As we have seen in both of the situations where this has been the case, the likely response in these circumstances is either inaccurate projections of what will be accomplished, frustrations both by lawmakers and voters, the feeling in Congress and the Administration that the job is so monumental and the political pain so great that it would be better for all concerned not to do what is needed to reduce the deficit to the target, or, the use of budget gimmicks and sleight of hand tricks that reduce the deficit now but do little or nothing to solve the longer term problem. In some cases the smoke, mirrors and budget ledger domain actually make the long term situation worse.

Accordingly, I'd like to urge this Commission to abandon the $36 billion a year reduction that Gramm-Rudman currently requires and put in something a little bit more reasonable and reachable. Something in the area of $15-20 billion. In light of the realities of today's federal budget, an annual $36 billion drop, I think, is all but impossible to achieve and will probably cause many or all the elements I just cited to be noted. A slower deficit reduction path is much more likely to be followed.

Finally, if this Commission does recommend changes in the budget process, I urge you in the strongest possible terms not to make it any more complex or complicated than it currently is. I've spent a great deal of time over the past two years speaking to different groups around the country. Everyone from senior federal officials to state and local government officials to business and community leaders. Their common complaint is that what is being done in Washington on the budget is too hard to understand and follow. Some even believe that this is done intentionally so that representatives, senators and the administration cannot be held accountable for their decisions. If there is one change in the budget debate that would make a greater difference than enabling voters to understand more about that's going on, why and who is responsible, I cannot think of it.

APPENDIX E

Testimony before the National Economic Coimmission in May, 1988 of Timothy Muris, Professor of Law and Economics at George Mason University and former Associate Executive Director of the Office of Management and Budget

Normally we think about the deficit as an absolute number. In 1987 it was $150 billion. ...There's this grand total deficit reduction, and the grand total deficit reduction adds up to about $76 billion over 2 years. Well, if the 1987 deficit was $150 billion, and you see, even the most optimistic projections don't have the 1988-89 deficit falling much below that, you might wonder, well, where does the $76 billion come from.... Most of your probably know there was a significant Social Security tax increase that went into effect on January lst of this year. That tax increase, in fact, raised Social Security receipts to the government by $29 billion. Well there's not a penny of that $29 in those numbers. On the other hand, there is this thing called the telephone excise tax which we extended at the same rate as it was last year, that's in here.... Another example, Medicare. ... Medicare has grown enormously in the 80's. When we're through by 1990, we will have roughly a tripling of Medicare. But yet here we see a $5.5 billion cut and .... that $5.5 billion reduction is part of about $50 billion in reductions in Medicare in the 1980's. ...

Now, what's up? How do we explain these numbers? Well, we explain them by something that we call baselines. All these numbers in the table are not changes to the deficit or changes to last year's level of spending, they are changes from the baseline. I think the best way to understand what the baseline is, is to call it a current policy baseline. What that means is that - it means at least two things - one is that you ask what would spending and receipts be under the laws as they now exist. Then you do something else. Many programs, under laws as they now exist, are not automatically inflated. You inflate everything that is not inflated. The stuff that is already inflated by law, you include that. That gets you your current policy baseline. Now this is sometimes called current services. It is often called current services. But I think that term is somewhat misleading. And the reason I think it is somewhat misleading is that the idea of current services implies that we take what we had last year and we inflate it for whatever it takes for the government to provide the same services that they provided last year. Well, that's not what the baseline that's used in the budget process does. What the baseline that's used in the budget process does, is it doesn't take current services as what's current, it takes current law as what's current. And I think that's what Senator Dominici was talking about a little while ago. Thus, if you've got a program that 3 years from now has a built-in increase of 20 percent in it, that spending is in the baseline. In the third year we don't say spending is increased by 20 percent — what we say is it hasn't increased at all because it is already law, therefore, it's already in the baseline.

Another fact to remember about the way we do these numbers is that we use the unit of the fiscal year and what that means is that some interesting things can happen. If, for example, as was done in the budget summit numbers, we accelerate taxes, where we're collecting them faster than we would be otherwise, we count the whole amount of the acceleration from say 1990 into 1989 as an increase, even though the benefit to the government is simply the fact that we get the money a little earlier. On the other hand, one of the things we did was we slowed down Medicare payments by a few days and if you slow them down by a few days by the time you get to the end of September you kick it into early October and that saves the government a little bit in reality because the government holds onto the money for a few more days and can presumably get interest from it. But in budget accounting we count all of that money that's shifted from the end of September into the beginning of October — that's counted as a reduction. And indeed that's part of these numbers. ...these numbers are all changes from this baseline. And this baseline takes law as given. In this baseline there are tax increases and spending increases but they don't show up anywhere for the year that they actually occur as increases of one type or the other because they are already "in the baseline". ...
What this means is that when you hear the word "cut", you always have to put quotes around it because most people think of the word "cut" as compared to last year, and that's not what we mean in the budget process. ...Think of it this way.... A former OMB director was at the home of a friend and the friend's 11 year old ran up and said "I just saved $1". And he (the director) said, "How did you save $1?" and he (the child) said, "I didn't take the bus I ran home along side of it." The OMB director said, "Well, next time run along side a cab and you'll save $2." ...

As Secretary Weinberger pointed out, the numbers under Defense, under discretionary for defense and domestic discretionary were obtained by a reduction from the baseline. The baseline assumed about 4% increase in spending and there was actually in the summit agreement a little less than 2% increase in spending. That's authority to spend, that's budget authority and it translates out into outlays.

There is no doubt that in year to year changes, which is the way everybody in the papers talks about defense, that defense in year to year is not growing and to the extent that it costs more obviously for weapons systems, and to the extent that we pay people more, that means there's less money for other things. That's absolutely true... Normally, what we do in the baseline, what the baseline does is to assume that federal pay will increase by the increase in private sector wages. Through the Regan administration that's been about a 5% increase a year. Since federal employees have had their pay increased by about 3 percent a year, that increase has been translated into billions of dollars of claimed savings. ... The only way you can reduce the deficit through cutting pay is to take money from the appropriators. Because when you give money to the appropriators the appropriators can spend it wherever they want. They can spend it on pay, they can spend it on other things. Appropriators get a big sum of money and they divide it up. They are not allowed to go over it. Unless you are cutting pay the only way you can reduce the deficit is to take the money away from the appropriators. The money wasn't taken from the appropriators so whatever you think of the idea that paying a 2 percent pay increase is a reduction there is no way...because the money wasn't taken from the appropriators. So that's so much for the $2.4 billion number. ...The allocation to Medicare was 5.5 billion over 2 years. In actuality CBO said that $5.9 billion over 2 years was cut. Well lets look a little bit at what happened. $1.1 billion over 2 years was a payment shift. That was taking a little money out of '88 and putting it into '89 and doing the same thing in September of '89 and putting it into October of '89 because the fiscal year breaks there. That was $1.1 billion of the savings. $1.7 billion of the savings was claimed from limiting the increase in reimbursements to hospitals. The way that works is as follows: Congress each year sets the increase and they have statutes that require recommendations from a private group and the secretary of HHS. Those people, when making the recommendations, are told to look at the input inflation which is called the "market basket". They're told to look at productivity, they're told to look at scientific advances, they're told to look at a whole host of factors. The baseline, however, reflects just one thing and that's the market basket. Before fiscal 1988 Congress had paid hospitals on average 1/4 of the market basket as an increase. In the budget summit, what happened is Congress decided we're going to pay hospitals 38 percent in '88, about 38 percent. This is on average, because different hospitals get different amounts, and about 60 percent in 1989 and they did that and the result of that was because the baseline was 100 percent, they claimed about $1.7 billion in savings.

Now it's not my point to say that it's good or bad to pay more of less for hospitals. The point is that relative to their past experience they paid hospitals a lot more but claimed a big savings. And that was caused, again, because of the way this baseline works.

Let me just be foreward looking and make three points that are relevant to next year and forget about past years.

Point 1 is the point that has been made by several people, which is confusion. I think the way we talk about baselines confuses the average person.

425

Point 2 is something is going to happen next year in several areas, but particularly Medicare. The baseline counts as a reduction, a continuation of an expiring cut ...If you look at Medicare as a whole, if Congress allocates to Medicare and says you go cut Medicare $6 billion, they can cut Medicare in 1990-1991, they can make that $6 billion target by simply extending policies that already existed in 1989 but that are in essence going to expire. So, you'll have to "cut" Medicare just to run in place. And Medicare is the biggest example because it's such a big program. But that's something to keep in mind.

Final point about the future. And again, this is something that happened in the budget. ... Program expansions are a significant part of what happens in these budget agreements and the way they work is they don't really show up in a 2 year manner like this. For example, Medicaid and income security were expanded over 5 years where HHS (Dept. of Health & Human Services) estimates there will be an extra $3.5 billion worth of spending. But those numbers were not required to be offset by the summit agreement and, because of the way program expansions work, that $3.5 billion does not show up in the first 3 years. 2/3 of it shows up in 4th and 5th year 1992 and 1993 and there are two reasons for that — one is that is takes a while to expand a program and the other is that a lot of these expansions are written so they don't take effect for a few years down the road, for whatever reason.

So you have got to be cognizant, I think, in terms of addressing the deficit picture, of the way baselines work; to be aware of the confusion problem, to be aware of the expiring law problem and to be aware of the expansions issue.

NOTES

FIRST STEP

1. *Pork Barrel*, by Randall Fitzgerald and Gerald Lipson, p.xix
2. *Wall Street Journal*, February 13, 1985, "Federal Bid to Update Agencies' Computers Faces Many Obstacles" by Leon Wynter
3. *Wealth*, Winter 1985, p. 15
4. *Underground Government*, by James Bennett and Thomas DiLorenzo Foreward by Gordon Tullock, p.xii
5. *Hoover Institution*, "An Economic Bill of Rights" by Martin Anderson, pp. 7-8
6. Wall Street Journal, January 23, 1988, "Rebuilding An International Monetary System" by Edouard Balladur, p.15
7. On this subject see Helen Roger's book: *Social Security: An Idea Whose Time Has Passed*

SECOND STEP

1. *The Atlantic*, October 1987, "The Morning After" by Peter Peterson, p. 49
2. Ibid
3. *Wall Street Journal*, January 15, 1988, "Trade Gap is Inevitable - And Good" by George Gilder
4. Ibid

5. President Reagan's annual Economic Report to Congress February 6, 1986
6. *The Rise and Fall of the Great Powers* by Paul Kennedy, pp.528-529
7. Ibid
8. *Everyone's Guide To Financial Planning* by Helen P. Rogers, p.258
9. *Wall Street Journal*, February 6, 1986, "New Building Blocks for Capital Formation" by David Boren
10. *Wall Street Journal*, December 30, 1987, "World Economy Doesn't Hang in the Imbalance" by Herbert Stein
11. Ibid
12. *Airline Pilot*, October 1984, p. 7
13. *Wall Street Journal*, "A Man Who Makes Good Use of the Numbers" by Alfred Malabre, Jr.
14. *How We Can Achieve Lifetime Employment* by Kelsos, 1983
15. Ibid
16. Ibid

THIRD STEP

1. *A New Social Contract* by Martin Carmoy, Derek Shearer and Russell Rumberger, p. 46
2. *Fortune*, March 2, 1987, "Europe Goes Wild Over Privatization" by Shawn Tully. Quote found on p. 68
3. *Insight*, July 6, 1987, "Would Privatization Make Postal Service Letter-perfect?" by Christopher Elias
4. *Wall Street Journal*, August 5, 1986
5. *Associated Press*, February 15, 1985, Rep. Barney Frank, D-MA
6. Ibid, Mayor Edward I. Koch of New York City
7. Ibid, Peter H. Bell, executive director of the National Housing Rehabilitation Assiciation
8. *CBO*, March 1984, Study "New Approaches to the Budgetary Treatment of Federal Credit Assistance"
9. *Redbook*, May 1987, "Madness In The Family" p. 188
10. The Dedham-Westwood Water District has access to Chapter 786 state funds (MA) to reimburse 50% of the cost of most improvements and repairs. Federal subsidies are in the form of tax savings, etc.
11. *Wall Street Journal*, June 2, 1987, "Is a Free Market for Electric Power On The Way?" by George Melloan
12. *Associated Press,* July 6, 1986, "Viewpoints Split on Private Firms Handling Governmental Services" by Kay Bartlett
13. Jack Anderson Column
14. *Business Week*, September 28, 1987, "Selling Uncle Sam's Assets: Why Reagan Has A Real Shot Now" by Stephen Wildstrom
15. *Wall Street Journal*, October 12, 1987, "Delaware Otsego Refuses To Be Shunted by Conrail" by Daniel Machalaba

16. *Atlas Shrugged* by Ayn Rand

17. *Time*, February 9. 1987, p. 54

FOURTH STEP

1. *Wall Street Journal*, May 16, 1985 "Pentagon Gosplan, Contd."
2. *Wall Street Journal*, "FDA Rule Changes May Rush New Drugs to Very Sick Patients" by Marilyn Chase
3. Rogers, Helen*The Election Process*, p. 86
4. Sears, Roebuck & Co. was sued unsuccessfully by EEOC in 1974 - James J. Kilpatrick Column, February 26, 1986
5. *Business Week*, August 5, 1985, pp. 48-54
6. Ibid
7. Ibid
8. *Forbes*, April 4, 1988 "I Went to Harvard With Liza" by Steve Weiner and Janis Bultman
9. *Insight*, January 11, 1988 "Coal Shippers Set Their Sights On Reviving Rail Regulation" by Holman Jenkins, Jr., p. 21
10. *Wall Street Journal*, April 7, 1987 "Unsafe Statistics"
11. *Insight*, April 20, 1987 "Coal Usage Feeding The Fuel Feud" by Carolyn Lockhead p.43
12. *Wall Street Journal*, September 17, 1985, "Hiding The True Costs of Energy Sources" by Richard Heede and Amory Lovins of the Rocky Mountain Institute
13. Ibid
14. *Regulation*, March/April 1985 "Helium—How Much Is Enough?" by Richard Stroup and Jane Shaw, pp. 17-22
15. Ibid, p.21-22
16. *Forbes*, April 4, 1988 "You Ain't Seen Nothing Yet" by George Gilder, p. 93
17. *Wall Street Journal*, June 12, 1985, "Arms Control Doesn't Save Money" by David Berkowitz
18. *The Mainspring of Human Progress* by Henry Grady Weaver
19. *Pork Barrel* by Randall Fitzgerald and Gerald Lipson, p. xxv
20. Ibid
21. *Business Week*, January 11, 1988 "Too Much Government Is What Ails The Third World" by Gary Becker, p. 28

FIFTH STEP

1. *Financial Planning*, January 1988 "Taxes Forever" by Rod Kuchio. Herb Stein quote found on p. 60
2. *The Atlantic*, "The Morning After" by Peter Peterson

3. *Business Week*, June 29, 1987 "Nowhere To Go But Up" p. 25
4. *Business Week*, November 16, 1987, The New Economy, "Say Hello to Lean Years" by Karen Pennar
5. Information and direct quotations were drawn from an article by Professor Marvin Olasky of the University of Texas at Austin titled "Income Tax, the Monstrosity That Wouldn't Die" which appeared in the *Wall Street Journal* on April 15, 1987
6. *Wall Street Journal*, November 23, 1987 "The Mitchell Curve"

SIXTH STEP

1. Enterprize zones are targeted to geographic areas where entrepreneuralism is subsidized by government.
2. *The Rule of Experts: Occupational Licensing in America* by David Young. Published by the Cato Institute, 224 Second St., S.E., Washington D.C. 20003
3. AT&T study by John P. Fernandez mentioned in *Business Week*, October 6, 1986
4. *Wall Street Journal*, March 3, 1988 "A Better Alternative to a Higher Minimum Wage" by J.D. Foster
5. *Business Week*, July 27, 1987 "The Real Costs of a Higher Minimum Wage" by Joan Berger and Susan Garland
6. *Wall Street Journal*, February 16, 1988 "Mandated Labor Costs"
7. *Wall Street Journal*, September 30, 1986 article by Peter Waldman
8. Ibid
9. *Fortune*, February 16, 1987 article by Fern Chapman
10. *Business Week*, October 10, 1986 "Business Starts Tailoring Itself To Suit Working Women" by Elizabeth Ehrlich
11. Ibid "Child Care: The Private Sector Can't Do It Alone" by Elizabeth Ehrlich
12. Ibid "Business Starts Tailoring Itself To Working Women"
"But the vast majority of working mothers do not fit the stereotype of the low-income mother working long hours to make ends meet. Two-earner families, for example, had a median income of $38,346 in 1986; "traditional" two-parent, one earner families $25,803...should a subsidy go to two-earner families that on average earn half again as much as traditional one-earner families?" *Wall Street Journal* - March 9, 1988 "The ABC of Child-Care Policies" by Douglas Besharov. Single mothers, not on welfare, earned 24% more than the median income of traditional, one-earner families. Again, the college-educated more affluent is getting the subsidy meant for the impoverished.
13. The Census Bureau found that 31% of college educated women use day care centers compared with 15% of women without even a high-school diploma. 55% of the less educated women use relatives and only 38% of this group *pay* the relatives. Child-care bills will subsidize day-care

centers, once again bypassing those who most need the help. *Wall Street Journal* - March 9, 1988 "The ABC of Child-Care Policies" by Douglas Besharov.

14. *Time*, June 22, 1987 "The Child-Care Dilemma" by Claudia Wallis p. 59
15. On January 21, 1987 the Supreme Court ruled that States may deny unemployment compensation to women who leave their jobs because they are pregnant and are not later rehired.
    Wimberly v. Labor and Industrial Relations Commission of Missouri
    On January 13, 1987 in *California Savings and Loan v. Guerra* the Supreme Court upheld a California law requiring reinstatement of women who sought to return to work after a pregnancy leave.
16. *Time*, June 22, 1987 "Day Care Bad for Babies?" by Claudia Wallis p. 63
17. *Cox v. Resilient Flooring Division*
18. *California Lawyer*, May 1987
19. *Business Week*, March 23, 1987 "The AIDS Epidemic And Business" pp. 122-132
20. *Heritage Foundation*, "Backgrounder" May 21, 1986 by Peter J. Ferrara
21. *National Underwriter*, January 26, 1987 "Social Investing: The Protest for 1980's" by Donald Luzzatto
22. *Wall Street Journal*, Michael Kinsley

SEVENTH STEP

1. *Insight*, March 30, 1987 "Fall of the Dollar Just a Start in Handling the Trade Deficit" by Carolyn Lockhead, p. 45
2. *The Mainspring Of Human Progress* by Henry Grady Weaver, p. 259
3. *Business Week*, January 26, 1987
4. American Enterprise Institute trade conference April 1987
5. *Wall Street Journal*, March 14, 1988 "High Yen Forces Japanese To Go American" by Sam Kusumoto
6. *Wall Street Journal*, January 28, 1988 "Bethlehem Steel Profit Doubled In 4th Quarter" by J. Ernest Beazley
7. See Chapter Six p. 162.
8. Mr. Baldridges testimony before Senate Government Affairs Committee on "Economic Competitiveness" whcih took place on March 25, 1987.
9. *Estrangement: America and the World*, edited by S.J. Unger "America Among Equals" by Lester Thurow, p. 163
10. *Associated Press* April 5, 1987 "Japanese, America Engaged In Volatile Economic Rivalry" by Charles J. Hanley
11. *Capitalism: The Unknown Ideal* by Ayn Rand, p. 216
12. Such a use of pension funds was hotly debated by the candidates for the Democratic presidential nomination in 1988 perhaps most forcefully by Jesse Jackson.
13. *Wall Street Journal*, March 14, 1988 (see #5 above)
14. *Wall Street Journal*, March 3, 1987 article by George Melloan, p. 32

15. From the speech given by Mr. Petersen before the "Emerging Issues Forum" held at North Carolina University.
16. *Wall Street Journal,* July 1, 1987 "What If It's Trade That Drives Currencies?" by David Ransom and Marc Miles
17. Ibid
18. *Time,* November 16, 1987 "The Declining Dollar: Not A Simple Cure" by Charles Alexander
19. *Wall Street Journal,* February 18, 1987 "The Dollar Must Keep Falling" by Martin Feldstein
20. *Wall Street Journal,* November 5, 1987 "Surprising Majority Agree On Need For Weaker Dollar" by Rudiger Dornbusch
21. The Reagan administration, at that time, expressed a desire to stabilize the dollar at closer to 150 yen as seen by James Baker's actions at Plaza II
22. *Wall Street Journal,* February 29, 1988 "Reagan's Legacy: America For Sale" by Alan Murray
23. *Wall Street Journal,* March 16, 1988 "Low Wages No Longer Give Competitive Edge" by Peter Drucker
24. According to a study released in April 1988, Japanese investors purchased $12.77 billion worth of U.S. real estate in 1987. The study was conducted by Kenneth Laventhal & Co., an accounting firm.
25. *Wall Street Journal,* February 29, 1988 (see #22 above)
26. *Wall Street Journal,* March 16, 1988 (see #23 above)
27. *Monterey Peninsula Herald,* January 24, 1988 "Future Will Find Human Ability Recognized as Capital" by John Diebold
28. *Wall Street Journal,* December 15, 1986 "Nissan Motor, Japan's No. 2 Auto Maker, Plunges Into the Red Amid Continuing Unior Problems" by Damon Darlin
29. *The Reckoning* by David Halberstam
30. *Forbes,* August 25, 1986 "A Barbarian Personality" by Andrew Tanzer
31. "The textile industry says it's being killed by imports from low-wage countries. But about half the industry actually operates at costs fully competitive with the lowest-wage producer anywhere..." Peter Drucker, *Wall Street Journal,* March 16, 1988 (see #23 above)
32. *Wall Street Journal,* March 30, 1987 "Europeans Take Similar Action On Japan Trade" by John Marcom, Jr.
33. *Wall Street Journal,* March 9, 1987 See related article. *Insight,* September 28, 1987 "U.S. Pension Insurer Feels the Heat of a Melting Industry" by Robert England and *Wall Street Journal* July 20, 1987 "Don't Cartelize the Steeel Industry" by Robert Crandall
34. Associated Press, April 12, 1987 "Japanese, America Engaged In Volatile Economic Rivalry" by Charles J. Hanley
35. *Wall Street Journal,* March 16, 1988 (see #23 above)
36. *Wall Street Journal,* August 21, 1986

EIGHTH STEP

1. *Business Week*, May 20, 1985 "How The Fed Lets The Deficit Flourish" by Thibaut De Saint Phalle
2. *Wall Street Journal*, November 5, 1987 "Time For Floating-Rate Treasuries" by Lowell Bryan
3. Ibid
4. *FRBSF Weekly Letter*, May 29, 1987 "Brave New World I" by Verle B. Johnston
5. *Business Week*, May 20, 1985 (same as #1 above)
6. *Fortune*, May 11, 1987 "Is The Dollar Too High—Or Too Low?" by Sylvia Nasar
7. Related articles *Wall Street Journal*, December 30, 1987 "World Economy Doesn't Hang in the Balance" by Herbert Stein — *AEI Economist*, July 1986 "The International Monetary System" by Gottfried Haberler — *Policy Review* "The Cure for Monetary Madness" by Allan Metzer
8. *Wall Street Journal*, June 10, 1987 "Tightening Won't Unravel Economic Knot" by David Hale
9. *Forbes*, March 7, 1987 "All the World's a Bank" by Edwin Finn, Jr.
10. *FRBSF Weekly Letter*, January 23, 1987 "Euromarkets and Monetary Policy" by Ramon Moreno
11. *Wall Street Journal*, January 15, 1988 "Trade Gap Is Inevitable — And Good" by George Gilder
12. Speech before the *American Enterprise Institute* on December 2, 1987 by Gottfried Haberler "The U.S. Economy, The Dollar & Gold"
13. Ibid
14. *The Atlantic*, October 1987 "The Morning After" by Peter Peterson, p. 46
15. *Wall Street Journal*, November 9, 1987 " The End of Policy Coordination" by Martin Feldstein

NINTH STEP

1. *"The Rise and Fall of the Great Powers"* by Paul Kennedy, pp. 389-390
2. Ibid, p. 529
3. *Wall Street Journal*, January 20, 1988 "Lack of U.S. Will Isn't Economy's Fault" by Herbert Stein
4. Kennedy, *"The Rise and Fall of the Great Powers*, p. 532
5. Ibid, p. 518
6. *Insight*, February 9, 1987
7. *FRBSF Weekly Letter*, January 8, 1988 "Capital Flight and LDC Debt" by Steven Plaut
8. Ibid
9. Ibid
10. Spoken before the Congressional Bretton Woods Committee on "Debt

and Development" which took place on January 22, 1987

11. Comment was made as Mr. Scheurer chaired a Congressional Subcommittee in 1987 which considered appropriating funds to preserve the African white rhinoceros, among other things.
12. *Insight*, February 9, 1987
13. *Wall Street Journal*, August 26, 1987 "London, Pyongyang & Moscow"
14. *Insight*, January 18, 1988 "Export-Import Bank Survives on Making Credit, Not Profit" by Holman Jenkins, Jr.
15. Ibid
16. *Insight*, February 15, 1988 "Bank's Mission Mired In Loan War" by Derk Kinnane-Roelofsma
17. *Insight*, February 9, 1988, p. 15
18. *Wall Street Journal*, January 8, 1988 "Some Big Banks Plan to Shun Mexican Plan" by Christian Hill, Peter Truell and Jeff Bailey
19. Discussed at the Congressional Bretton Woods Committee meeting on "Debt and Development" held on Janurary 22, 1987
20. *Wall Street Journal*, March 12, 1987 "International-Debt Experts Worry That Congress Will Tinker With the Problem and Make It Worse" by Art Pine

TENTH STEP

1. *Wall Street Journal*, April 23, 1987 "Capital Guidelines Could Weaken Banks" by Lowell Bryan
2. *Wall Street Journal*, March 12, 1987 "What We Need Are A Few Good Bank Runs" by Lindley Clark, Jr. Quote attributed to George Kaufman, an economist at Loyola University of Chicago.
3. *Jack Anderson's Column*, March 12, 1987 "Lousy Track Record"
4. *Financial Planning News*, April 1987 "New Efforts to Deregulate Banks Ignore Lessons Learned Long Ago" by David Silver
5. See related articles *Business Week*, June 15, 1987 "What's In Store At the Fed" and *Business Week*, June 22, 1987 "How Does the Street Spell Relief? G-R-E-E-N-S-P-A-N" and *Time*, August 10, 1987 p.33
6. On March 30, 1988 the Senate voted overwhelmingly to pass S. 1886, the banking deregulation bill to be referred to as The Proxmire Financial Modernization Act of 1988. See *Congressional Quarterly* 1988, p. 843-849
7. *FRBSF Weekly Letter*, May 8, 1987 "Mortgage Securitization & REMICs" by Randall Pozdena
8. *Wall Street Journal*, July 20, 1987 "1/8 Over LIBOR?"
9. *Wall Street Journal*, January 19, 1988 "Legal Services Corp.'s Attacks On Banks" by William F. Harvey
10. Ibid Willam Harvey was chairman of the Legal Service Corp's Board in 1982 and is now a professor at Indiana University's School of Law

11. Ibid
12. See glossary
13. *Business Week,* April 6, 1987 "Are Banks Obsolete?" by Sarah Bartlett p.75
14. *Wall Street Journal,* January 28, 1988 "Japan's Banks Become Ever-Bigger Lenders To American Business" by Michael Sesit
15. CNN'S "Moneyline" February 17, 1988
16. C-SPAN Interview with Martha Seger, Federal Reserve Governor, on February 6, 1988
17. *FRBSF Weekly Letter,* May 22, 1987 "Regulating Bank Capital" by Michael Keeley and Frederick Furlong

ELEVENTH STEP

1. *Wall Street Journal,* March 7, 1988 "Line Item Veto: Older Than Constitution" by Forrest McDonald
2. *Wall Street Journal,* "GAAP's Budget Gaps Will Suprise" by Representative Joseph DioGuardi
3. *U.S. Code Congressional & Administrative News,* Vol 11A, p. 6206
4. *Underground Government: The Off-Budget Public Sector* by James T. Bennett & Thomas J. DiLorenzo published by Cato Institute 1983, p. 176
5. January 12, 1988 Byron Mandell on "Moneyline"
6. See *The American Deficit: Fulfillment of a Prophecy?* by Helen P. Rogers, pp. 21-24
7. *Insight,* January 26, 1987
8. Refers to a study conducted by Duncan & Cole at the University of Michigan and called *Years of Poverty, Years of Plenty* and Charles Murray's book *Losing Ground.* They were discussed by Helen Rogers on pp. 40-41 in the supplemental section of her book *Social Security: An Idea Whose Time Has Passed*
9. *Wall Street Journal,* November 24, 1987 "Compromise: Spend and Tax"
10. *Wall Street Journal,* December 3, 1987 "Budget Accord Is Top Heavy With Taxes" by William V. Roth, Jr.
11. *The Atlantic Monthly,* October 1987 "The Morning After" by Peter G. Peterson, p. 46

INDEX

438

440

441

443

451